Jim Henson's Legends of THE DARK CRYSTAL™

THE Garthim Wars

VOLUME 1

Written by Barbara Randall Kesel
Illustrated by Heidi Arnhold and Max Kim
Cover Art by Jae-Hwan Kim

Based on the film "The Dark Crystal"
Directed by Jim Henson and Frank Oz
Screenplay by David Odell
Story by Jim Henson

Original designs by Brian Froud

TOKYOPOP®

HAMBURG // LONDON // LOS ANGELES // TOKYO

Jim Henson's Legends of The Dark Crystal Vol. 1: The Garthim Wars

Written by Barbara Randall Kesel

Illustrated by Heidi Arnhold and Max Kim

Tones - Jessica Feinberg
Lettering - Lucas Rivera
Cover Art - Jae-Hwan Kim
Cover Design - Jose Macasocol, Jr.

Consulting Editor - Michael Polis
Assistant Editor - Sarah Tangney

Editor - Tim Beedle
Digital Imaging Manager - Chris Buford
Pre-Production Supervisor - Erika Terriquez
Managing Editor - Elisabeth Brizzi
Creative Director - Anne Marie Horne
Editor-in-Chief - Rob Tokar
Publisher - Mike Kiley
President and C.O.O. - John Parker
C.E.O. and Chief Creative Officer - Stuart Levy

A TOKYOPOP® Manga

TOKYOPOP Inc.
5900 Wilshire Blvd. Suite 2000
Los Angeles, CA 90036

E-mail: info@TOKYOPOP.com
Come visit us online at www.TOKYOPOP.com

ISBN: 978-1-59816-701-6

First TOKYOPOP printing: November 2007
10 9 8 7 6 5 4 3 2 1
Printed in the USA

Jim Henson's
LEGENDS OF
THE DARK CRYSTAL
THE GARTHIM WARS

CONTENTS

Chapter One

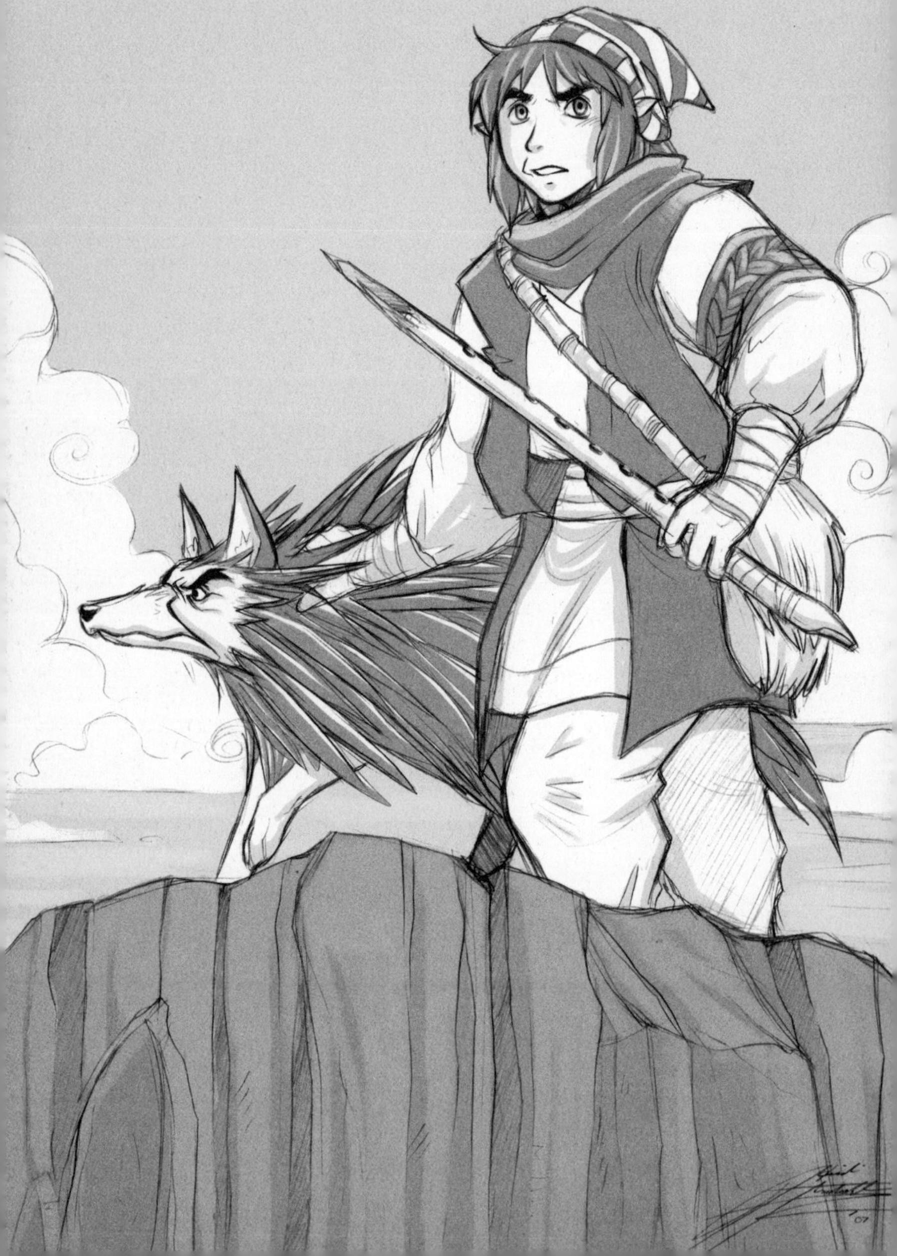

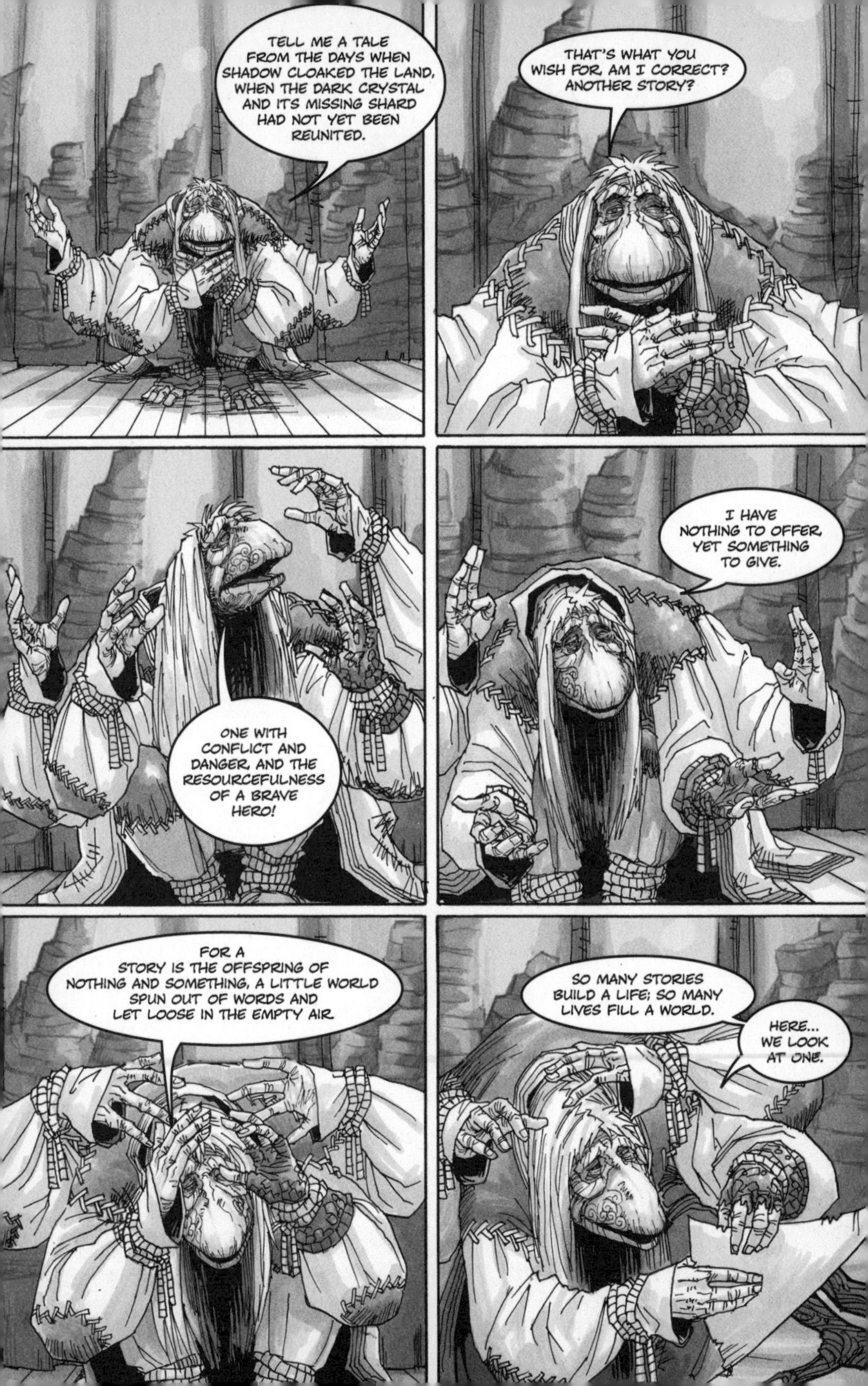
TELL ME A TALE FROM THE DAYS WHEN SHADOW CLOAKED THE LAND, WHEN THE DARK CRYSTAL AND ITS MISSING SHARD HAD NOT YET BEEN REUNITED.
THAT'S WHAT YOU WISH FOR, AM I CORRECT? ANOTHER STORY?
ONE WITH CONFLICT AND DANGER, AND THE RESOURCEFULNESS OF A BRAVE HERO!
I HAVE NOTHING TO OFFER, YET SOMETHING TO GIVE.
FOR A STORY IS THE OFFSPRING OF NOTHING AND SOMETHING, A LITTLE WORLD SPUN OUT OF WORDS AND LET LOOSE IN THE EMPTY AIR.
SO MANY STORIES BUILD A LIFE; SO MANY LIVES FILL A WORLD.
HERE... WE LOOK AT ONE.

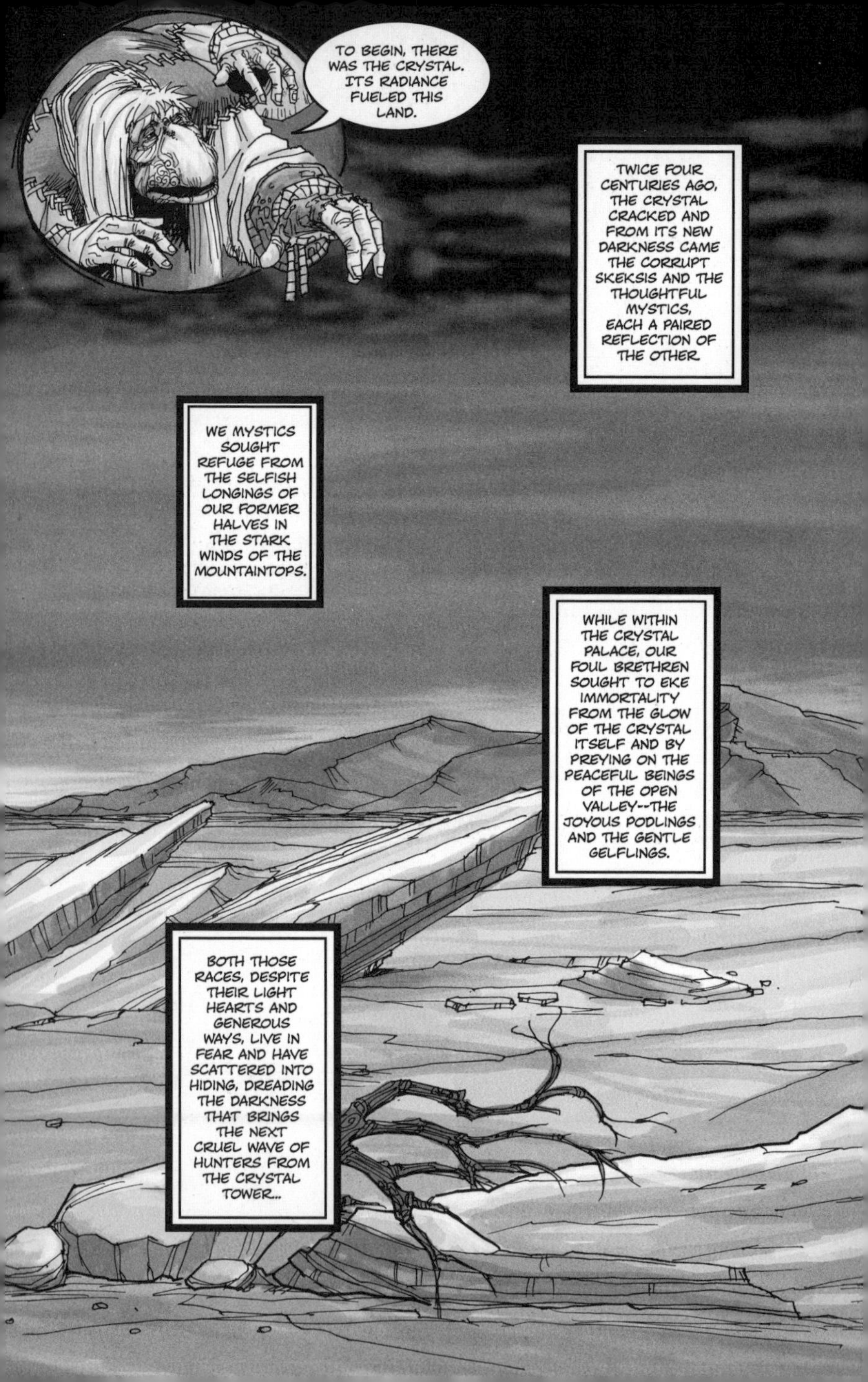
TO BEGIN, THERE WAS THE CRYSTAL. ITS RADIANCE FUELED THIS LAND.
TWICE FOUR CENTURIES AGO, THE CRYSTAL CRACKED AND FROM ITS NEW DARKNESS CAME THE CORRUPT SKEKSIS AND THE THOUGHTFUL MYSTICS, EACH A PAIRED REFLECTION OF THE OTHER
WE MYSTICS SOUGHT REFUGE FROM THE SELFISH LONGINGS OF OUR FORMER HALVES IN THE STARK WINDS OF THE MOUNTAINTOPS.
WHILE WITHIN THE CRYSTAL PALACE, OUR FOUL BRETHREN SOUGHT TO EKE IMMORTALITY FROM THE GLOW OF THE CRYSTAL ITSELF AND BY PREYING ON THE PEACEFUL BEINGS OF THE OPEN VALLEY--THE JOYOUS PODLINGS AND THE GENTLE GELFLINGS.
BOTH THOSE RACES, DESPITE THEIR LIGHT HEARTS AND GENEROUS WAYS, LIVE IN FEAR AND HAVE SCATTERED INTO HIDING, DREADING THE DARKNESS THAT BRINGS THE NEXT CRUEL WAVE OF HUNTERS FROM THE CRYSTAL TOWER...

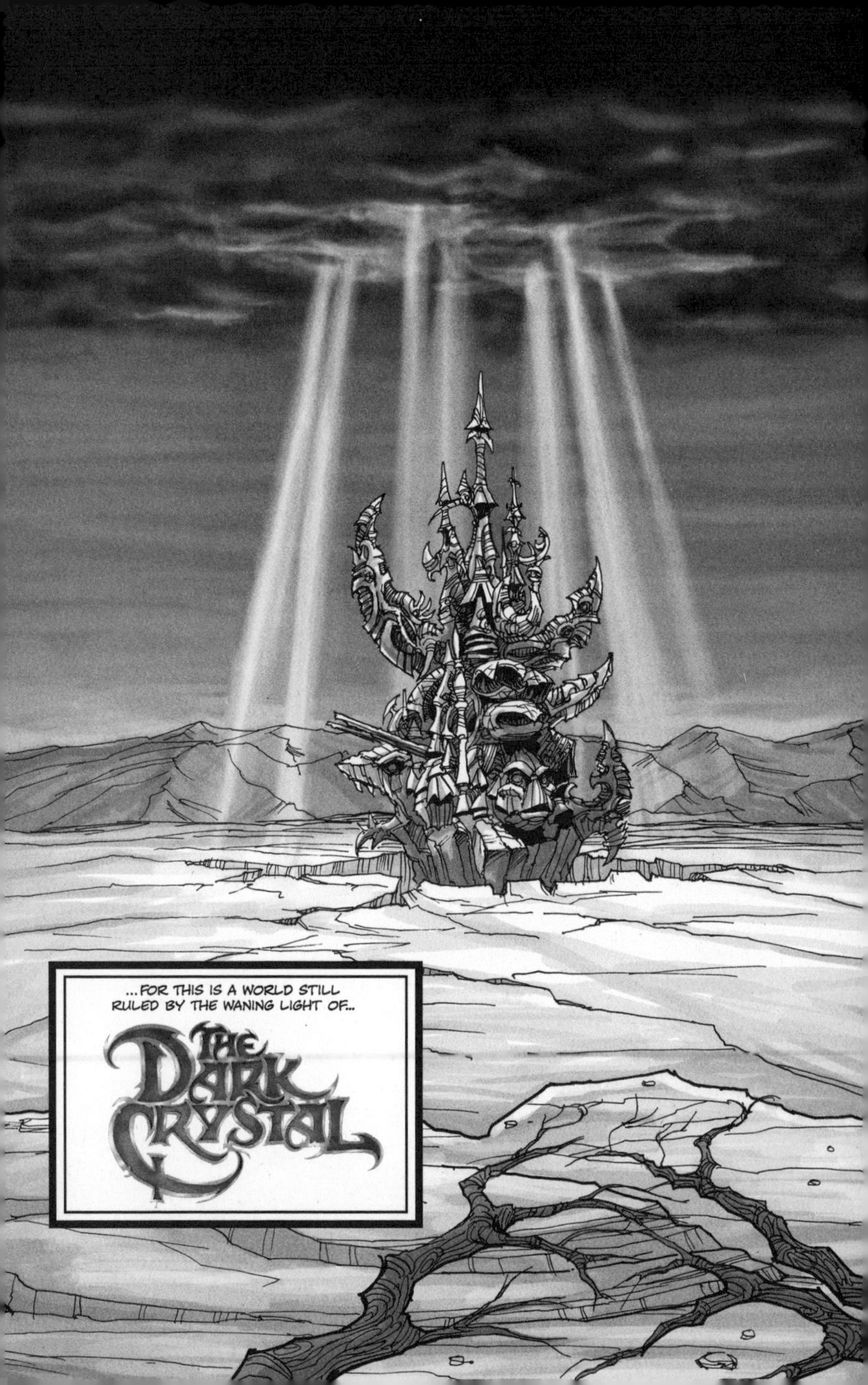
...FOR THIS IS A WORLD STILL RULED BY THE WANING LIGHT OF...
THE DARK CRYSTAL

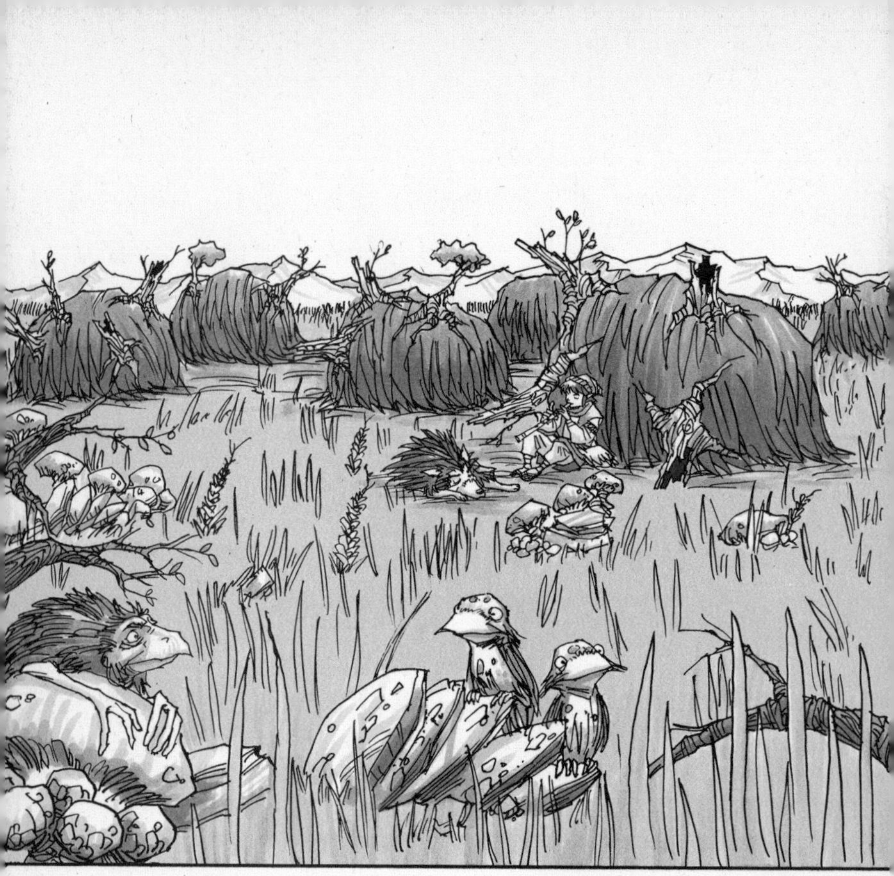

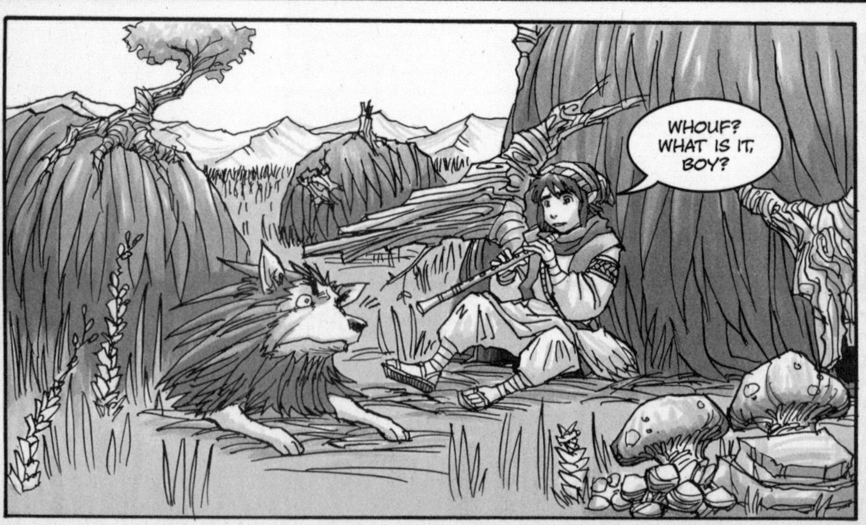
WHOUF? WHAT IS IT, BOY?

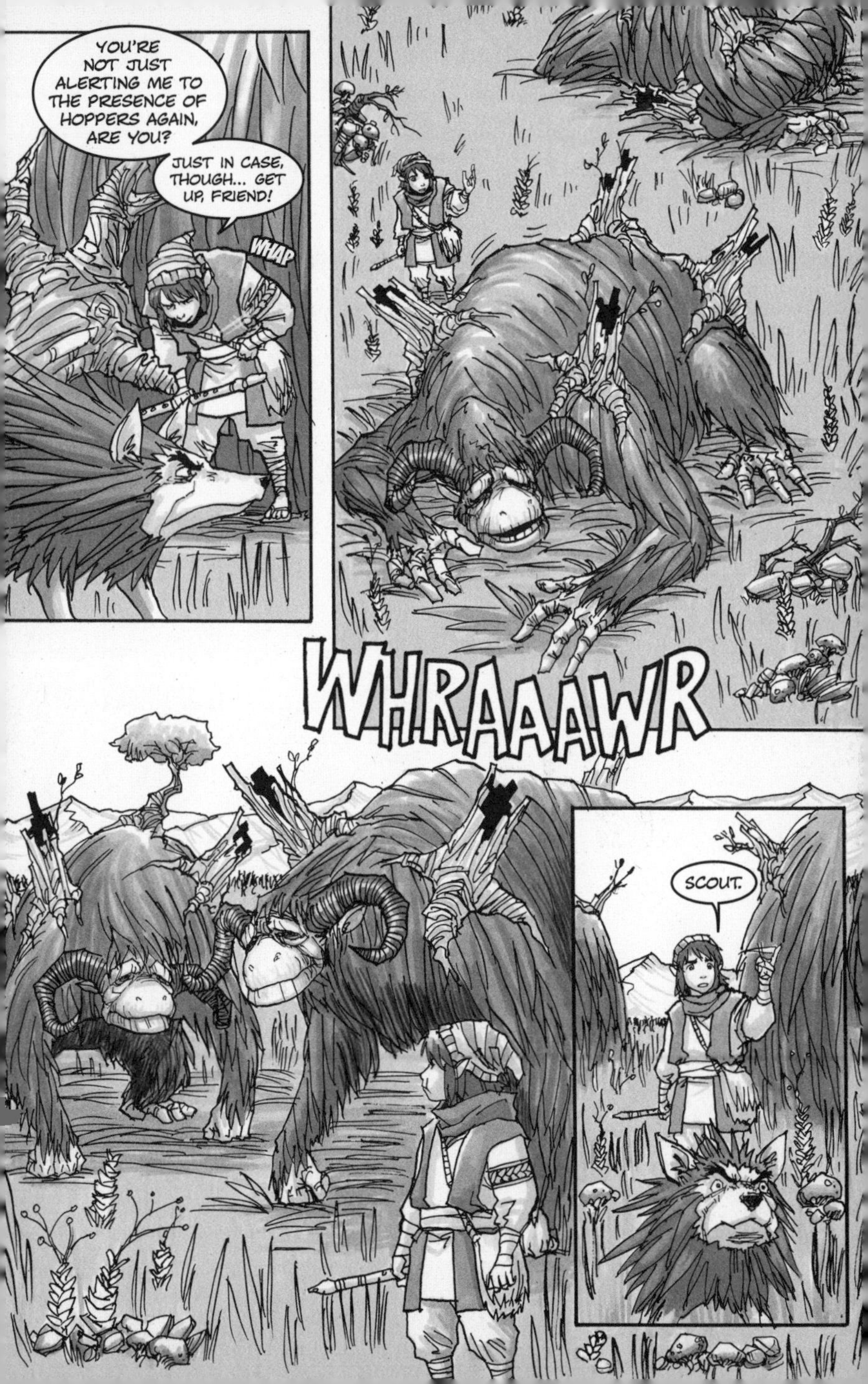
YOU'RE NOT JUST ALERTING ME TO THE PRESENCE OF HOPPERS AGAIN, ARE YOU?
JUST IN CASE, THOUGH... GET UP, FRIEND!
WHAP
WHRAAAWR
SCOUT.

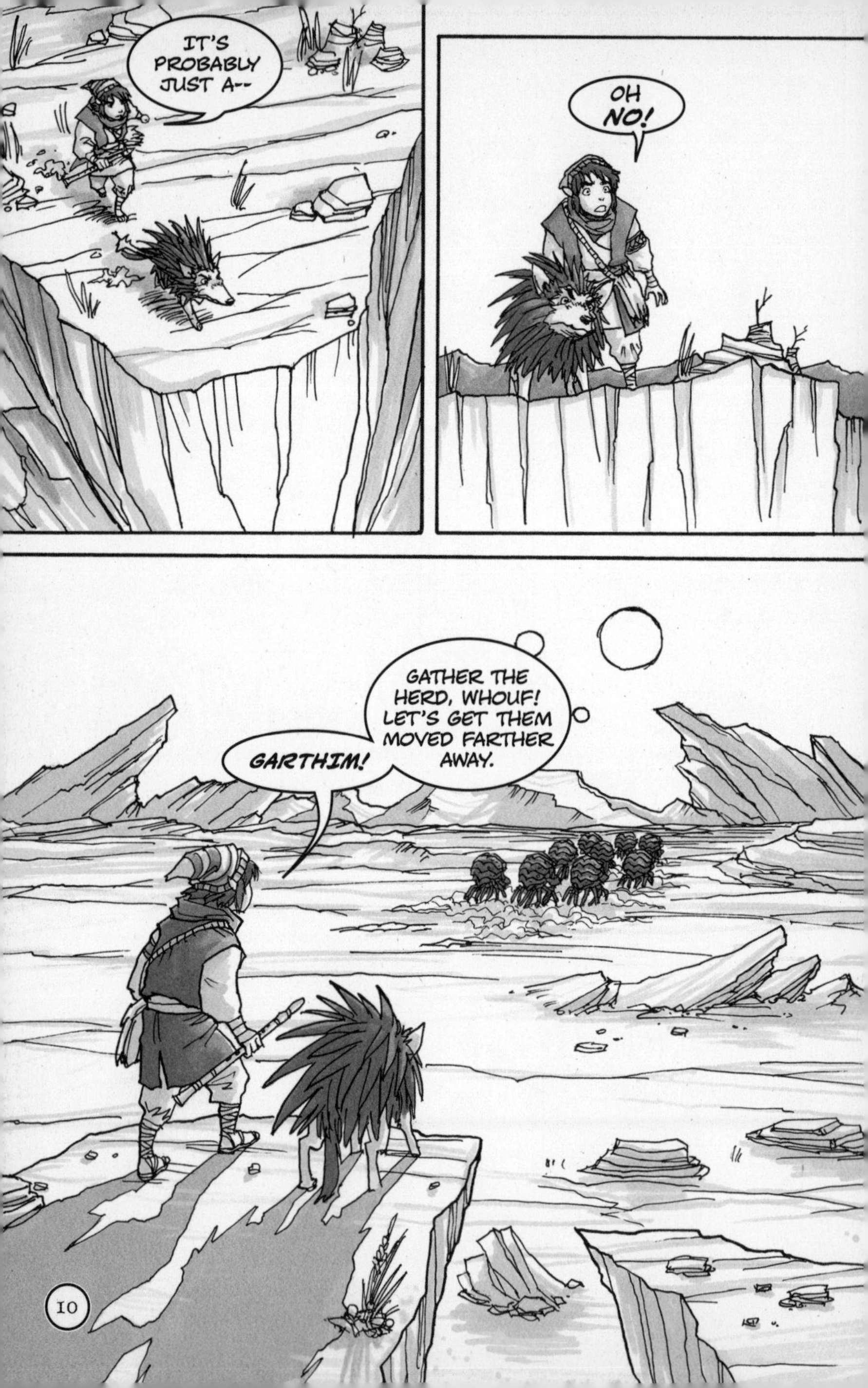
IT'S PROBABLY JUST A--
OH NO!
GARTHIM!
GATHER THE HERD, WHOUF! LET'S GET THEM MOVED FARTHER AWAY.

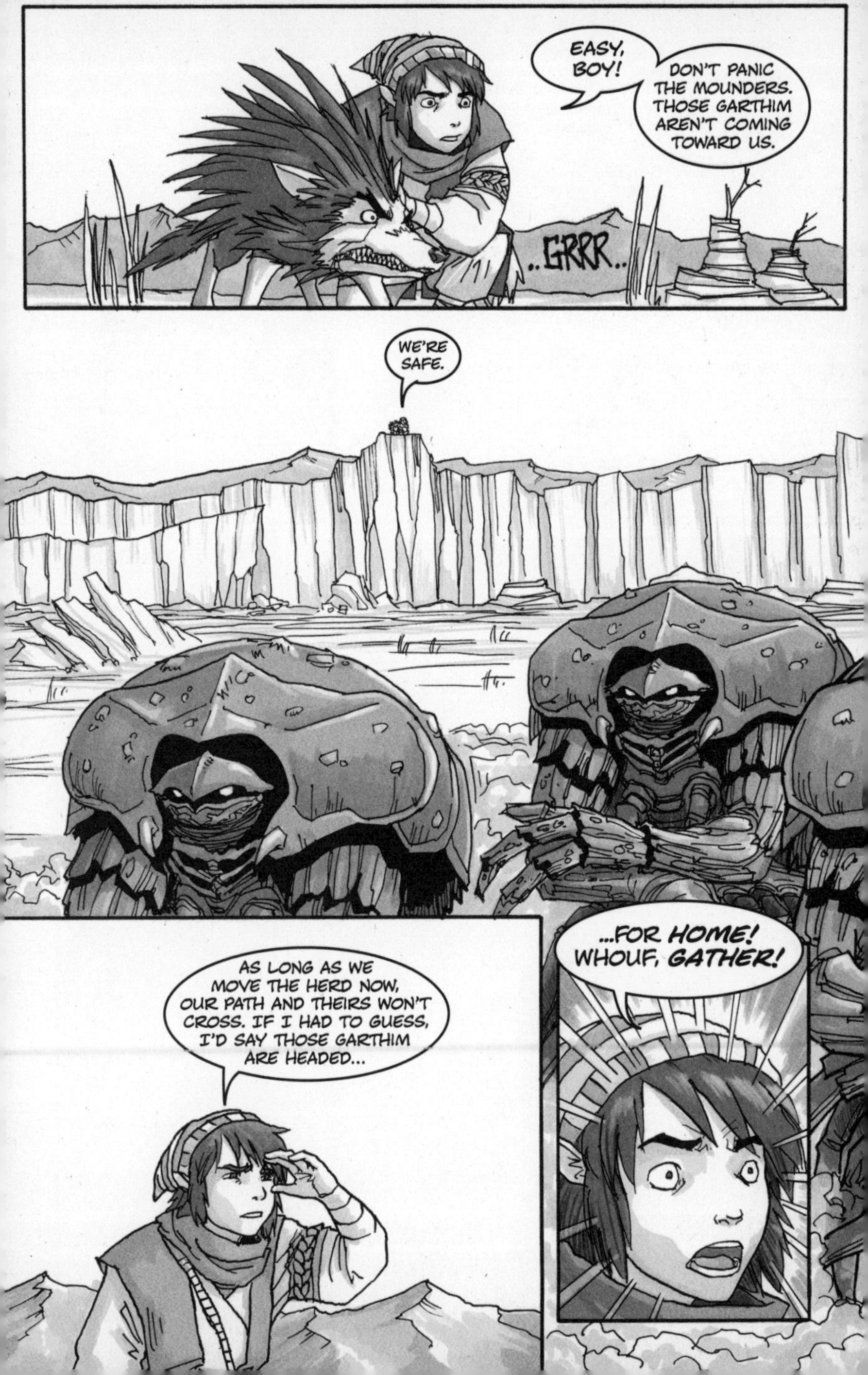
EASY, BOY!
DON'T PANIC THE MOUNDERS. THOSE GARTHIM AREN'T COMING TOWARD US.
..GRRR..
WE'RE SAFE.
AS LONG AS WE MOVE THE HERD NOW, OUR PATH AND THEIRS WON'T CROSS. IF I HAD TO GUESS, I'D SAY THOSE GARTHIM ARE HEADED...
...FOR HOME! WHOUF, GATHER!

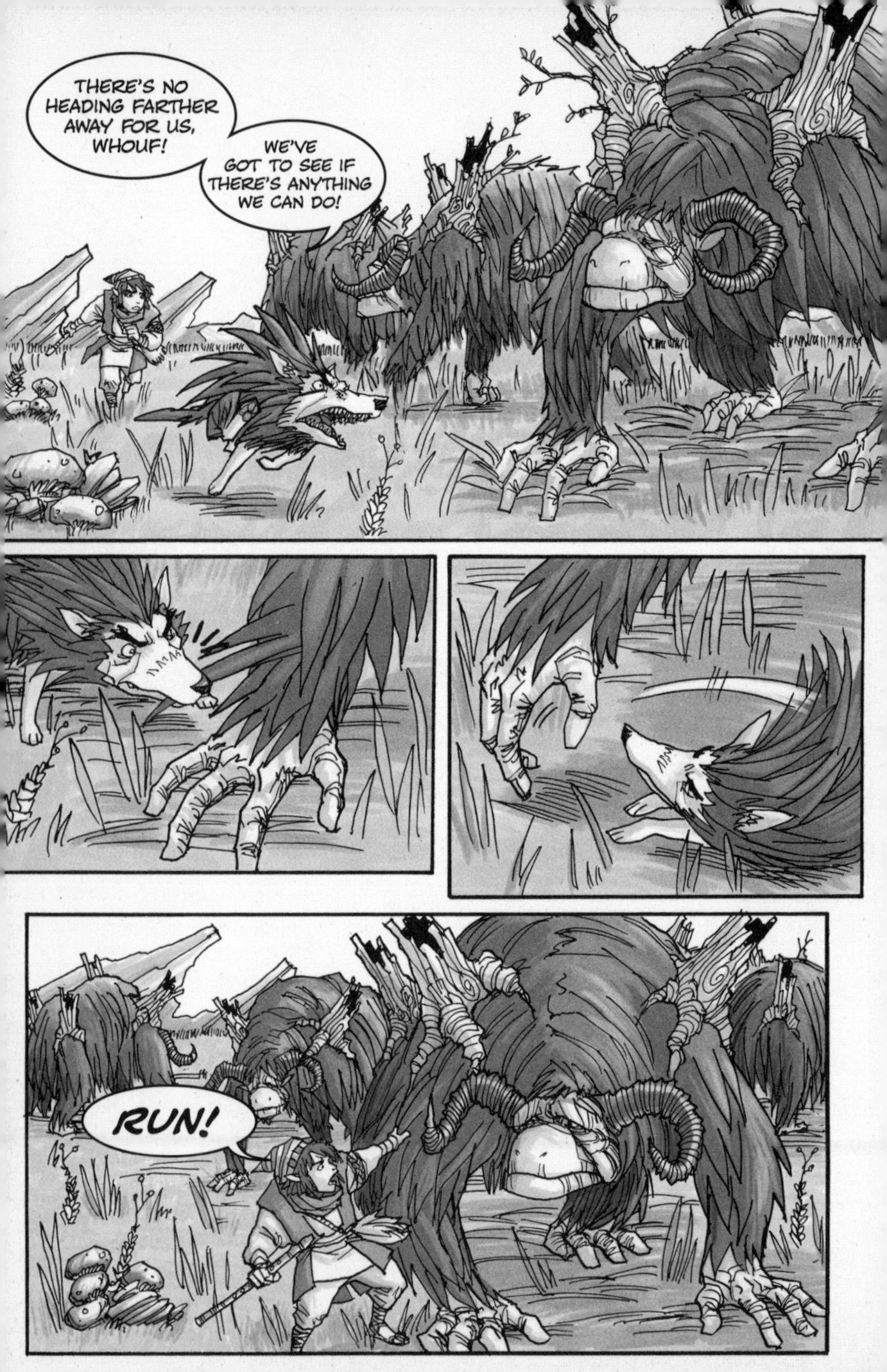
THERE'S NO HEADING FARTHER AWAY FOR US, WHOUF!
WE'VE GOT TO SEE IF THERE'S ANYTHING WE CAN DO!
RUN!

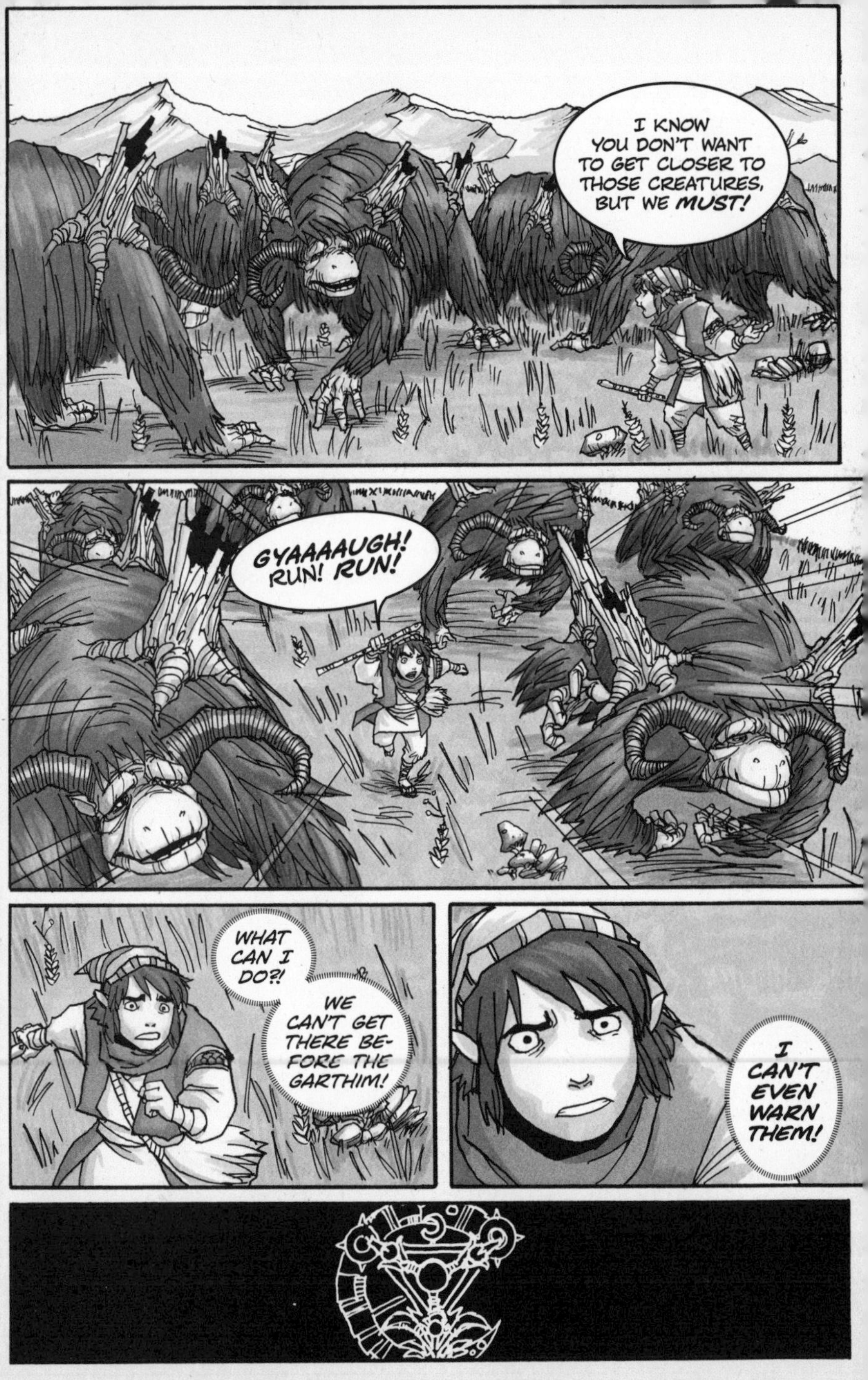
I KNOW YOU DON'T WANT TO GET CLOSER TO THOSE CREATURES, BUT WE MUST!
GYAAAAUGH! RUN! RUN!
WHAT CAN I DO?!
WE CAN'T GET THERE BE-FORE THE GARTHIM!
I CAN'T EVEN WARN THEM!

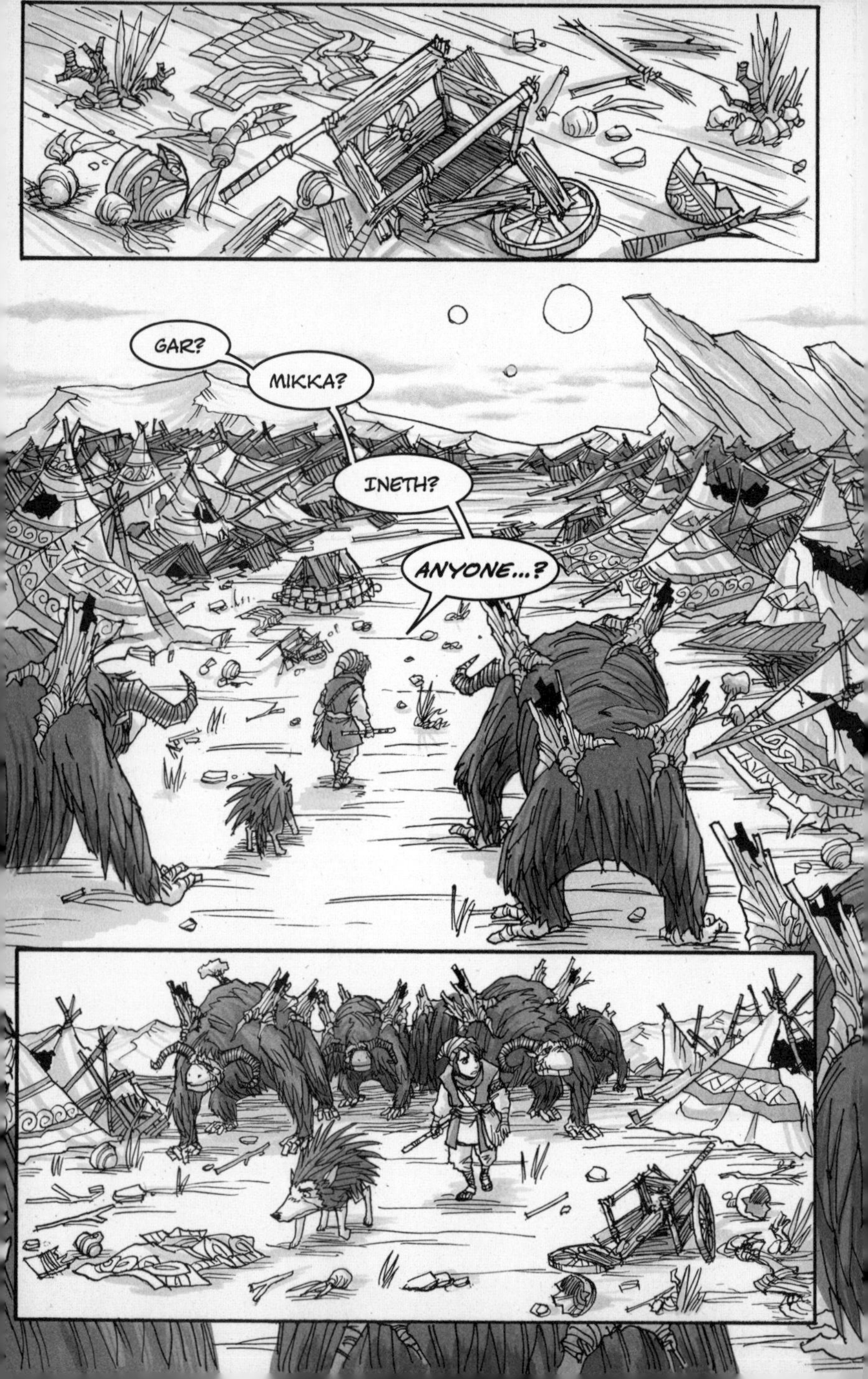
GAR?
MIKKA?
INETH?
ANYONE...?

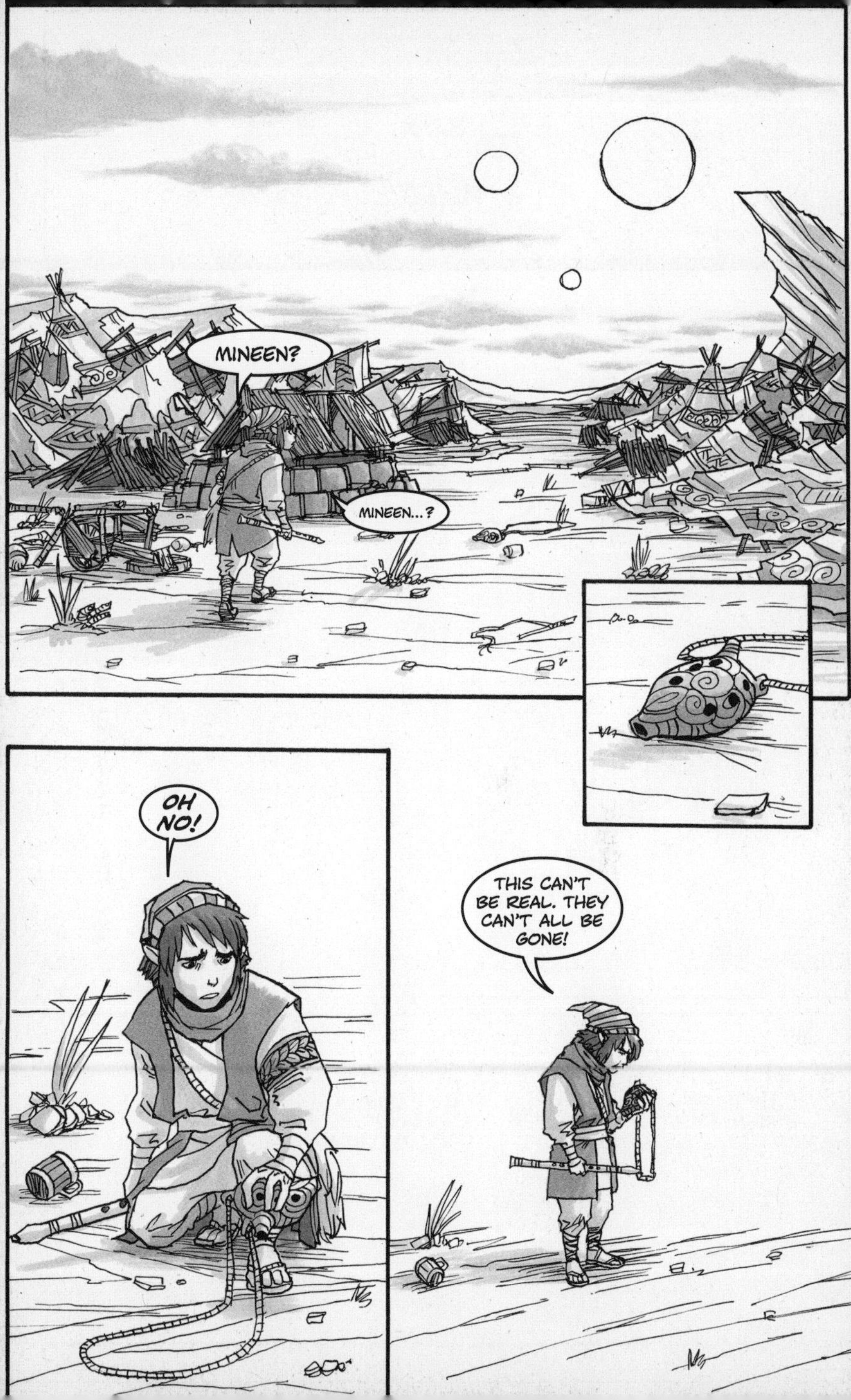
MINEEN?
MINEEN...?
OH NO!
THIS CAN'T BE REAL. THEY CAN'T ALL BE GONE!

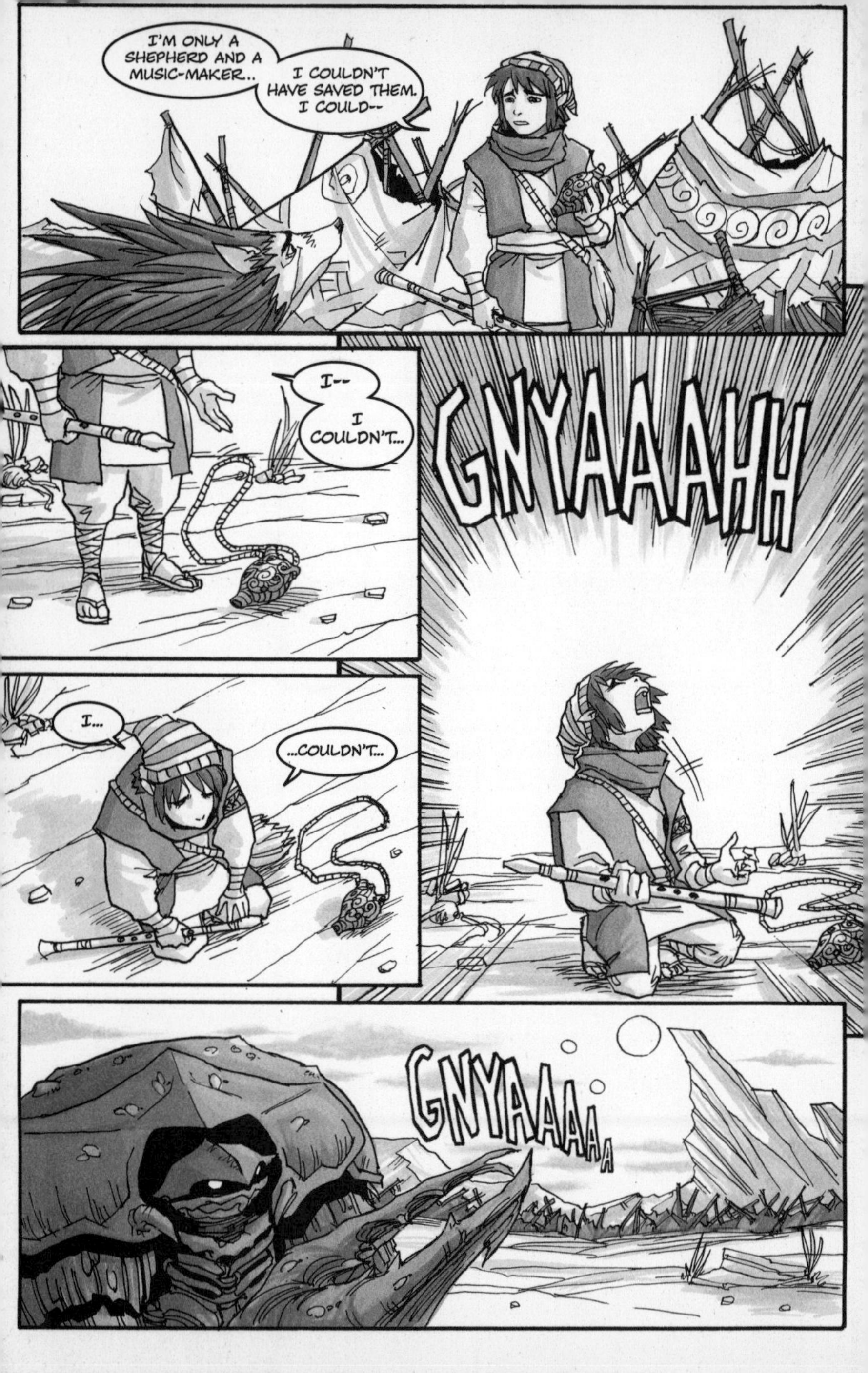
I'M ONLY A SHEPHERD AND A MUSIC-MAKER..
I COULDN'T HAVE SAVED THEM. I COULD--
I--
I COULDN'T...
I...
...COULDN'T...
GNYAAAAH
GNYAAAAA

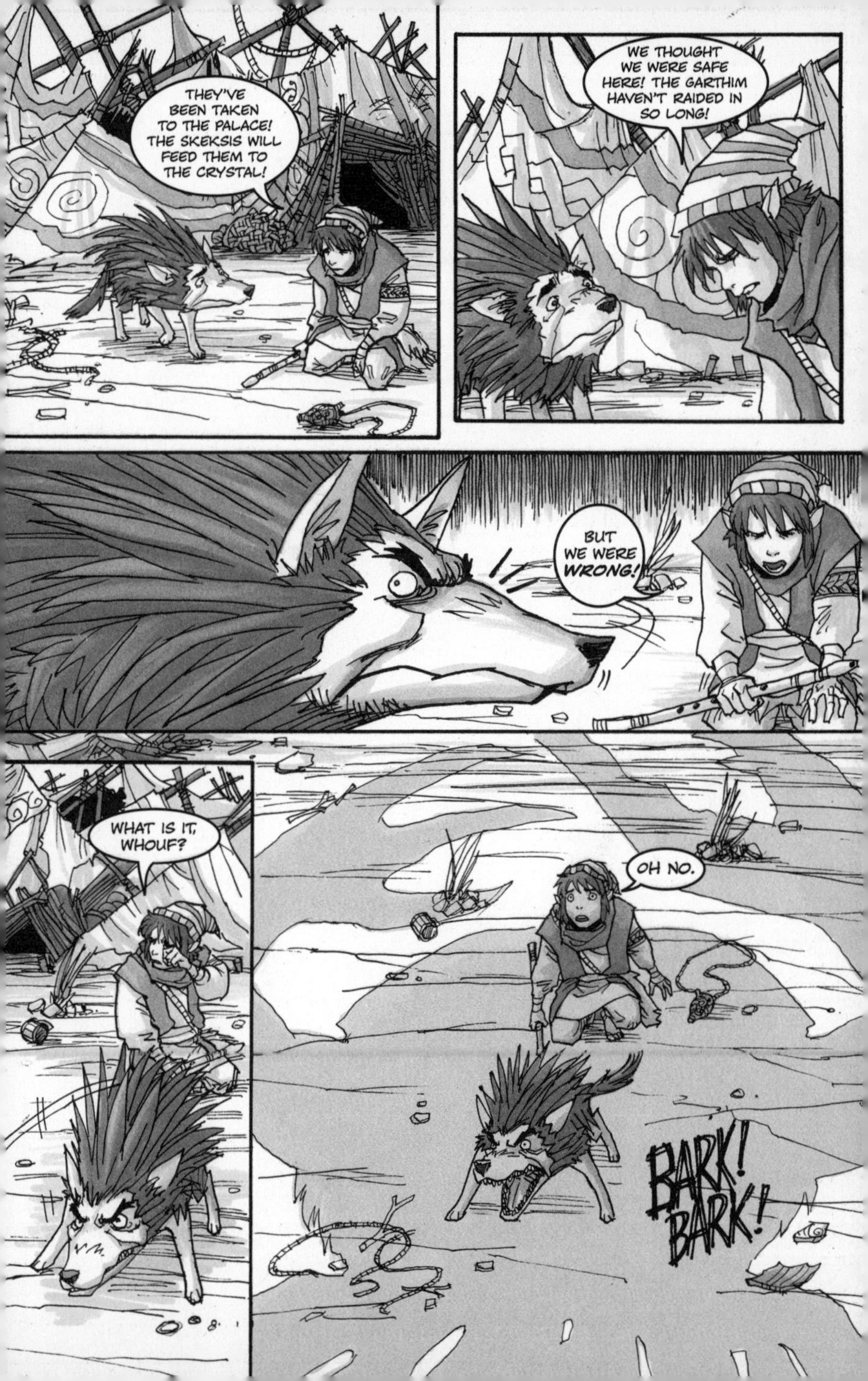
THEY'VE BEEN TAKEN TO THE PALACE! THE SKEKSIS WILL FEED THEM TO THE CRYSTAL!
WE THOUGHT WE WERE SAFE HERE! THE GARTHIM HAVEN'T RAIDED IN SO LONG!
BUT WE WERE **WRONG!**
WHAT IS IT, WHOUF?
OH NO.
BARK! BARK!

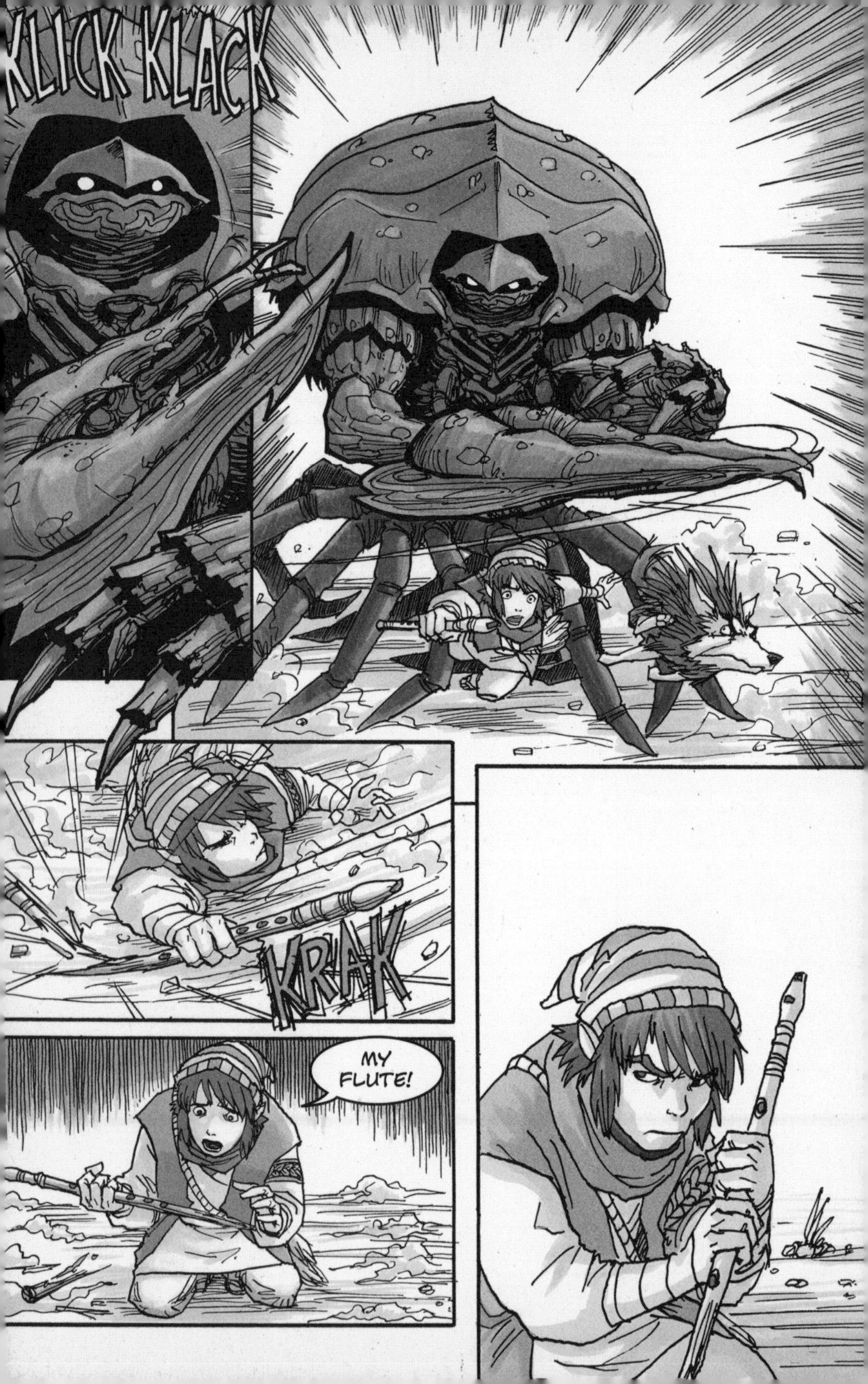
KLICK KLACK
KRAK
MY FLUTE!

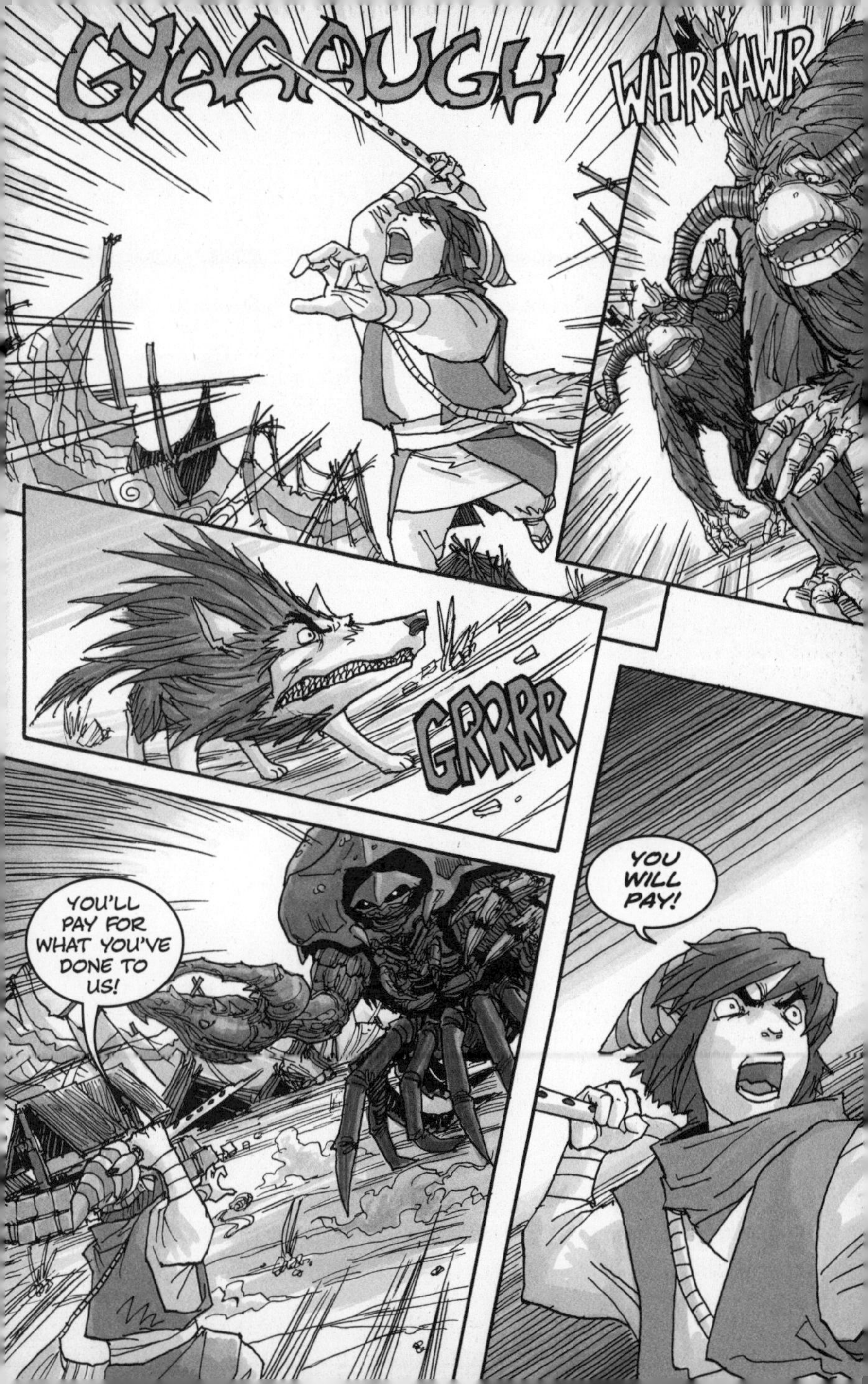
GYAAAUGH
WHRAAWR
GRRRR
YOU'LL PAY FOR WHAT YOU'VE DONE TO US!
YOU WILL PAY!

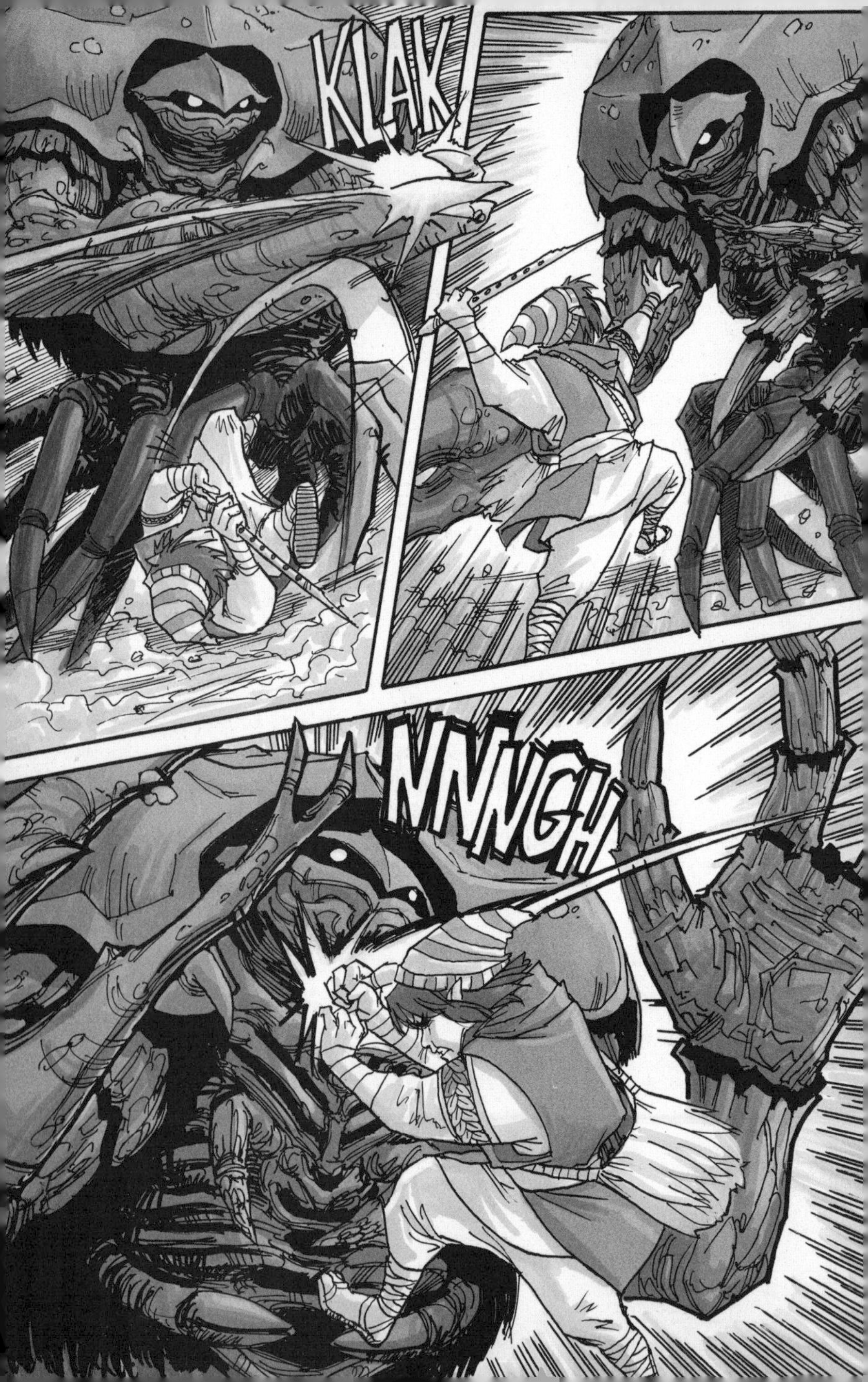
KLAK!
NNNGH!

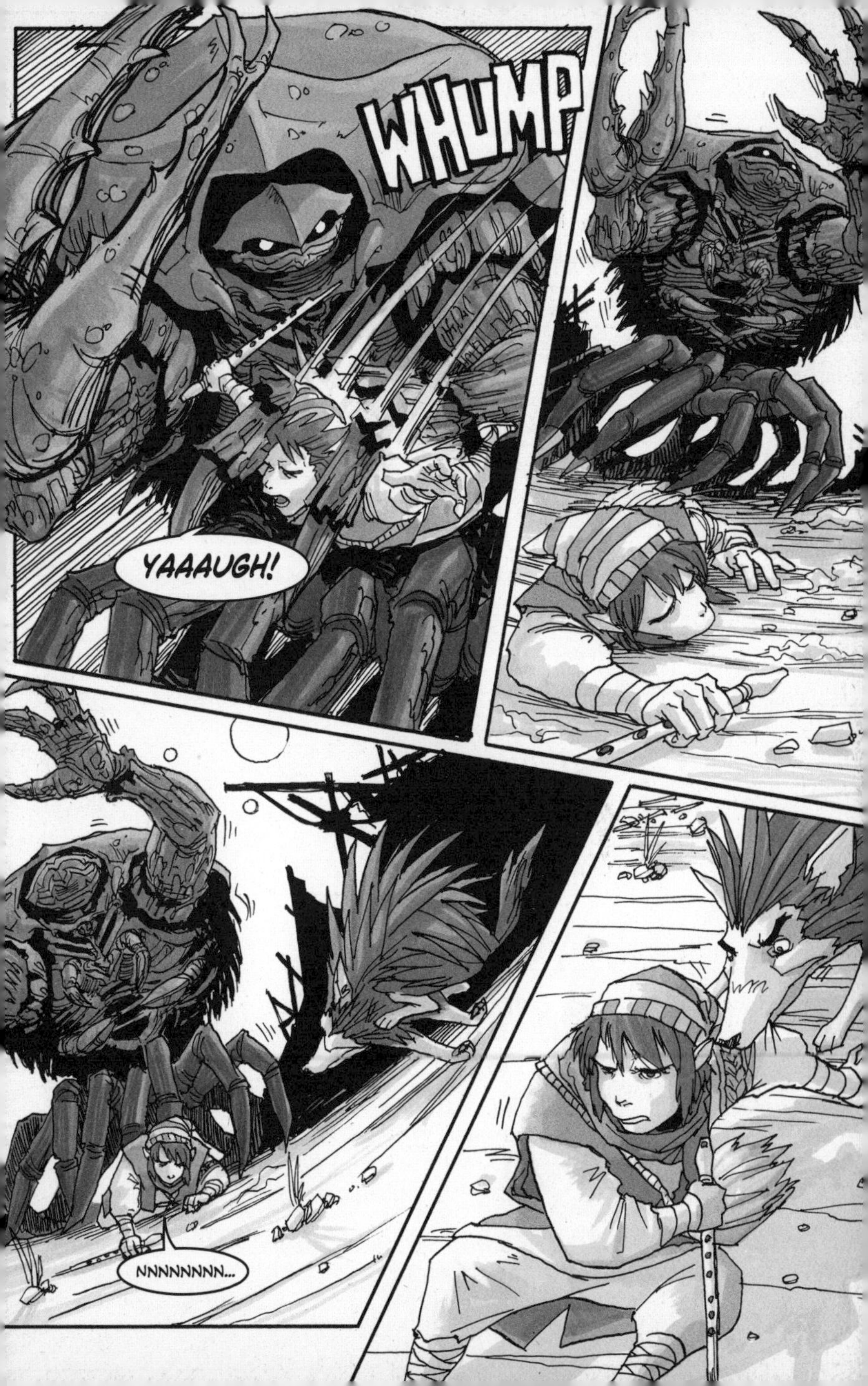
WHUMP
YAAAUGH!
NNNNNNNN...

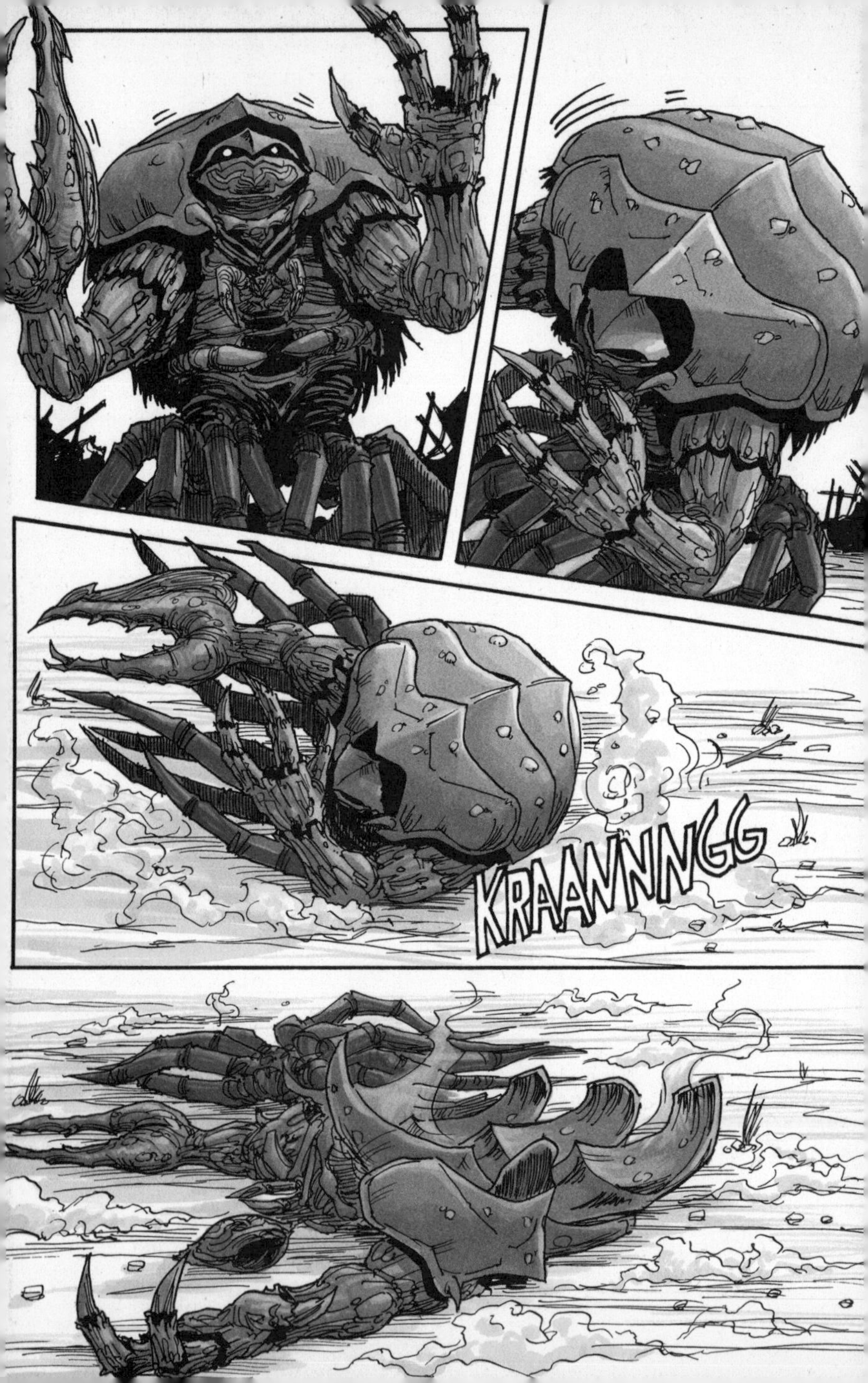
KRAANNNGG

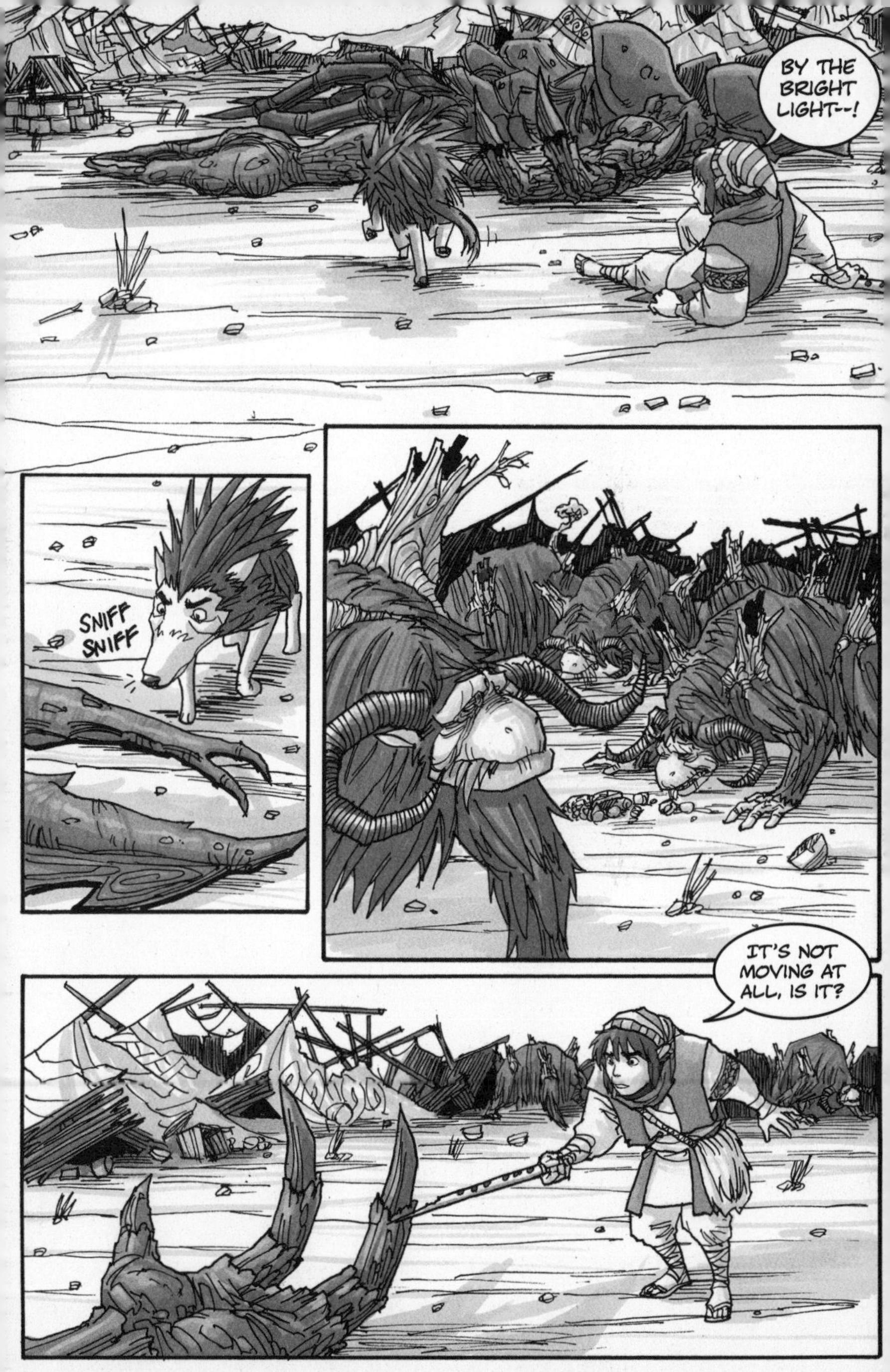
BY THE BRIGHT LIGHT--!
SNIFF SNIFF
IT'S NOT MOVING AT ALL, IS IT?

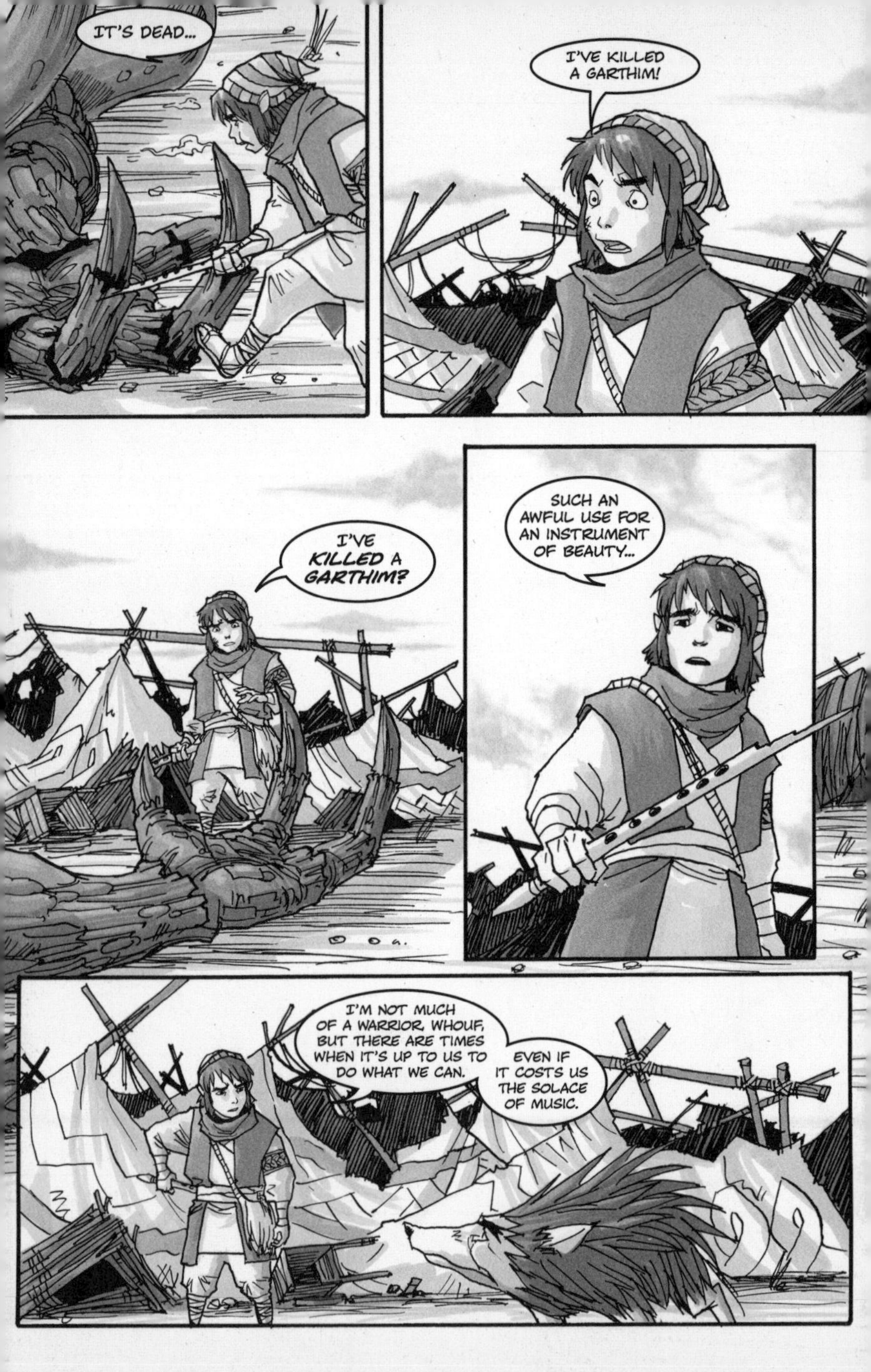
IT'S DEAD...
I'VE KILLED A GARTHIM!
I'VE KILLED A GARTHIM?
SUCH AN AWFUL USE FOR AN INSTRUMENT OF BEAUTY...
I'M NOT MUCH OF A WARRIOR, WHOUF, BUT THERE ARE TIMES WHEN IT'S UP TO US TO DO WHAT WE CAN.
EVEN IF IT COSTS US THE SOLACE OF MUSIC.

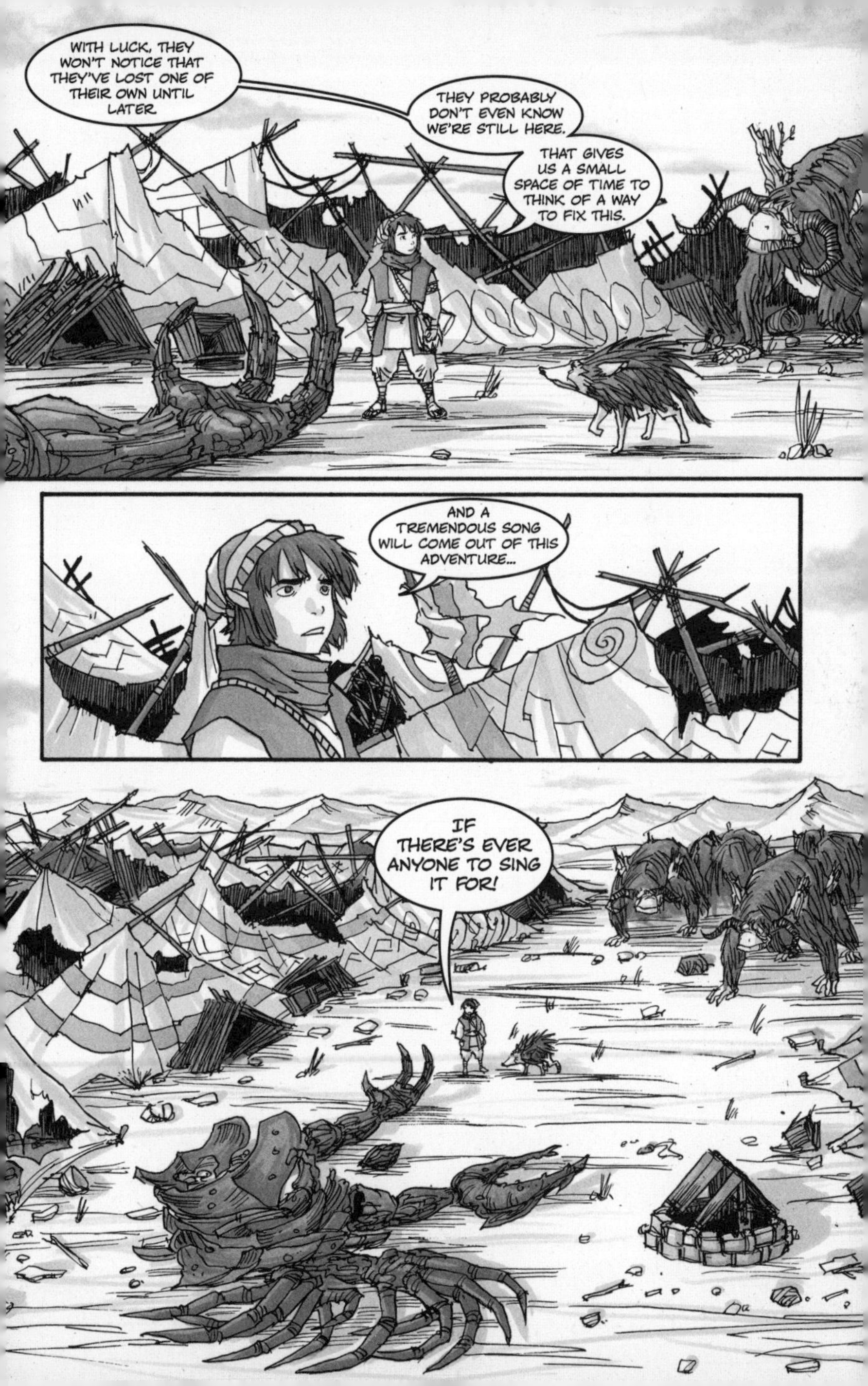
WITH LUCK, THEY WON'T NOTICE THAT THEY'VE LOST ONE OF THEIR OWN UNTIL LATER.
THEY PROBABLY DON'T EVEN KNOW WE'RE STILL HERE.
THAT GIVES US A SMALL SPACE OF TIME TO THINK OF A WAY TO FIX THIS.
AND A TREMENDOUS SONG WILL COME OUT OF THIS ADVENTURE...
IF THERE'S EVER ANYONE TO SING IT FOR!

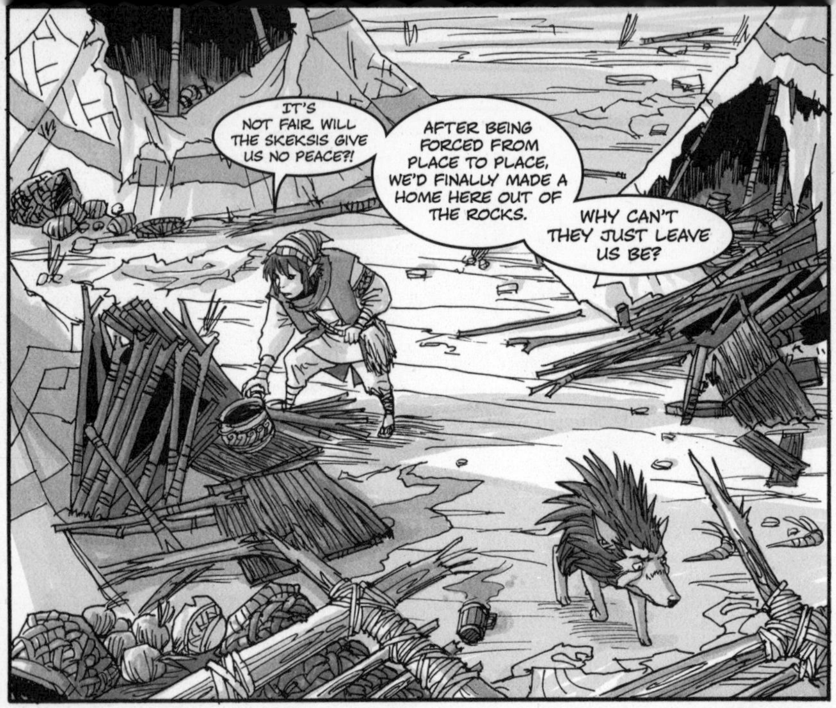
IT'S NOT FAIR. WILL THE SKEKSIS GIVE US NO PEACE?!
AFTER BEING FORCED FROM PLACE TO PLACE, WE'D FINALLY MADE A HOME HERE OUT OF THE ROCKS.
WHY CAN'T THEY JUST LEAVE US BE?
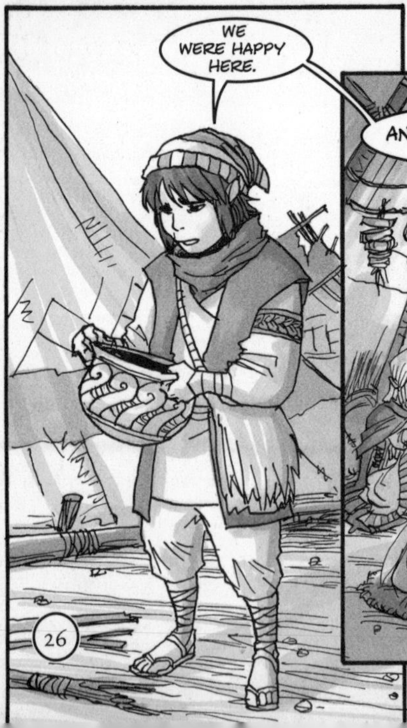
WE WERE HAPPY HERE.
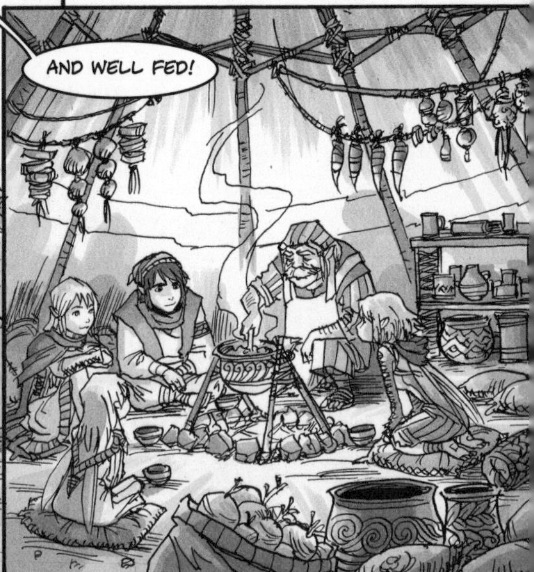
AND WELL FED!

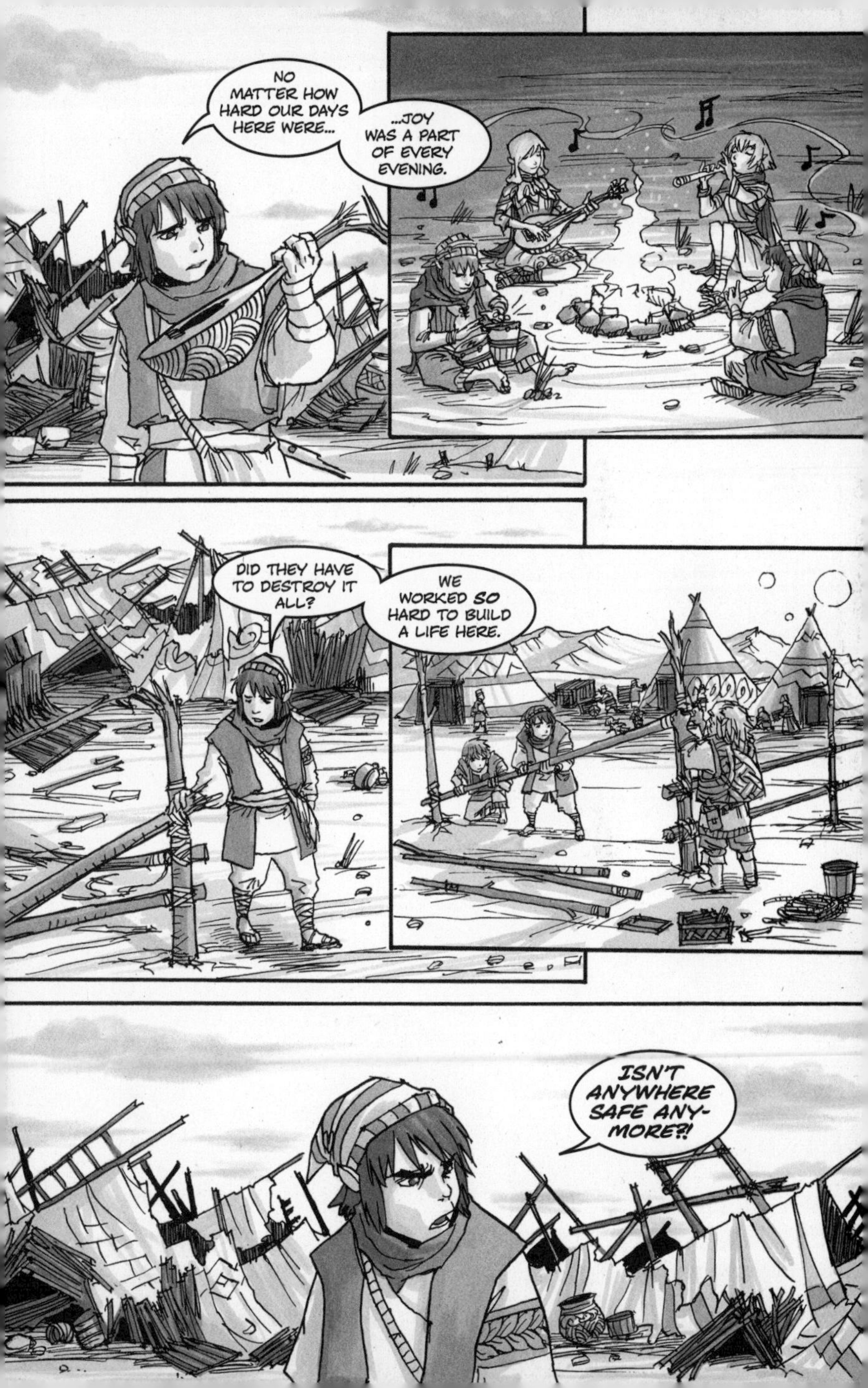
NO MATTER HOW HARD OUR DAYS HERE WERE...
...JOY WAS A PART OF EVERY EVENING.
DID THEY HAVE TO DESTROY IT ALL?
WE WORKED SO HARD TO BUILD A LIFE HERE.
ISN'T ANYWHERE SAFE ANY-MORE?!

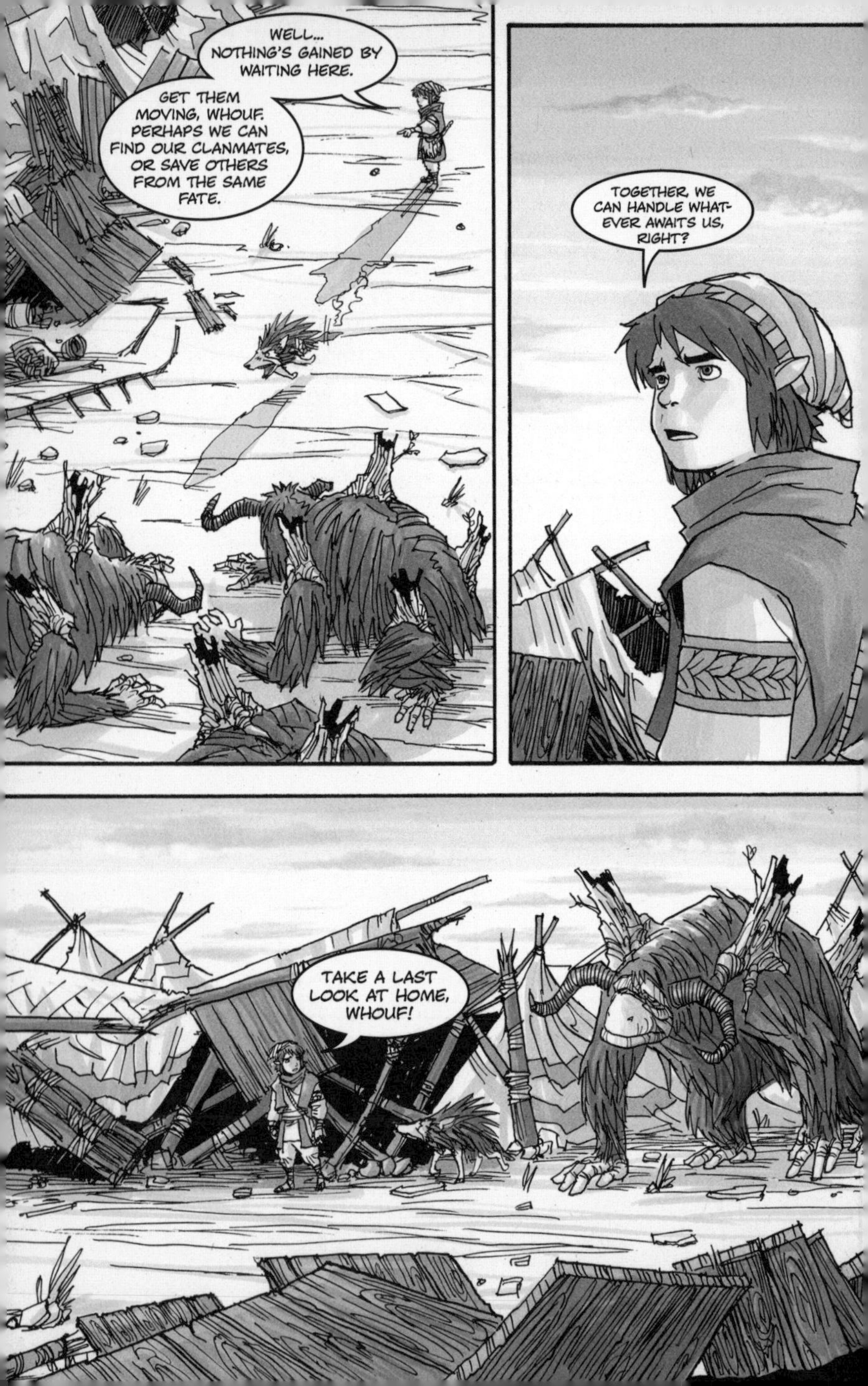
WELL... NOTHING'S GAINED BY WAITING HERE.
GET THEM MOVING, WHOUF. PERHAPS WE CAN FIND OUR CLANMATES, OR SAVE OTHERS FROM THE SAME FATE.
TOGETHER, WE CAN HANDLE WHAT-EVER AWAITS US, RIGHT?
TAKE A LAST LOOK AT HOME, WHOUF!

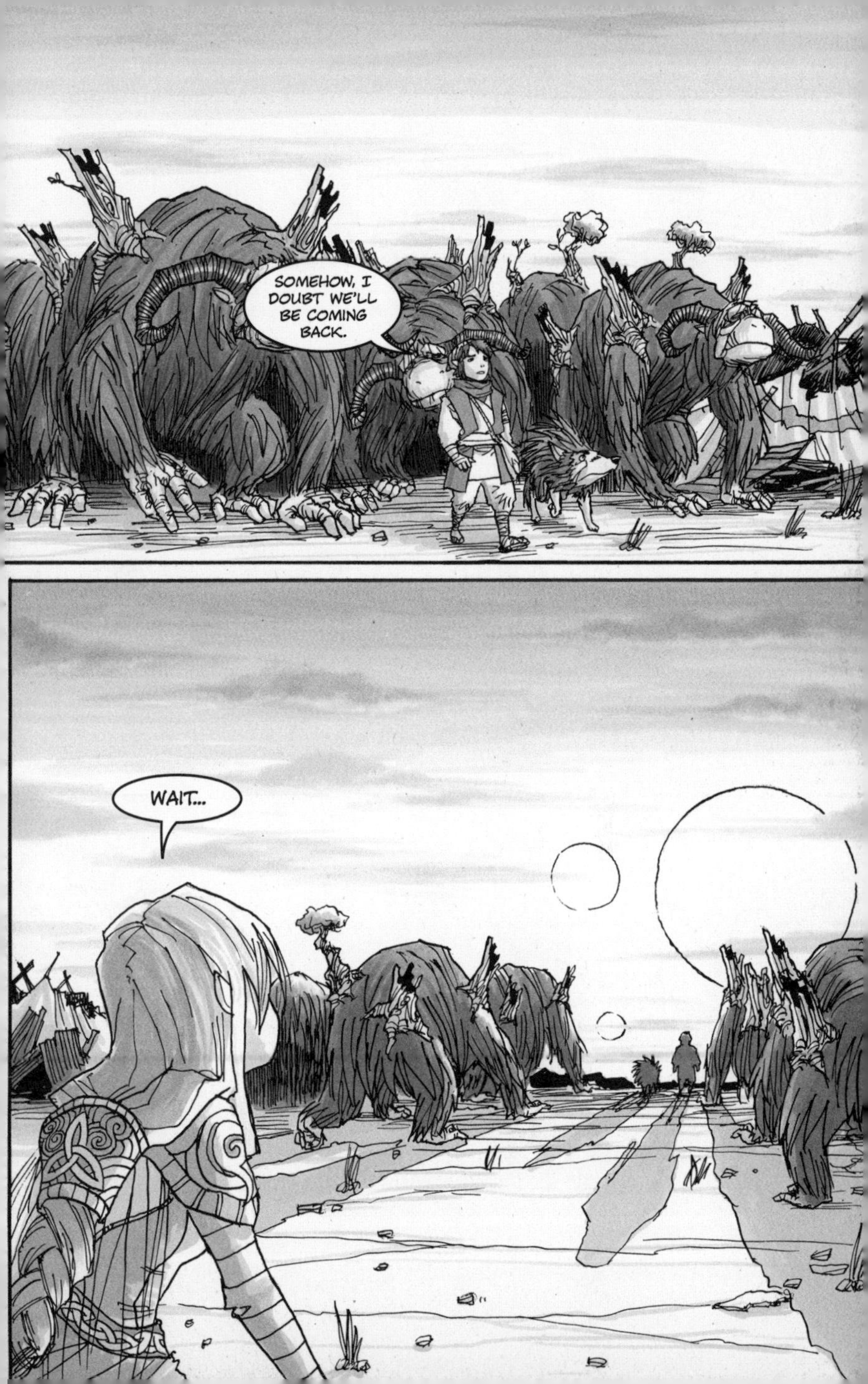
SOMEHOW, I DOUBT WE'LL BE COMING BACK.
WAIT...

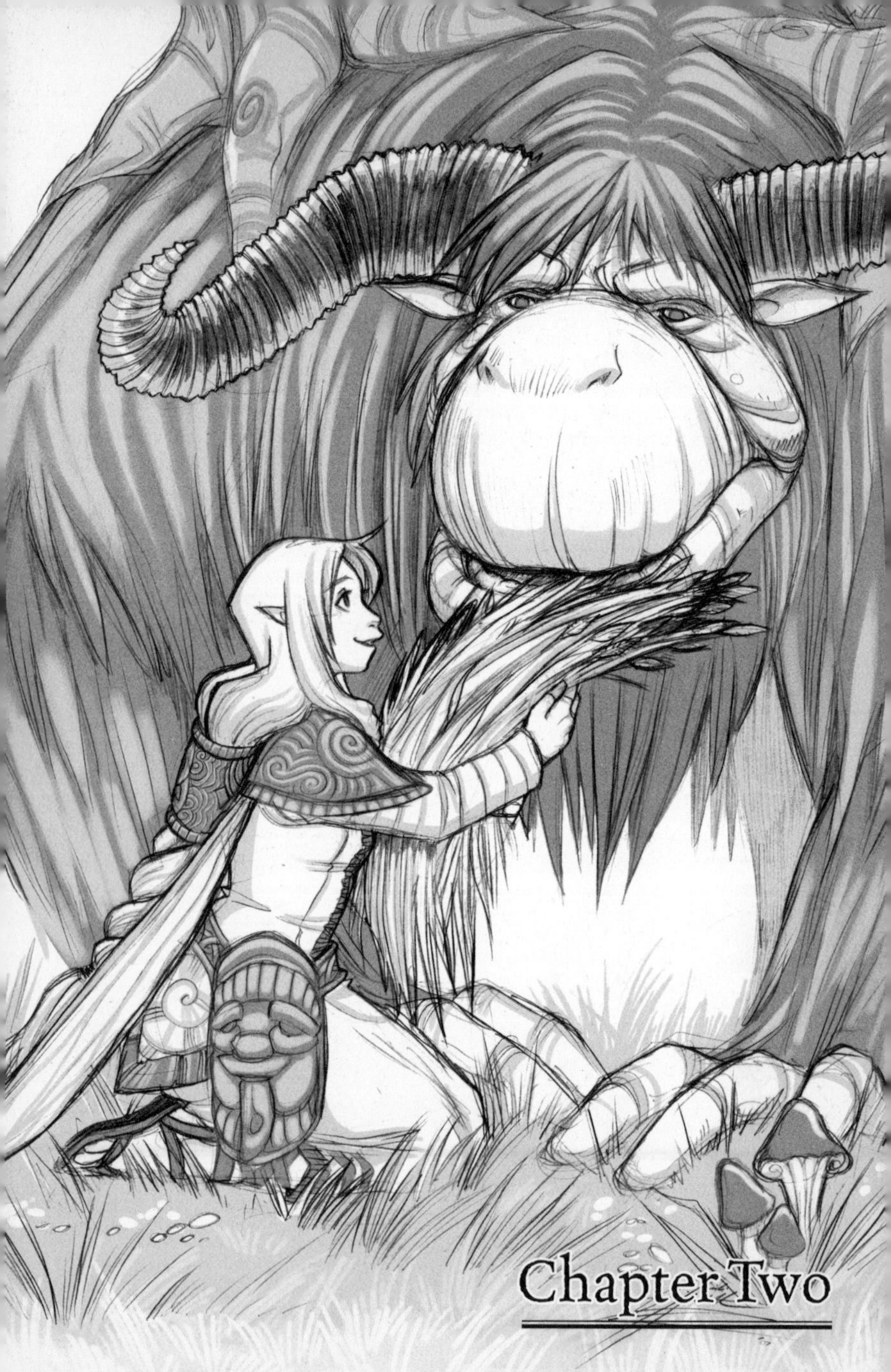

Chapter Two

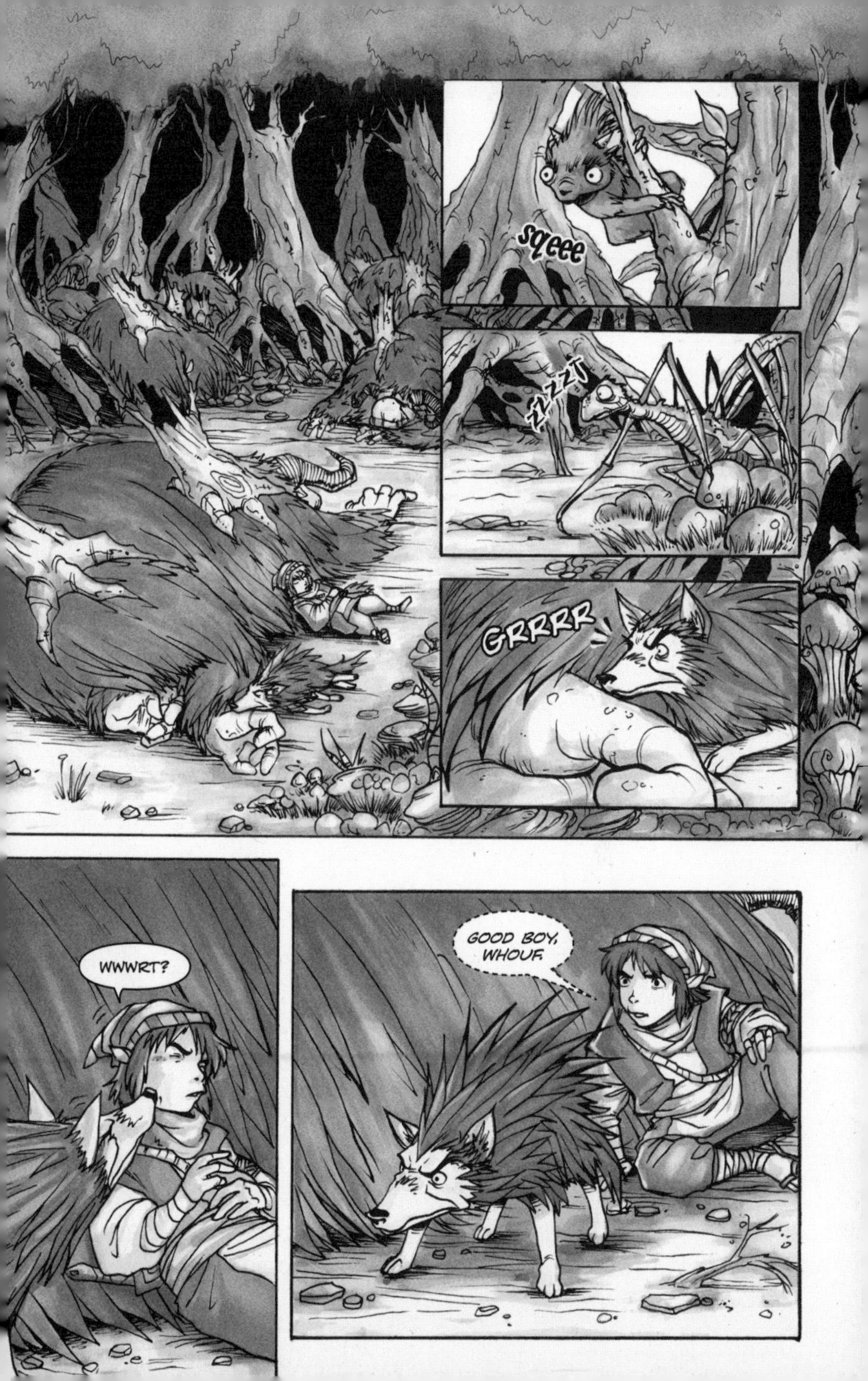
sqeee
zzzzt
GRRRR
WWWRT?
GOOD BOY, WHOUF.

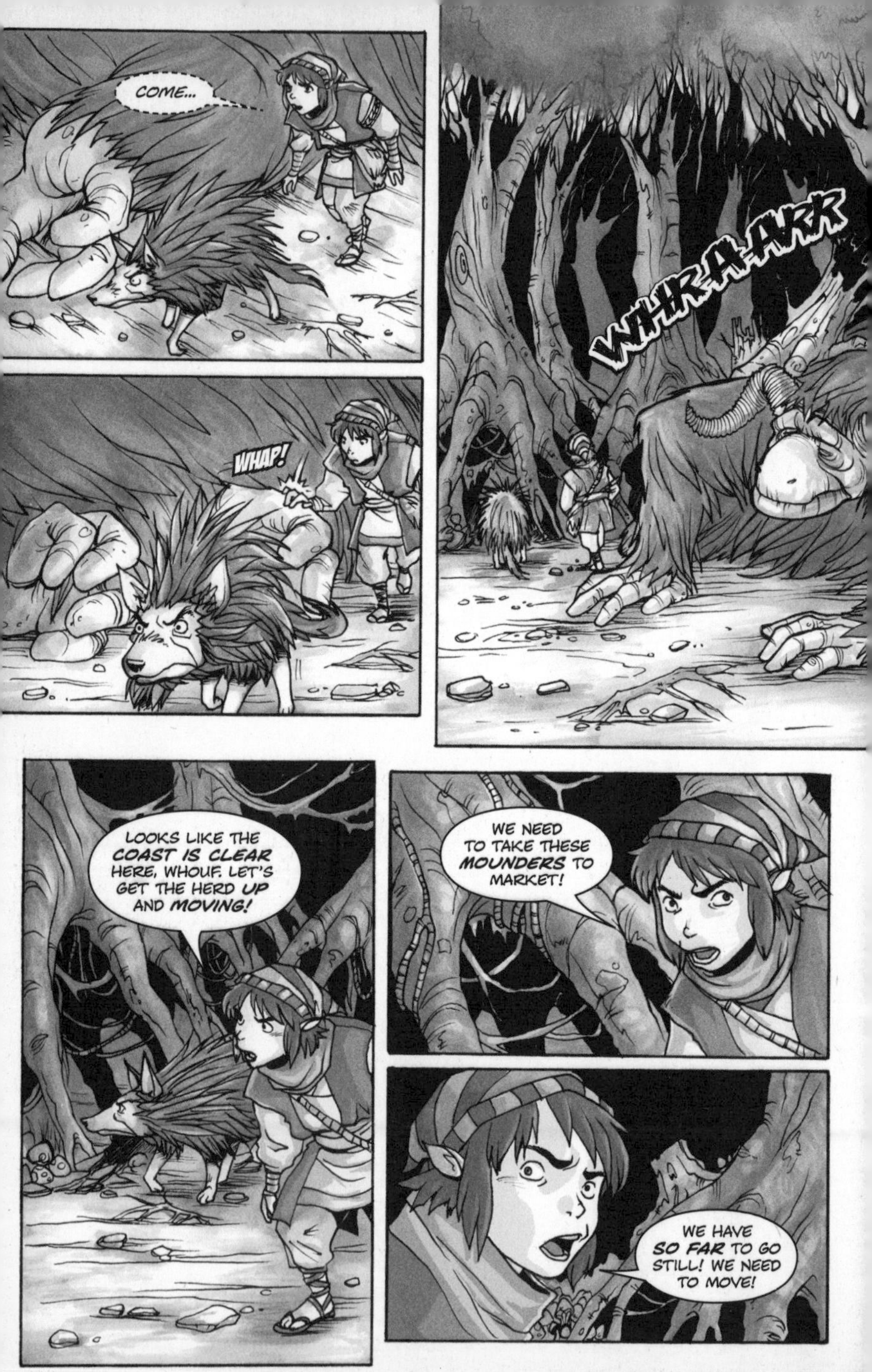
COME...
WHAP!
WHR A-ARR
LOOKS LIKE THE **COAST IS CLEAR** HERE, WHOUF. LET'S GET THE HERD **UP** AND **MOVING!**
WE NEED TO TAKE THESE **MOUNDERS** TO MARKET!
WE HAVE **SO FAR** TO GO STILL! WE NEED TO MOVE!

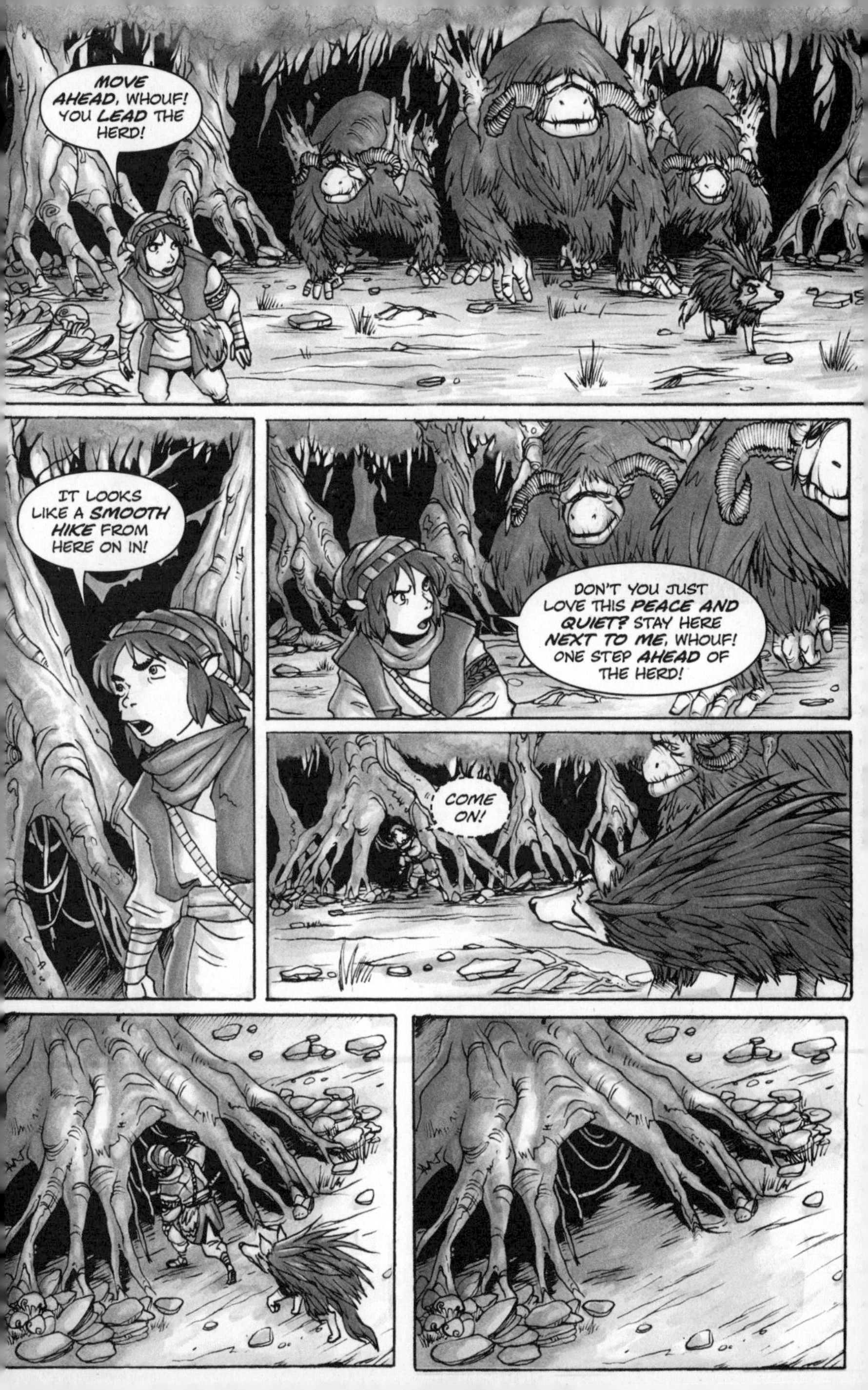
MOVE AHEAD, WHOUF! YOU LEAD THE HERD!
IT LOOKS LIKE A SMOOTH HIKE FROM HERE ON IN!
DON'T YOU JUST LOVE THIS PEACE AND QUIET? STAY HERE NEXT TO ME, WHOUF! ONE STEP AHEAD OF THE HERD!
COME ON!

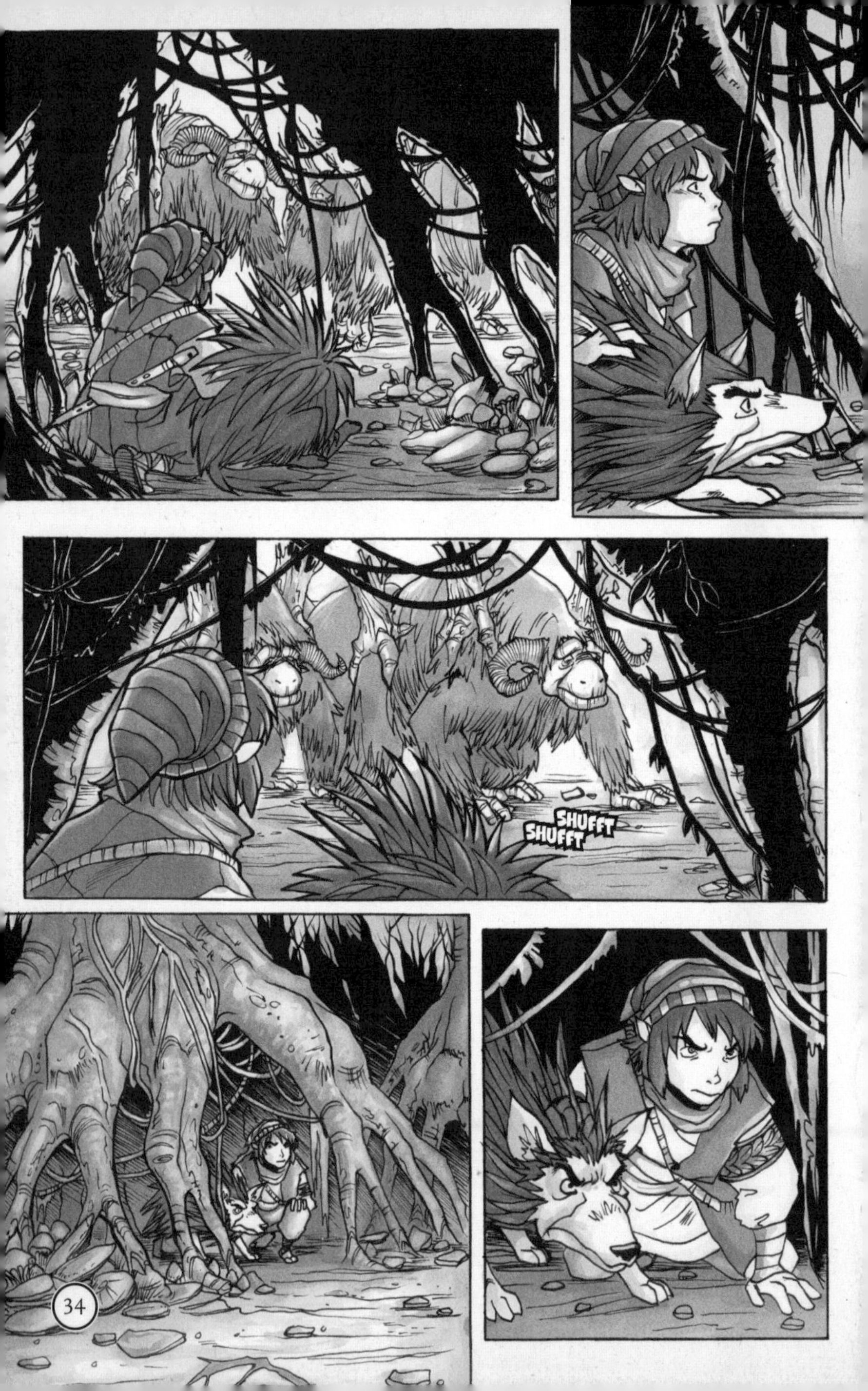
SHUFFT
SHUFFT

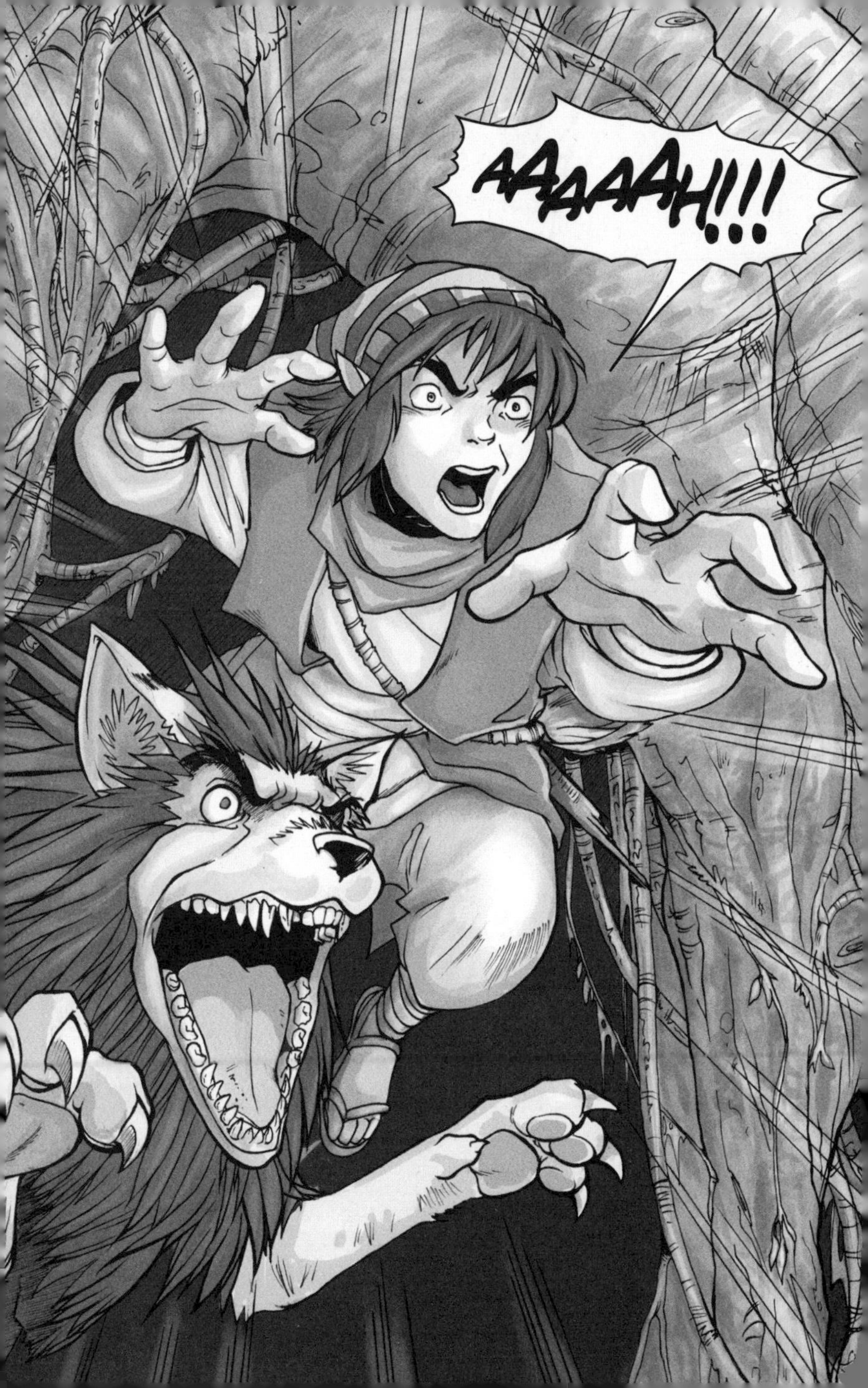
AAAAAH!!!

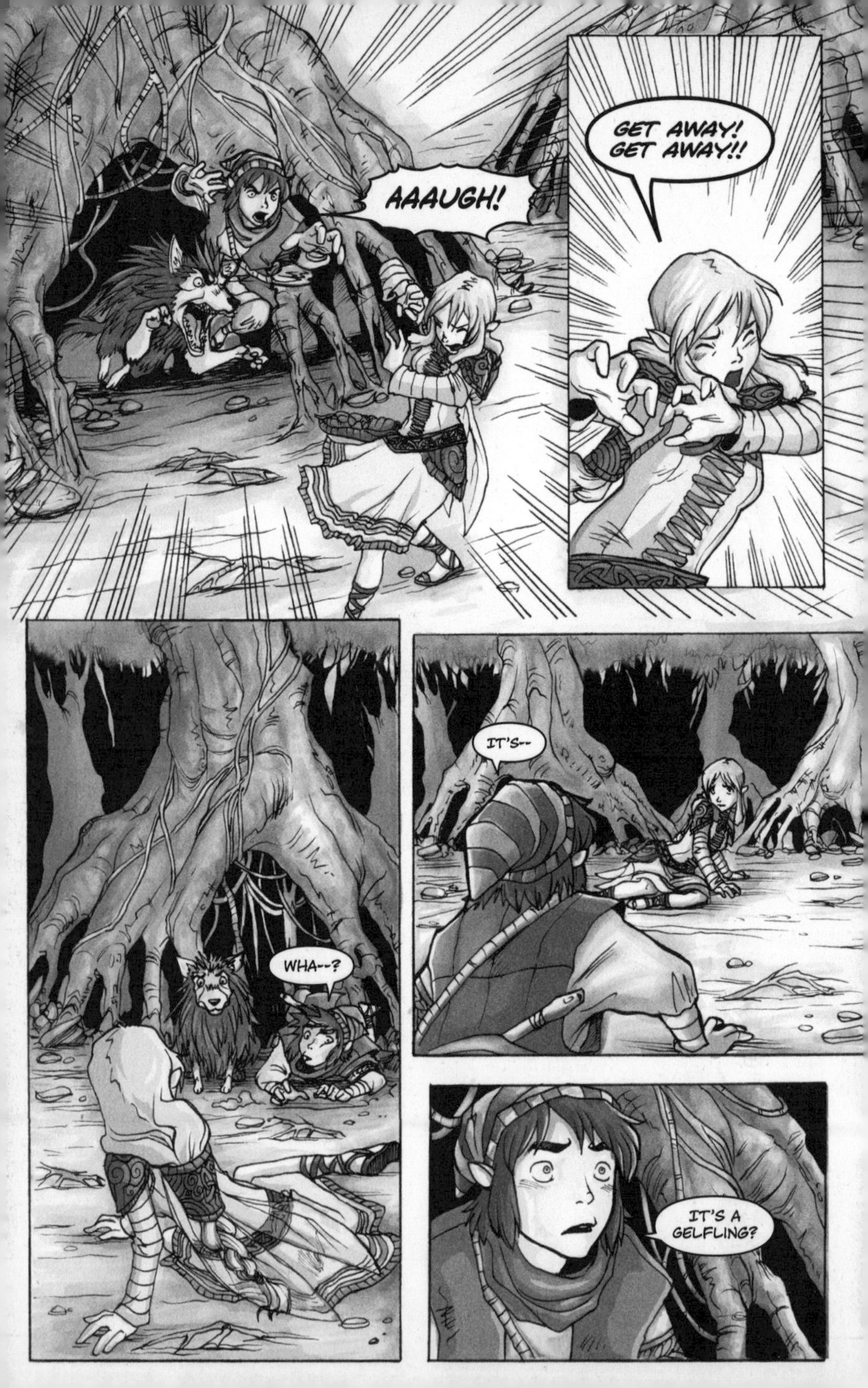
AAAUGH!
GET AWAY! GET AWAY!!
WHA--?
IT'S--
IT'S A GELFLING?

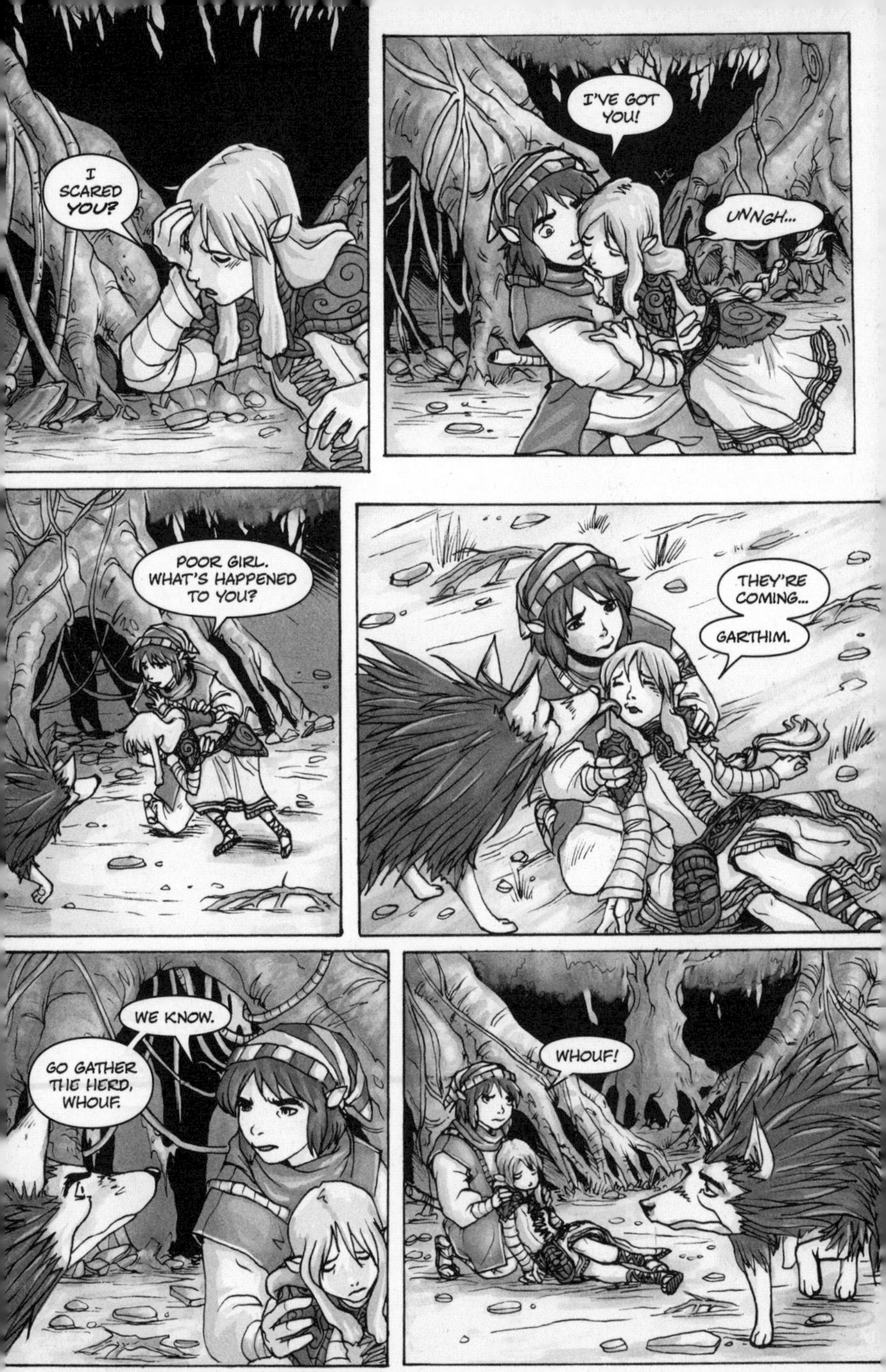
I SCARED YOU?
I'VE GOT YOU!
UNNGH...
POOR GIRL. WHAT'S HAPPENED TO YOU?
THEY'RE COMING...
GARTHIM.
WE KNOW.
GO GATHER THE HERD, WHOUF.
WHOUF!

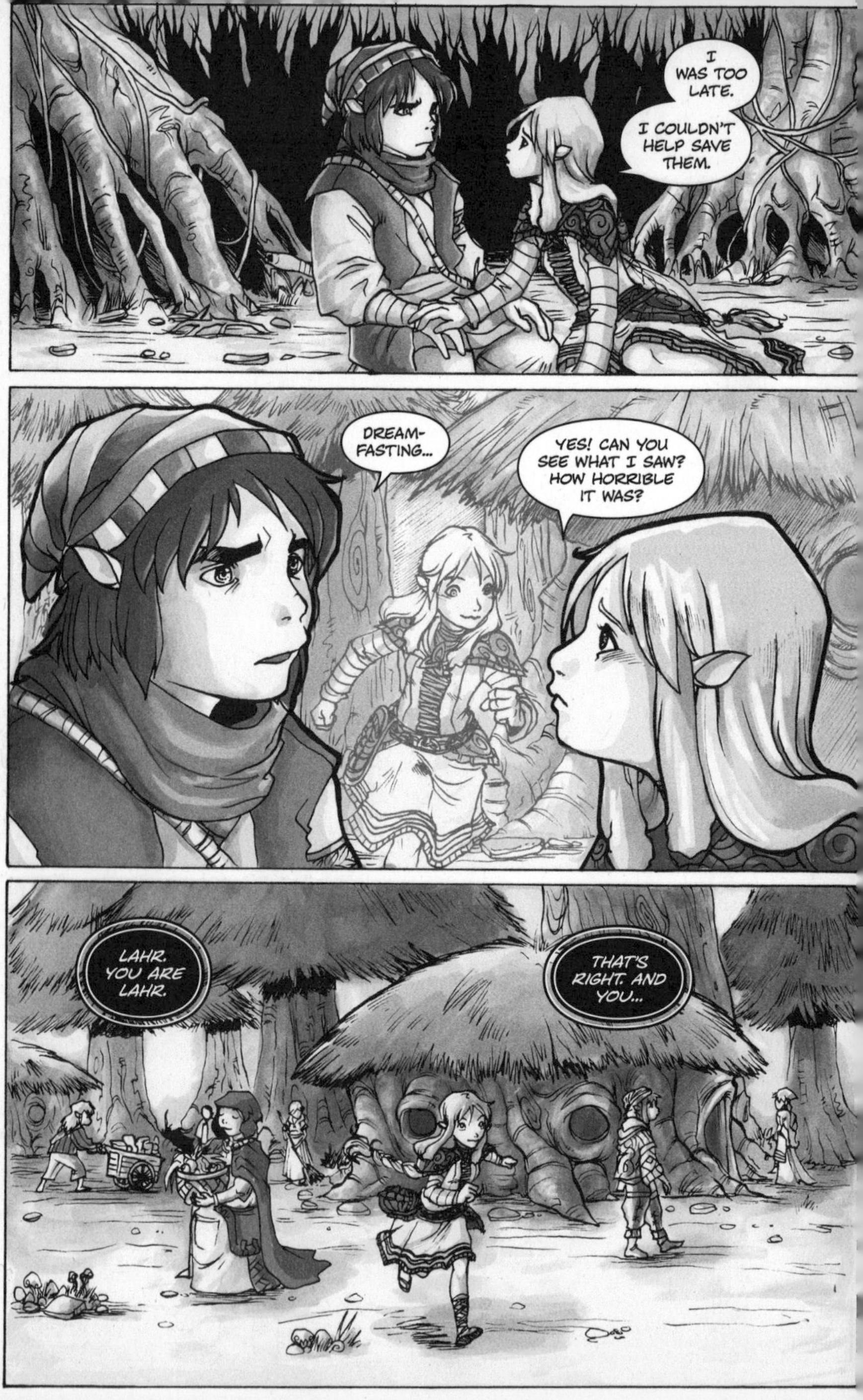
I WAS TOO LATE.
I COULDN'T HELP SAVE THEM.
DREAM-FASTING...
YES! CAN YOU SEE WHAT I SAW? HOW HORRIBLE IT WAS?
LAHR. YOU ARE LAHR.
THAT'S RIGHT. AND YOU...

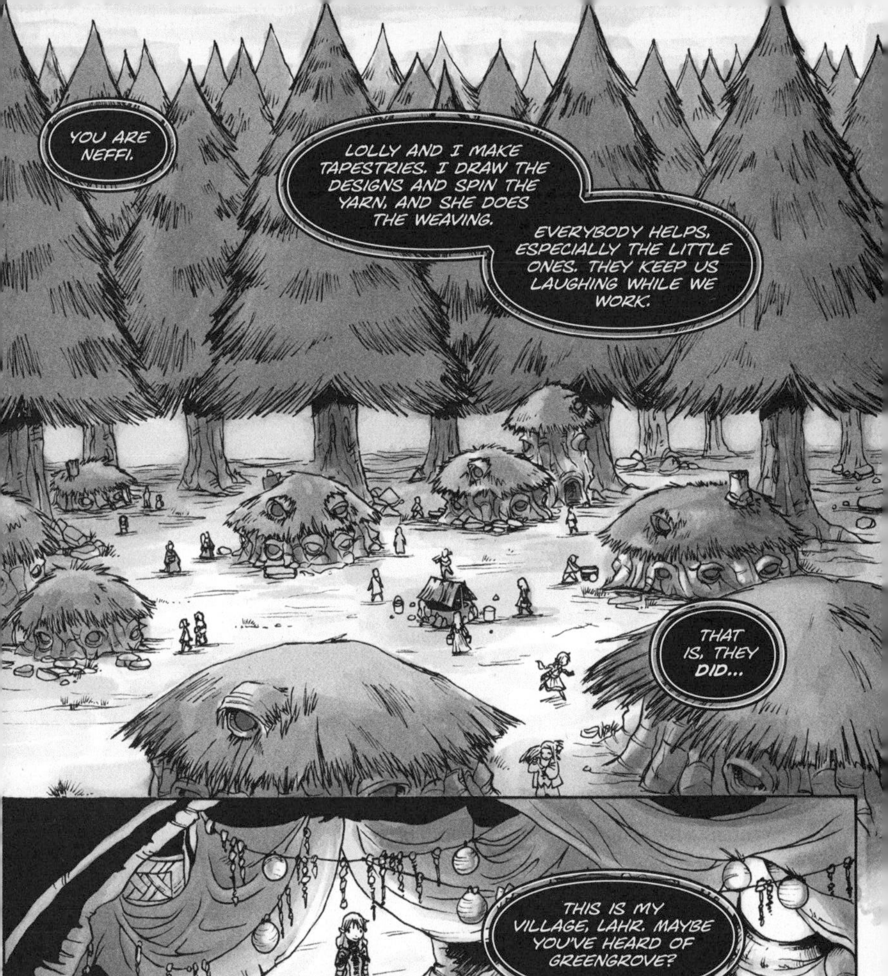
YOU ARE NEFFI.
LOLLY AND I MAKE TAPESTRIES. I DRAW THE DESIGNS AND SPIN THE YARN, AND SHE DOES THE WEAVING.
EVERYBODY HELPS, ESPECIALLY THE LITTLE ONES. THEY KEEP US LAUGHING WHILE WE WORK.
THAT IS, THEY *DID*...
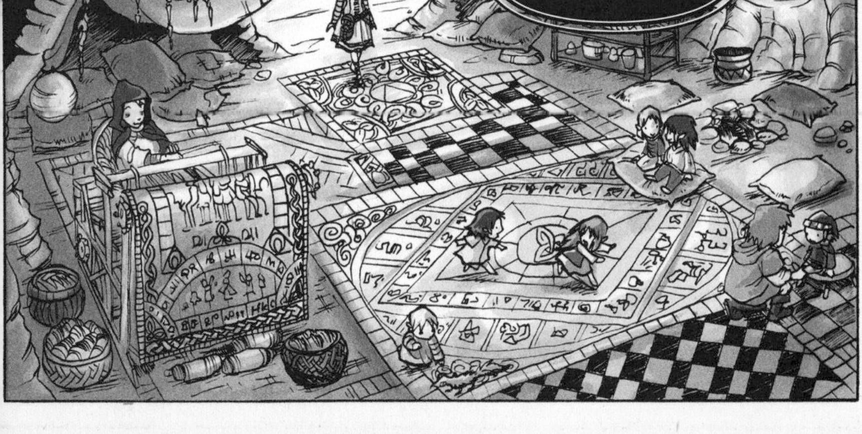
THIS IS MY VILLAGE, LAHR. MAYBE YOU'VE HEARD OF GREENGROVE?

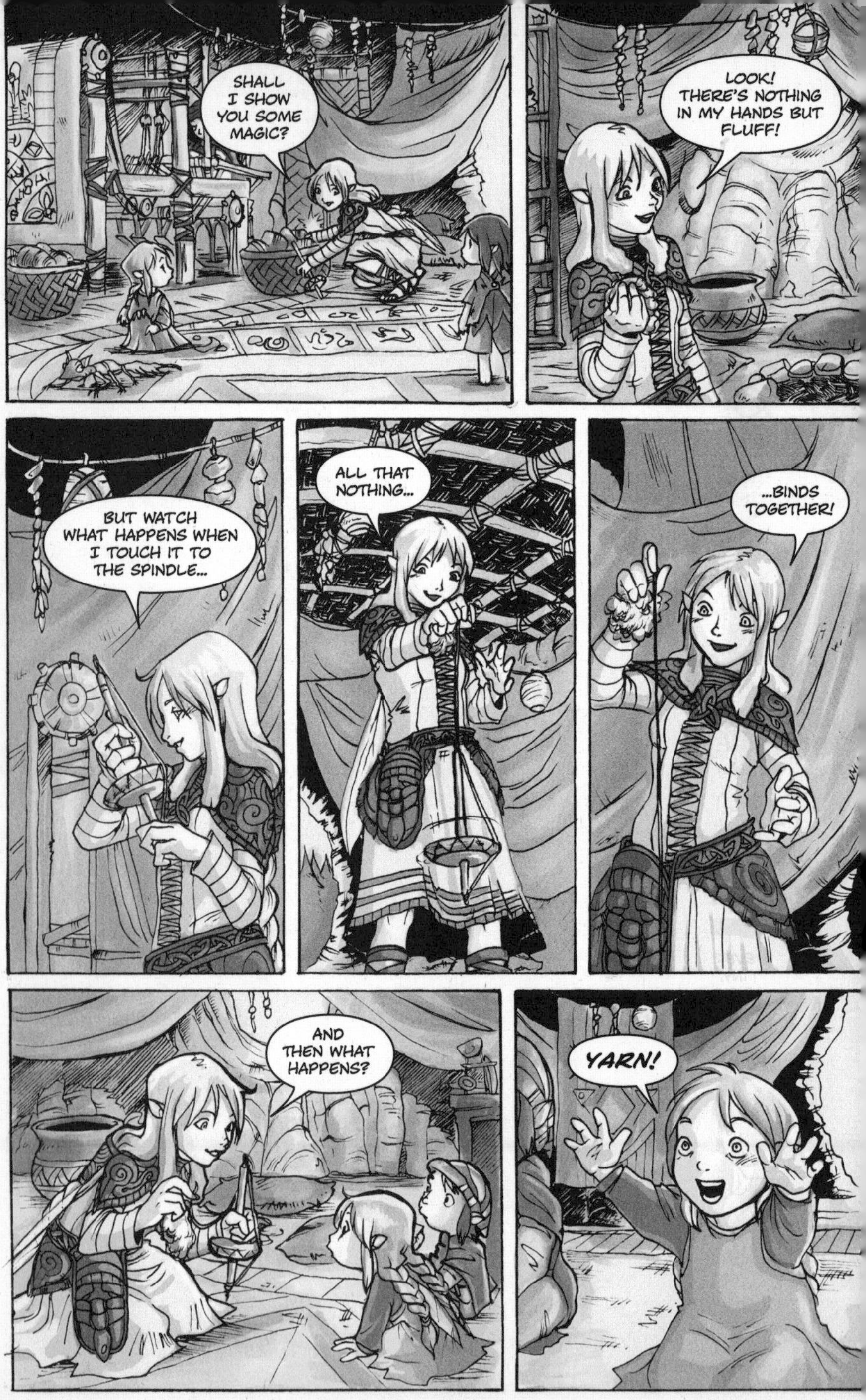
SHALL I SHOW YOU SOME MAGIC?
LOOK! THERE'S NOTHING IN MY HANDS BUT FLUFF!
BUT WATCH WHAT HAPPENS WHEN I TOUCH IT TO THE SPINDLE...
ALL THAT NOTHING...
...BINDS TOGETHER!
AND THEN WHAT HAPPENS?
YARN!

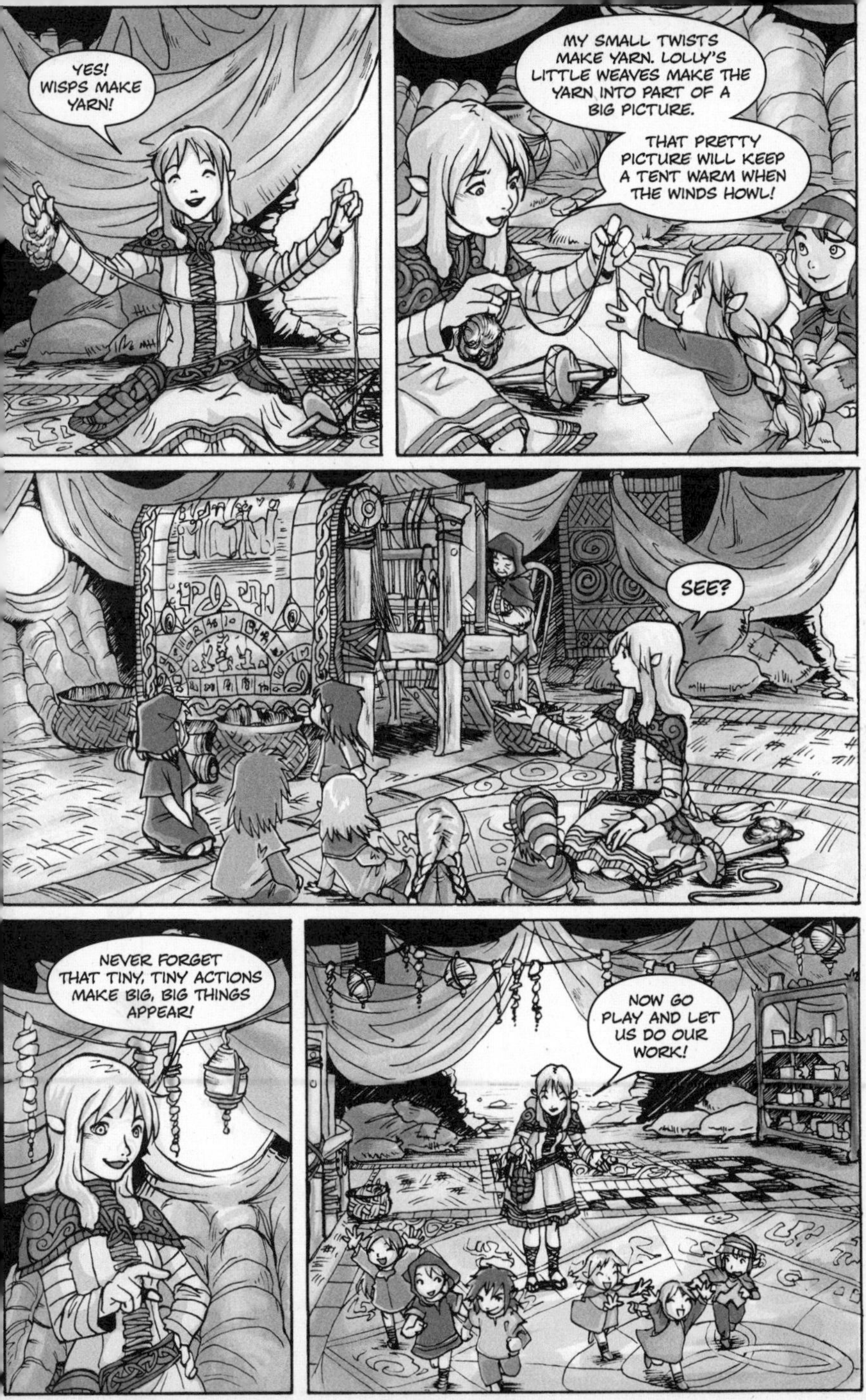
YES! WISPS MAKE YARN!
MY SMALL TWISTS MAKE YARN. LOLLY'S LITTLE WEAVES MAKE THE YARN INTO PART OF A BIG PICTURE.
THAT PRETTY PICTURE WILL KEEP A TENT WARM WHEN THE WINDS HOWL!
SEE?
NEVER FORGET THAT TINY, TINY ACTIONS MAKE BIG, BIG THINGS APPEAR!
NOW GO PLAY AND LET US DO OUR WORK!

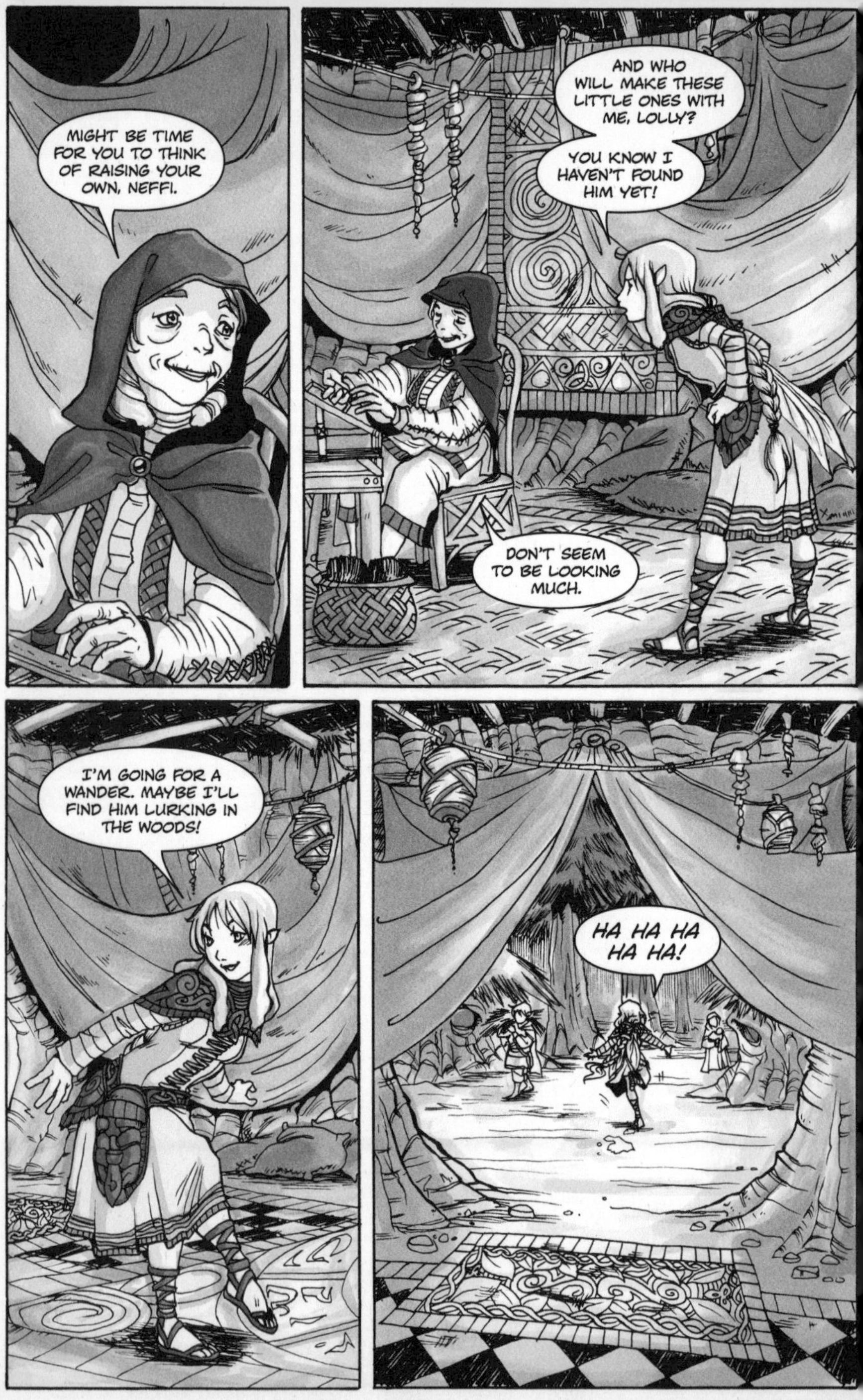
MIGHT BE TIME FOR YOU TO THINK OF RAISING YOUR OWN, NEFFI.
AND WHO WILL MAKE THESE LITTLE ONES WITH ME, LOLLY?
YOU KNOW I HAVEN'T FOUND HIM YET!
DON'T SEEM TO BE LOOKING MUCH.
I'M GOING FOR A WANDER. MAYBE I'LL FIND HIM LURKING IN THE WOODS!
HA HA HA HA HA!

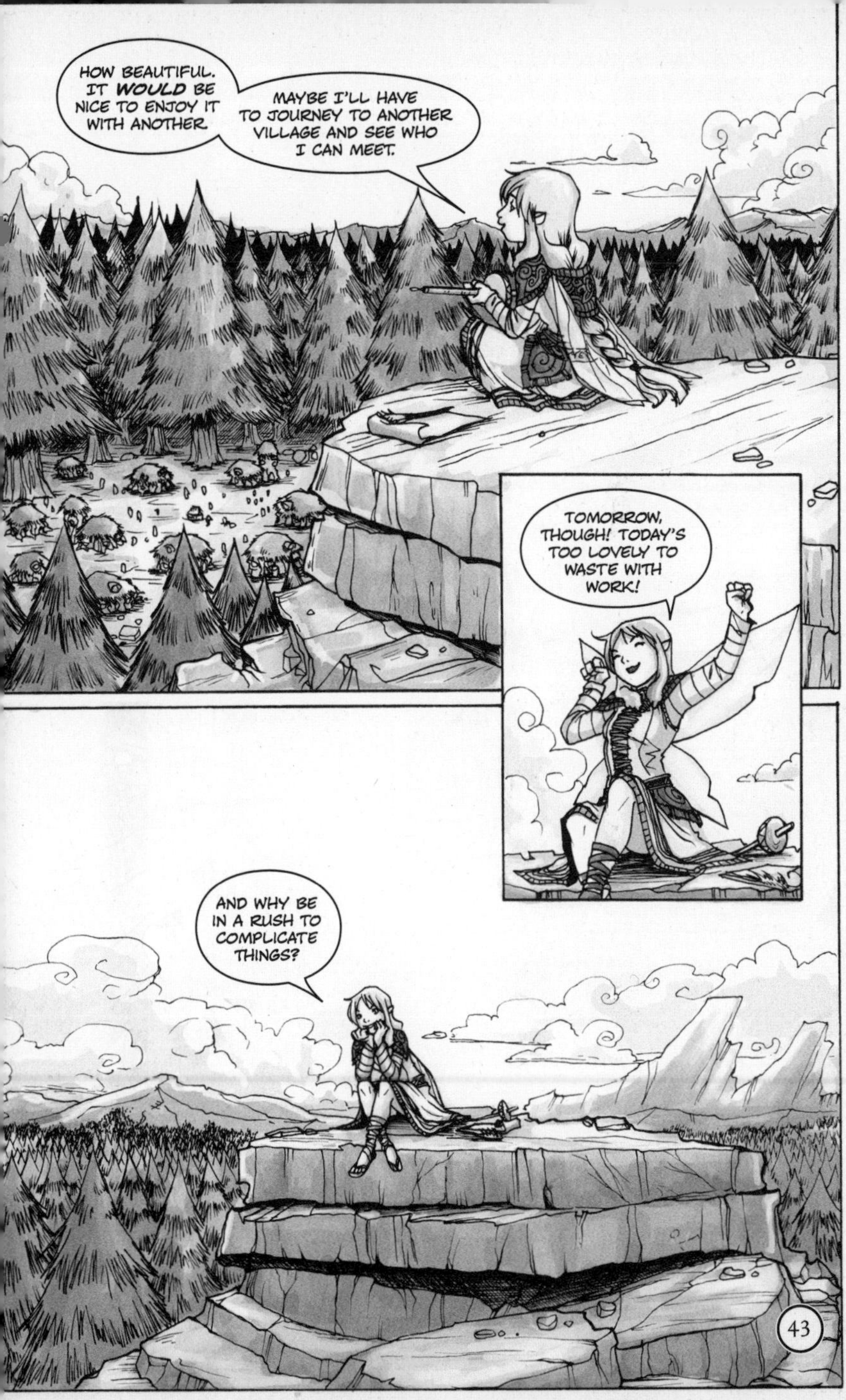
HOW BEAUTIFUL. IT ***WOULD*** BE NICE TO ENJOY IT WITH ANOTHER.
MAYBE I'LL HAVE TO JOURNEY TO ANOTHER VILLAGE AND SEE WHO I CAN MEET.
TOMORROW, THOUGH! TODAY'S TOO LOVELY TO WASTE WITH WORK!
AND WHY BE IN A RUSH TO COMPLICATE THINGS?

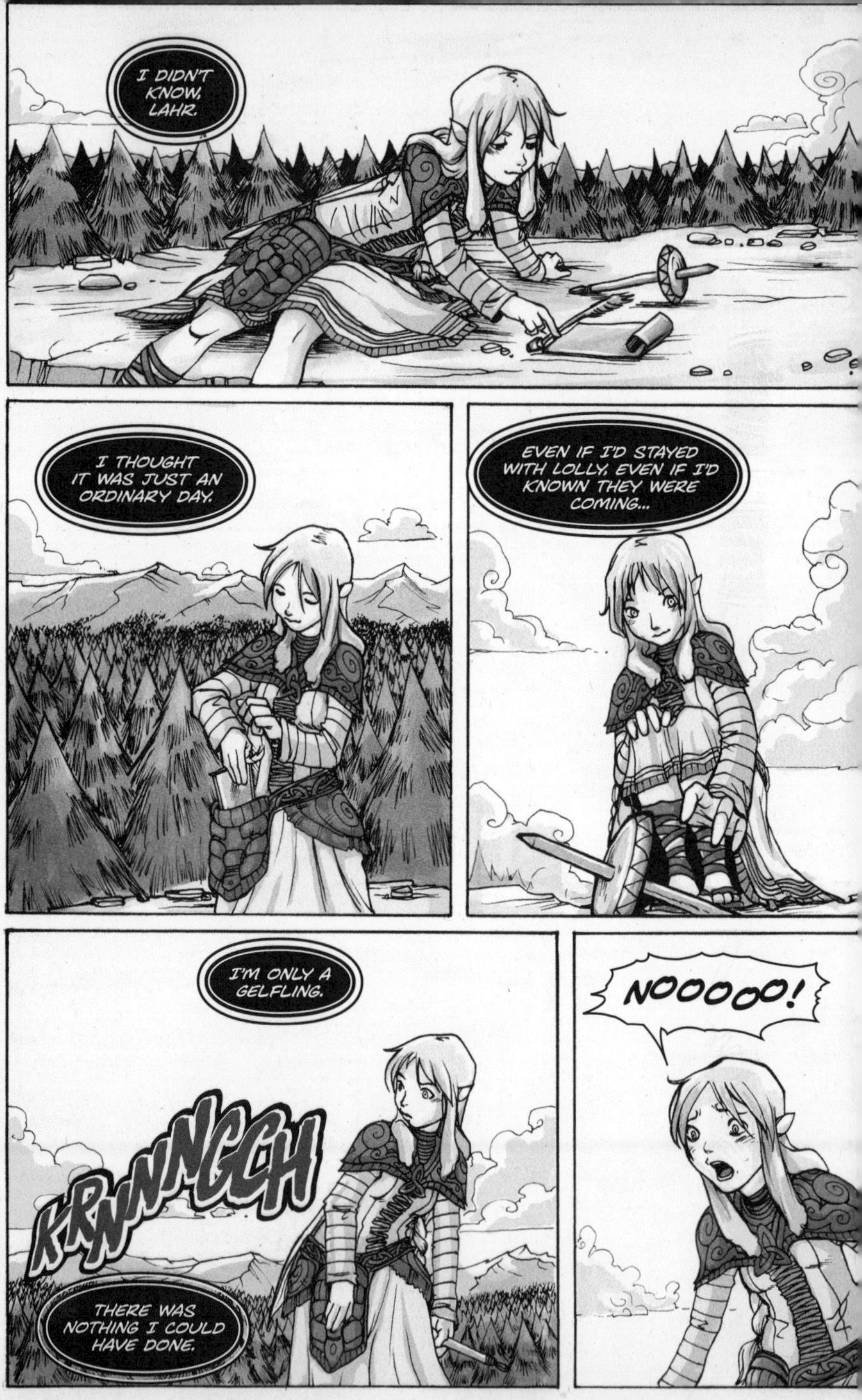
I DIDN'T KNOW, LAHR.
I THOUGHT IT WAS JUST AN ORDINARY DAY.
EVEN IF I'D STAYED WITH LOLLY, EVEN IF I'D KNOWN THEY WERE COMING...
I'M ONLY A GELFLING.
KRNNNGCH
THERE WAS NOTHING I COULD HAVE DONE.
NOOOOO!

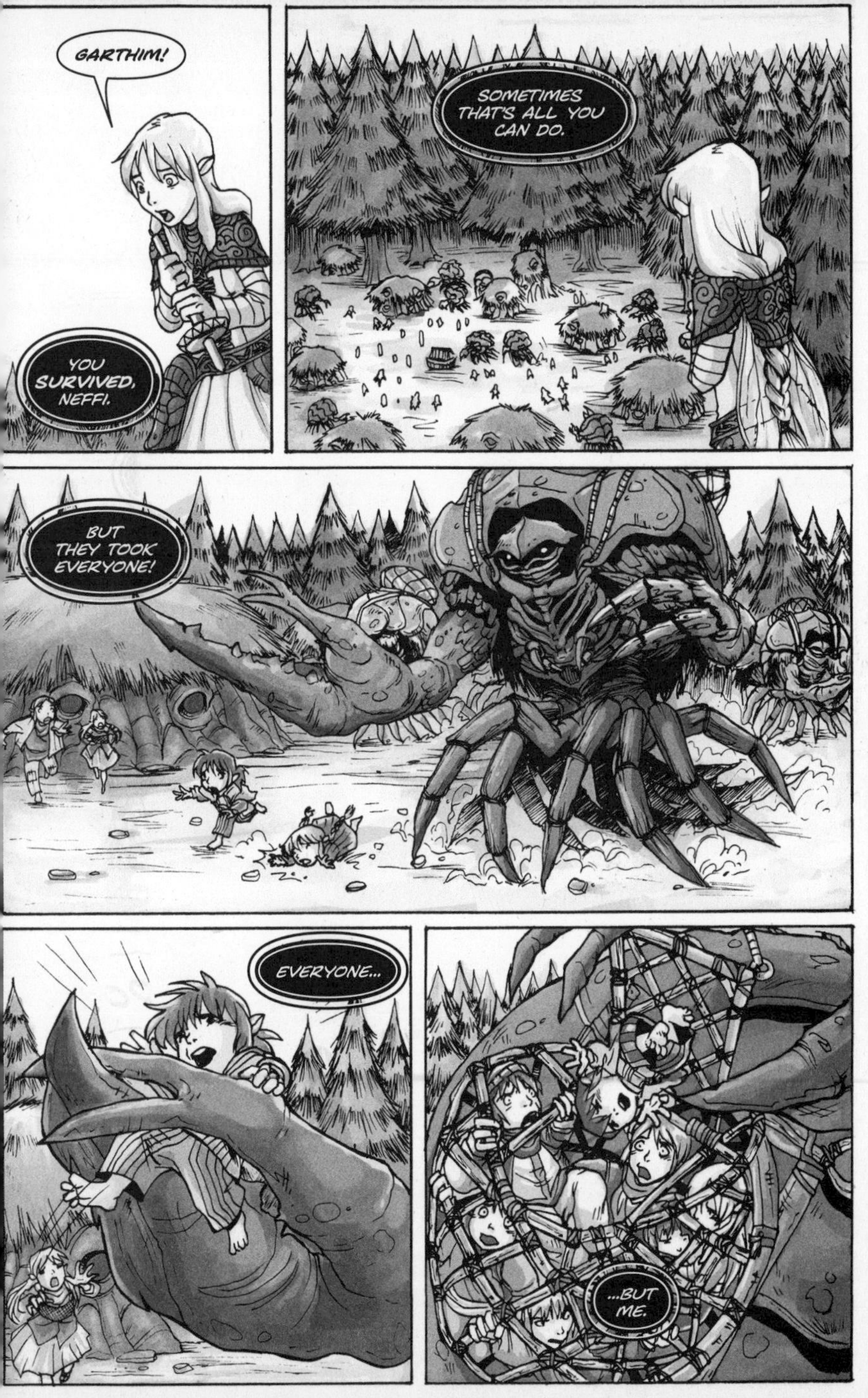
GARTHIM!
YOU SURVIVED, NEFFI.
SOMETIMES THAT'S ALL YOU CAN DO.
BUT THEY TOOK EVERYONE!
EVERYONE...
...BUT ME.

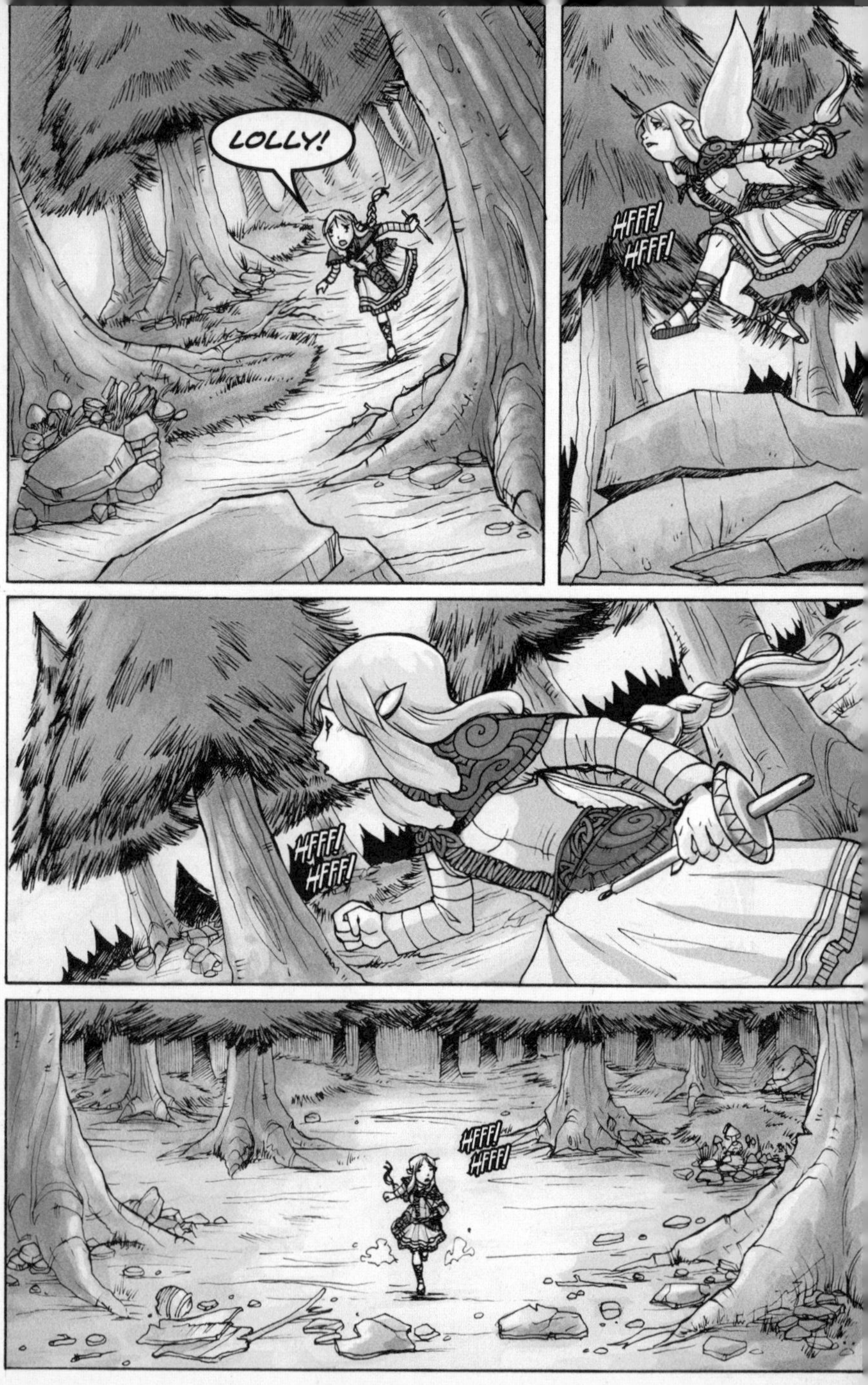
LOLLY!
HFFF! HFFF!
HFFF! HFFF!
HFFF! HFFF!

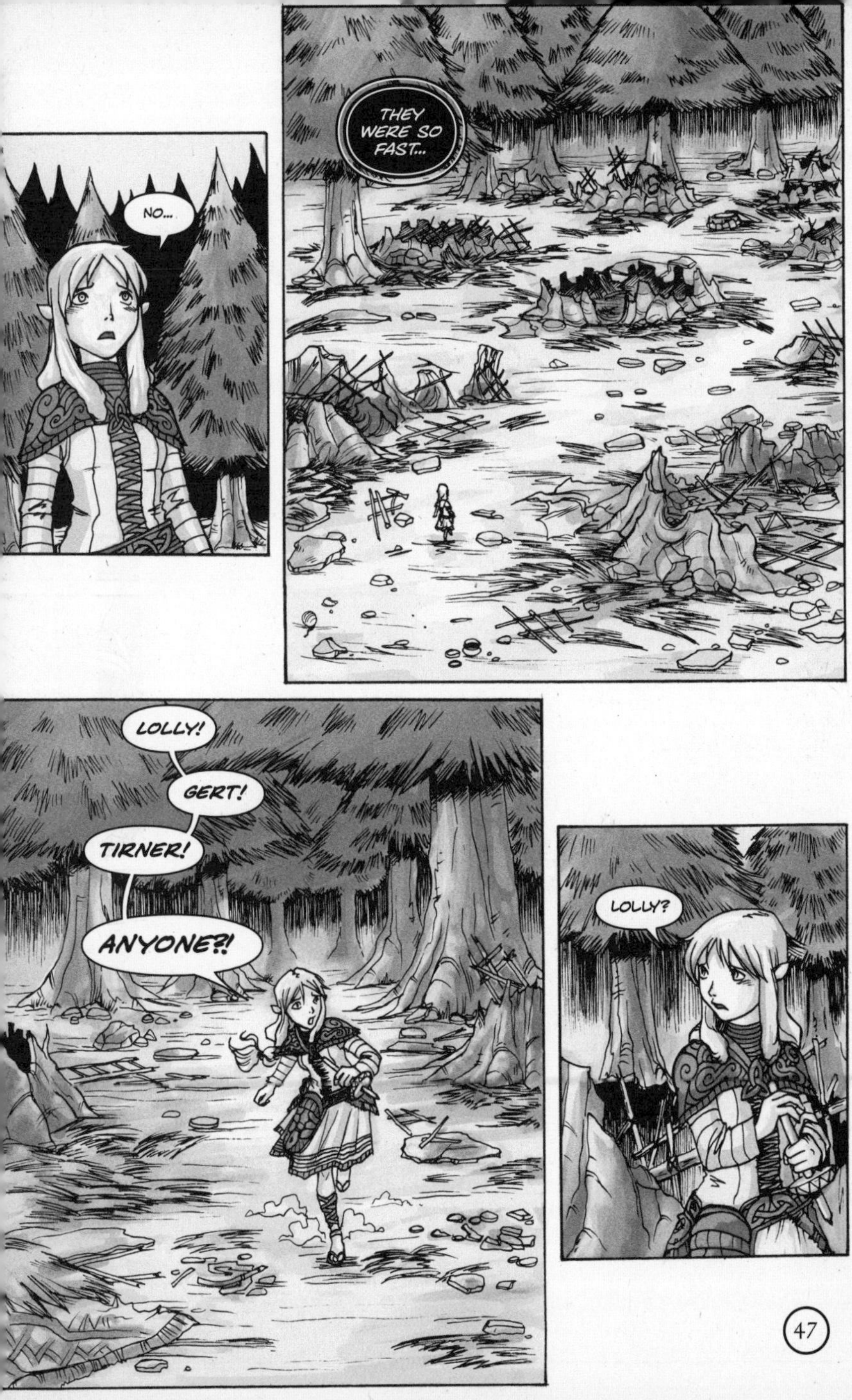
NO...
THEY WERE SO FAST...
LOLLY!
GERT!
TIRNER!
ANYONE?!
LOLLY?

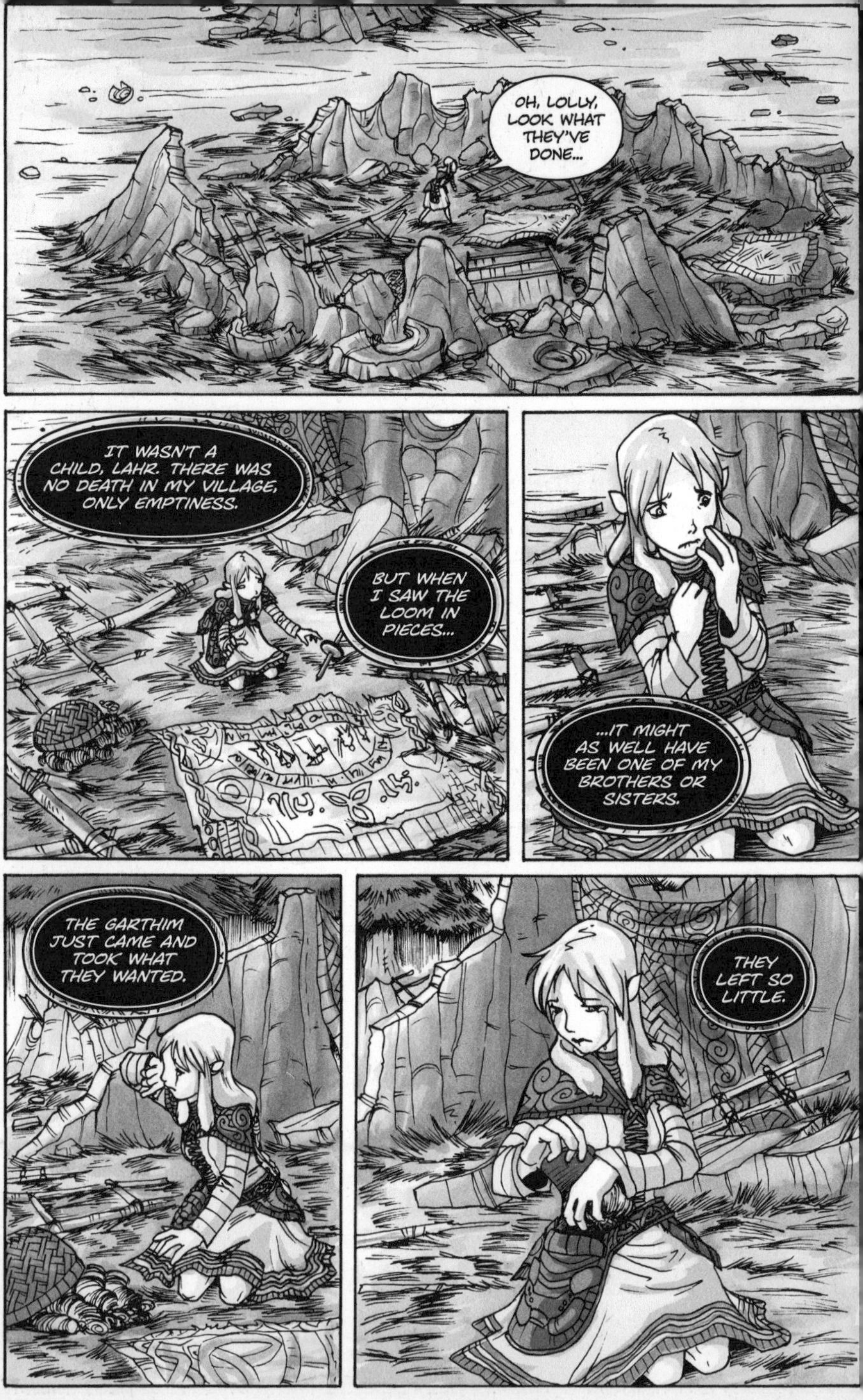
OH, LOLLY, LOOK WHAT THEY'VE DONE...
IT WASN'T A CHILD, LAHR. THERE WAS NO DEATH IN MY VILLAGE, ONLY EMPTINESS.
BUT WHEN I SAW THE LOOM IN PIECES...
...IT MIGHT AS WELL HAVE BEEN ONE OF MY BROTHERS OR SISTERS.
THE GARTHIM JUST CAME AND TOOK WHAT THEY WANTED.
THEY LEFT SO LITTLE.

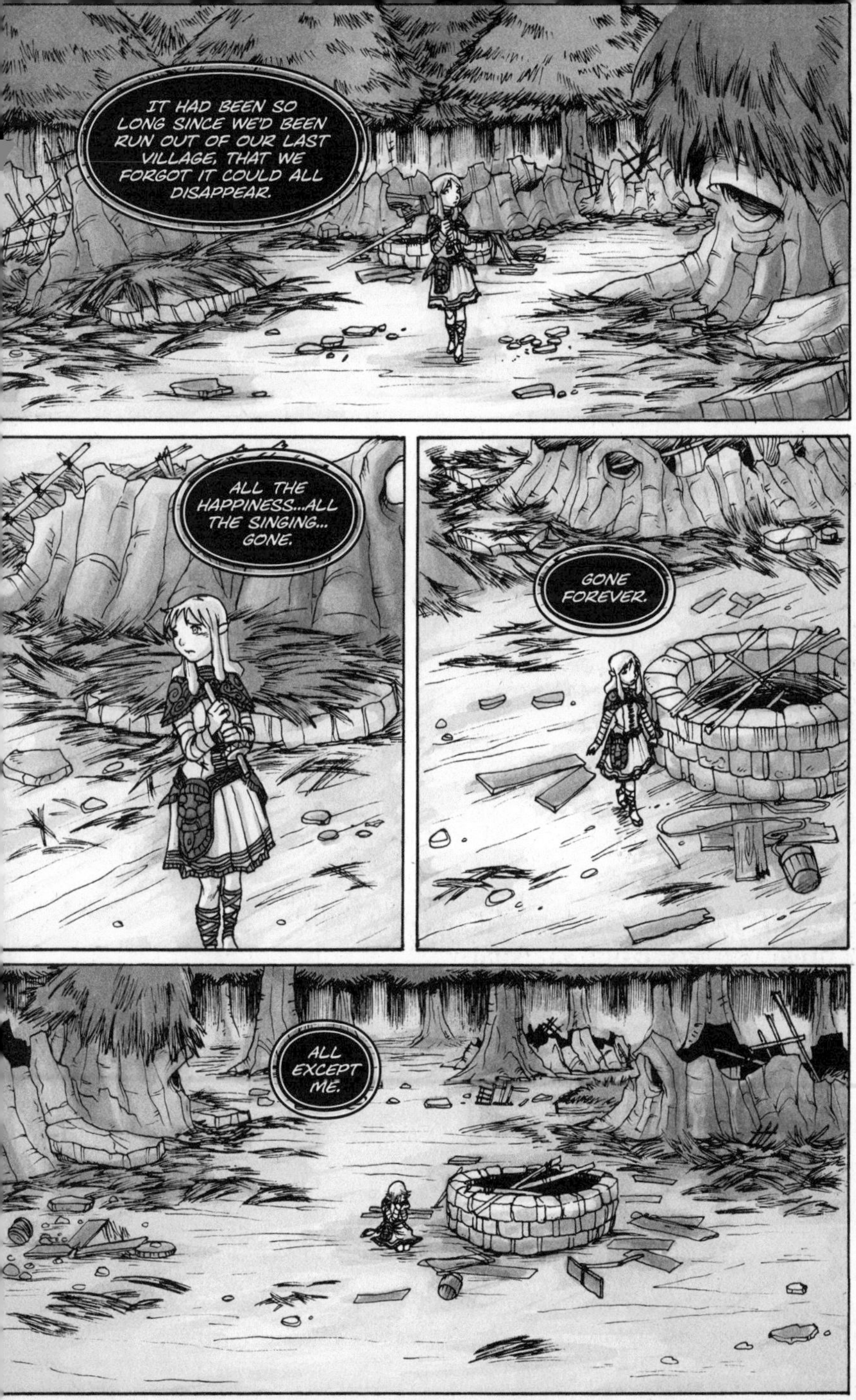
IT HAD BEEN SO LONG SINCE WE'D BEEN RUN OUT OF OUR LAST VILLAGE, THAT WE FORGOT IT COULD ALL DISAPPEAR.
ALL THE HAPPINESS...ALL THE SINGING... GONE.
GONE FOREVER.
ALL EXCEPT ME.

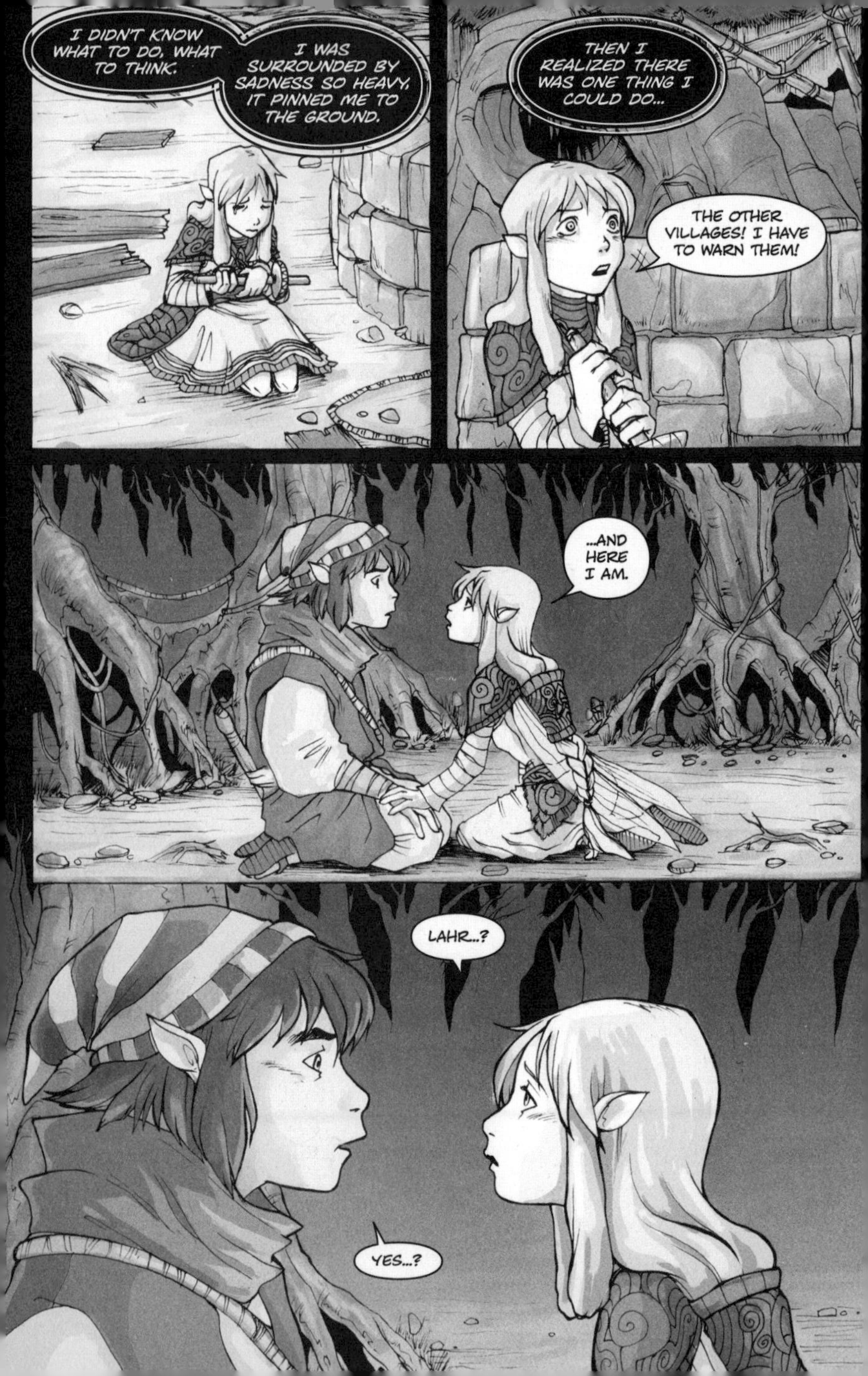
I DIDN'T KNOW WHAT TO DO, WHAT TO THINK.
I WAS SURROUNDED BY SADNESS SO HEAVY, IT PINNED ME TO THE GROUND.
THEN I REALIZED THERE WAS ONE THING I COULD DO...
THE OTHER VILLAGES! I HAVE TO WARN THEM!
...AND HERE I AM.
LAHR...?
YES...?

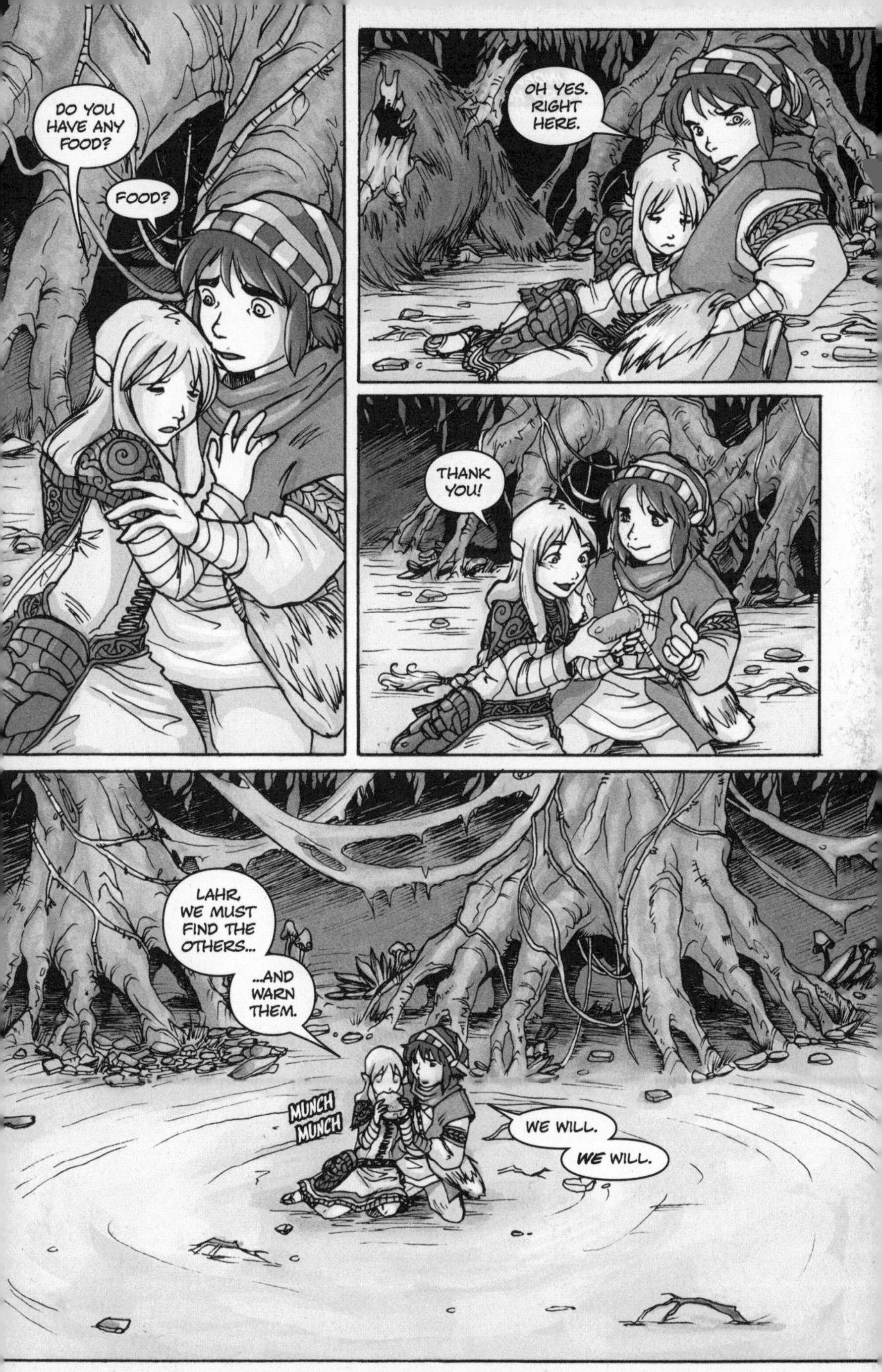
DO YOU HAVE ANY FOOD?
FOOD?
OH YES. RIGHT HERE.
THANK YOU!
LAHR, WE MUST FIND THE OTHERS...
...AND WARN THEM.
MUNCH MUNCH
WE WILL.
WE WILL.

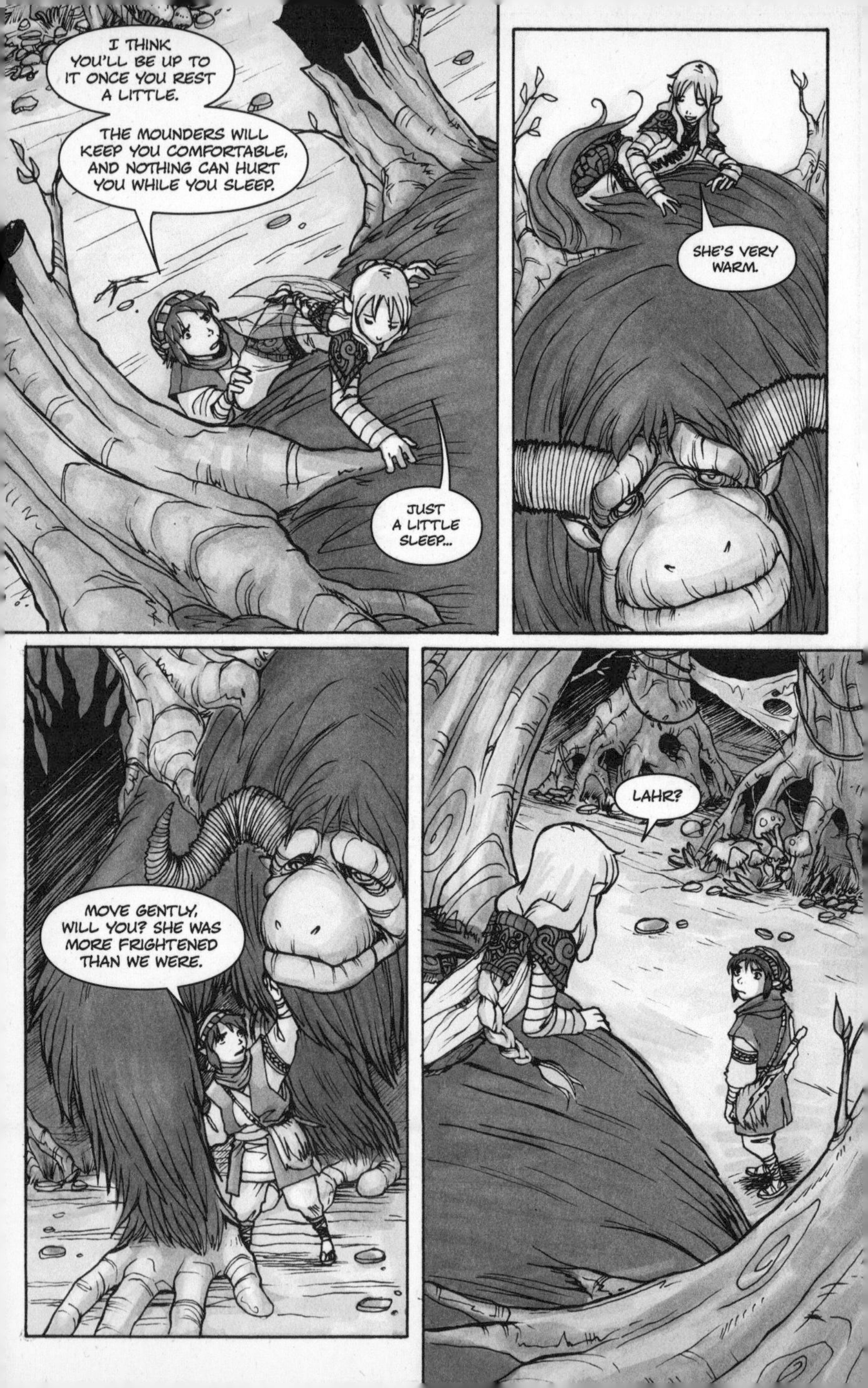
I THINK YOU'LL BE UP TO IT ONCE YOU REST A LITTLE.
THE MOUNDERS WILL KEEP YOU COMFORTABLE, AND NOTHING CAN HURT YOU WHILE YOU SLEEP.
JUST A LITTLE SLEEP...
SHE'S VERY WARM.
MOVE GENTLY, WILL YOU? SHE WAS MORE FRIGHTENED THAN WE WERE.
LAHR?

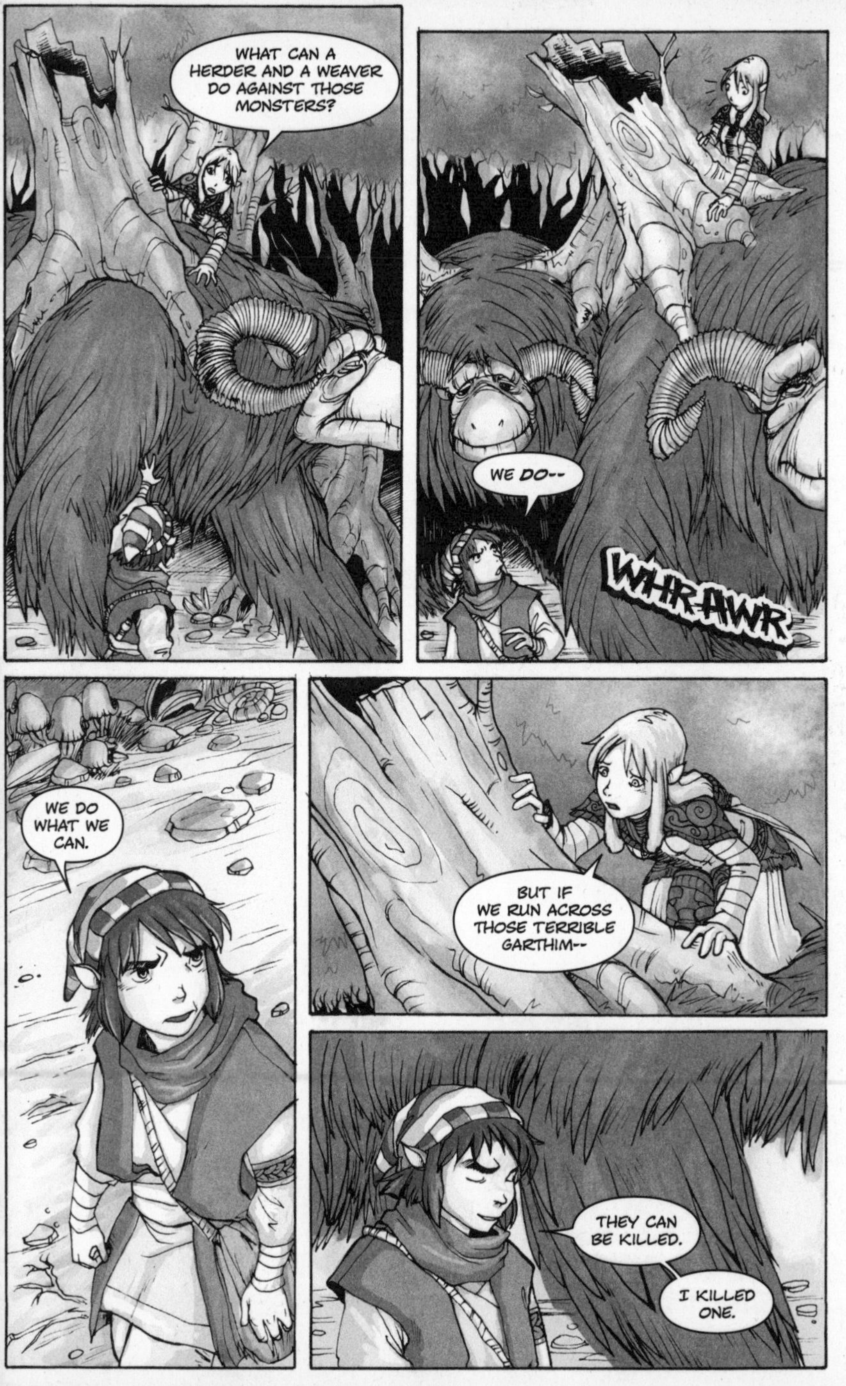
WHAT CAN A HERDER AND A WEAVER DO AGAINST THOSE MONSTERS?
WE DO--
WHRAWR
WE DO WHAT WE CAN.
BUT IF WE RUN ACROSS THOSE TERRIBLE GARTHIM--
THEY CAN BE KILLED.
I KILLED ONE.

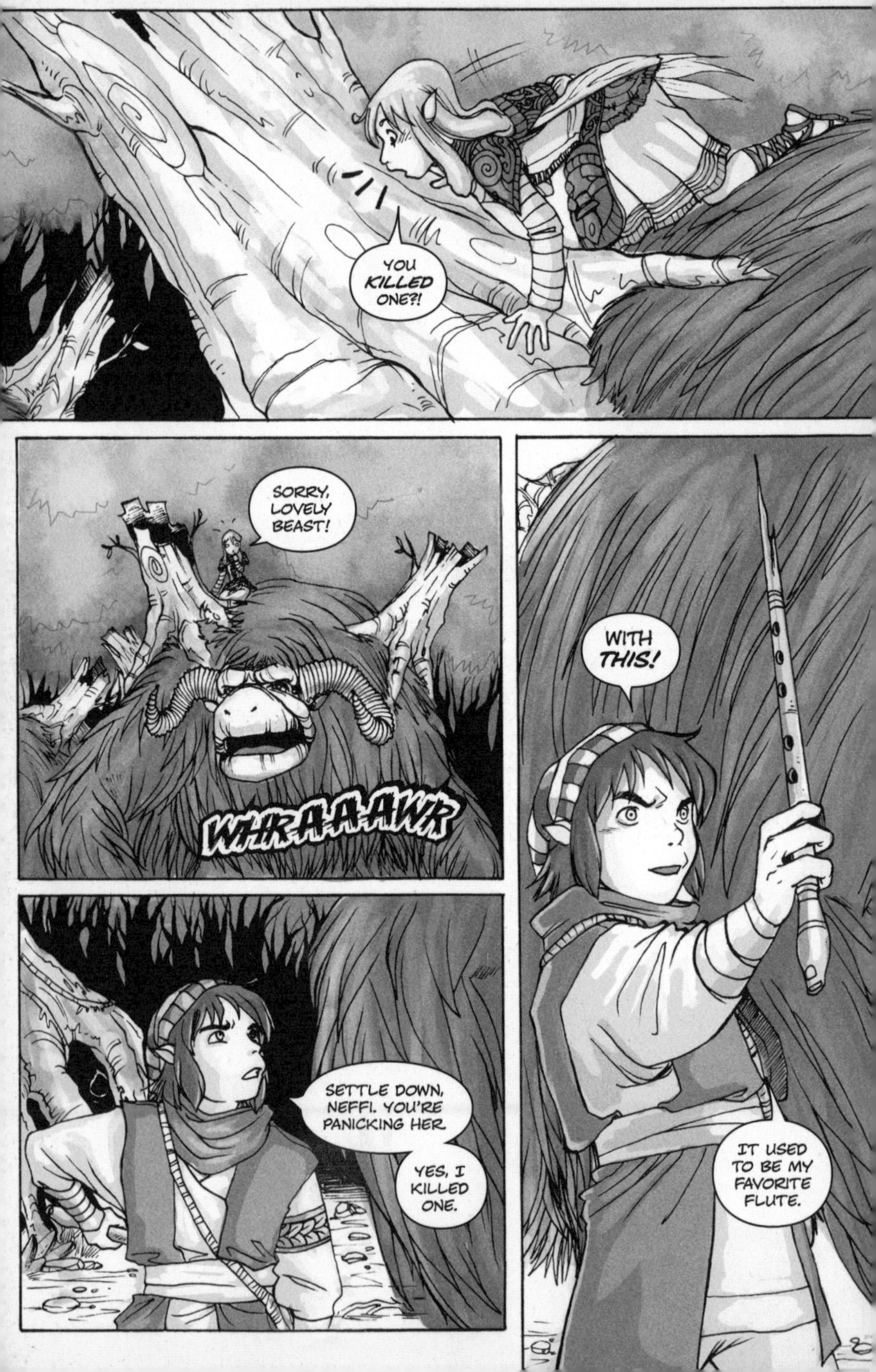

YOU KILLED ONE?!
SORRY, LOVELY BEAST!
WHRAAAWR
SETTLE DOWN, NEFFI. YOU'RE PANICKING HER
YES, I KILLED ONE.
WITH THIS!
IT USED TO BE MY FAVORITE FLUTE.

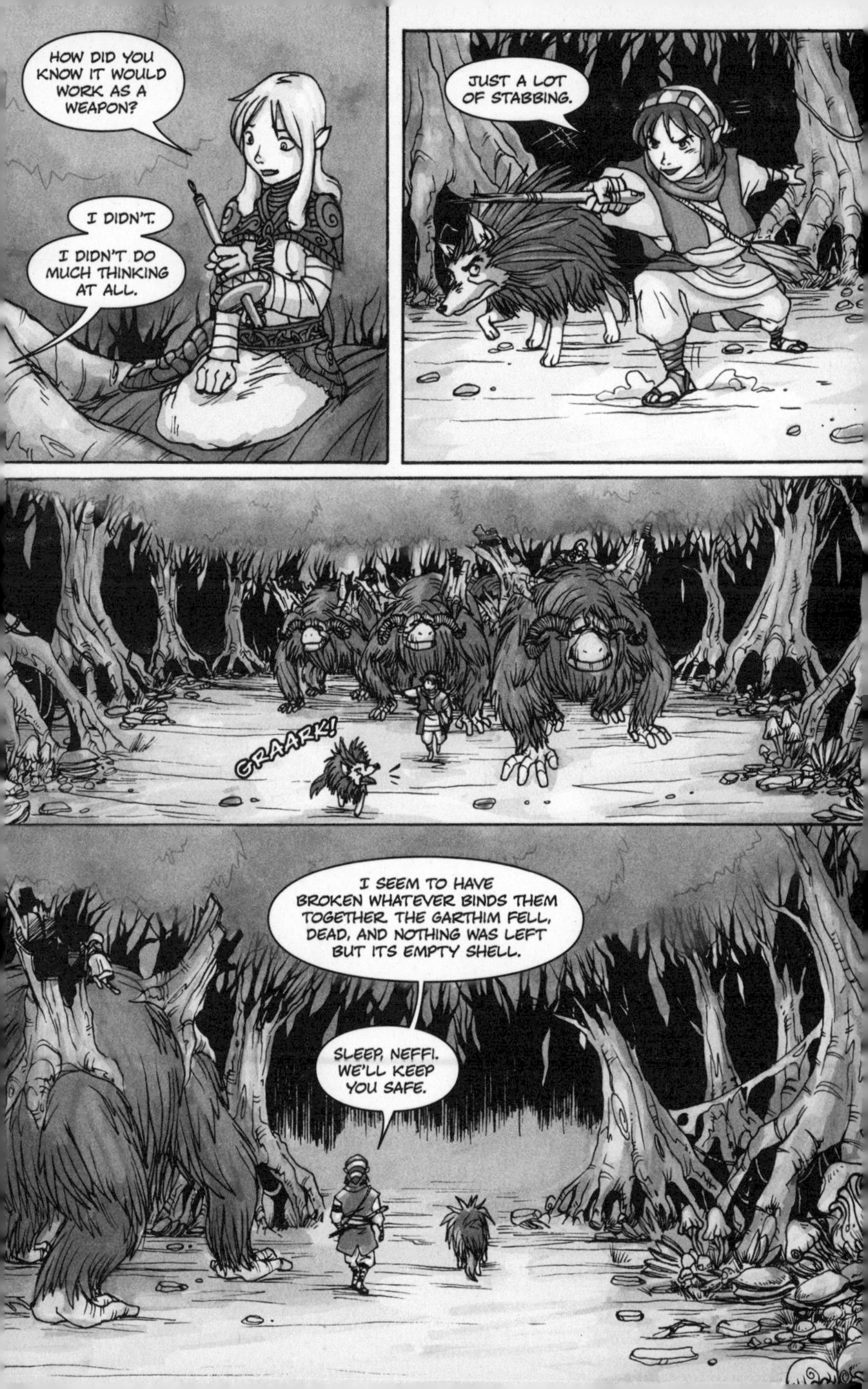
HOW DID YOU KNOW IT WOULD WORK AS A WEAPON?
I DIDN'T.
I DIDN'T DO MUCH THINKING AT ALL.
JUST A LOT OF STABBING.
GRAARK!
I SEEM TO HAVE BROKEN WHATEVER BINDS THEM TOGETHER. THE GARTHIM FELL, DEAD, AND NOTHING WAS LEFT BUT ITS EMPTY SHELL.
SLEEP, NEFFI. WE'LL KEEP YOU SAFE.

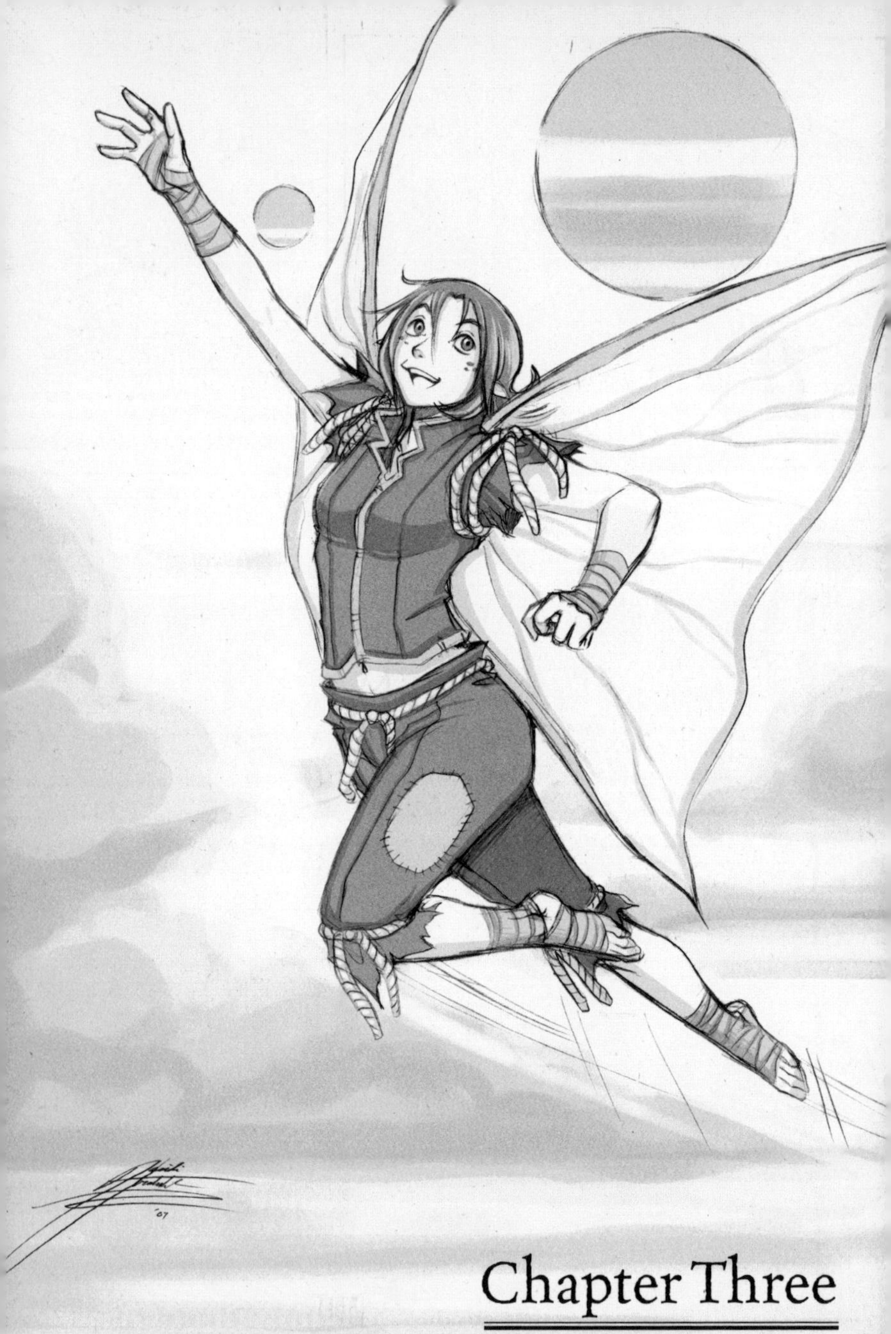

Chapter Three

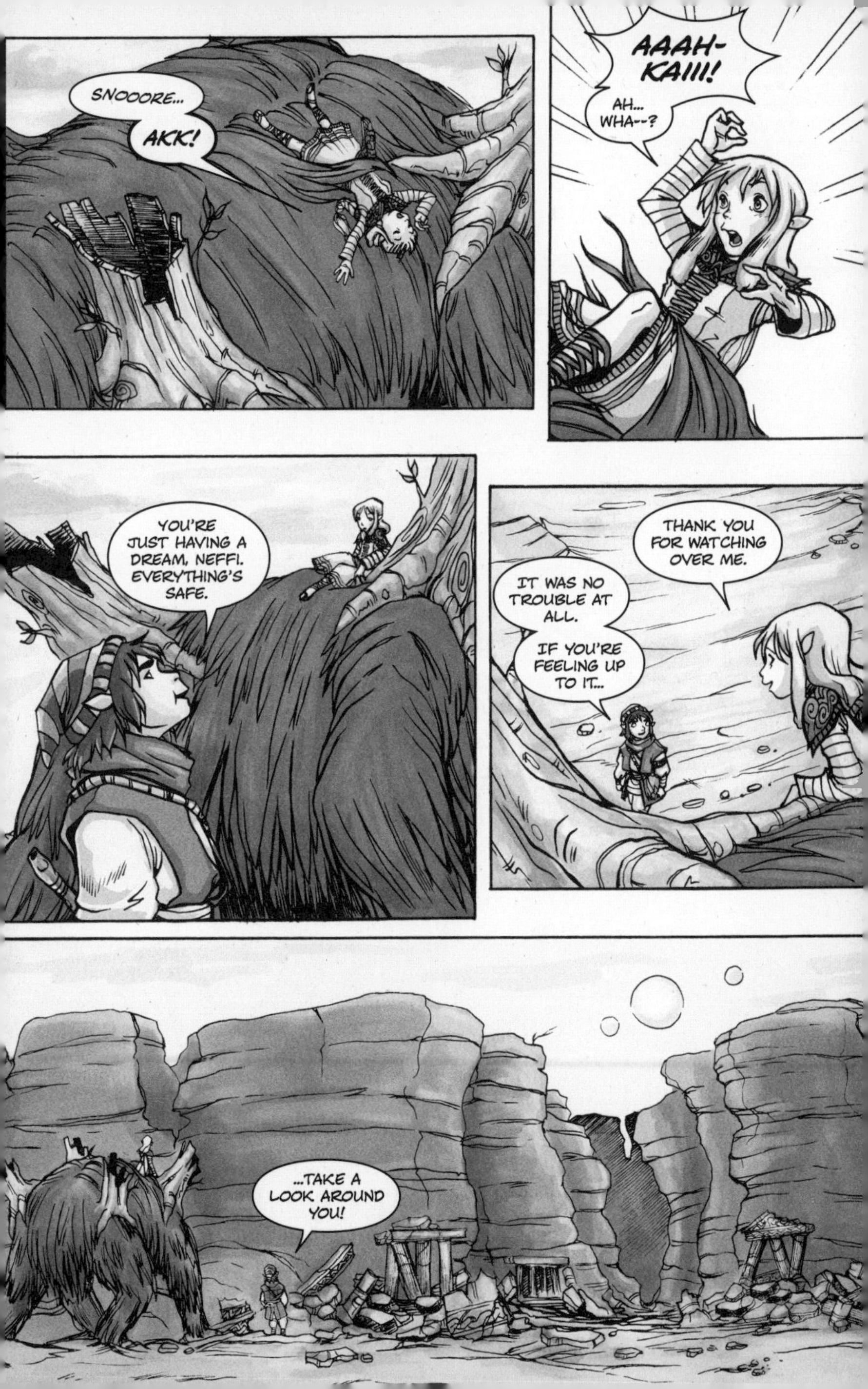
SNOOORE...
AKK!
AAAH-KAIII!
AH... WHA--?
YOU'RE JUST HAVING A DREAM, NEFFI. EVERYTHING'S SAFE.
THANK YOU FOR WATCHING OVER ME.
IT WAS NO TROUBLE AT ALL.
IF YOU'RE FEELING UP TO IT...
...TAKE A LOOK AROUND YOU!

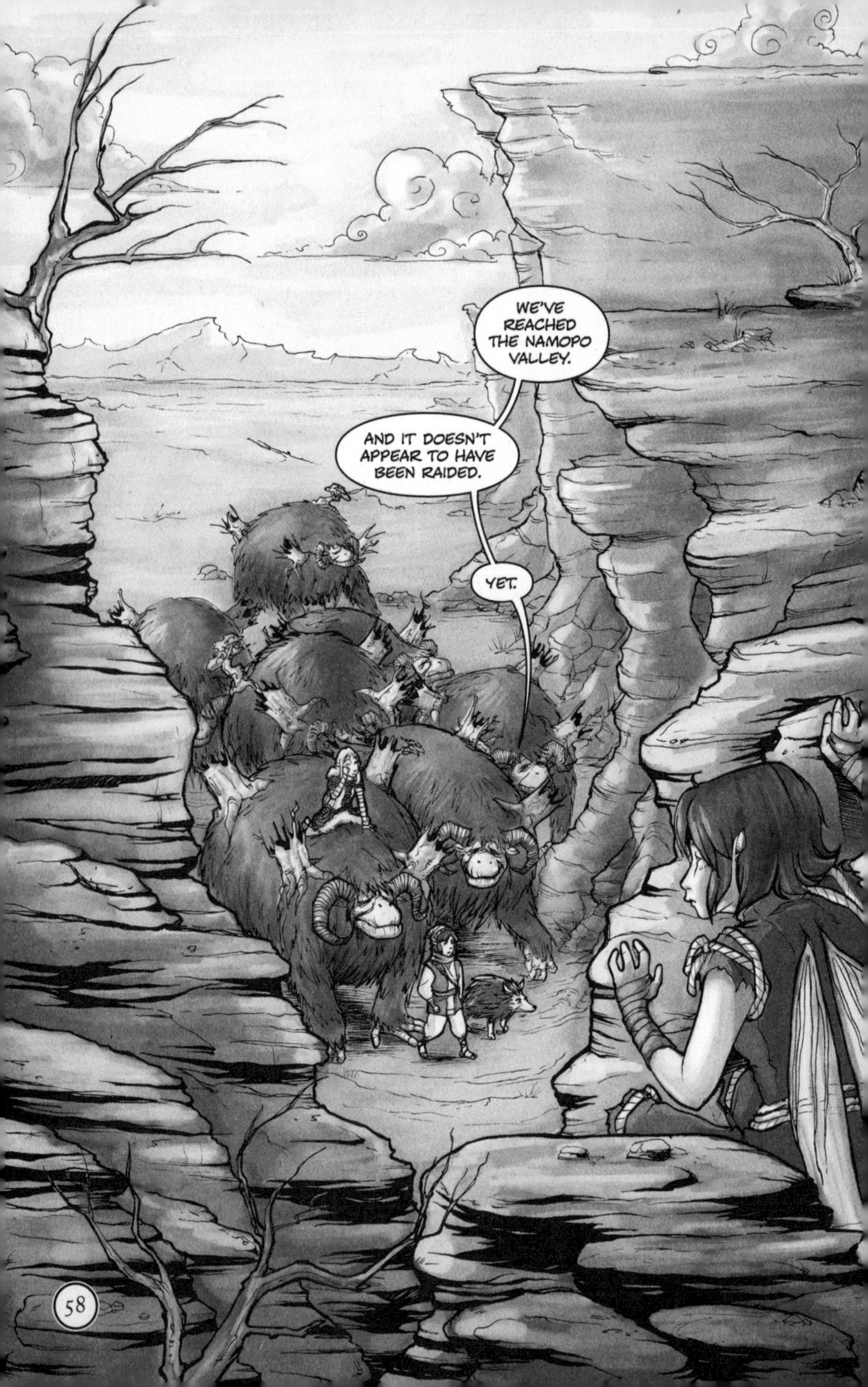
WE'VE REACHED THE NAMOPO VALLEY.
AND IT DOESN'T APPEAR TO HAVE BEEN RAIDED.
YET.

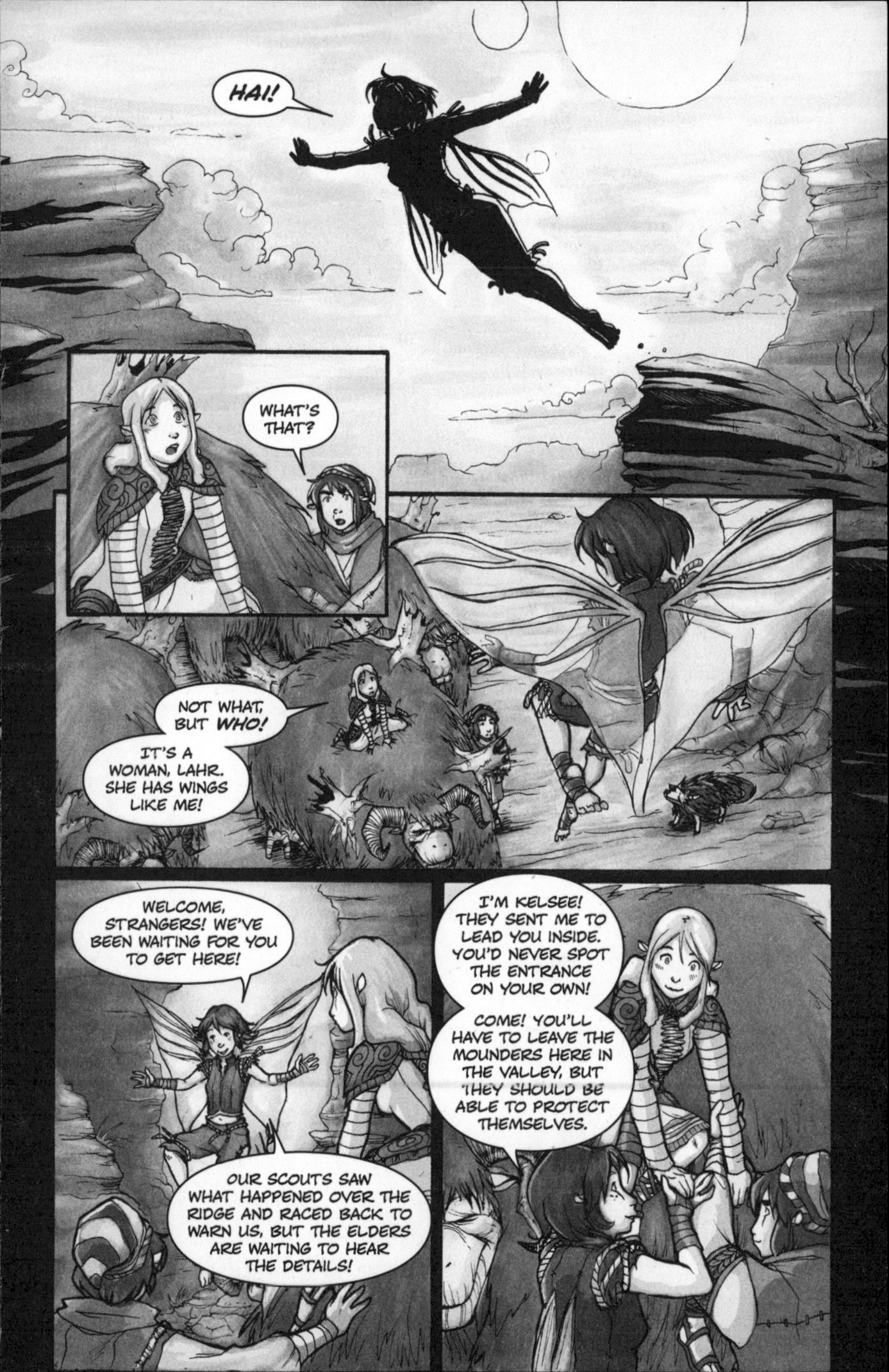
HAI!
WHAT'S THAT?
NOT WHAT, BUT WHO!
IT'S A WOMAN, LAHR. SHE HAS WINGS LIKE ME!
WELCOME, STRANGERS! WE'VE BEEN WAITING FOR YOU TO GET HERE!
OUR SCOUTS SAW WHAT HAPPENED OVER THE RIDGE AND RACED BACK TO WARN US, BUT THE ELDERS ARE WAITING TO HEAR THE DETAILS!
I'M KELSEE! THEY SENT ME TO LEAD YOU INSIDE. YOU'D NEVER SPOT THE ENTRANCE ON YOUR OWN!
COME! YOU'LL HAVE TO LEAVE THE MOUNDERS HERE IN THE VALLEY, BUT THEY SHOULD BE ABLE TO PROTECT THEMSELVES.

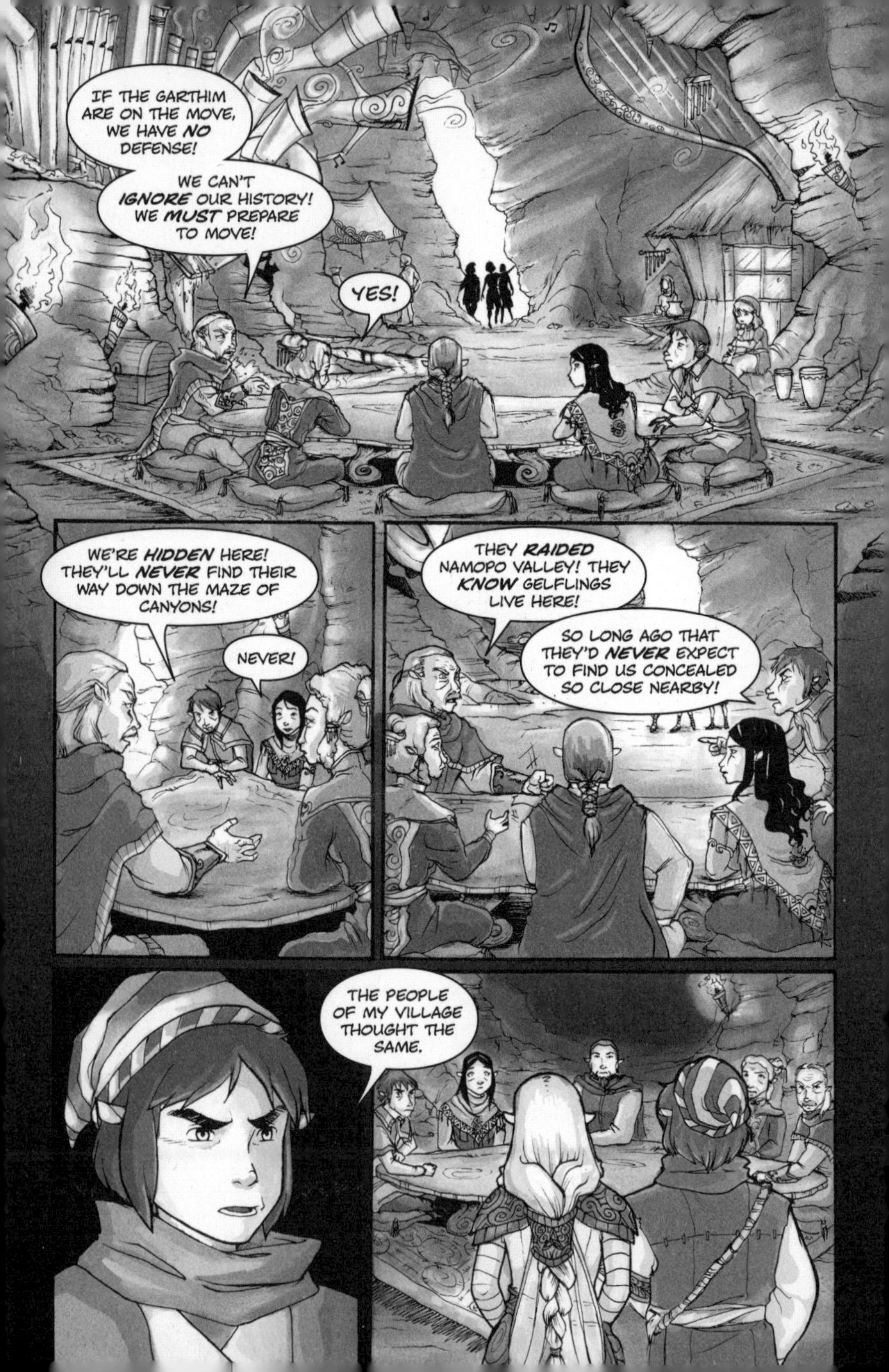
IF THE GARTHIM ARE ON THE MOVE, WE HAVE NO DEFENSE!
WE CAN'T IGNORE OUR HISTORY! WE MUST PREPARE TO MOVE!
YES!
WE'RE HIDDEN HERE! THEY'LL NEVER FIND THEIR WAY DOWN THE MAZE OF CANYONS!
NEVER!
THEY RAIDED NAMOPO VALLEY! THEY KNOW GELFLINGS LIVE HERE!
SO LONG AGO THAT THEY'D NEVER EXPECT TO FIND US CONCEALED SO CLOSE NEARBY!
THE PEOPLE OF MY VILLAGE THOUGHT THE SAME.

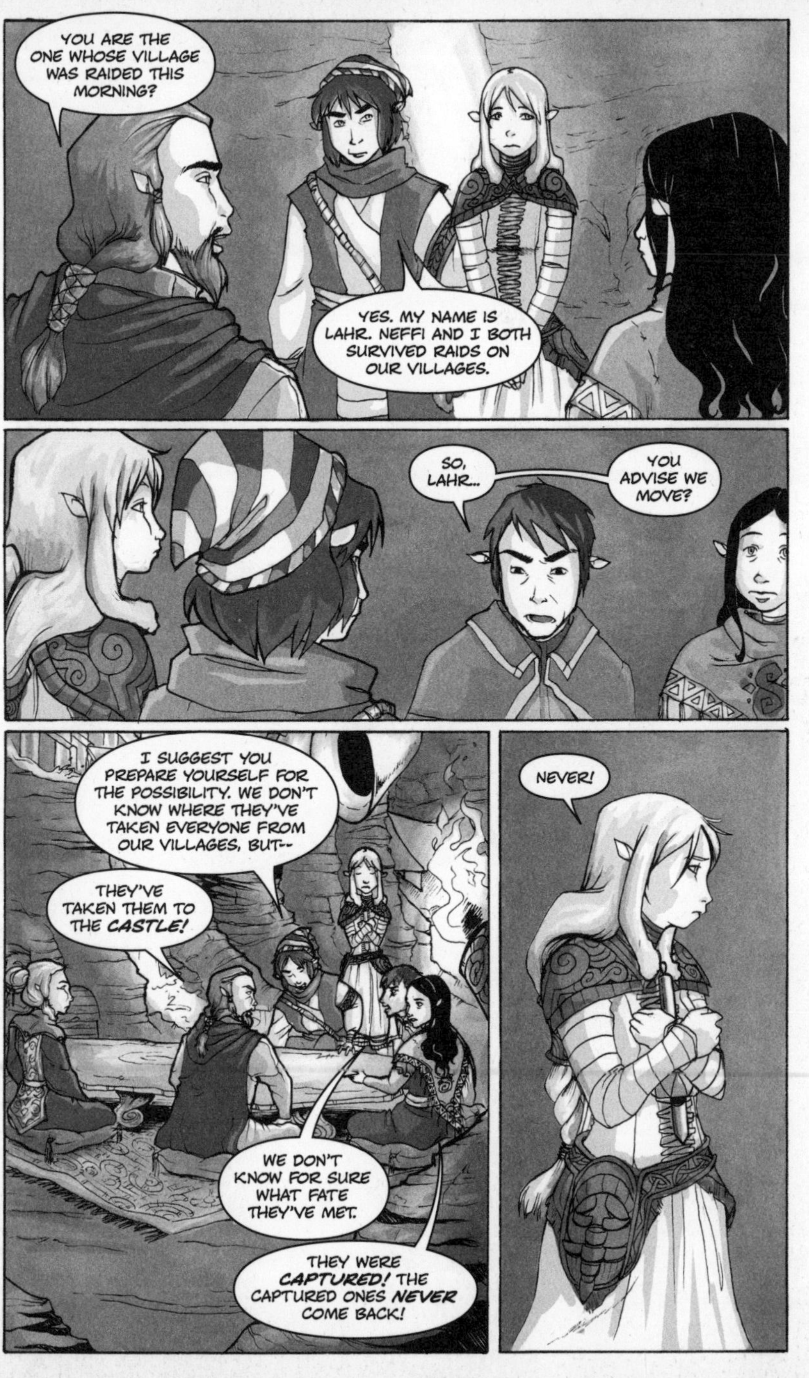
YOU ARE THE ONE WHOSE VILLAGE WAS RAIDED THIS MORNING?
YES. MY NAME IS LAHR. NEFFI AND I BOTH SURVIVED RAIDS ON OUR VILLAGES.
SO, LAHR...
YOU ADVISE WE MOVE?
I SUGGEST YOU PREPARE YOURSELF FOR THE POSSIBILITY. WE DON'T KNOW WHERE THEY'VE TAKEN EVERYONE FROM OUR VILLAGES, BUT--
THEY'VE TAKEN THEM TO THE *CASTLE!*
WE DON'T KNOW FOR SURE WHAT FATE THEY'VE MET.
THEY WERE *CAPTURED!* THE CAPTURED ONES *NEVER* COME BACK!
NEVER!

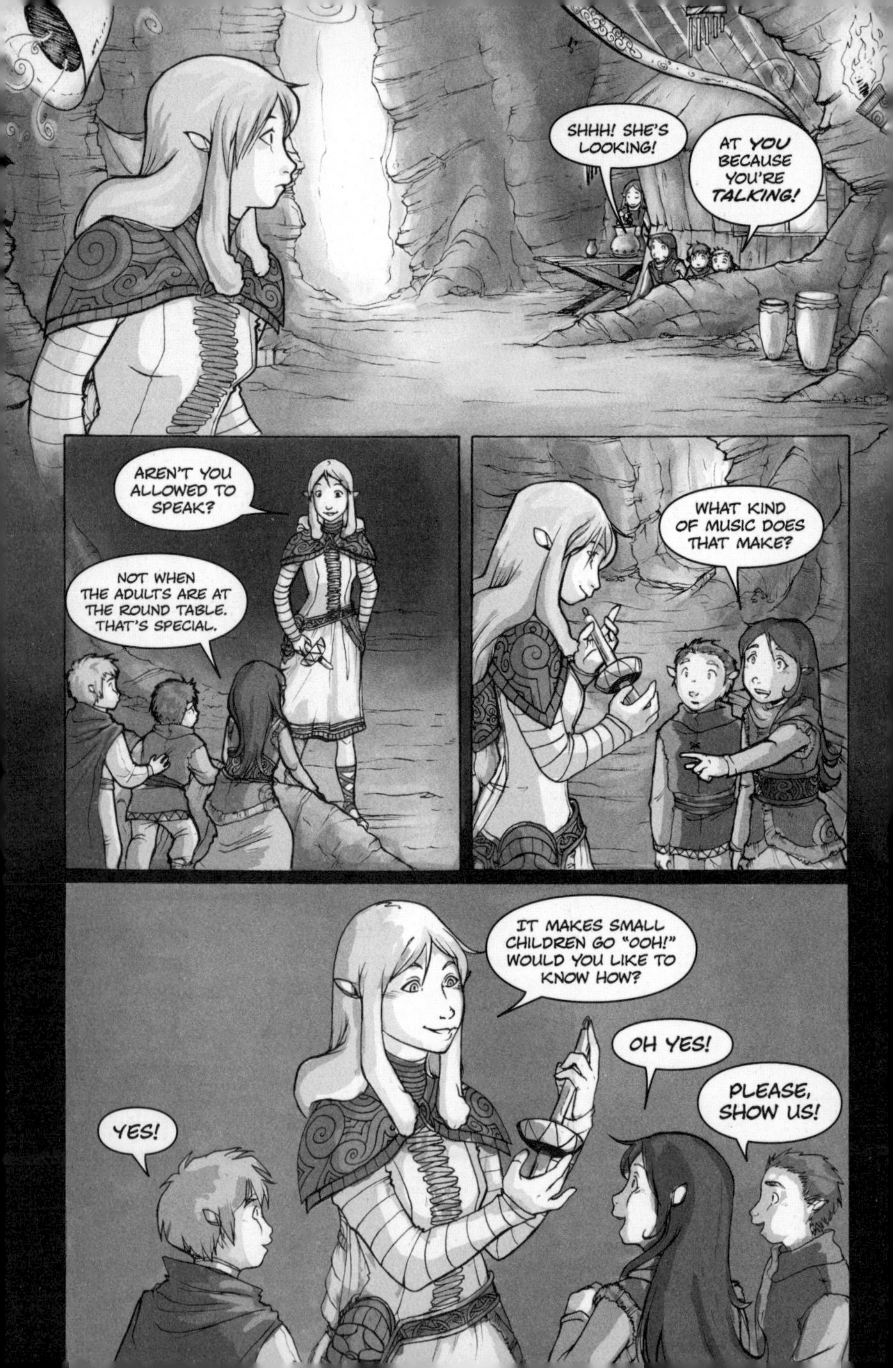
SHHH! SHE'S LOOKING!
AT *YOU* BECAUSE YOU'RE *TALKING!*
AREN'T YOU ALLOWED TO SPEAK?
NOT WHEN THE ADULTS ARE AT THE ROUND TABLE. THAT'S SPECIAL.
WHAT KIND OF MUSIC DOES THAT MAKE?
IT MAKES SMALL CHILDREN GO "OOH!" WOULD YOU LIKE TO KNOW HOW?
YES!
OH YES!
PLEASE, SHOW US!

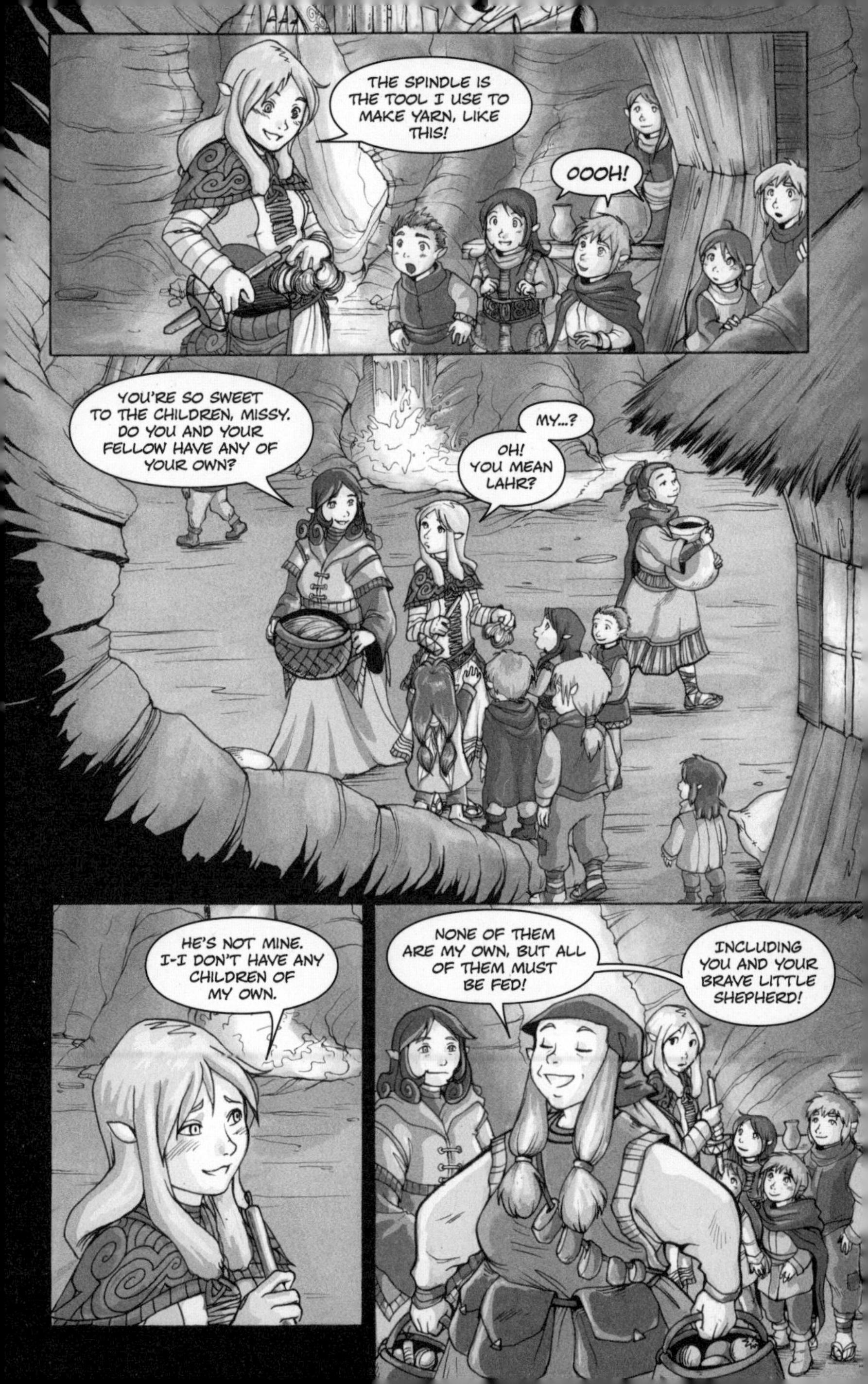
THE SPINDLE IS THE TOOL I USE TO MAKE YARN, LIKE THIS!
OOOH!
YOU'RE SO SWEET TO THE CHILDREN, MISSY. DO YOU AND YOUR FELLOW HAVE ANY OF YOUR OWN?
MY...?
OH! YOU MEAN LAHR?
HE'S NOT MINE. I-I DON'T HAVE ANY CHILDREN OF MY OWN.
NONE OF THEM ARE MY OWN, BUT ALL OF THEM MUST BE FED!
INCLUDING YOU AND YOUR BRAVE LITTLE SHEPHERD!

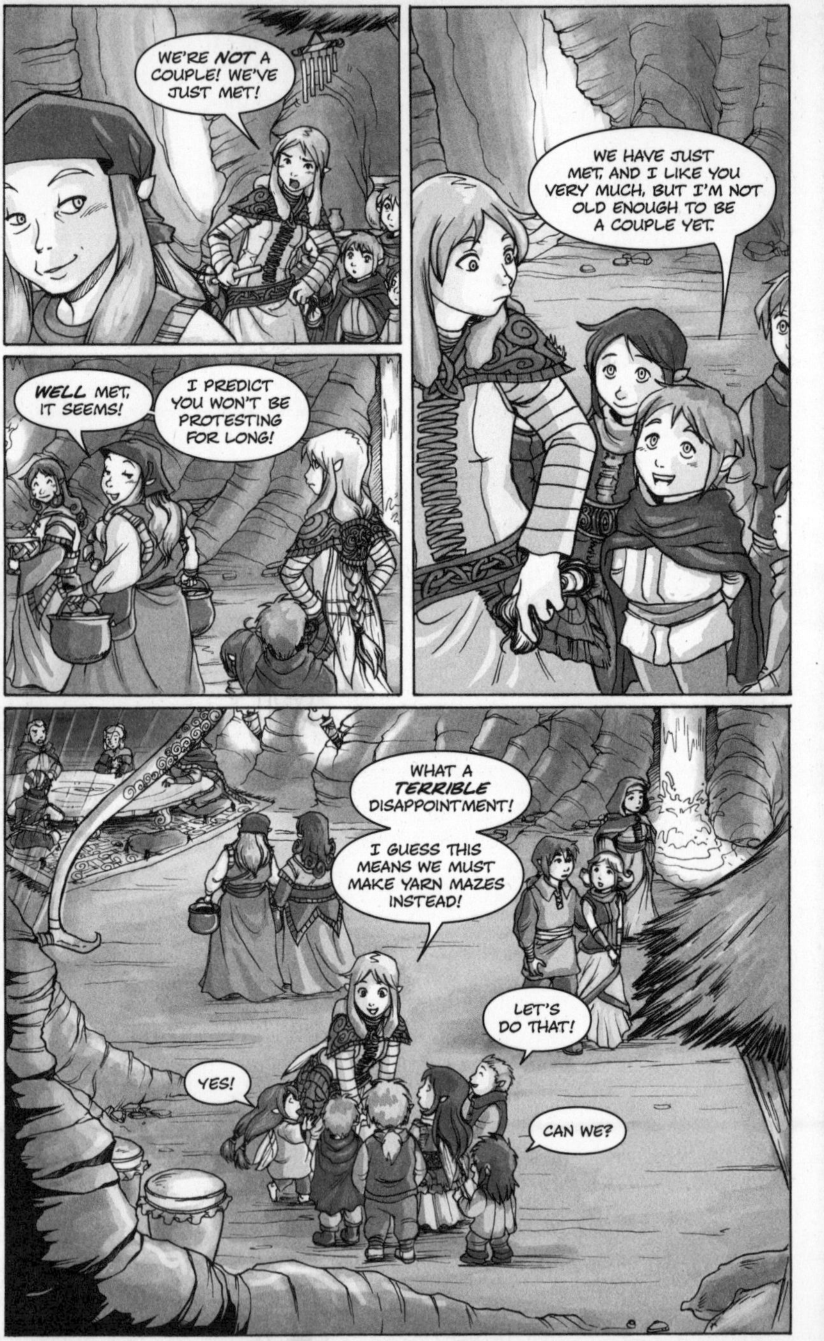
WE'RE NOT A COUPLE! WE'VE JUST MET!
WE HAVE JUST MET, AND I LIKE YOU VERY MUCH, BUT I'M NOT OLD ENOUGH TO BE A COUPLE YET.
WELL MET, IT SEEMS!
I PREDICT YOU WON'T BE PROTESTING FOR LONG!
WHAT A TERRIBLE DISAPPOINTMENT!
I GUESS THIS MEANS WE MUST MAKE YARN MAZES INSTEAD!
LET'S DO THAT!
YES!
CAN WE?

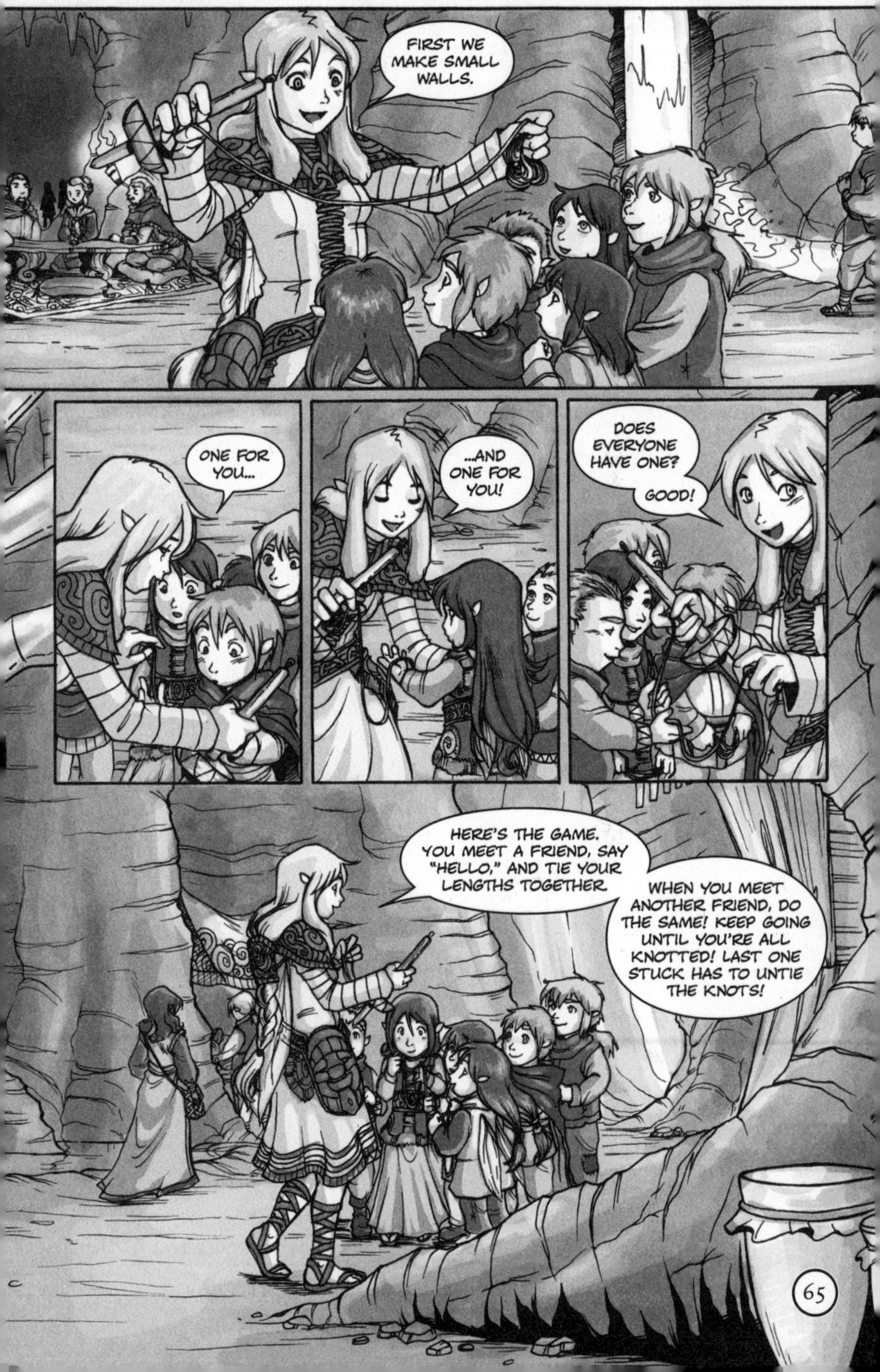
FIRST WE MAKE SMALL WALLS.
ONE FOR YOU...
...AND ONE FOR YOU!
DOES EVERYONE HAVE ONE?
GOOD!
HERE'S THE GAME. YOU MEET A FRIEND, SAY "HELLO," AND TIE YOUR LENGTHS TOGETHER
WHEN YOU MEET ANOTHER FRIEND, DO THE SAME! KEEP GOING UNTIL YOU'RE ALL KNOTTED! LAST ONE STUCK HAS TO UNTIE THE KNOTS!

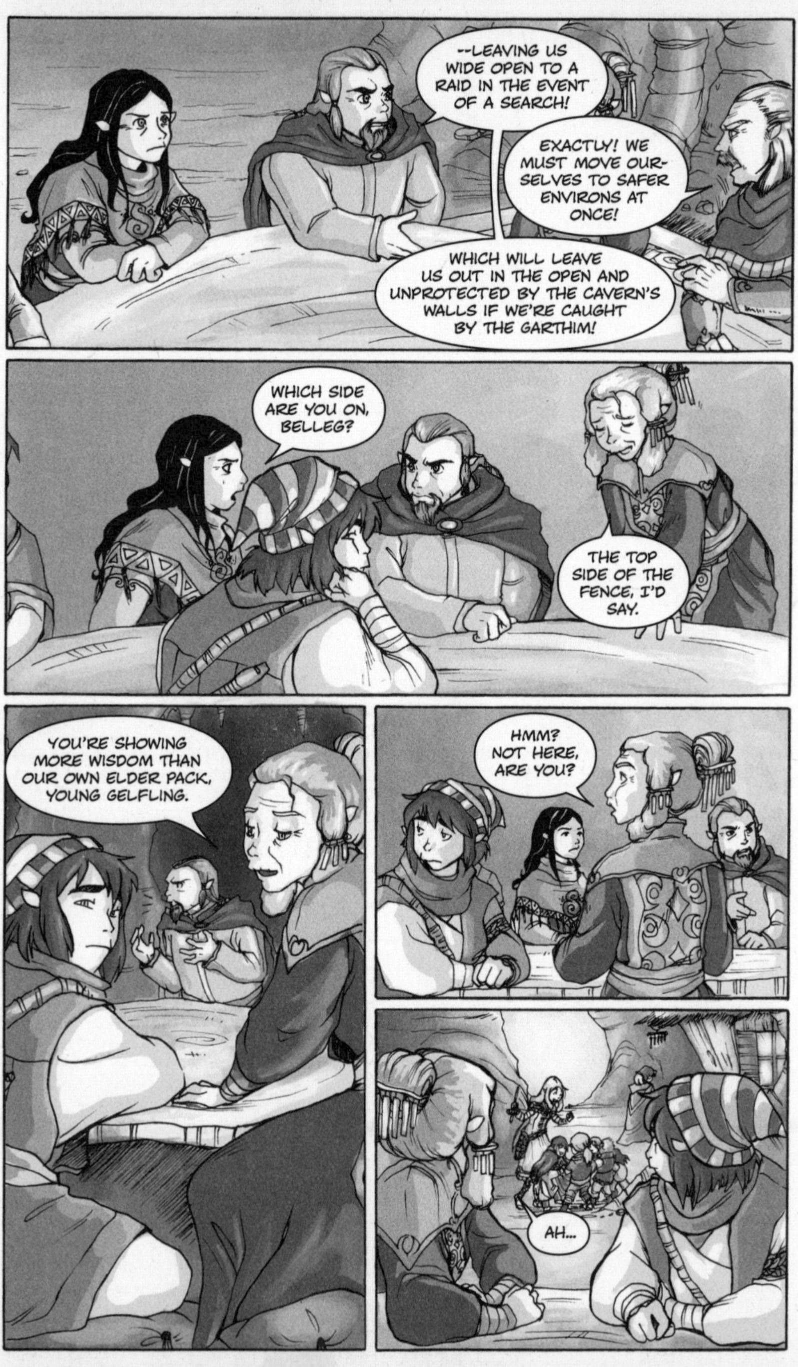
--LEAVING US WIDE OPEN TO A RAID IN THE EVENT OF A SEARCH!
EXACTLY! WE MUST MOVE OUR-SELVES TO SAFER ENVIRONS AT ONCE!
WHICH WILL LEAVE US OUT IN THE OPEN AND UNPROTECTED BY THE CAVERN'S WALLS IF WE'RE CAUGHT BY THE GARTHIM!
WHICH SIDE ARE YOU ON, BELLEG?
THE TOP SIDE OF THE FENCE, I'D SAY.
YOU'RE SHOWING MORE WISDOM THAN OUR OWN ELDER PACK, YOUNG GELFLING.
HMM? NOT HERE, ARE YOU?
AH...

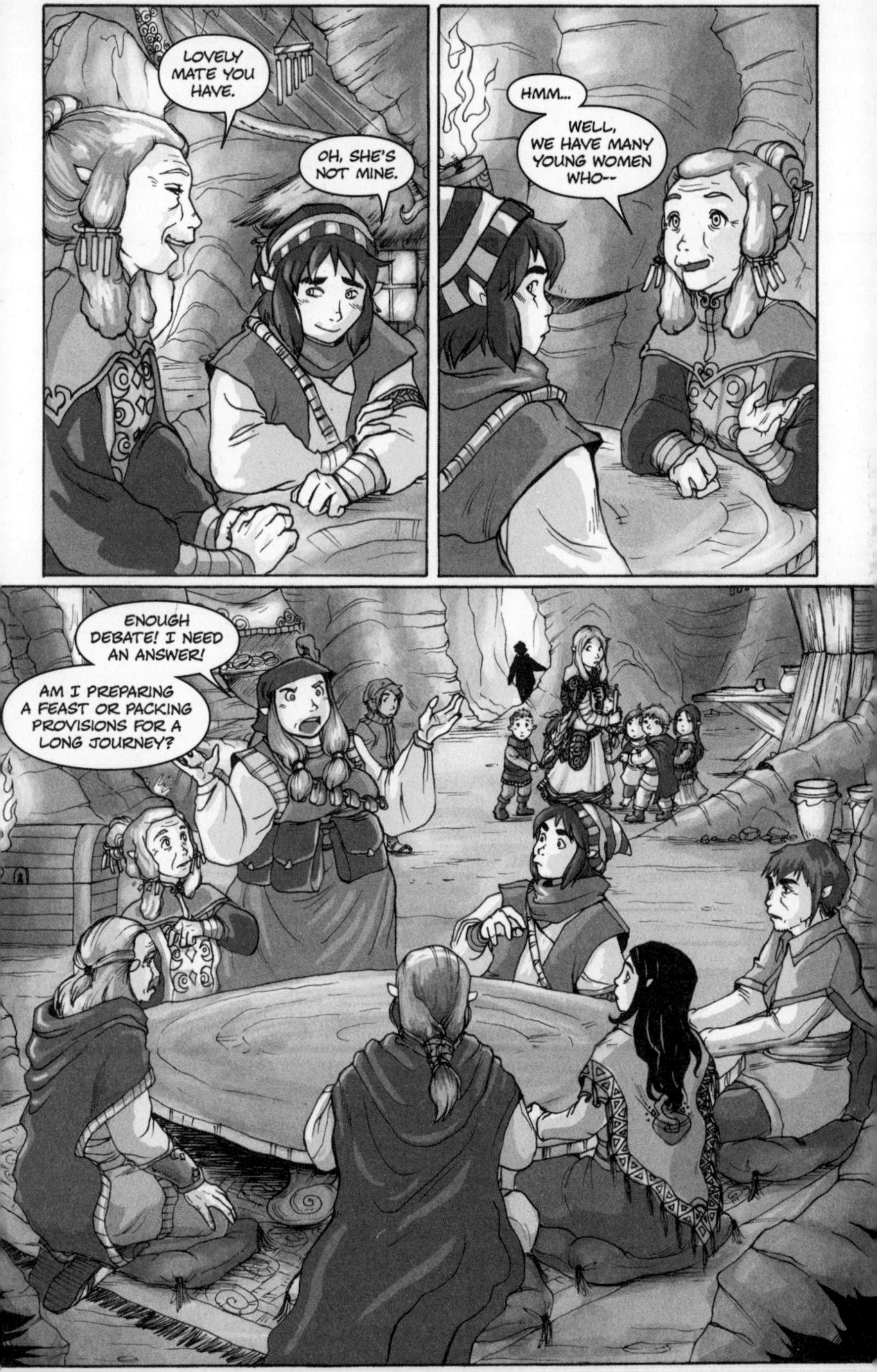
LOVELY MATE YOU HAVE.
OH, SHE'S NOT MINE.
HMM...
WELL, WE HAVE MANY YOUNG WOMEN WHO--
ENOUGH DEBATE! I NEED AN ANSWER!
AM I PREPARING A FEAST OR PACKING PROVISIONS FOR A LONG JOURNEY?

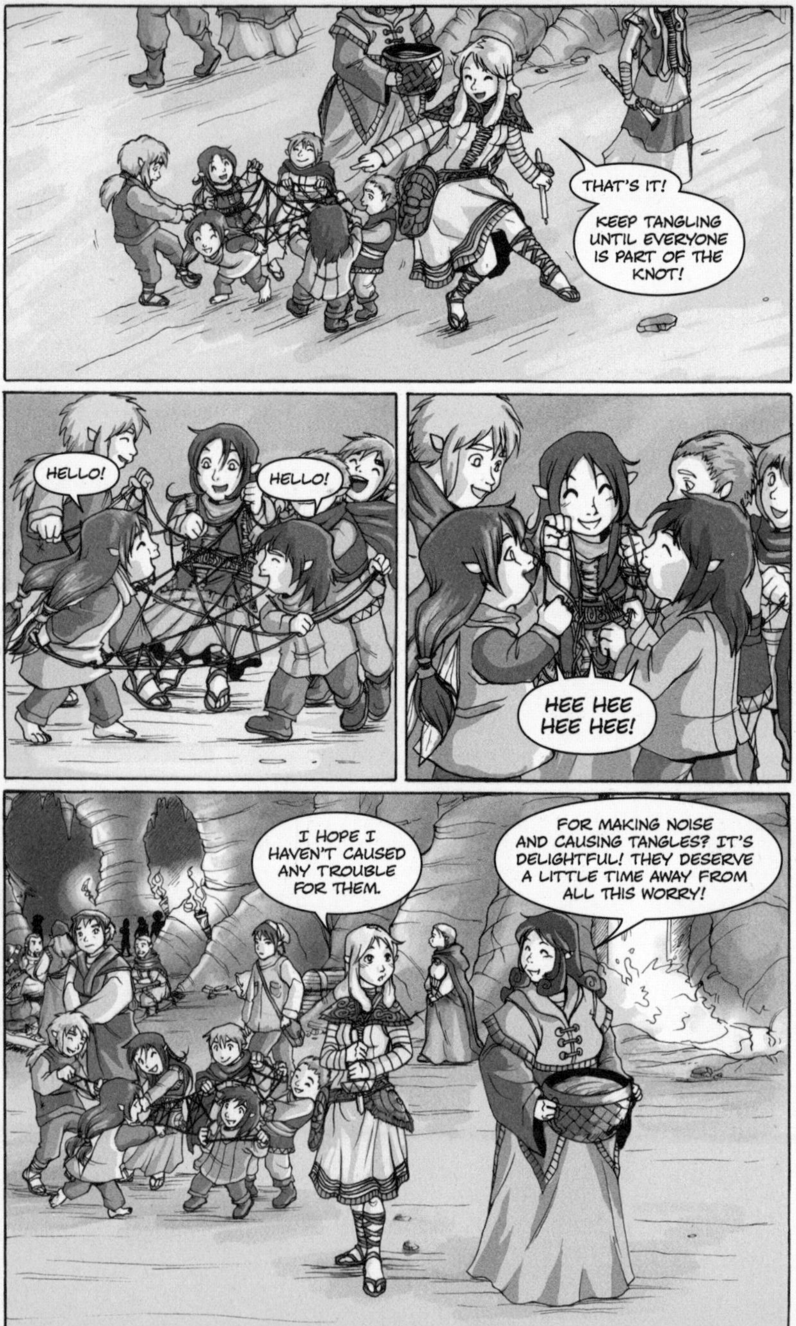

THAT'S IT!
KEEP TANGLING UNTIL EVERYONE IS PART OF THE KNOT!
HELLO!
HELLO!
HEE HEE HEE HEE!
I HOPE I HAVEN'T CAUSED ANY TROUBLE FOR THEM.
FOR MAKING NOISE AND CAUSING TANGLES? IT'S DELIGHTFUL! THEY DESERVE A LITTLE TIME AWAY FROM ALL THIS WORRY!

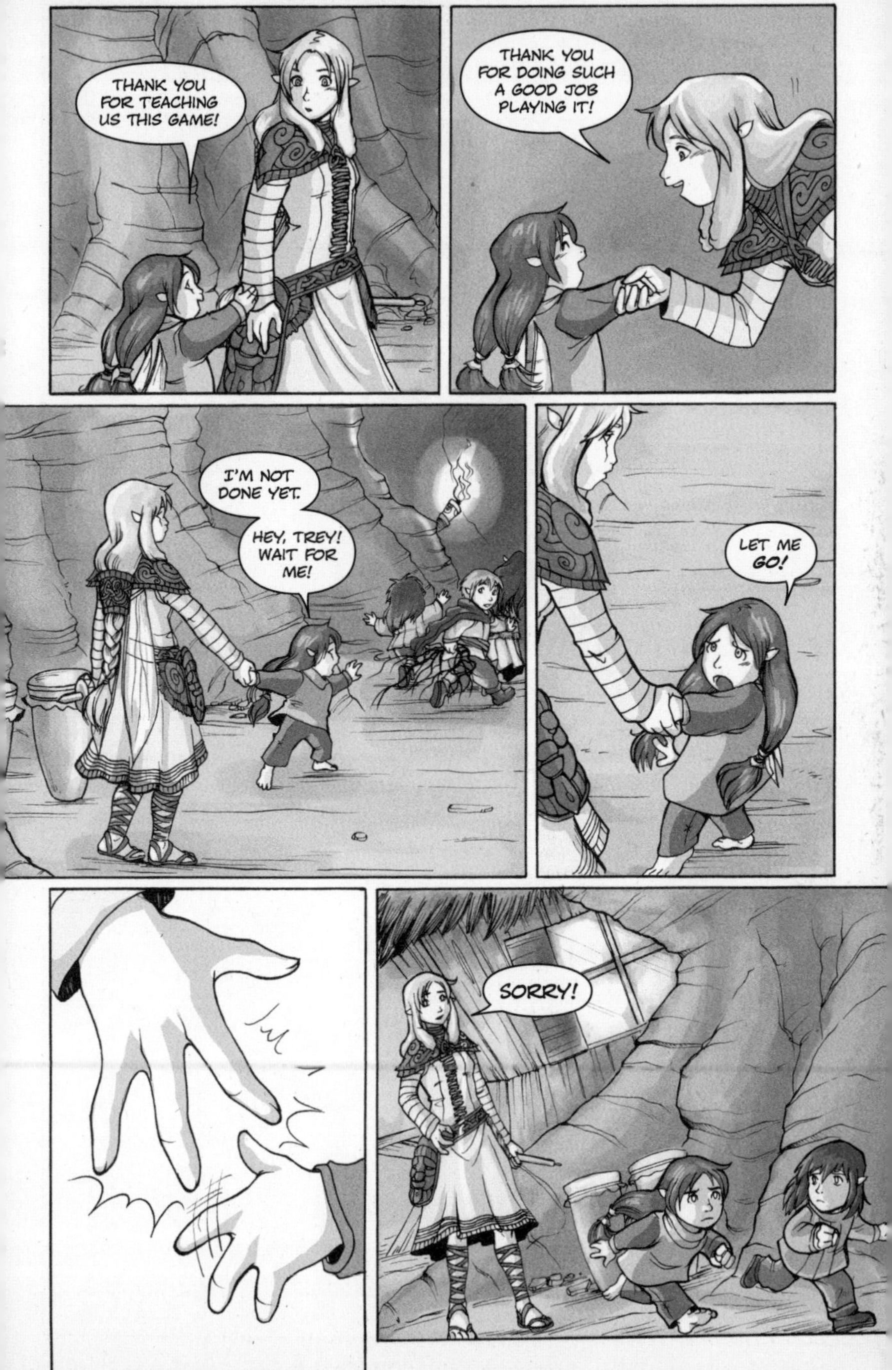
THANK YOU FOR TEACHING US THIS GAME!
THANK YOU FOR DOING SUCH A GOOD JOB PLAYING IT!
I'M NOT DONE YET.
HEY, TREY! WAIT FOR ME!
LET ME GO!
SORRY!

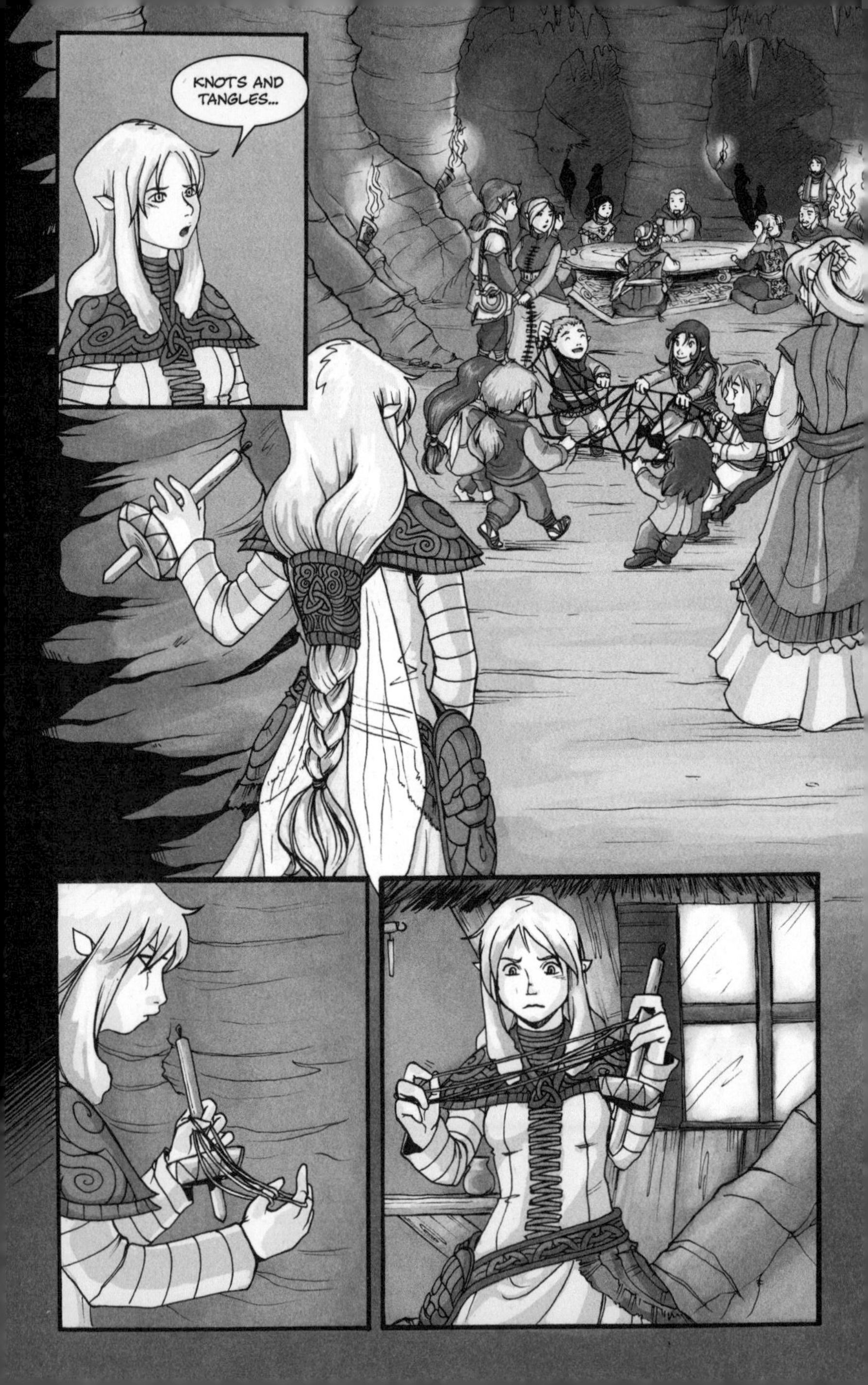
KNOTS AND TANGLES...

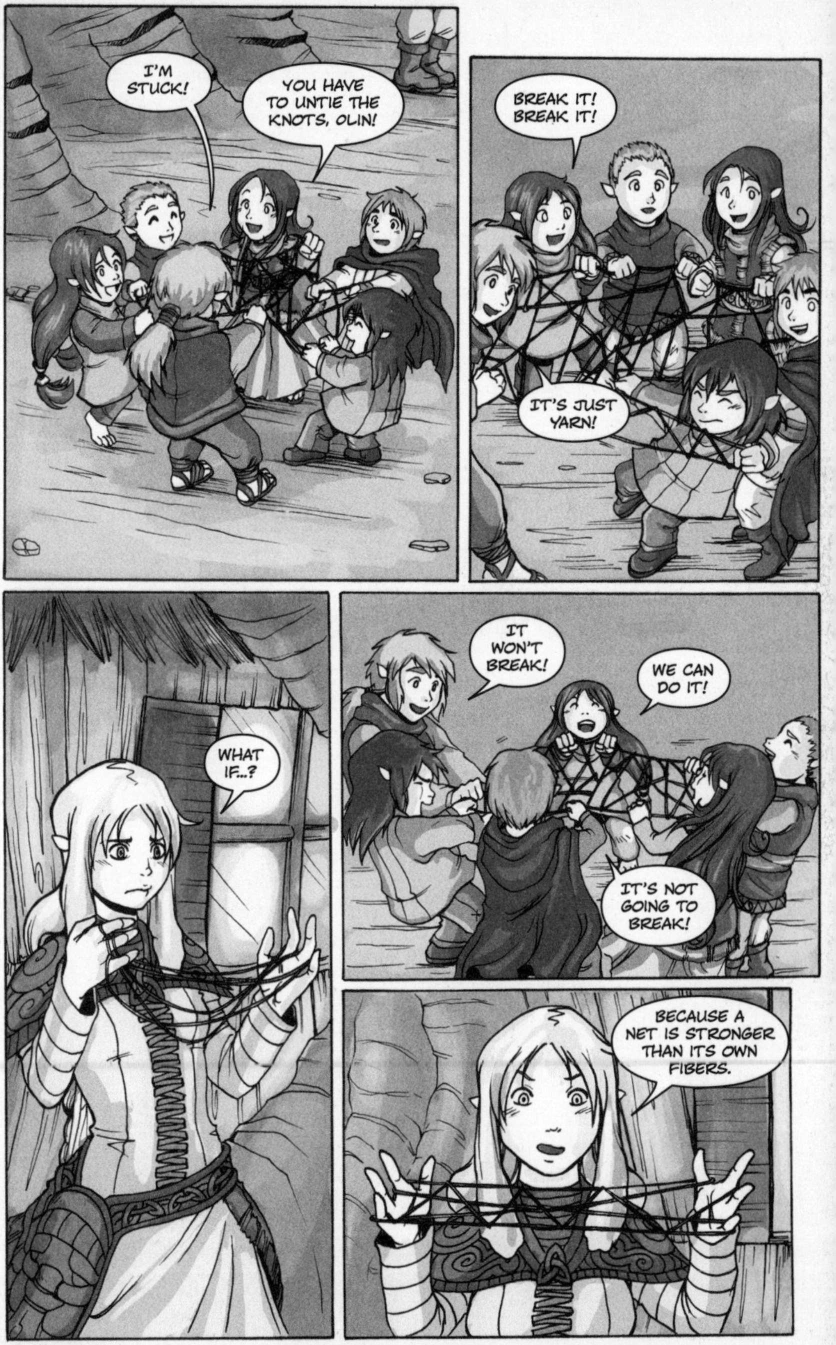
I'M STUCK!
YOU HAVE TO UNTIE THE KNOTS, OLIN!
BREAK IT! BREAK IT!
IT'S JUST YARN!
WHAT IF...?
IT WON'T BREAK!
WE CAN DO IT!
IT'S NOT GOING TO BREAK!
BECAUSE A NET IS STRONGER THAN ITS OWN FIBERS.

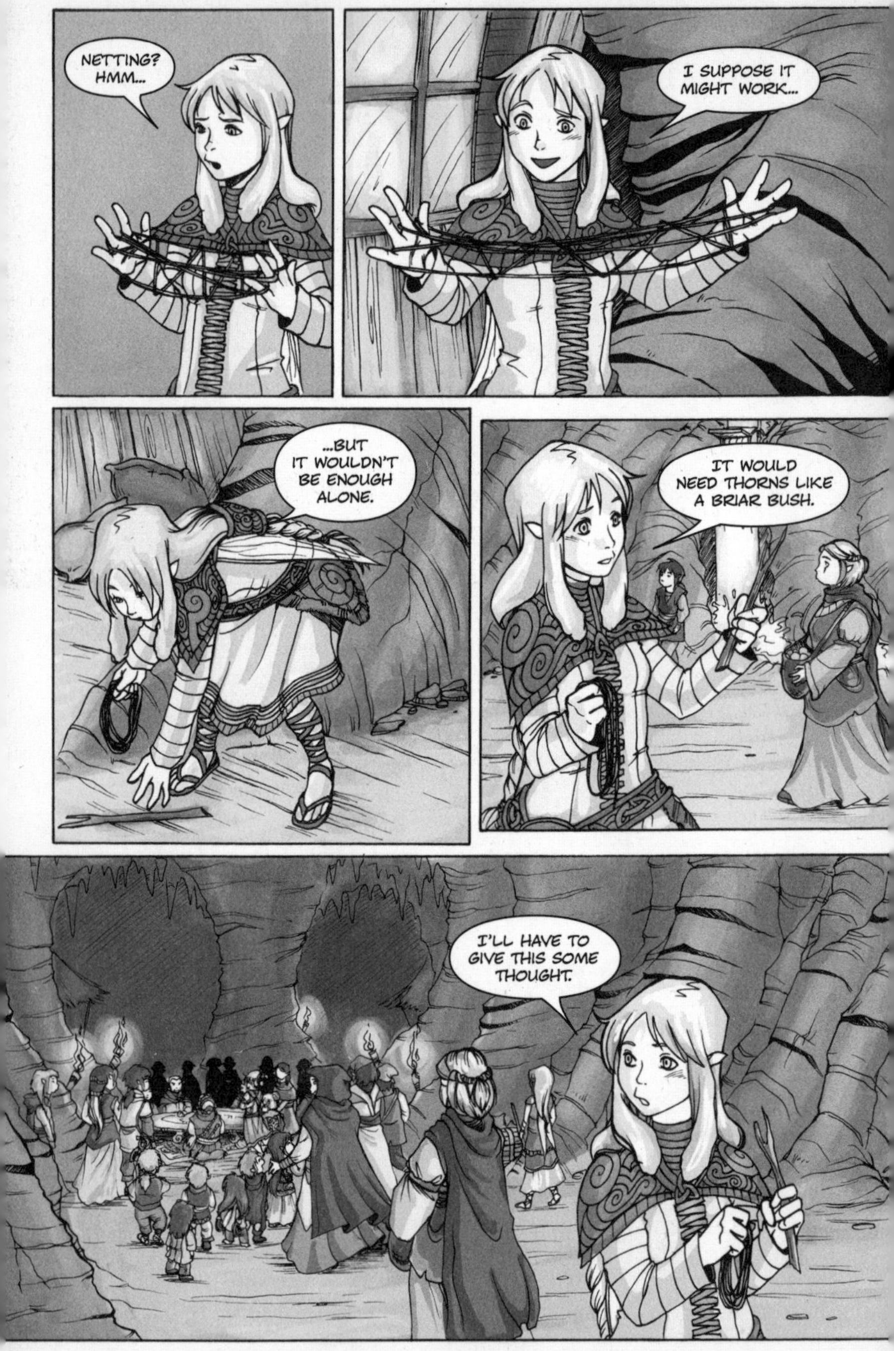
NETTING? HMM...
I SUPPOSE IT MIGHT WORK...
...BUT IT WOULDN'T BE ENOUGH ALONE.
IT WOULD NEED THORNS LIKE A BRIAR BUSH.
I'LL HAVE TO GIVE THIS SOME THOUGHT.

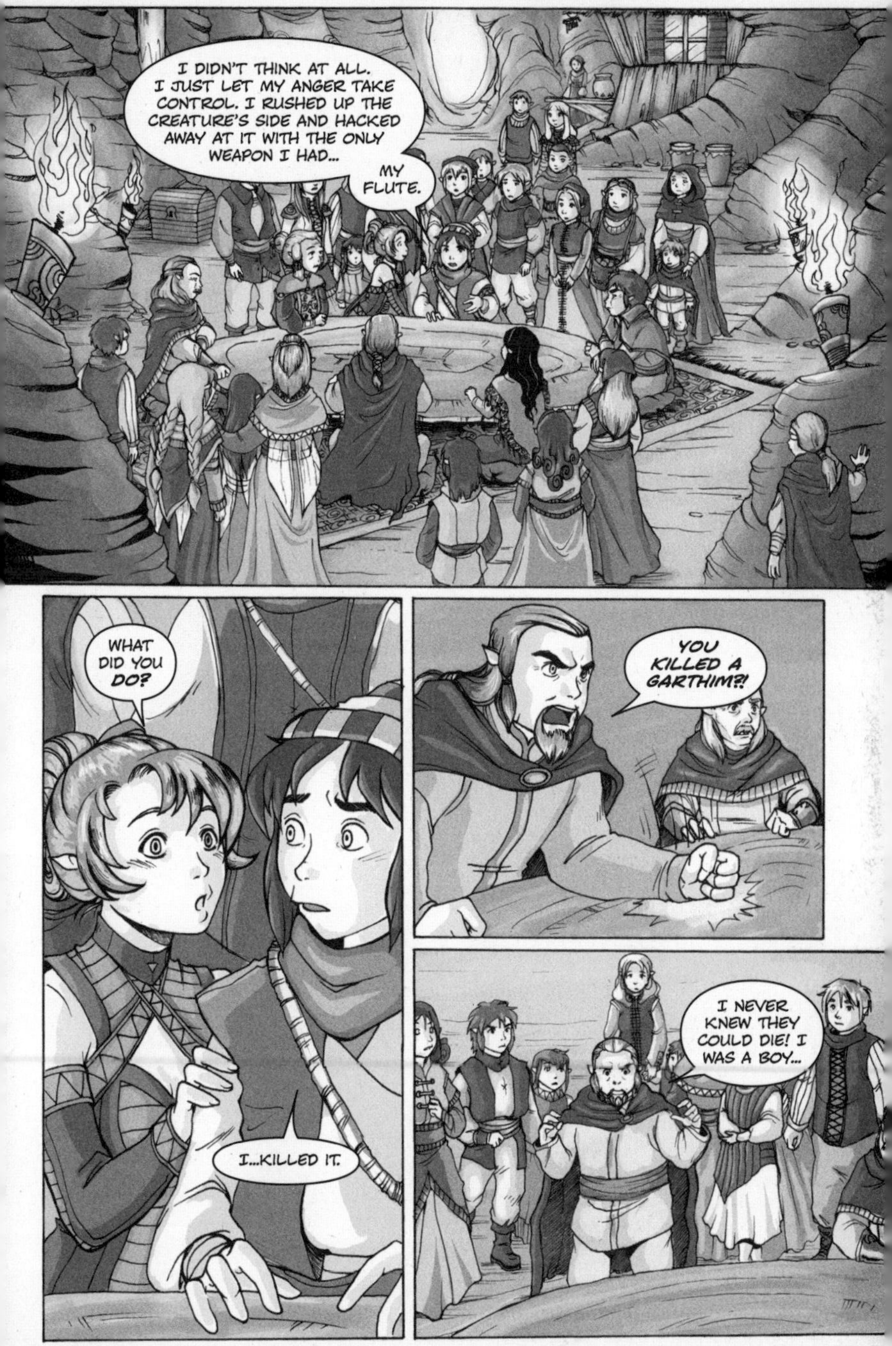
I DIDN'T THINK AT ALL. I JUST LET MY ANGER TAKE CONTROL. I RUSHED UP THE CREATURE'S SIDE AND HACKED AWAY AT IT WITH THE ONLY WEAPON I HAD...
MY FLUTE.
WHAT DID YOU DO?
I...KILLED IT.
YOU KILLED A GARTHIM?!
I NEVER KNEW THEY COULD DIE! I WAS A BOY...

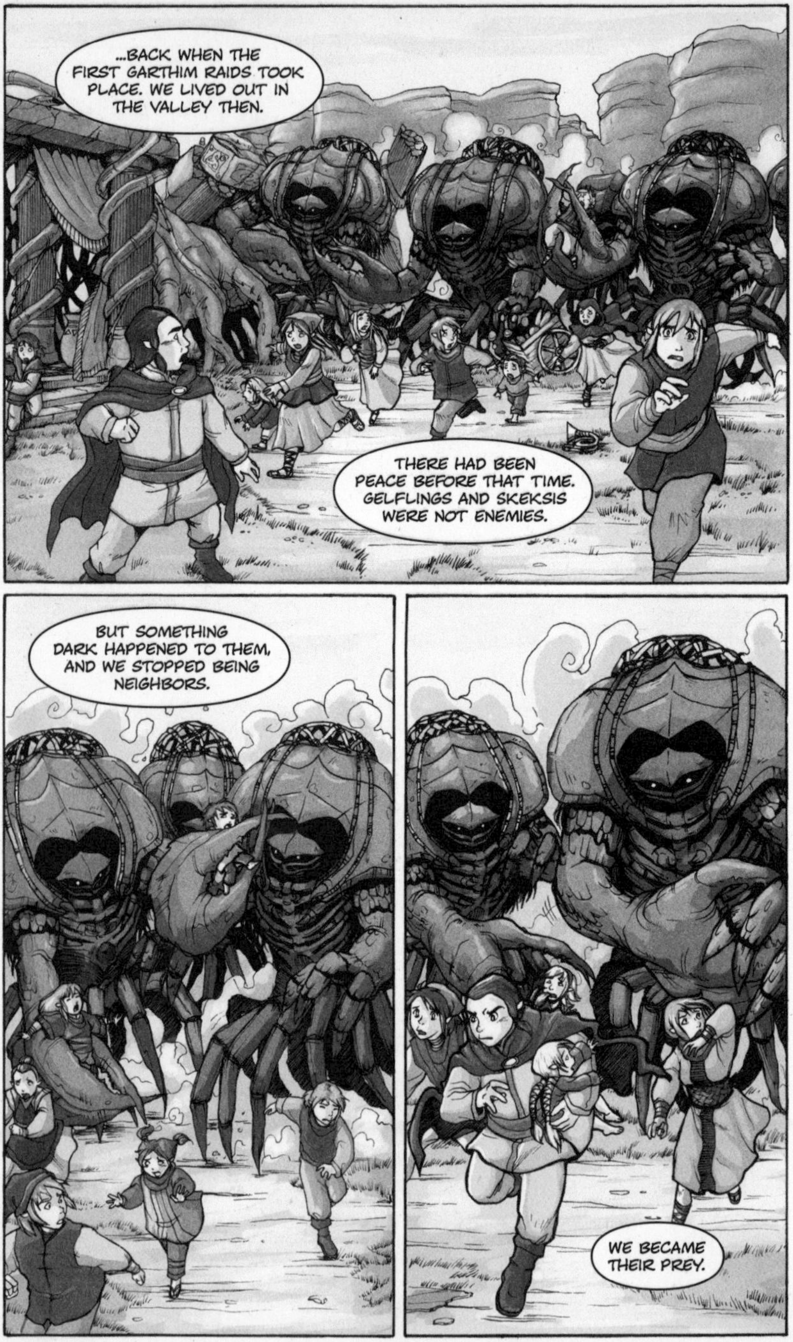
...BACK WHEN THE FIRST GARTHIM RAIDS TOOK PLACE. WE LIVED OUT IN THE VALLEY THEN.
THERE HAD BEEN PEACE BEFORE THAT TIME. GELFLINGS AND SKEKSIS WERE NOT ENEMIES.
BUT SOMETHING DARK HAPPENED TO THEM, AND WE STOPPED BEING NEIGHBORS.
WE BECAME THEIR PREY.

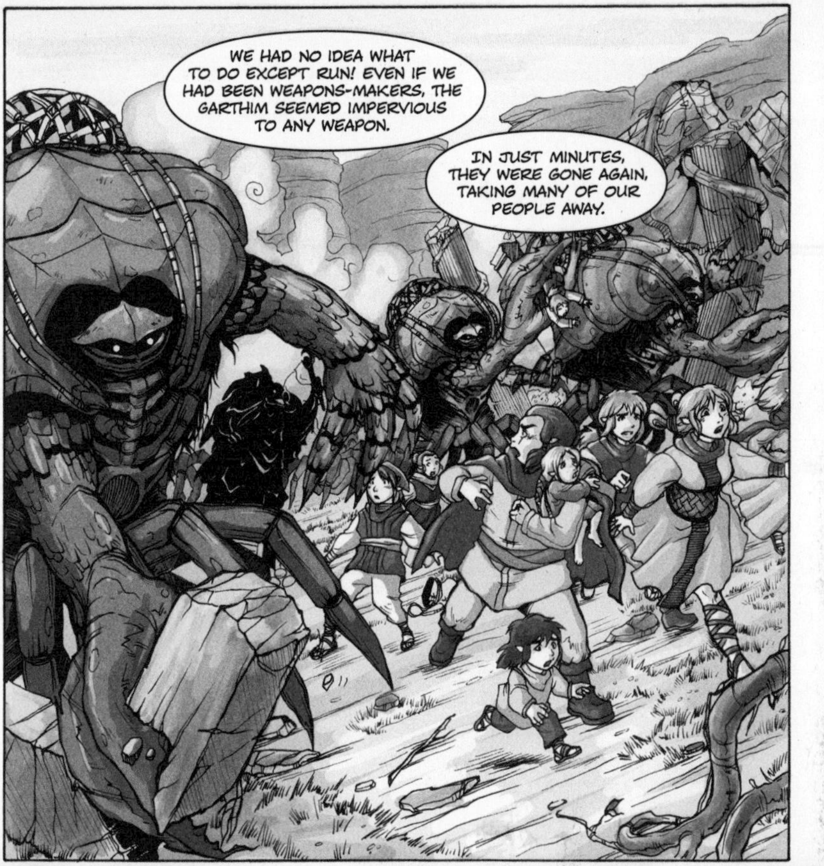
WE HAD NO IDEA WHAT TO DO EXCEPT RUN! EVEN IF WE HAD BEEN WEAPONS-MAKERS, THE GARTHIM SEEMED IMPERVIOUS TO ANY WEAPON.
IN JUST MINUTES, THEY WERE GONE AGAIN, TAKING MANY OF OUR PEOPLE AWAY.
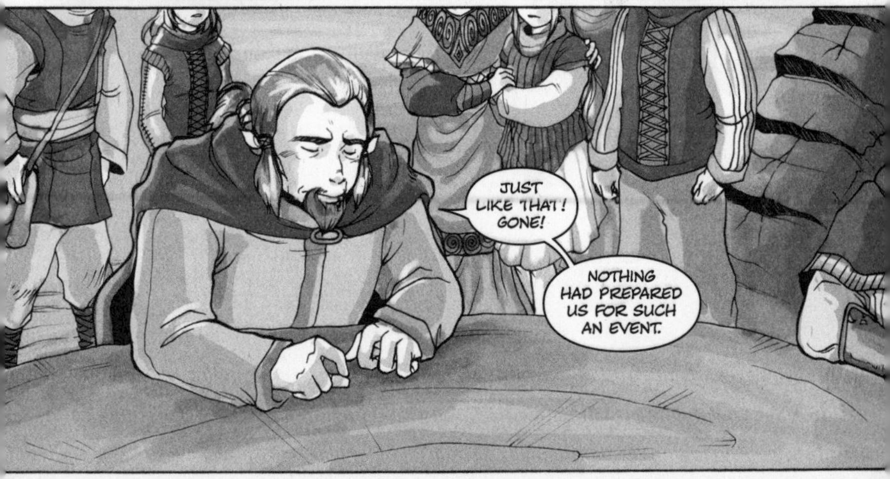
JUST LIKE THAT! GONE!
NOTHING HAD PREPARED US FOR SUCH AN EVENT.

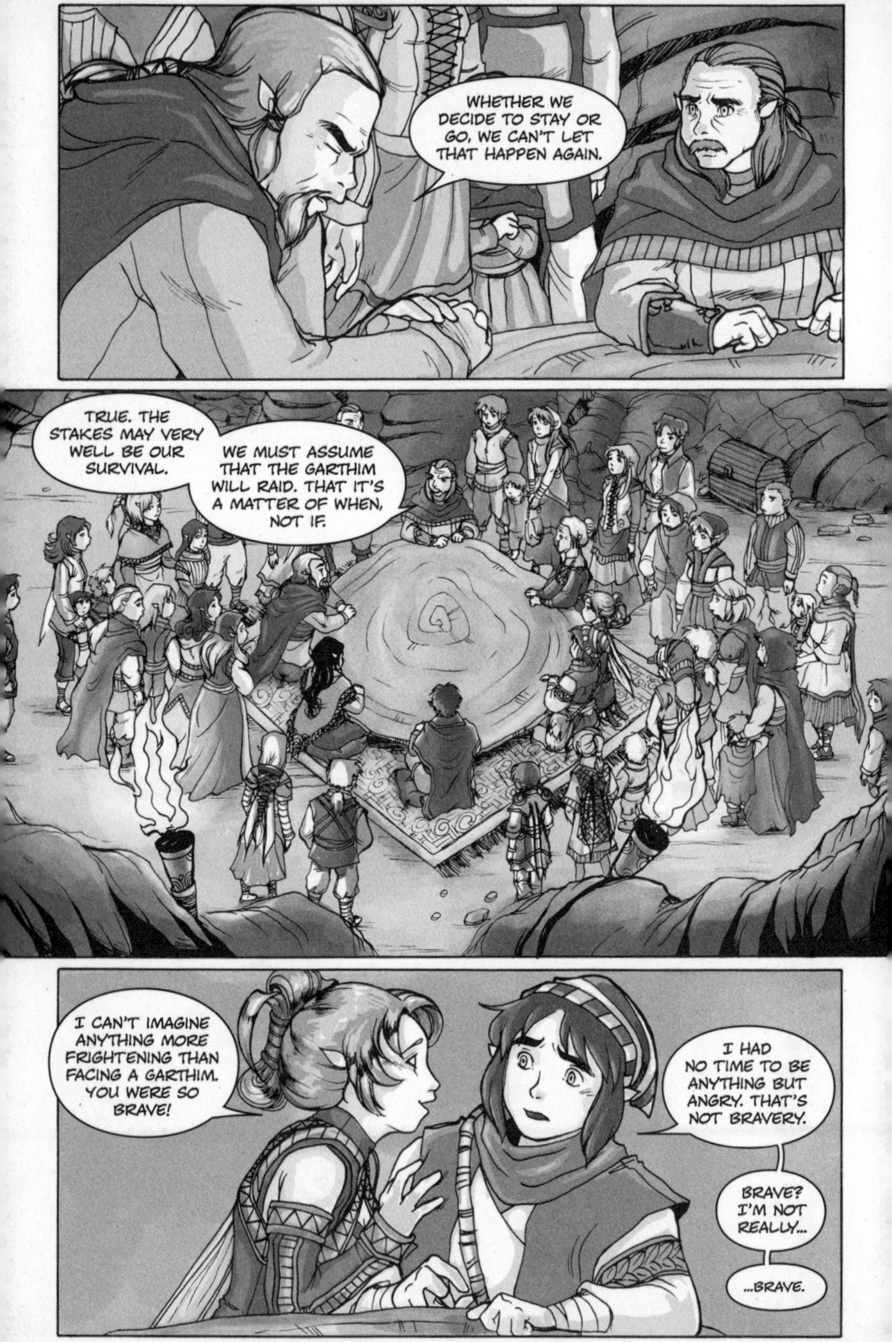
WHETHER WE DECIDE TO STAY OR GO, WE CAN'T LET THAT HAPPEN AGAIN.
TRUE. THE STAKES MAY VERY WELL BE OUR SURVIVAL.
WE MUST ASSUME THAT THE GARTHIM WILL RAID. THAT IT'S A MATTER OF WHEN, NOT IF.
I CAN'T IMAGINE ANYTHING MORE FRIGHTENING THAN FACING A GARTHIM. YOU WERE SO BRAVE!
I HAD NO TIME TO BE ANYTHING BUT ANGRY. THAT'S NOT BRAVERY.
BRAVE? I'M NOT REALLY...
...BRAVE.

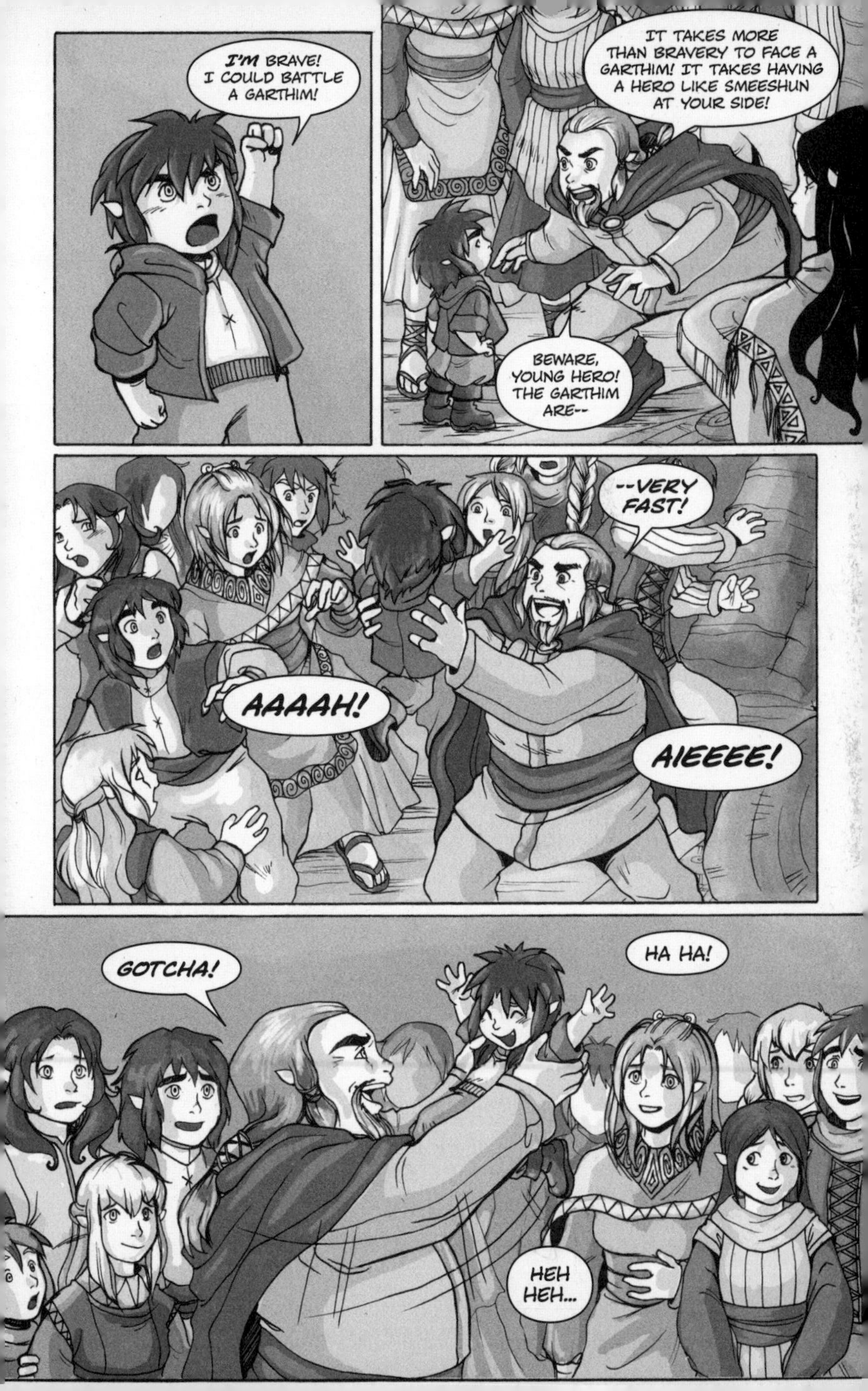
I'M BRAVE! I COULD BATTLE A GARTHIM!
IT TAKES MORE THAN BRAVERY TO FACE A GARTHIM! IT TAKES HAVING A HERO LIKE SMEESHUN AT YOUR SIDE!
BEWARE, YOUNG HERO! THE GARTHIM ARE--
--VERY FAST!
AAAAH!
AIEEEE!
GOTCHA!
HA HA!
HEH HEH...

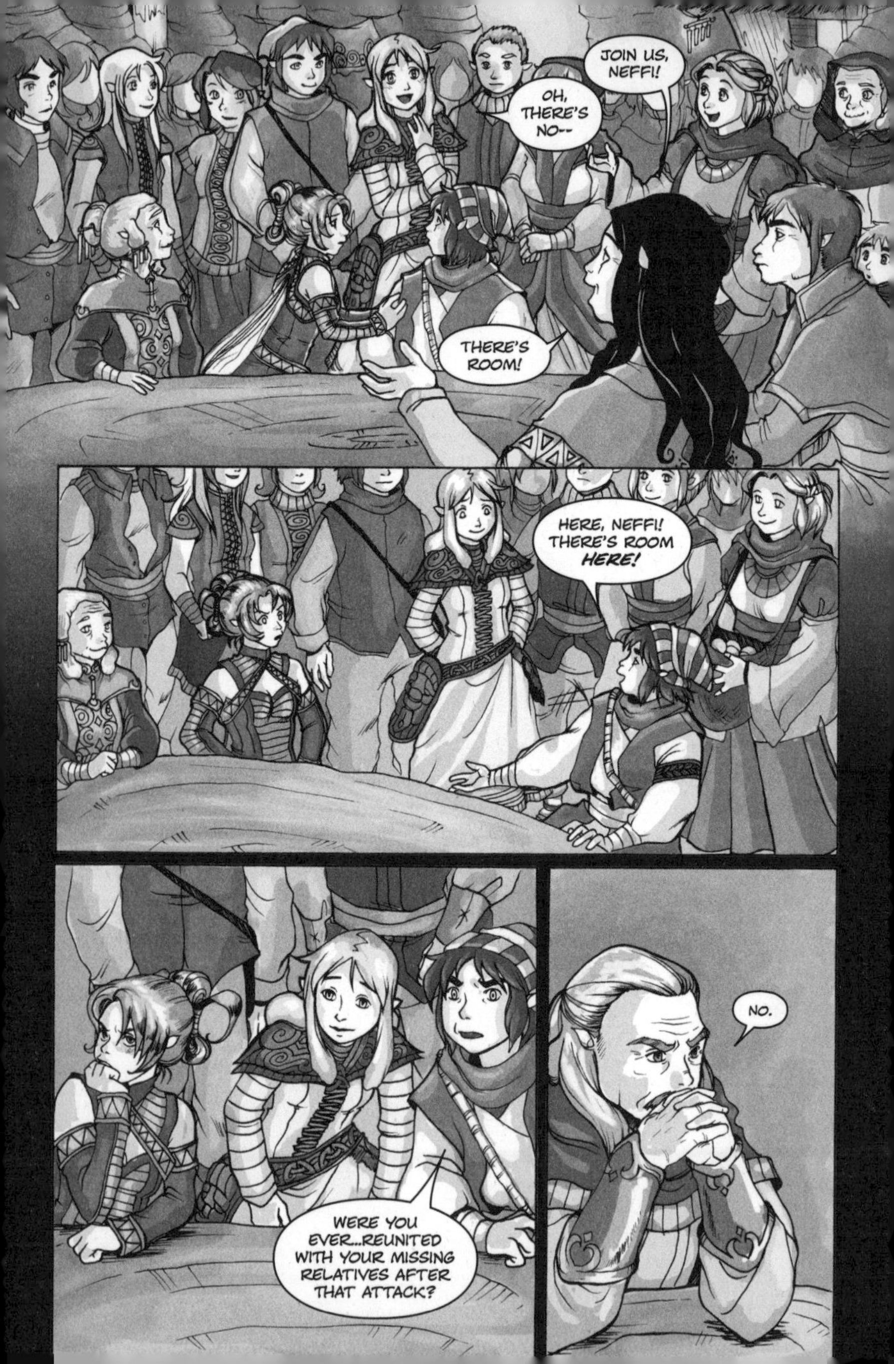
OH, THERE'S NO--
JOIN US, NEFFI!
THERE'S ROOM!
HERE, NEFFI! THERE'S ROOM *HERE!*
WERE YOU EVER...REUNITED WITH YOUR MISSING RELATIVES AFTER THAT ATTACK?
NO.

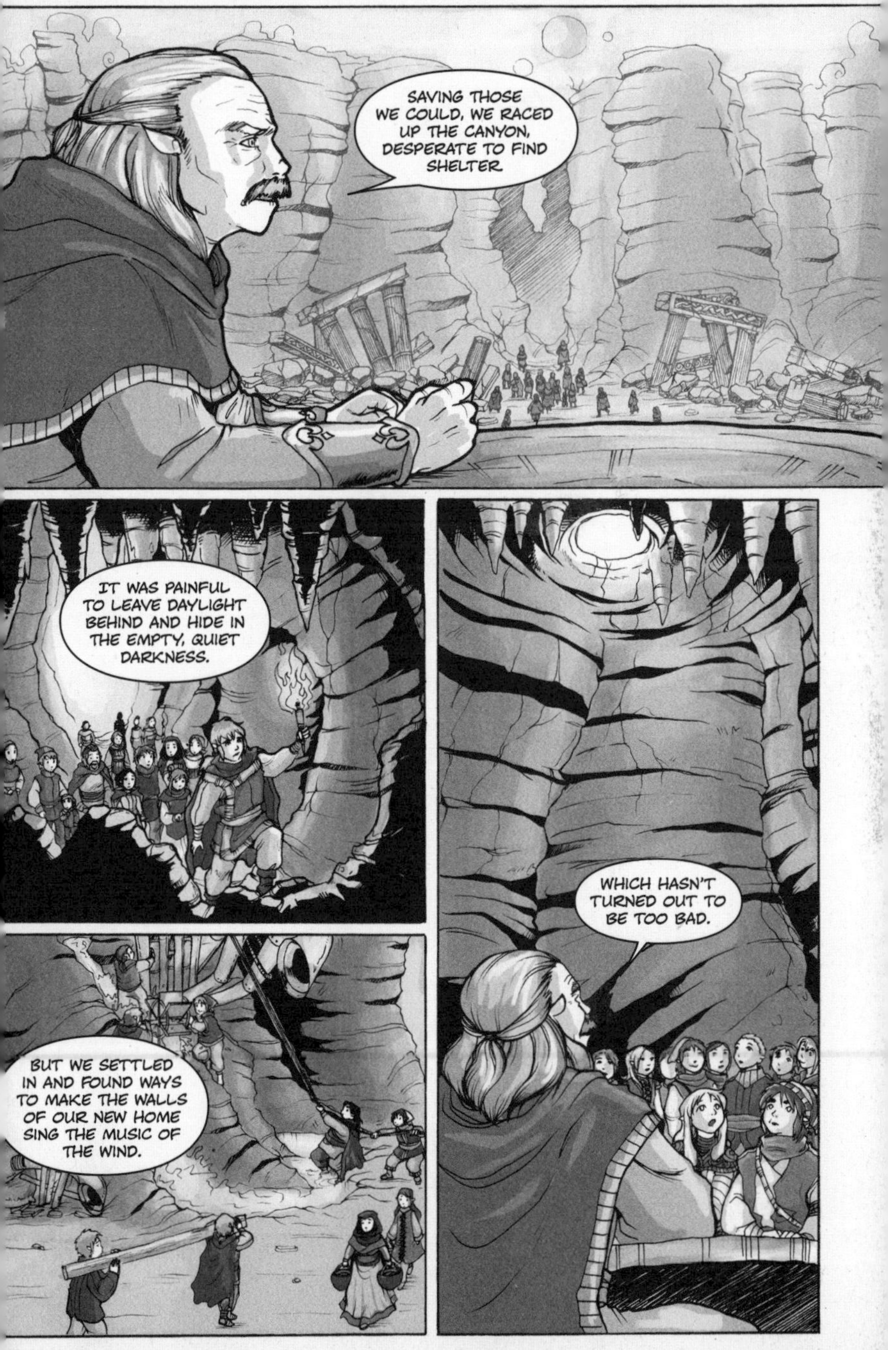
SAVING THOSE WE COULD, WE RACED UP THE CANYON, DESPERATE TO FIND SHELTER
IT WAS PAINFUL TO LEAVE DAYLIGHT BEHIND AND HIDE IN THE EMPTY, QUIET DARKNESS.
BUT WE SETTLED IN AND FOUND WAYS TO MAKE THE WALLS OF OUR NEW HOME SING THE MUSIC OF THE WIND.
WHICH HASN'T TURNED OUT TO BE TOO BAD.

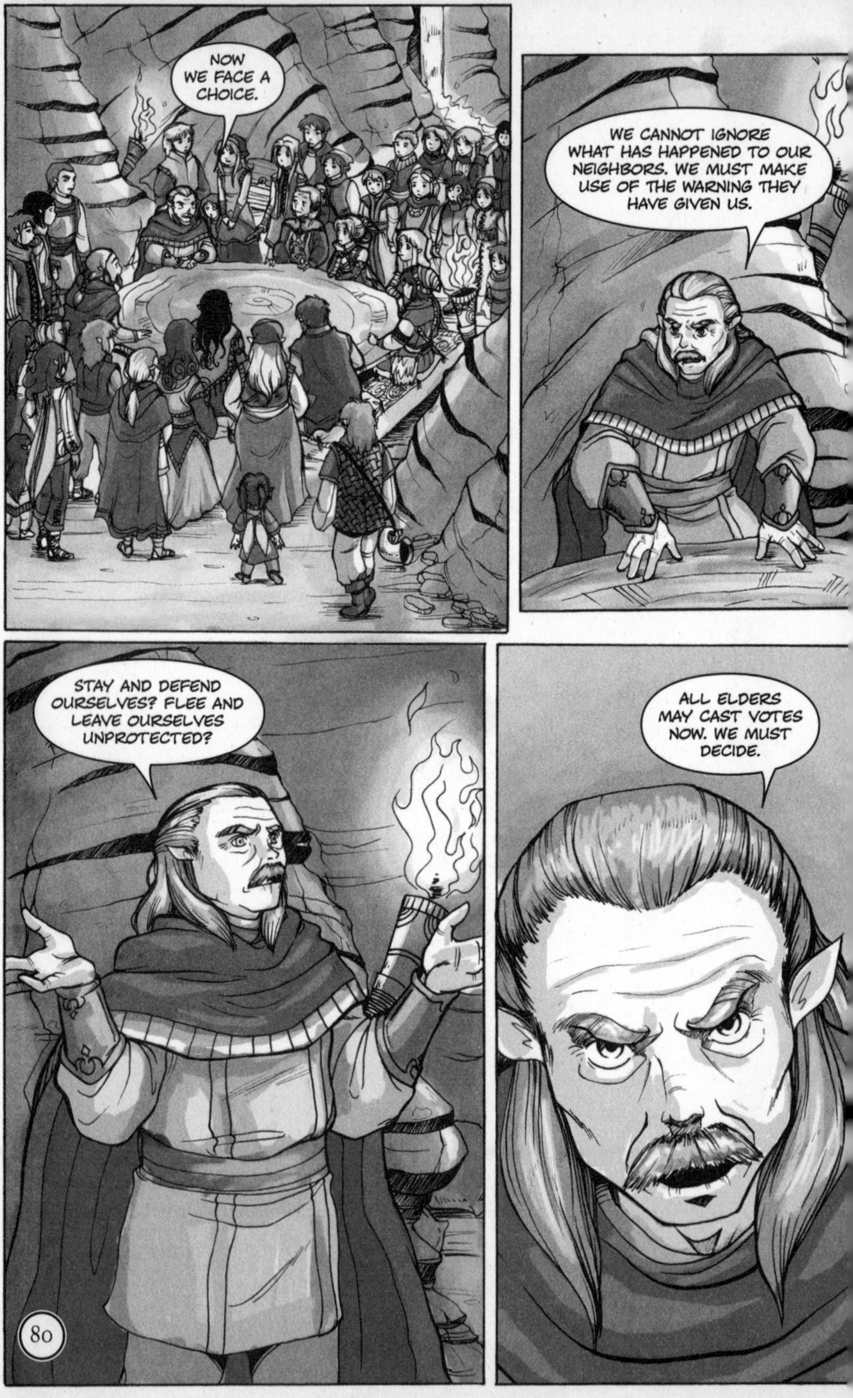
NOW WE FACE A CHOICE.
WE CANNOT IGNORE WHAT HAS HAPPENED TO OUR NEIGHBORS. WE MUST MAKE USE OF THE WARNING THEY HAVE GIVEN US.
STAY AND DEFEND OURSELVES? FLEE AND LEAVE OURSELVES UNPROTECTED?
ALL ELDERS MAY CAST VOTES NOW. WE MUST DECIDE.

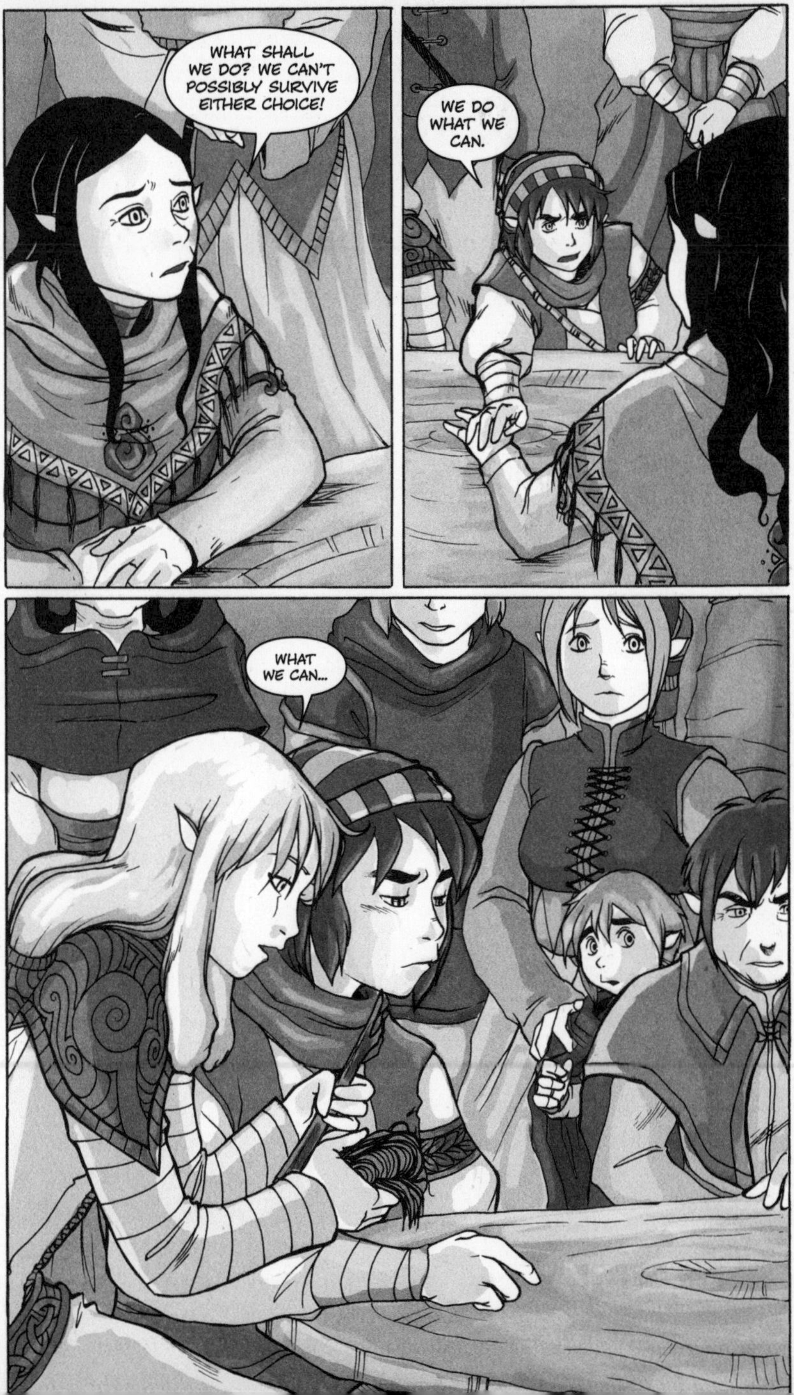
WHAT SHALL WE DO? WE CAN'T POSSIBLY SURVIVE EITHER CHOICE!
WE DO WHAT WE CAN.
WHAT WE CAN...

Chapter Four

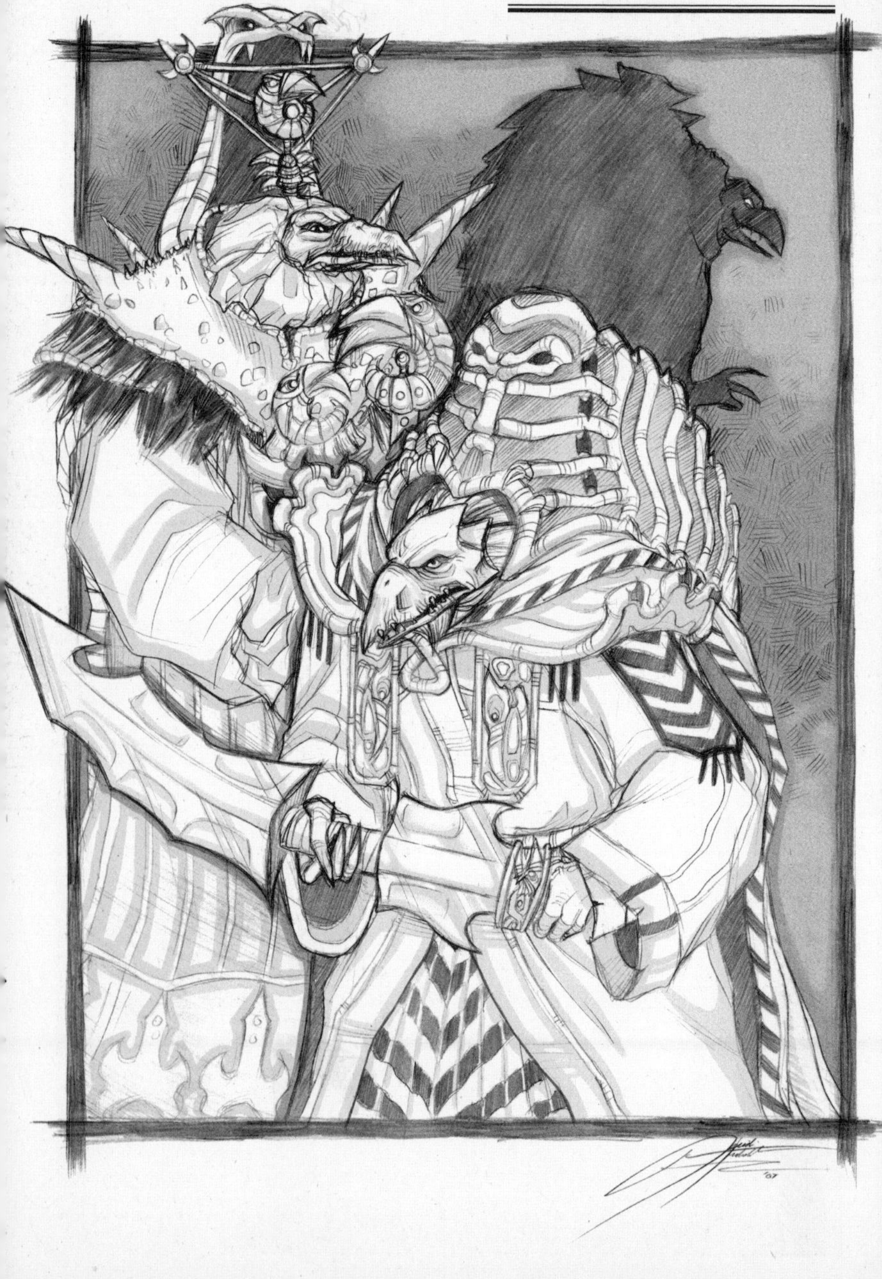

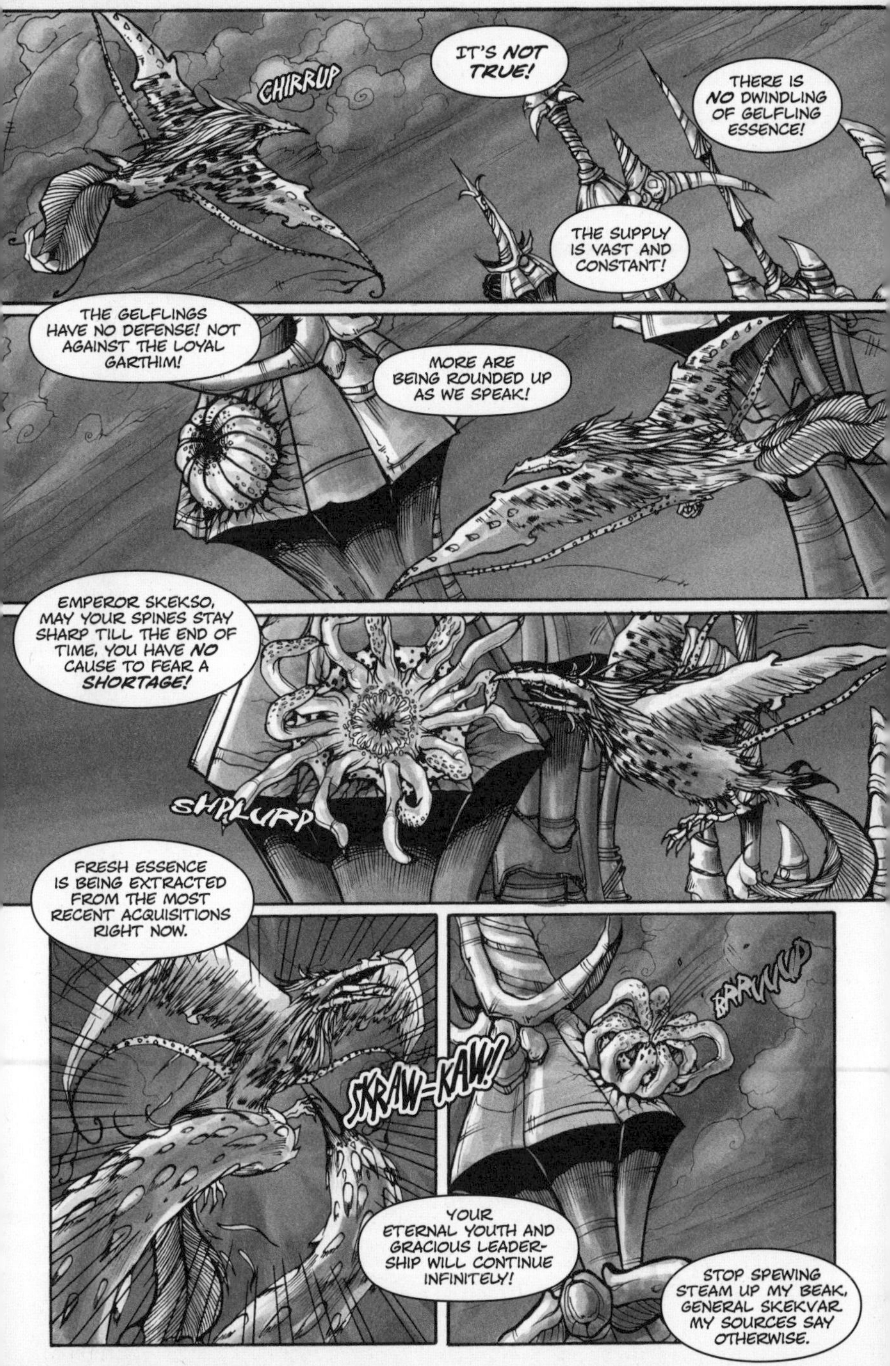
CHIRRUP
IT'S NOT TRUE!
THERE IS NO DWINDLING OF GELFLING ESSENCE!
THE SUPPLY IS VAST AND CONSTANT!
THE GELFLINGS HAVE NO DEFENSE! NOT AGAINST THE LOYAL GARTHIM!
MORE ARE BEING ROUNDED UP AS WE SPEAK!
EMPEROR SKEKSO, MAY YOUR SPINES STAY SHARP TILL THE END OF TIME, YOU HAVE NO CAUSE TO FEAR A SHORTAGE!
SHPLURP
FRESH ESSENCE IS BEING EXTRACTED FROM THE MOST RECENT ACQUISITIONS RIGHT NOW.
SKRAW-KAW!
BRRVUUP
YOUR ETERNAL YOUTH AND GRACIOUS LEADER-SHIP WILL CONTINUE INFINITELY!
STOP SPEWING STEAM UP MY BEAK, GENERAL SKEKVAR MY SOURCES SAY OTHERWISE.

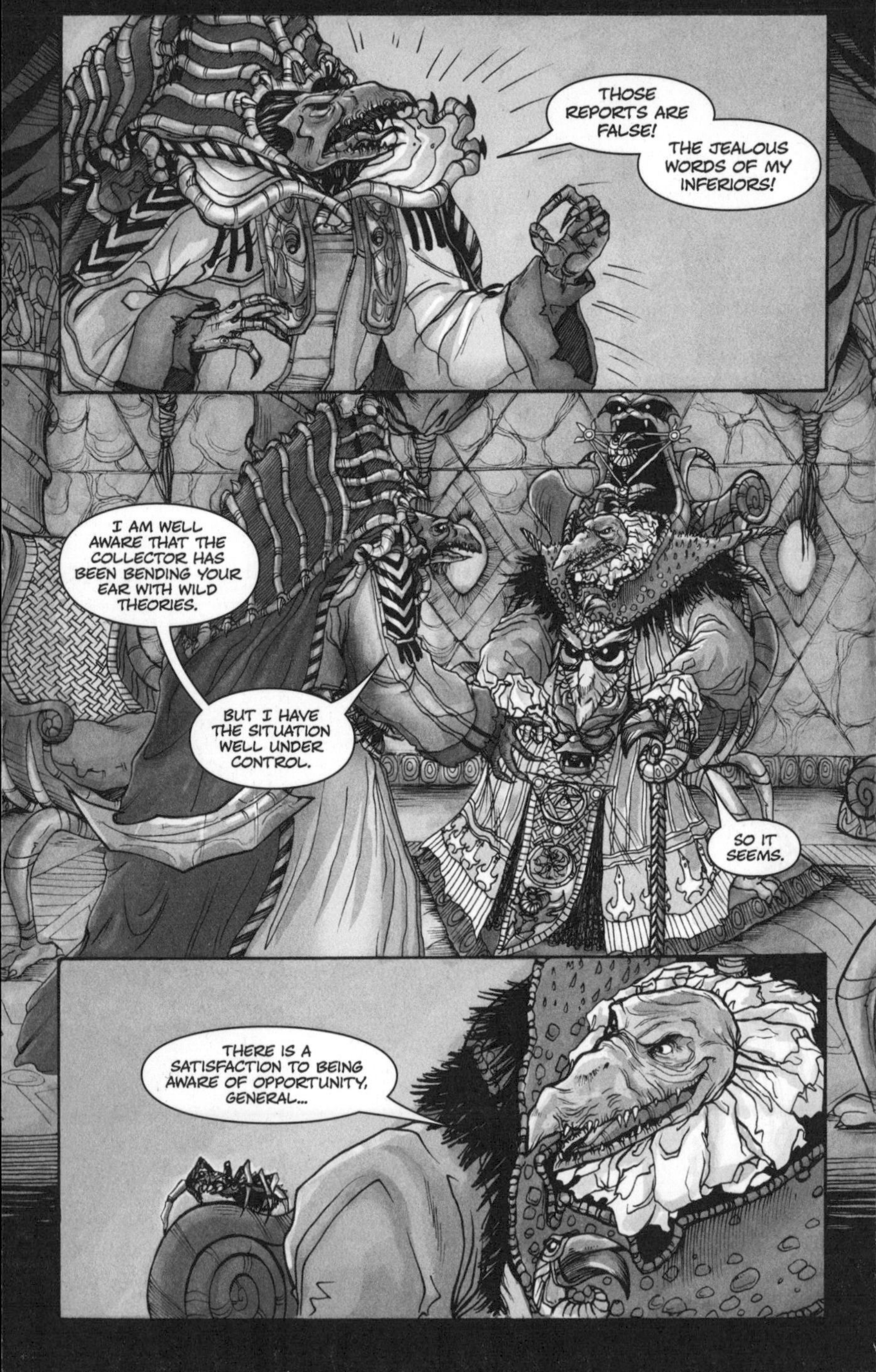
THOSE REPORTS ARE FALSE!
THE JEALOUS WORDS OF MY INFERIORS!
I AM WELL AWARE THAT THE COLLECTOR HAS BEEN BENDING YOUR EAR WITH WILD THEORIES.
BUT I HAVE THE SITUATION WELL UNDER CONTROL.
SO IT SEEMS.
THERE IS A SATISFACTION TO BEING AWARE OF OPPORTUNITY, GENERAL...

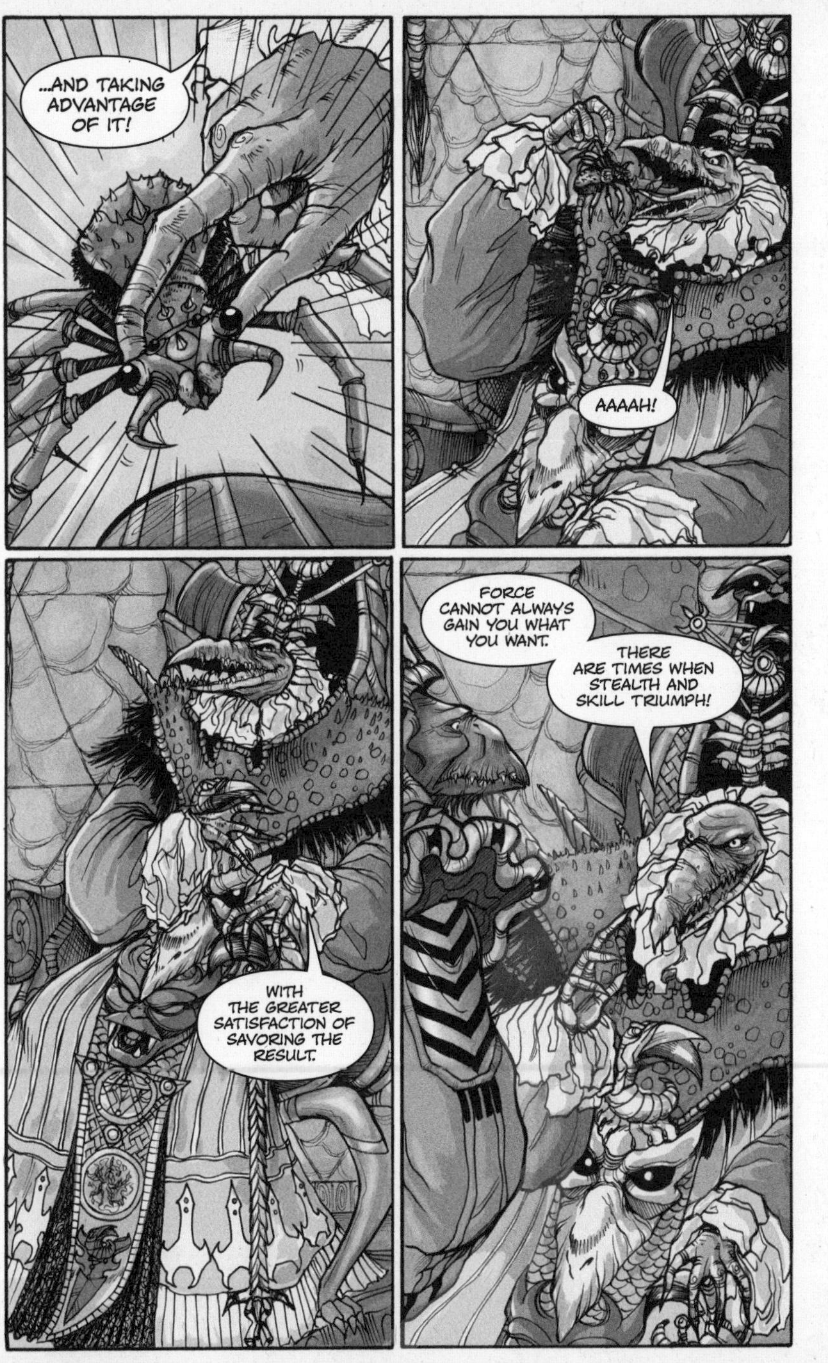
...AND TAKING ADVANTAGE OF IT!
AAAAH!
WITH THE GREATER SATISFACTION OF SAVORING THE RESULT.
FORCE CANNOT ALWAYS GAIN YOU WHAT YOU WANT.
THERE ARE TIMES WHEN STEALTH AND SKILL TRIUMPH!

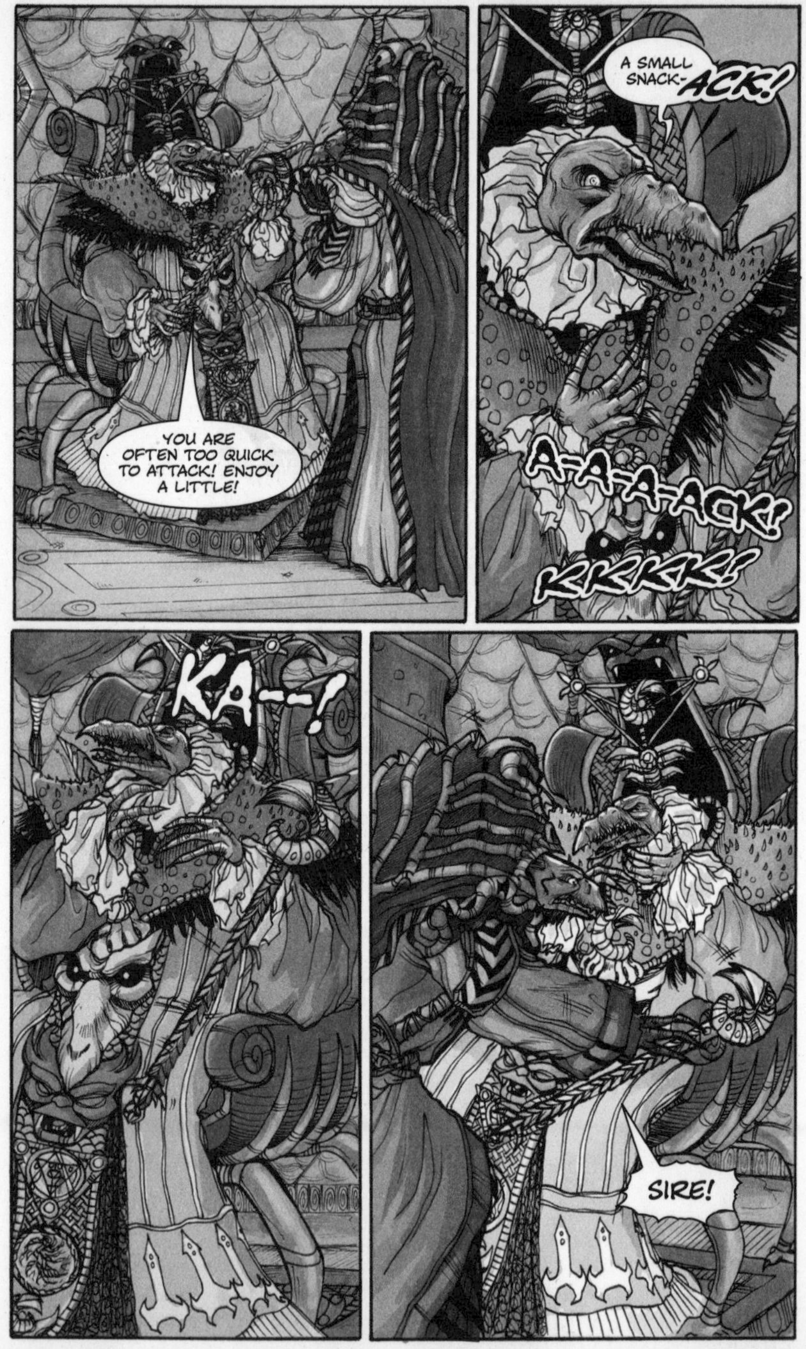
YOU ARE OFTEN TOO QUICK TO ATTACK! ENJOY A LITTLE!
A SMALL SNACK-ACK!
A-A-A-ACK!
KKKKK!
KA--!
SIRE!

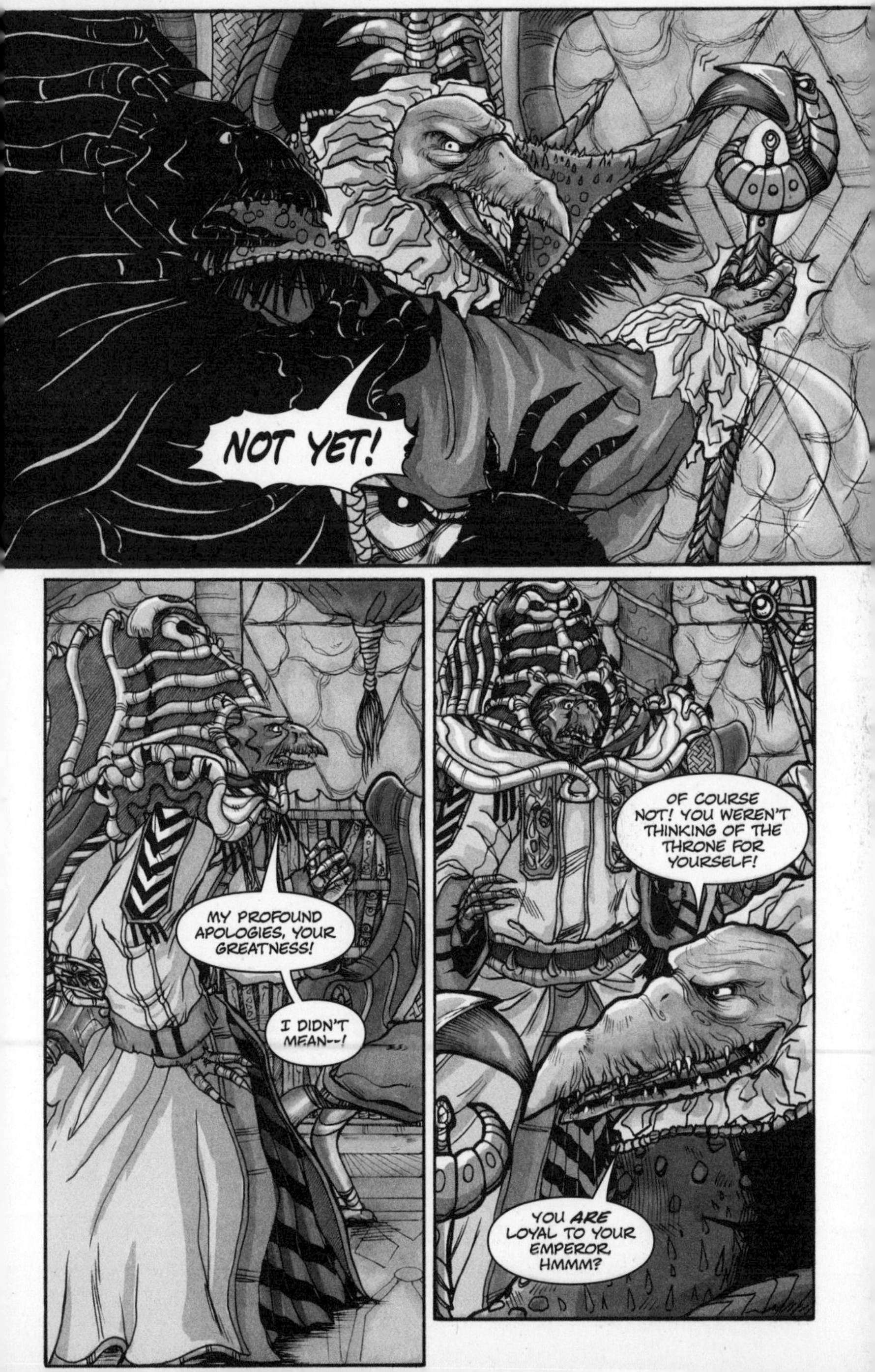
NOT YET!
MY PROFOUND APOLOGIES, YOUR GREATNESS!
I DIDN'T MEAN--!
OF COURSE NOT! YOU WEREN'T THINKING OF THE THRONE FOR YOURSELF!
YOU ARE LOYAL TO YOUR EMPEROR, HMMM?

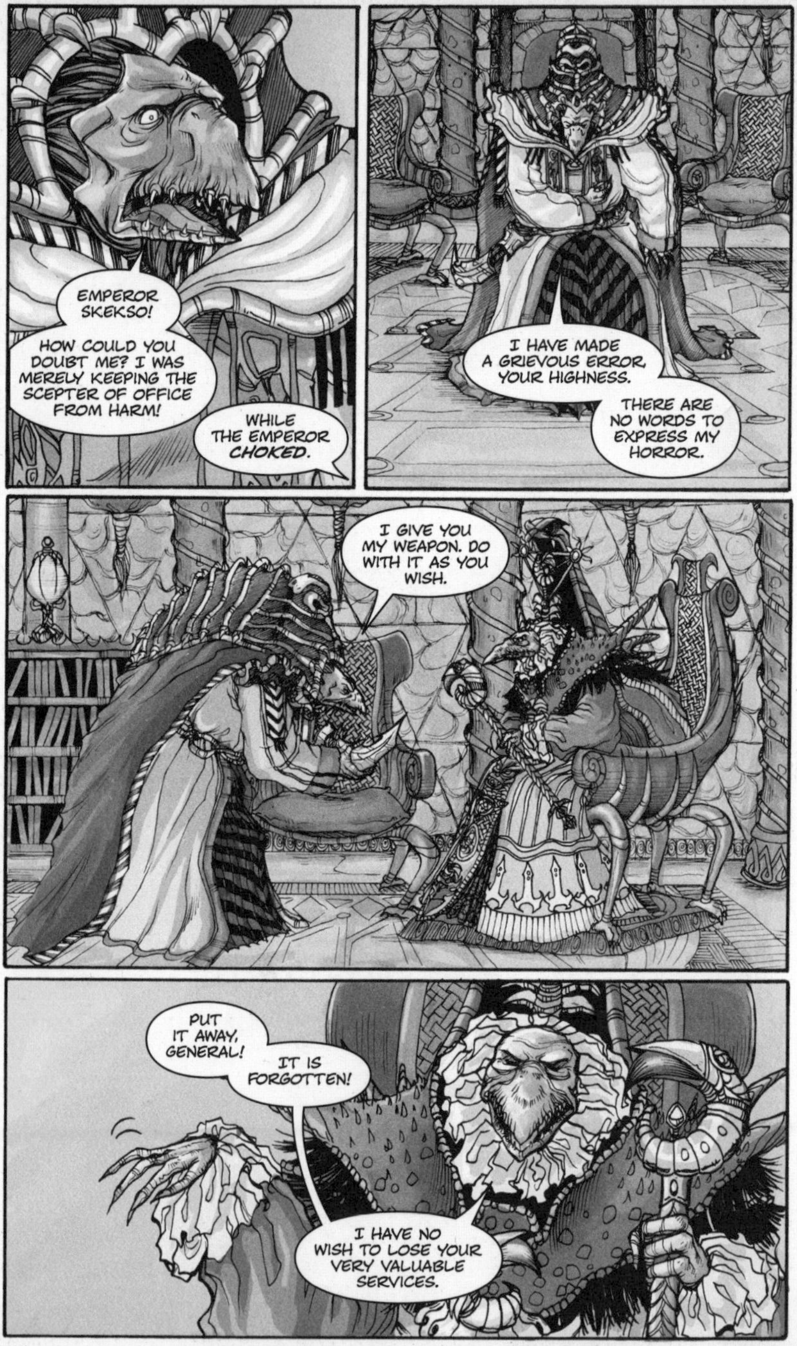
EMPEROR SKEKSO!
HOW COULD YOU DOUBT ME? I WAS MERELY KEEPING THE SCEPTER OF OFFICE FROM HARM!
WHILE THE EMPEROR *CHOKED*.
I HAVE MADE A GRIEVOUS ERROR, YOUR HIGHNESS.
THERE ARE NO WORDS TO EXPRESS MY HORROR.
I GIVE YOU MY WEAPON. DO WITH IT AS YOU WISH.
PUT IT AWAY, GENERAL!
IT IS FORGOTTEN!
I HAVE NO WISH TO LOSE YOUR VERY VALUABLE SERVICES.

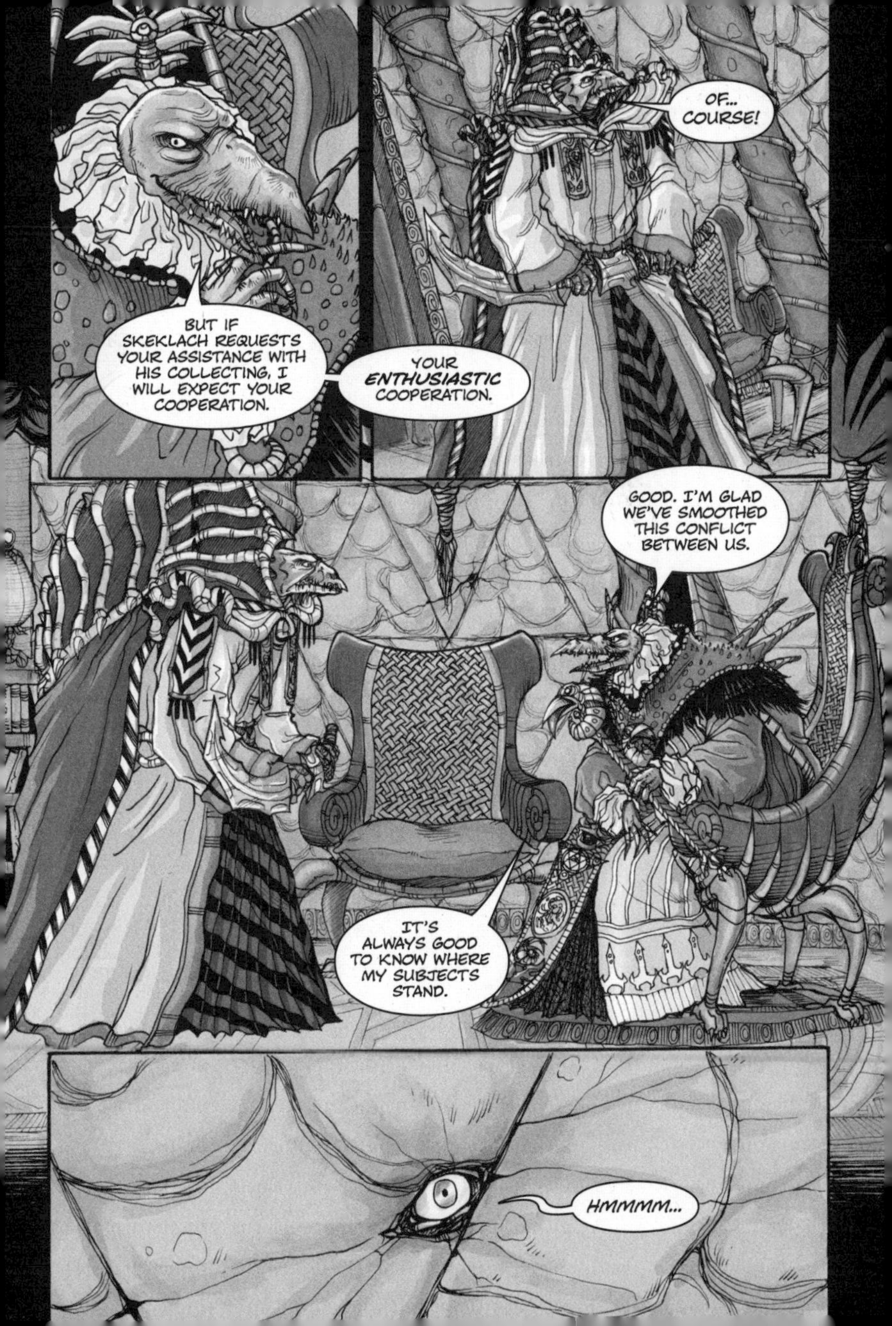
BUT IF SKEKLACH REQUESTS YOUR ASSISTANCE WITH HIS COLLECTING, I WILL EXPECT YOUR COOPERATION.
YOUR *ENTHUSIASTIC* COOPERATION.
OF... COURSE!
GOOD. I'M GLAD WE'VE SMOOTHED THIS CONFLICT BETWEEN US.
IT'S ALWAYS GOOD TO KNOW WHERE MY SUBJECTS STAND.
HMMMM...

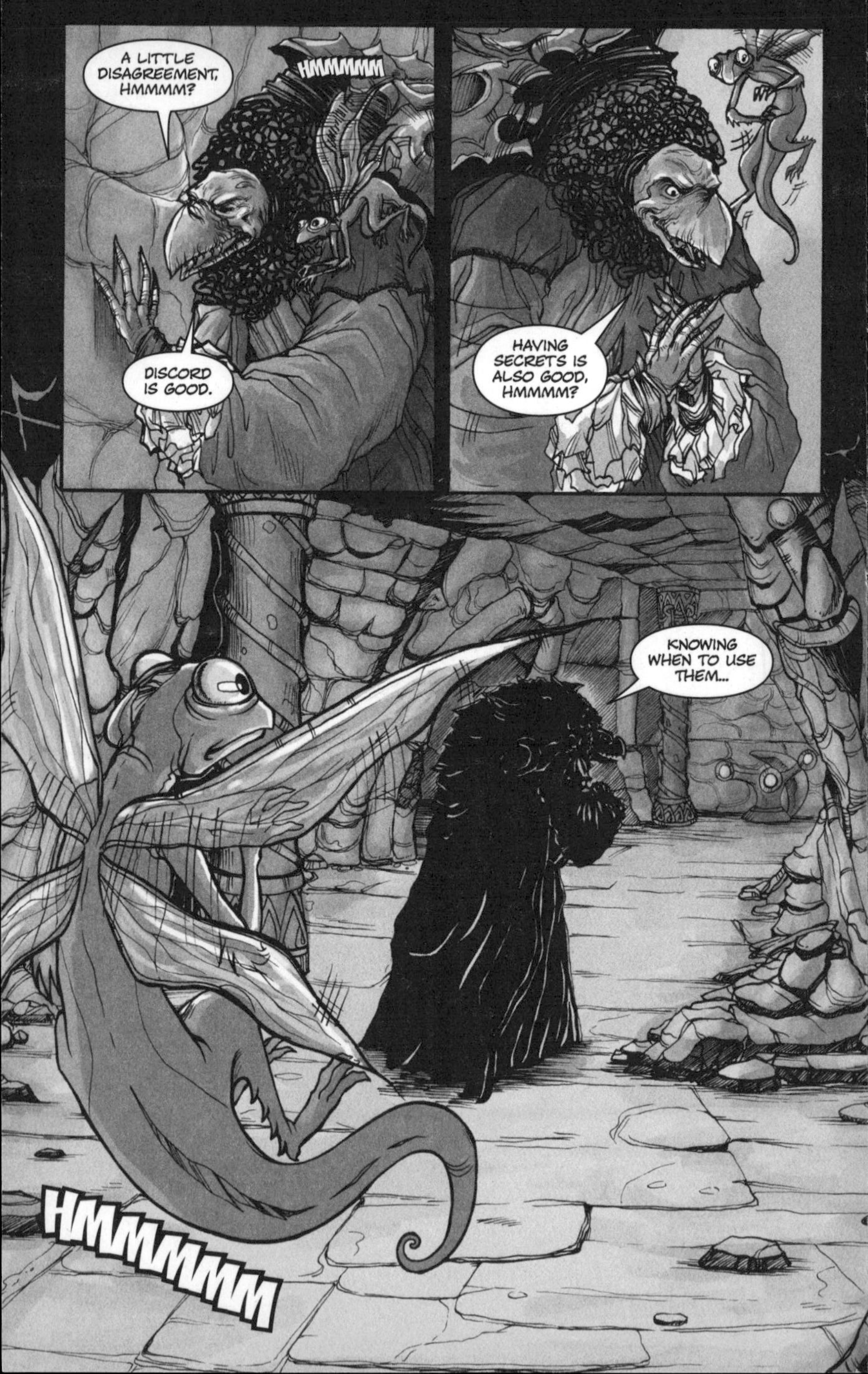
A LITTLE DISAGREEMENT, HMMMM?
HMMMMM
DISCORD IS GOOD.
HAVING SECRETS IS ALSO GOOD, HMMMM?
KNOWING WHEN TO USE THEM...
HMMMMMM

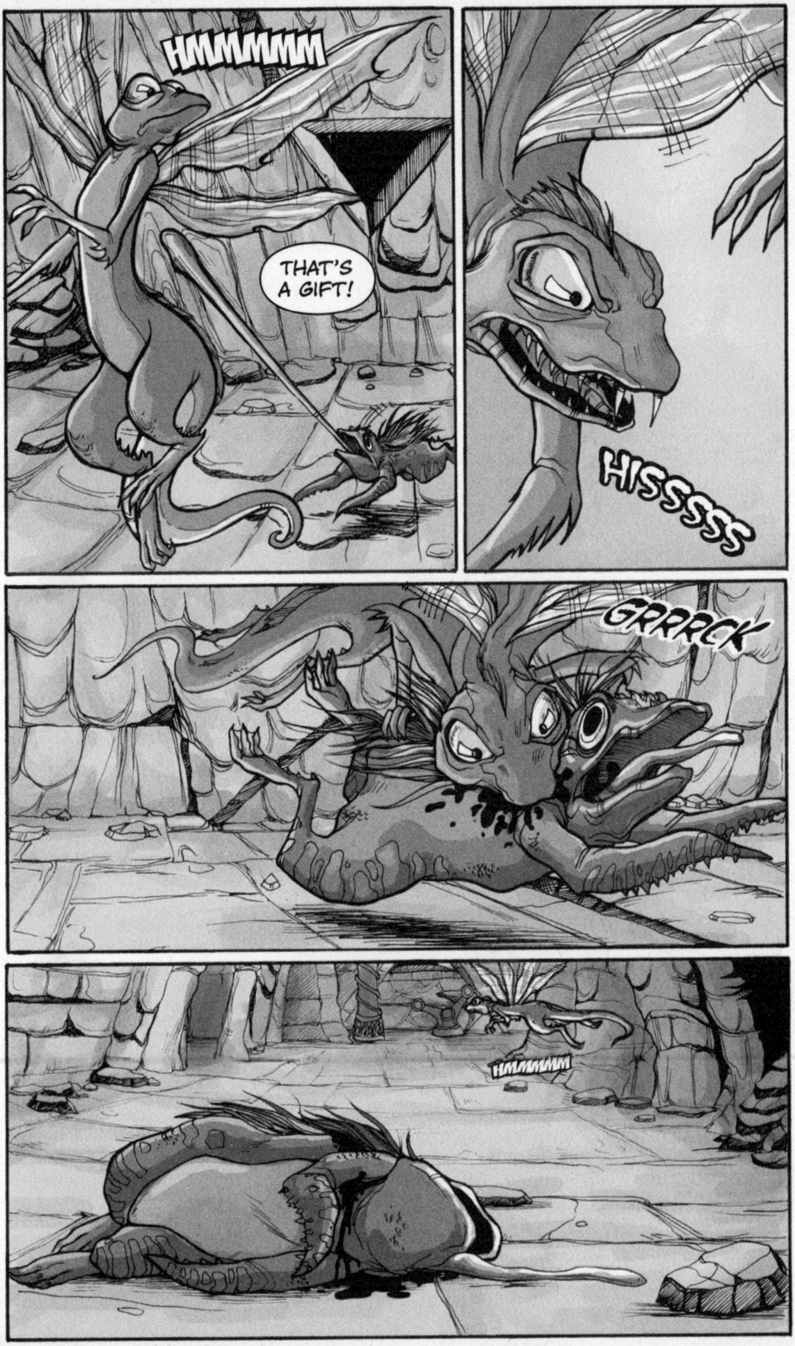
HMMMMMM
THAT'S A GIFT!
HISSSSS
GRRRCK
HMMMMMM

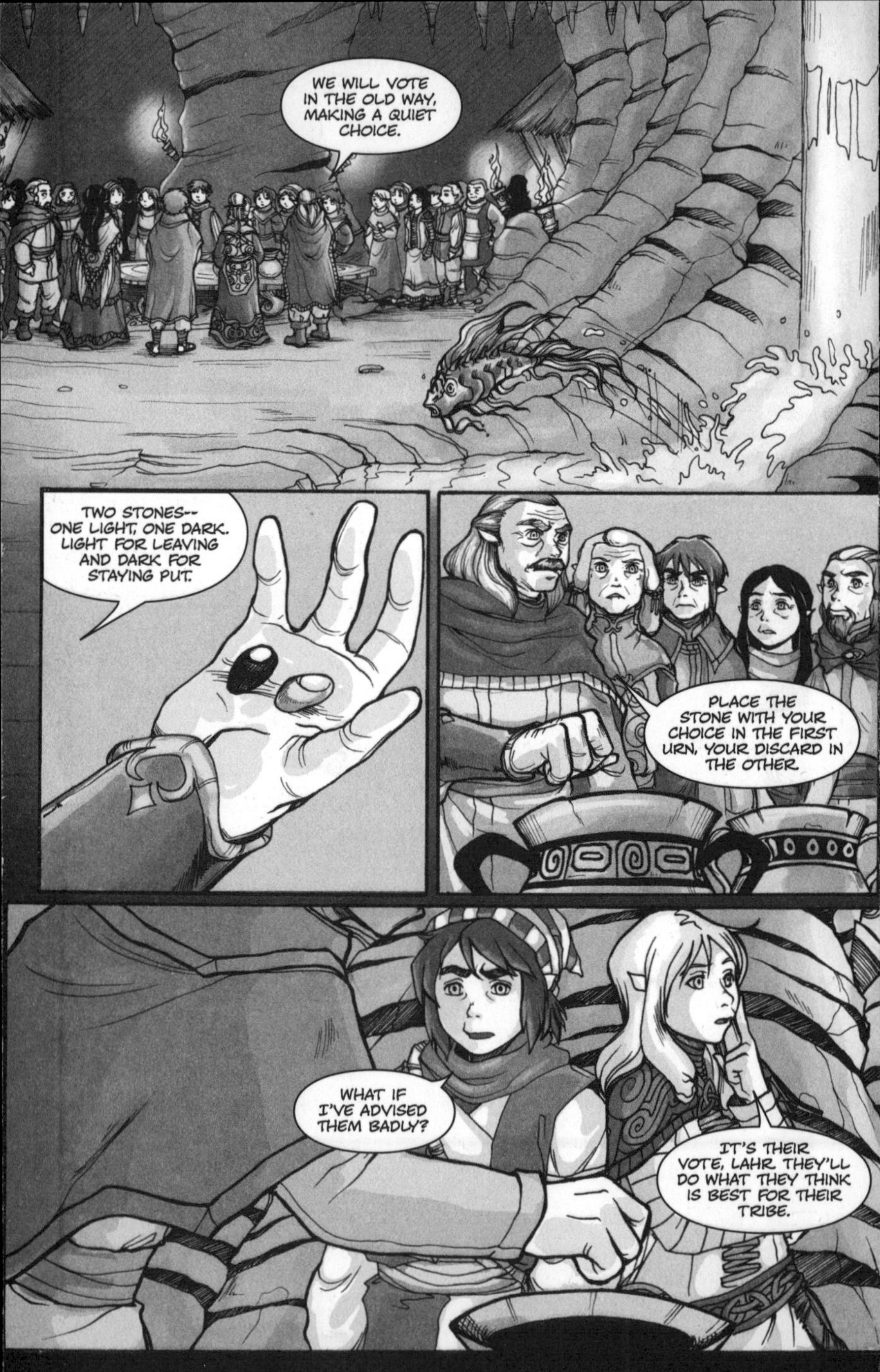
WE WILL VOTE IN THE OLD WAY, MAKING A QUIET CHOICE.
TWO STONES-- ONE LIGHT, ONE DARK. LIGHT FOR LEAVING AND DARK FOR STAYING PUT.
PLACE THE STONE WITH YOUR CHOICE IN THE FIRST URN, YOUR DISCARD IN THE OTHER.
WHAT IF I'VE ADVISED THEM BADLY?
IT'S THEIR VOTE, LAHR. THEY'LL DO WHAT THEY THINK IS BEST FOR THEIR TRIBE.

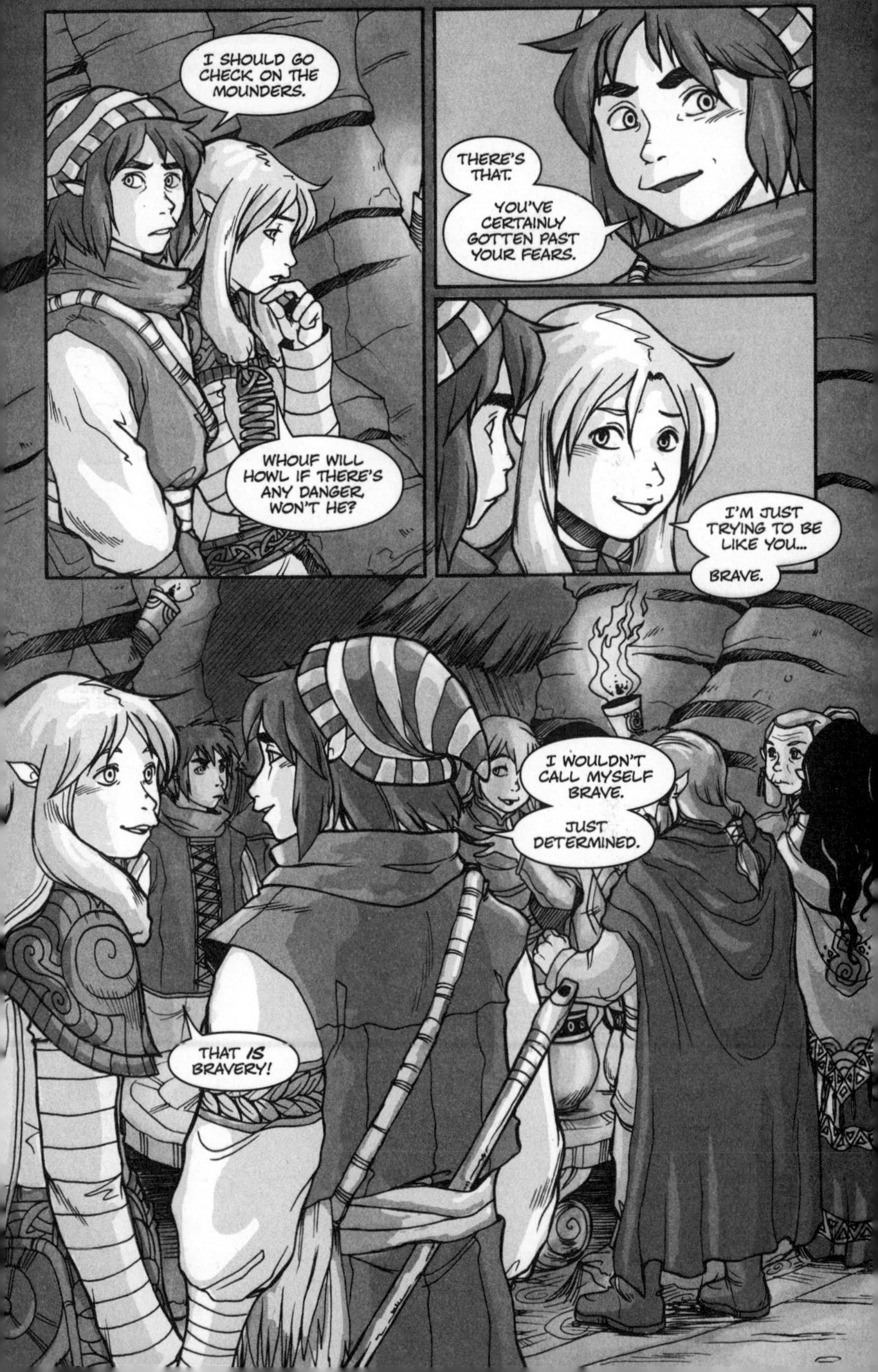
I SHOULD GO CHECK ON THE MOUNDERS.
WHOUF WILL HOWL IF THERE'S ANY DANGER, WON'T HE?
THERE'S THAT.
YOU'VE CERTAINLY GOTTEN PAST YOUR FEARS.
I'M JUST TRYING TO BE LIKE YOU...
BRAVE.
I WOULDN'T CALL MYSELF BRAVE.
JUST DETERMINED.
THAT *IS* BRAVERY!

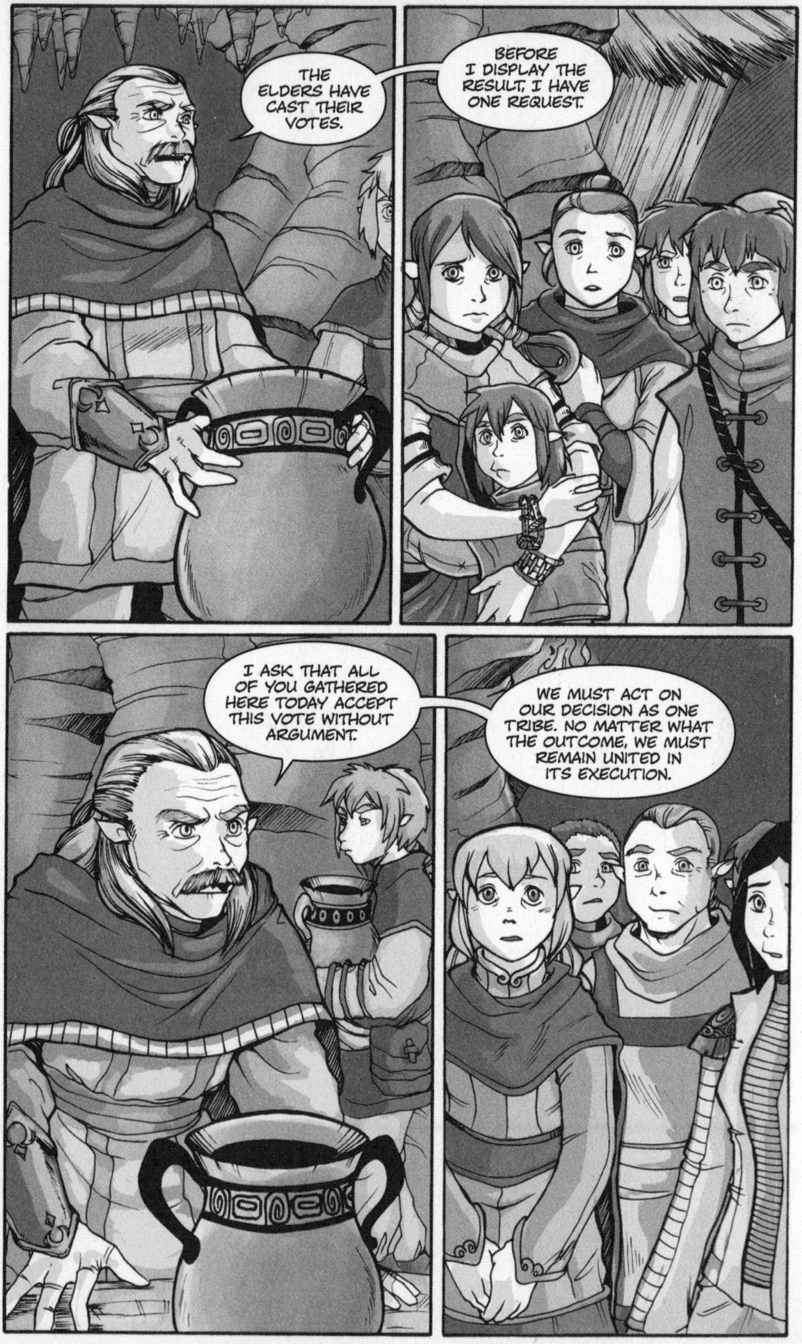
THE ELDERS HAVE CAST THEIR VOTES.
BEFORE I DISPLAY THE RESULT, I HAVE ONE REQUEST.
I ASK THAT ALL OF YOU GATHERED HERE TODAY ACCEPT THIS VOTE WITHOUT ARGUMENT.
WE MUST ACT ON OUR DECISION AS ONE TRIBE. NO MATTER WHAT THE OUTCOME, WE MUST REMAIN UNITED IN ITS EXECUTION.

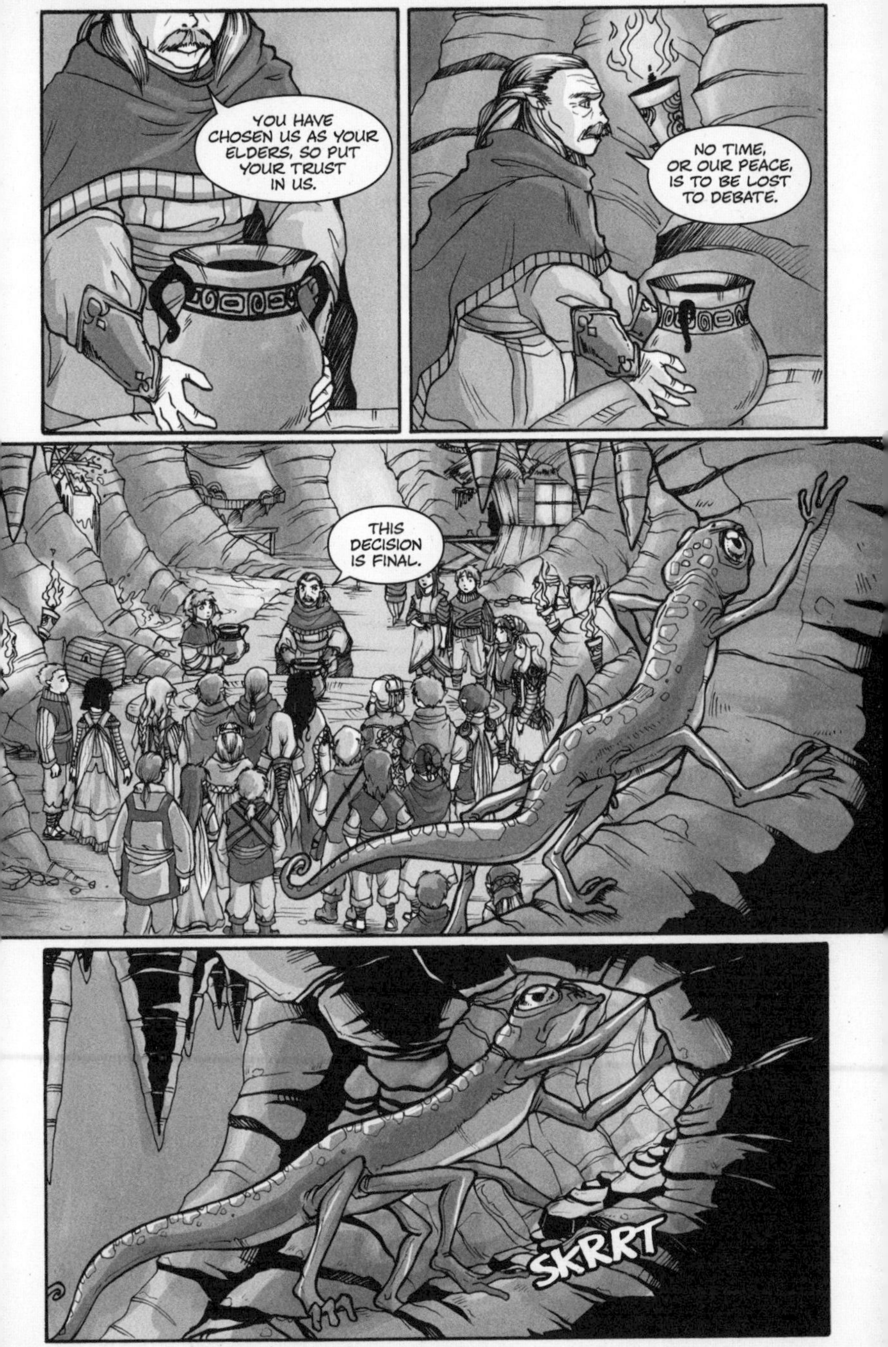
YOU HAVE CHOSEN US AS YOUR ELDERS, SO PUT YOUR TRUST IN US.
NO TIME, OR OUR PEACE, IS TO BE LOST TO DEBATE.
THIS DECISION IS FINAL.
SKRRT

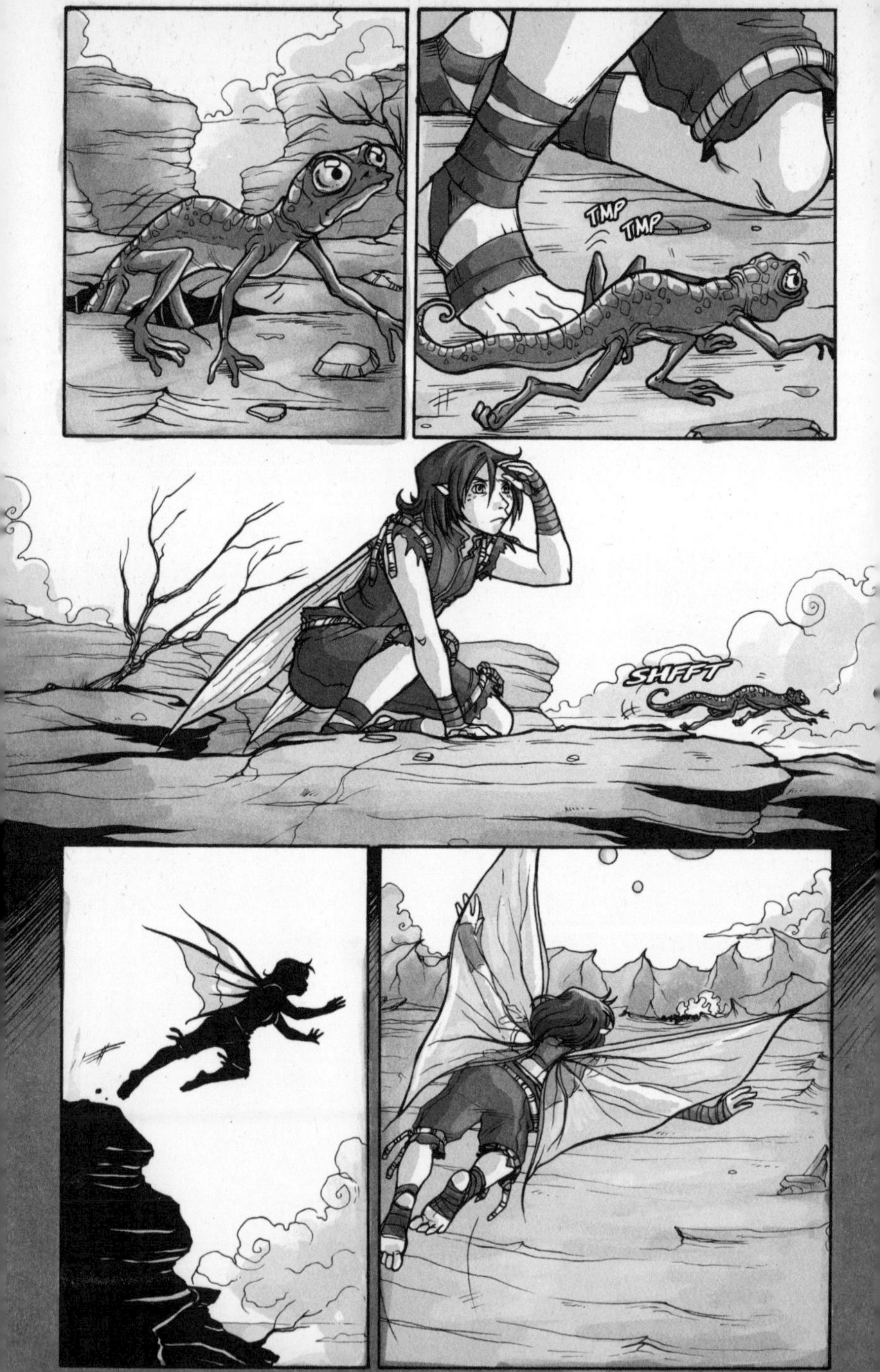
TMP
TMP
SHFFT

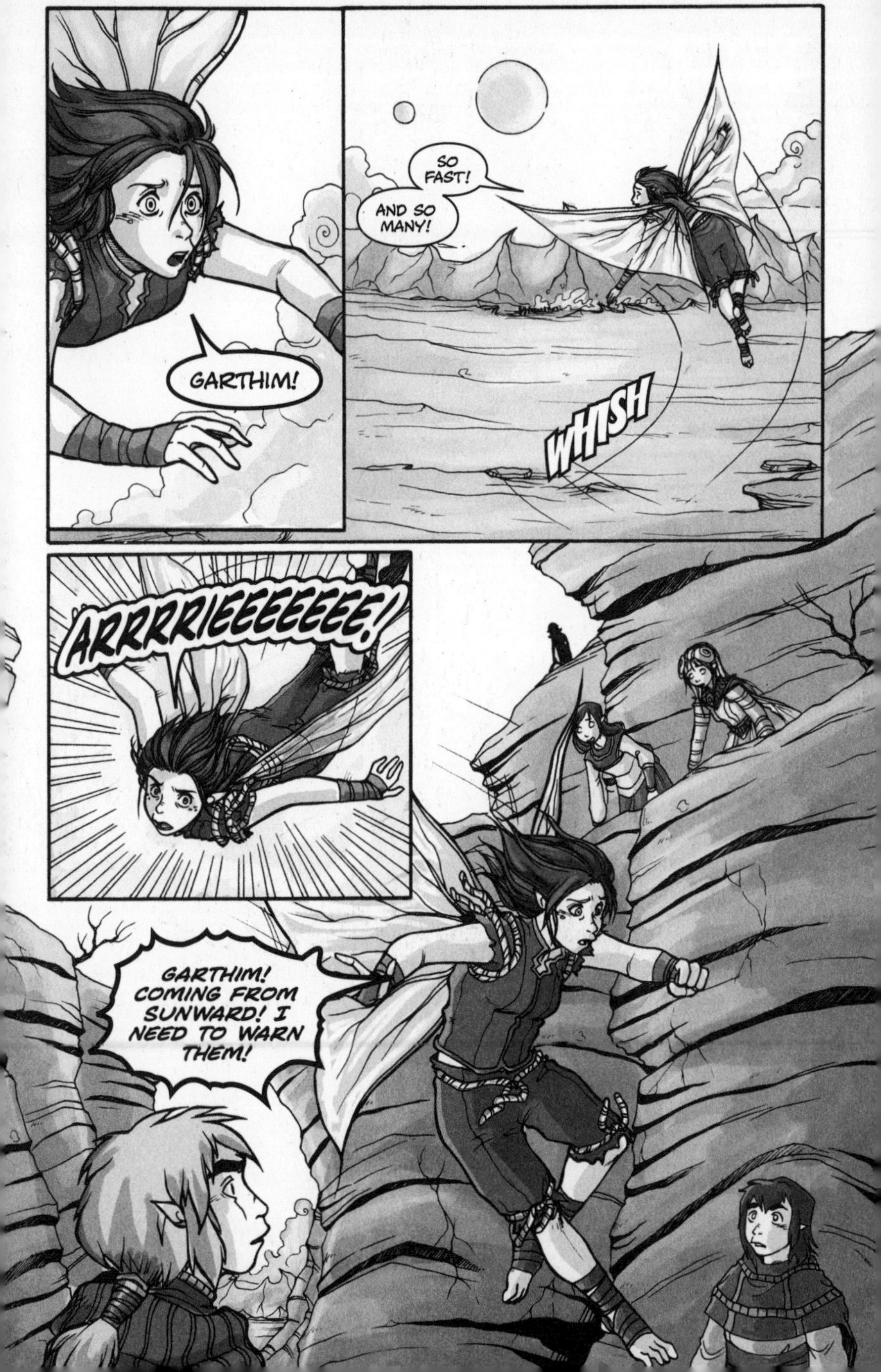
GARTHIM!
SO FAST!
AND SO MANY!
WHISH
ARRRRIEEEEEEEE!
GARTHIM! COMING FROM SUNWARD! I NEED TO WARN THEM!

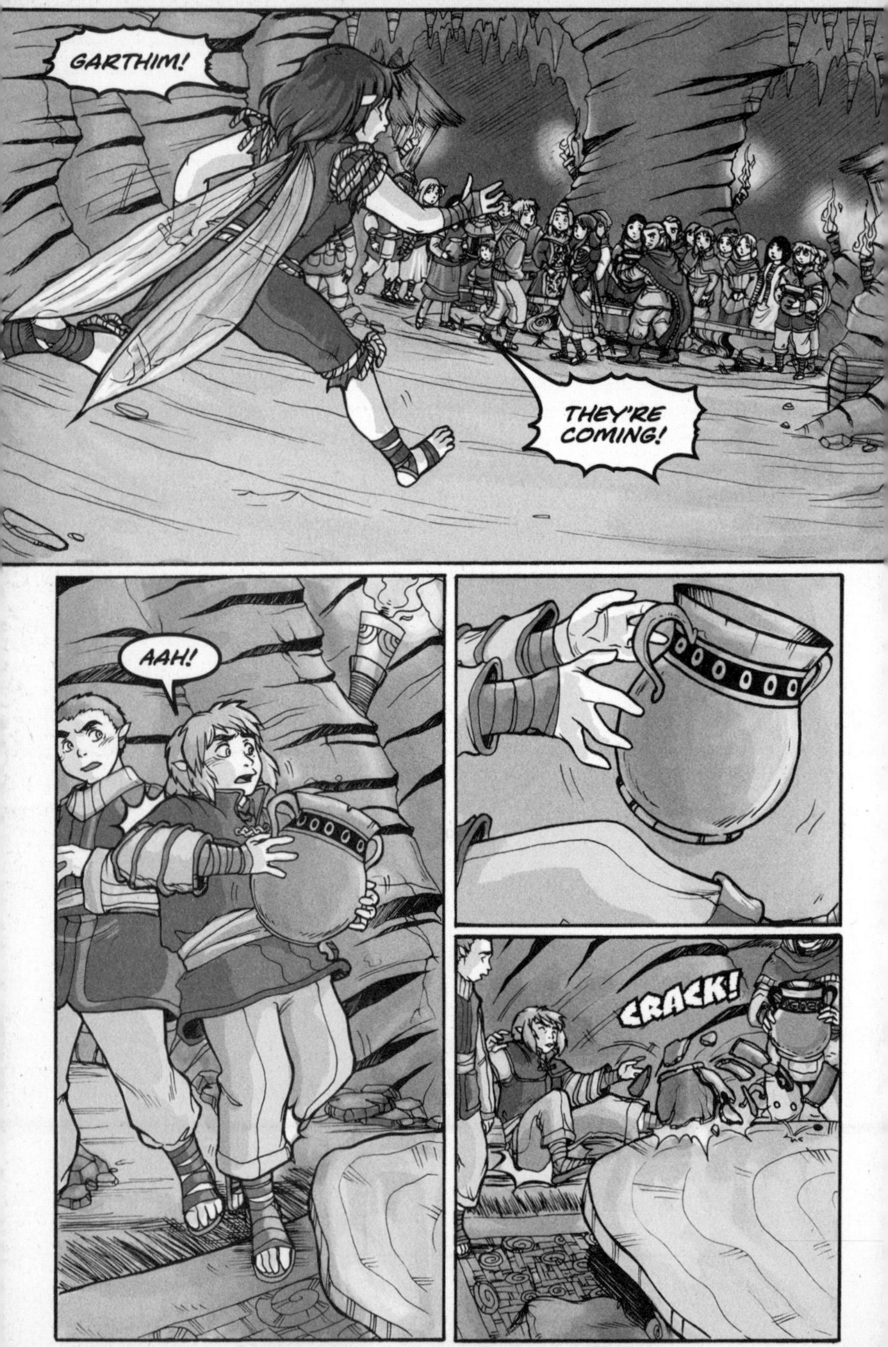
GARTHIM!
THEY'RE COMING!
AAH!
CRACK!

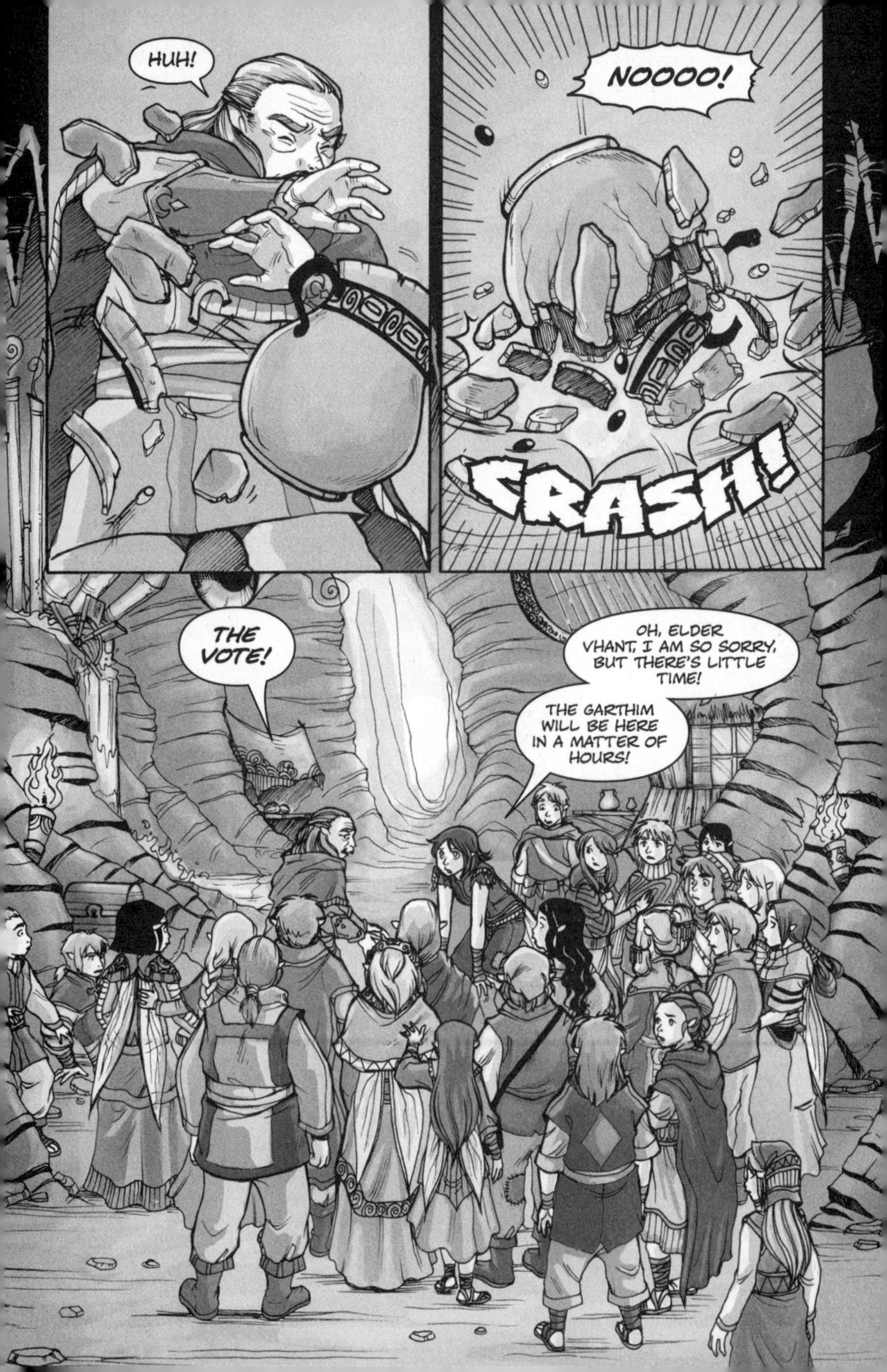
HUH!
NOOOO!
CRASH!
THE VOTE!
OH, ELDER VHANT, I AM SO SORRY, BUT THERE'S LITTLE TIME!
THE GARTHIM WILL BE HERE IN A MATTER OF HOURS!

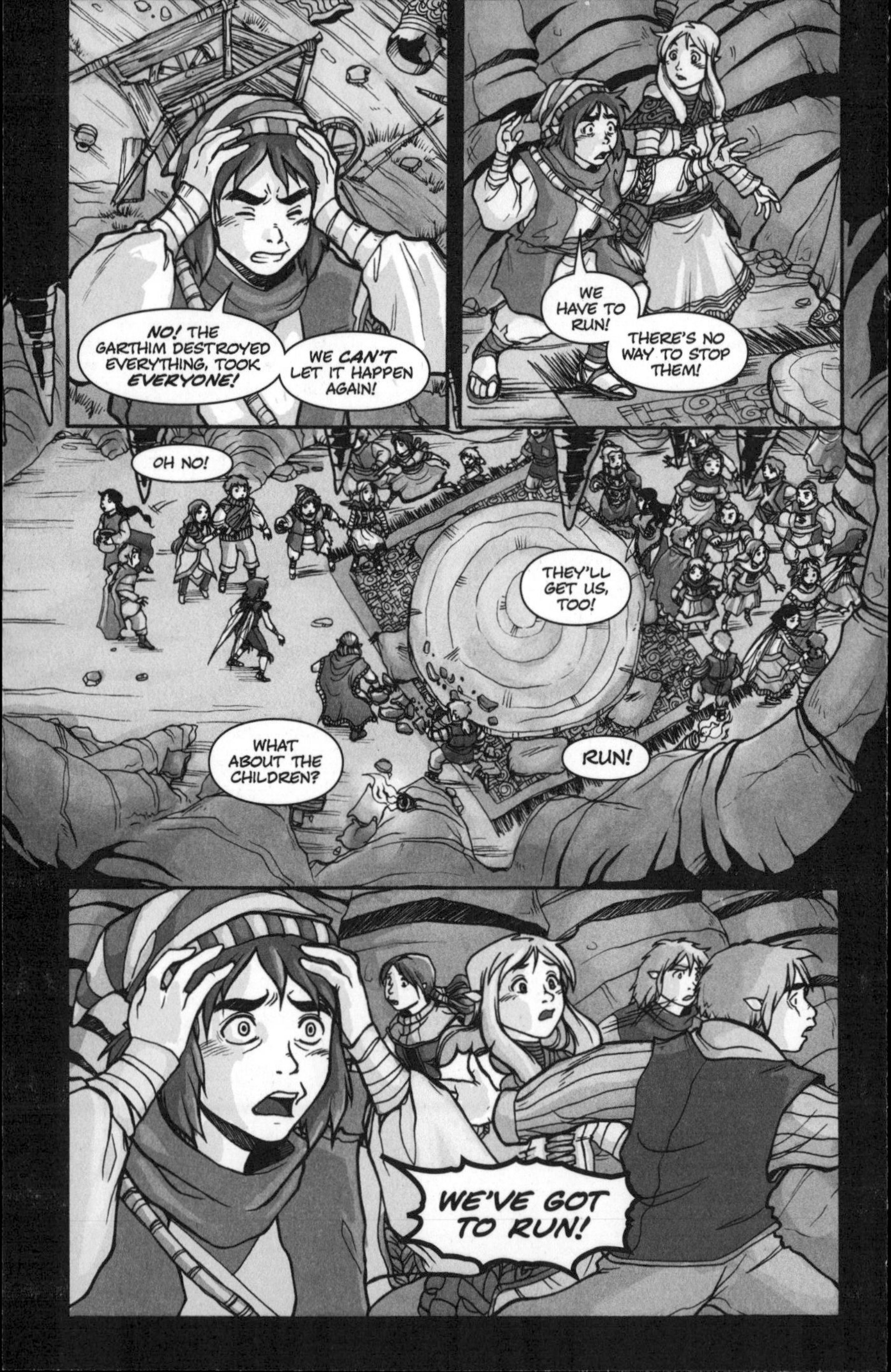
NO! THE GARTHIM DESTROYED EVERYTHING, TOOK EVERYONE!
WE CAN'T LET IT HAPPEN AGAIN!
WE HAVE TO RUN!
THERE'S NO WAY TO STOP THEM!
OH NO!
THEY'LL GET US, TOO!
WHAT ABOUT THE CHILDREN?
RUN!
WE'VE GOT TO RUN!

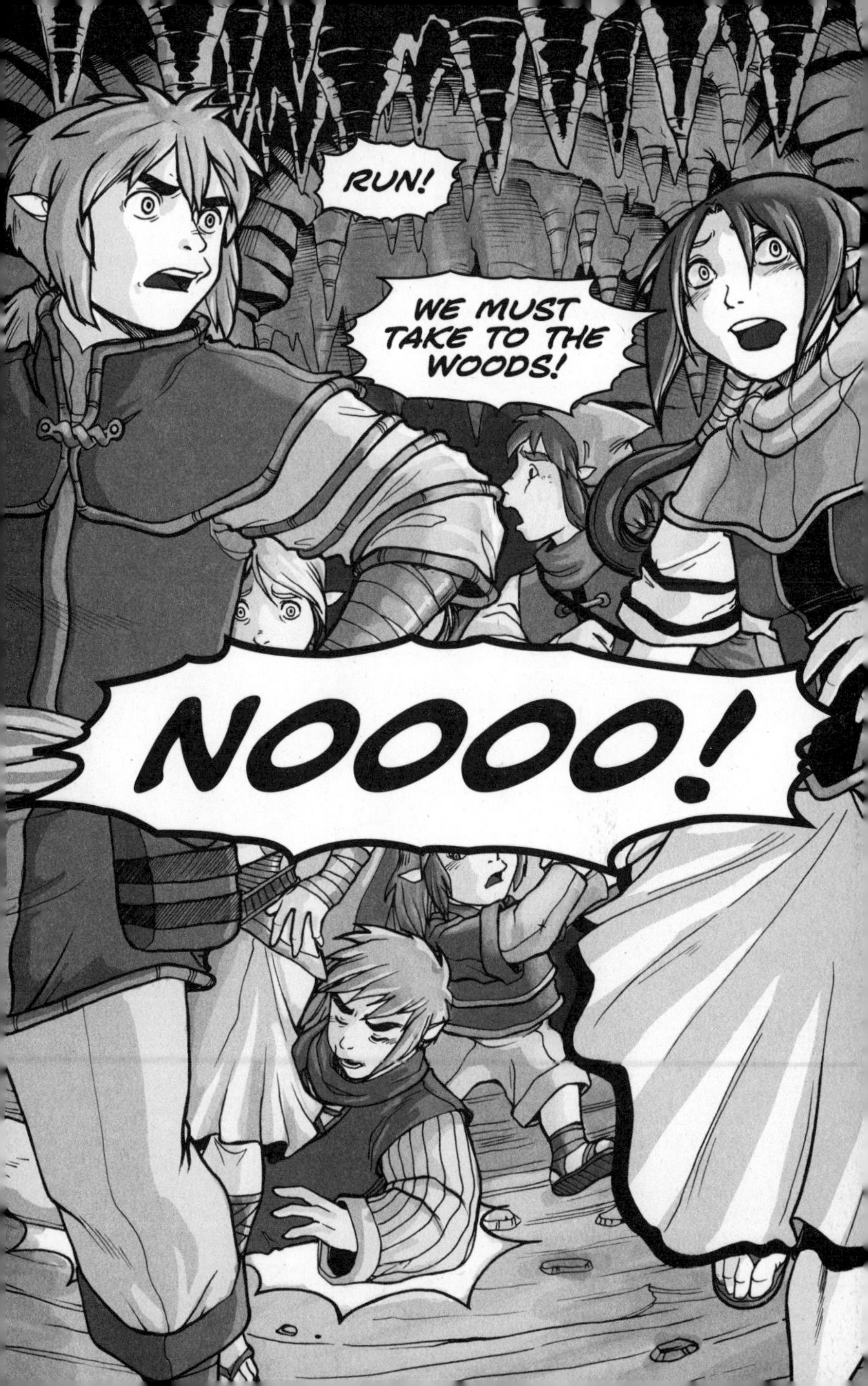
RUN!
WE MUST TAKE TO THE WOODS!
NOOOO!

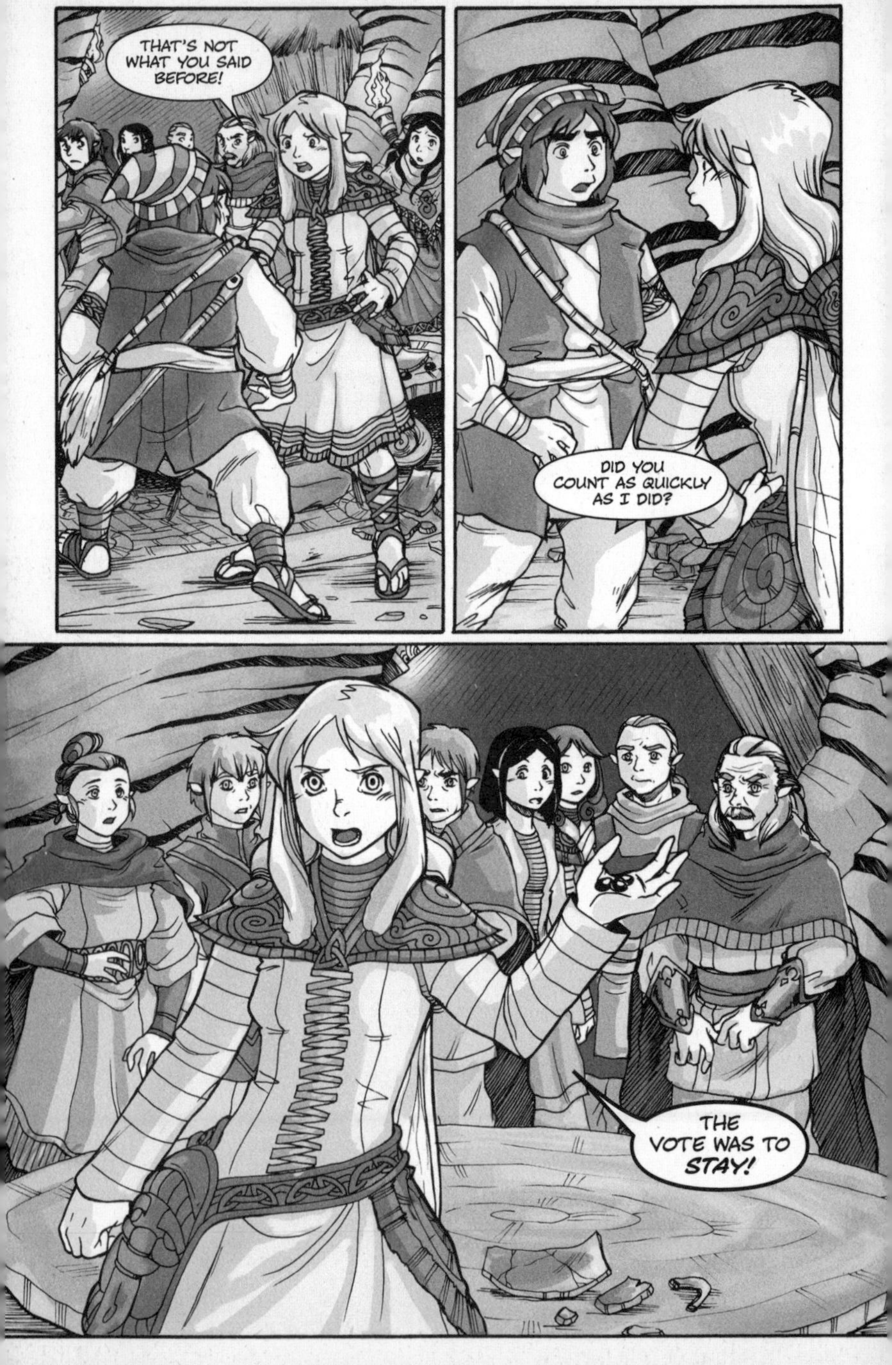
THAT'S NOT WHAT YOU SAID BEFORE!
DID YOU COUNT AS QUICKLY AS I DID?
THE VOTE WAS TO *STAY!*

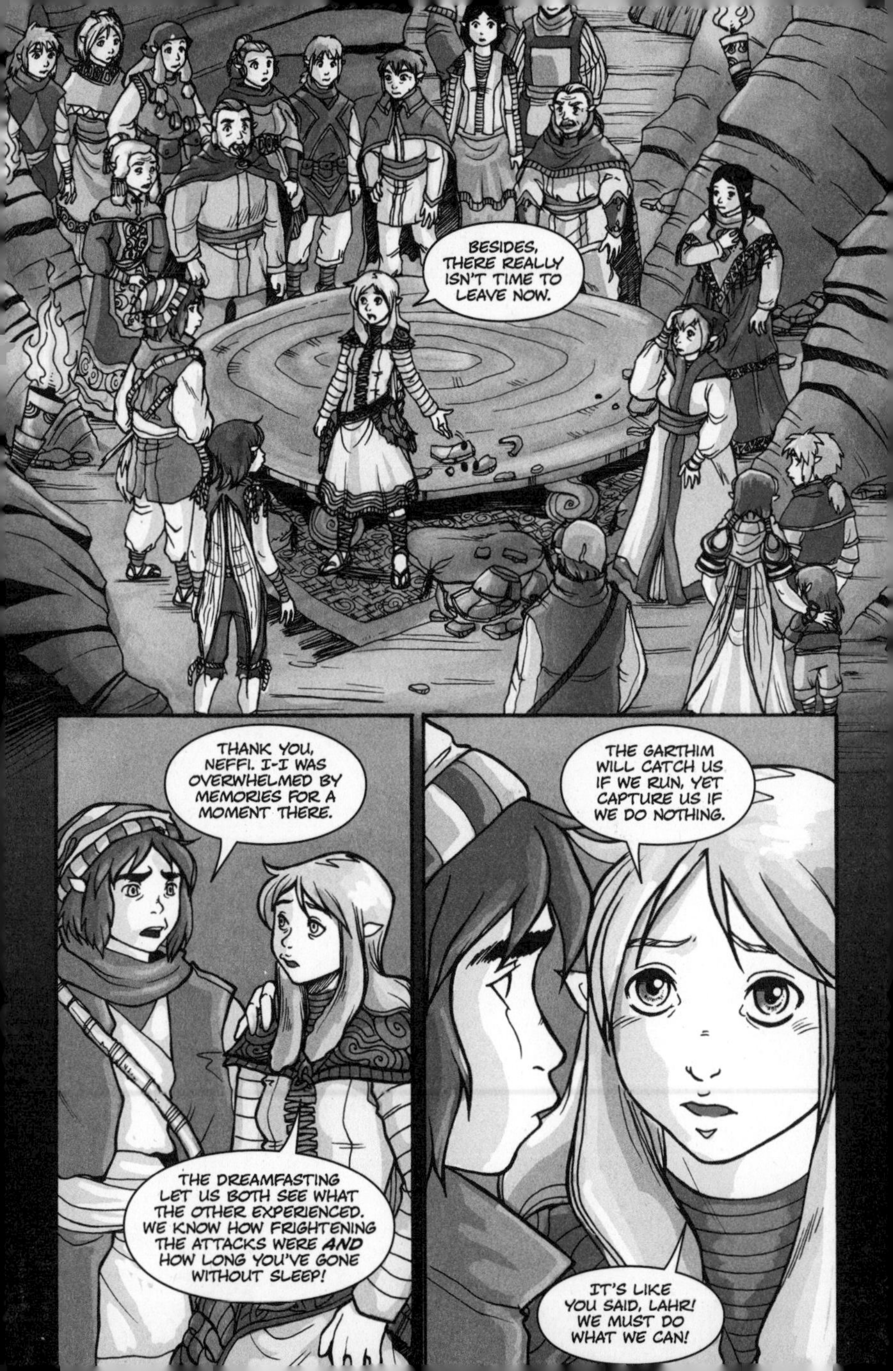
BESIDES, THERE REALLY ISN'T TIME TO LEAVE NOW.
THANK YOU, NEFFI. I-I WAS OVERWHELMED BY MEMORIES FOR A MOMENT THERE.
THE DREAMFASTING LET US BOTH SEE WHAT THE OTHER EXPERIENCED. WE KNOW HOW FRIGHTENING THE ATTACKS WERE AND HOW LONG YOU'VE GONE WITHOUT SLEEP!
THE GARTHIM WILL CATCH US IF WE RUN, YET CAPTURE US IF WE DO NOTHING.
IT'S LIKE YOU SAID, LAHR! WE MUST DO WHAT WE CAN!

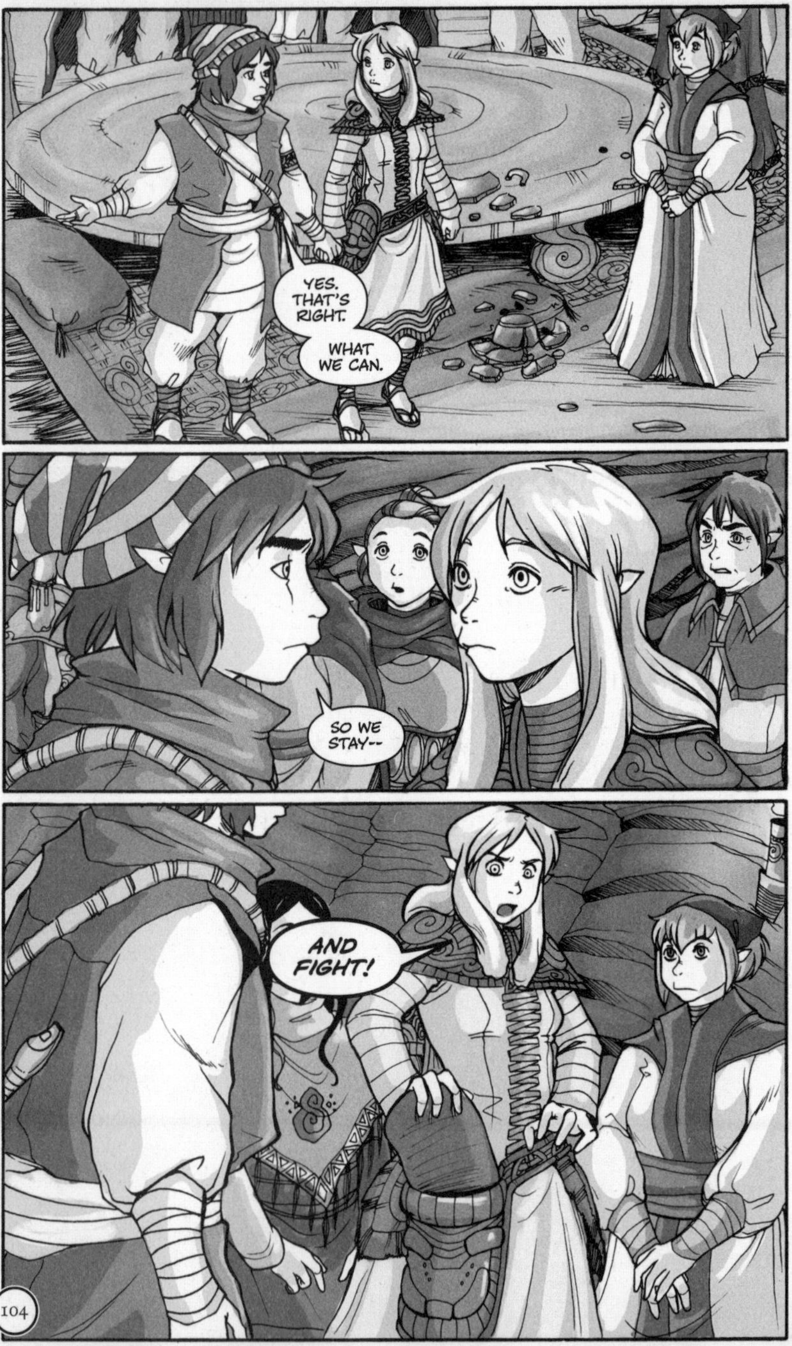
YES. THAT'S RIGHT.
WHAT WE CAN.
SO WE STAY--
AND FIGHT!

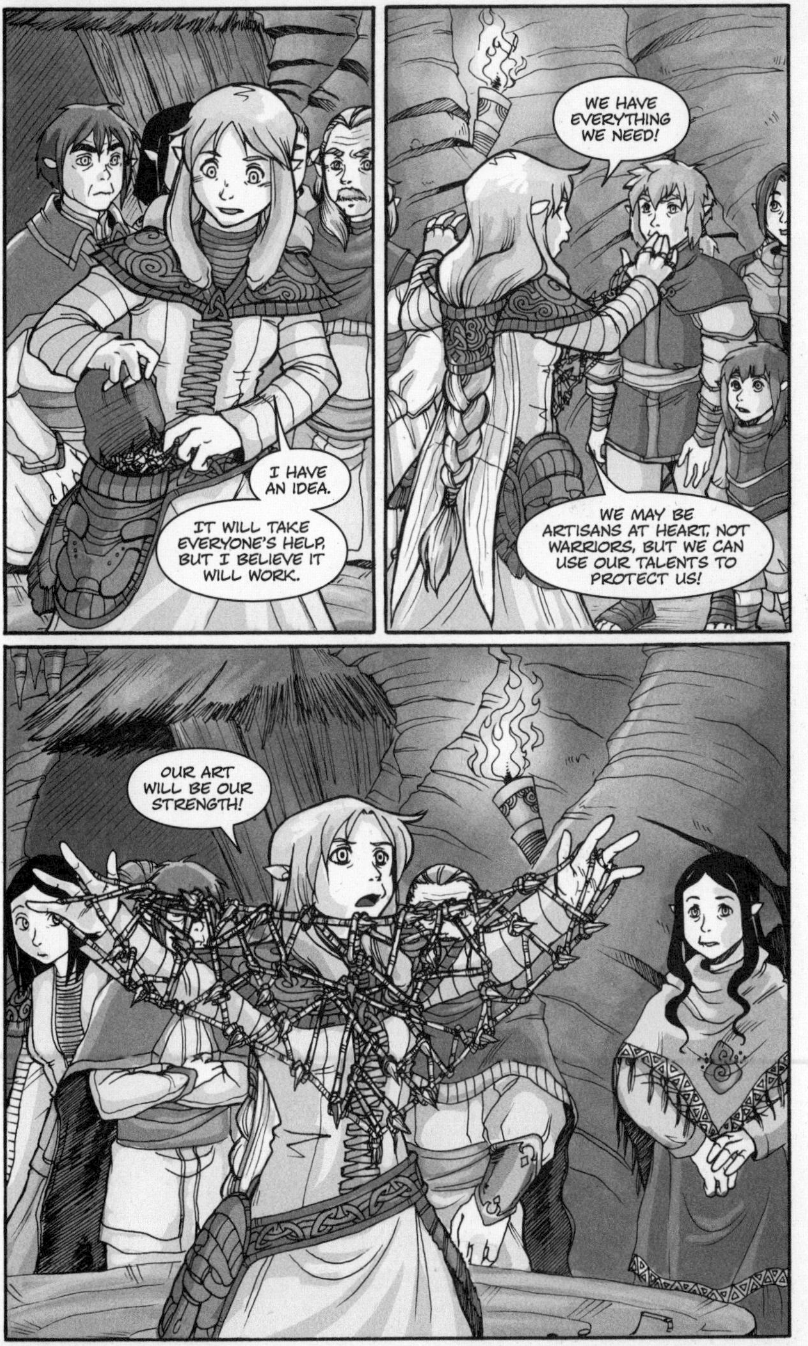
I HAVE AN IDEA.
IT WILL TAKE EVERYONE'S HELP, BUT I BELIEVE IT WILL WORK.
WE HAVE EVERYTHING WE NEED!
WE MAY BE ARTISANS AT HEART, NOT WARRIORS, BUT WE CAN USE OUR TALENTS TO PROTECT US!
OUR ART WILL BE OUR STRENGTH!

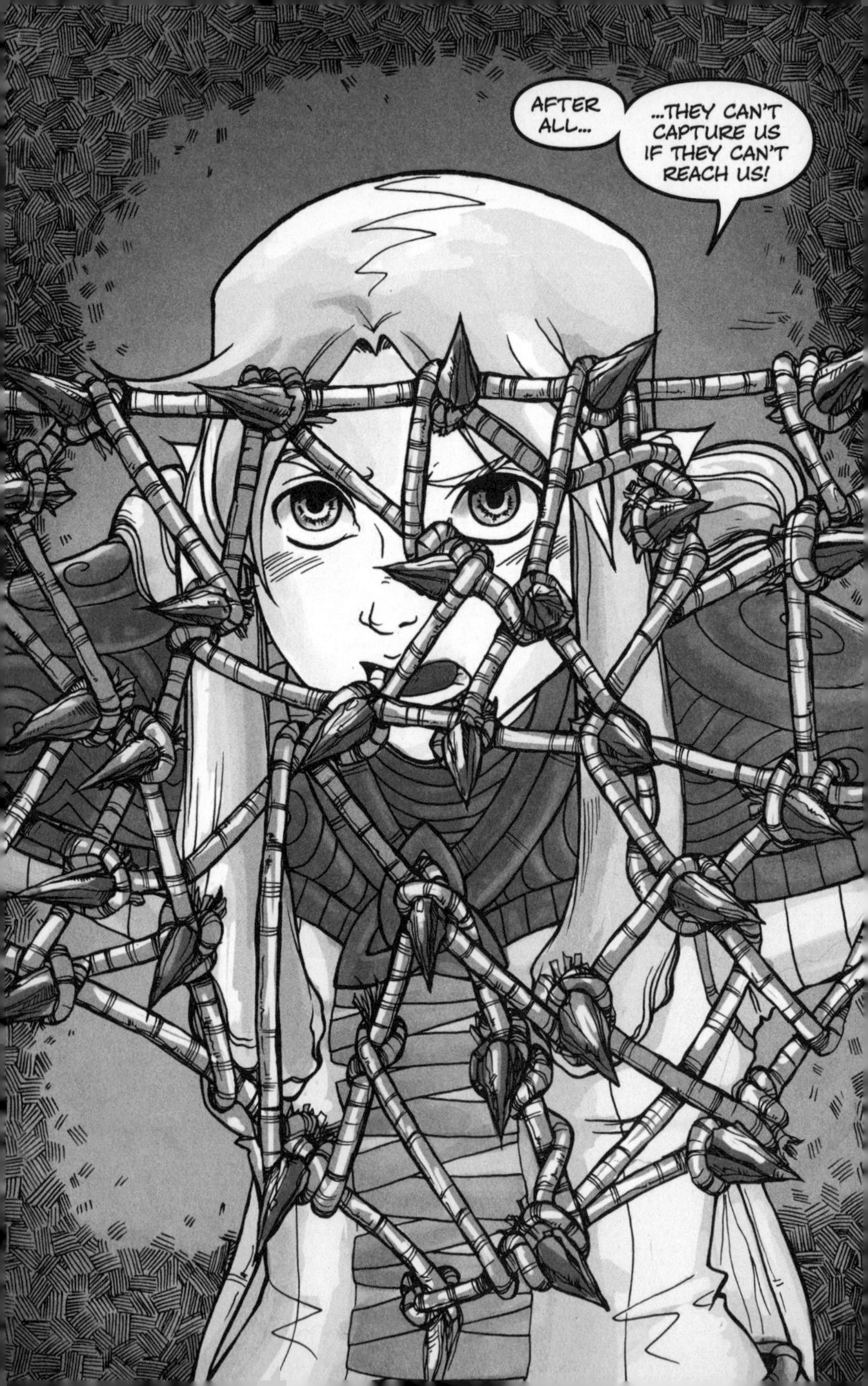
AFTER ALL...
...THEY CAN'T CAPTURE US IF THEY CAN'T REACH US!

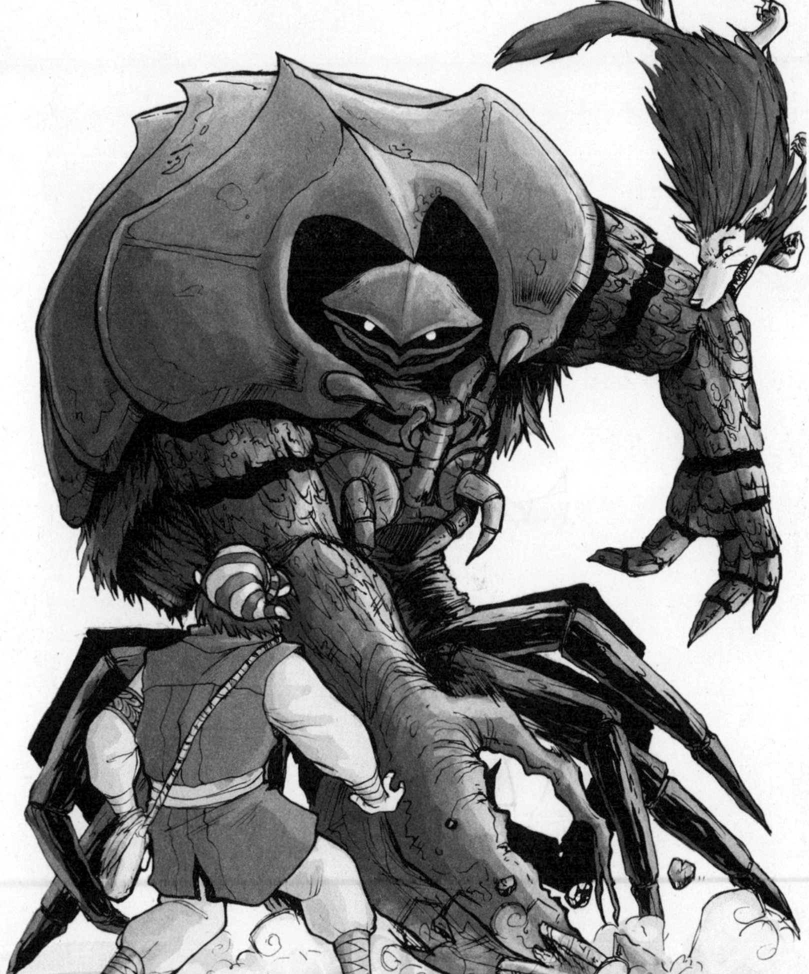

Chapter Five

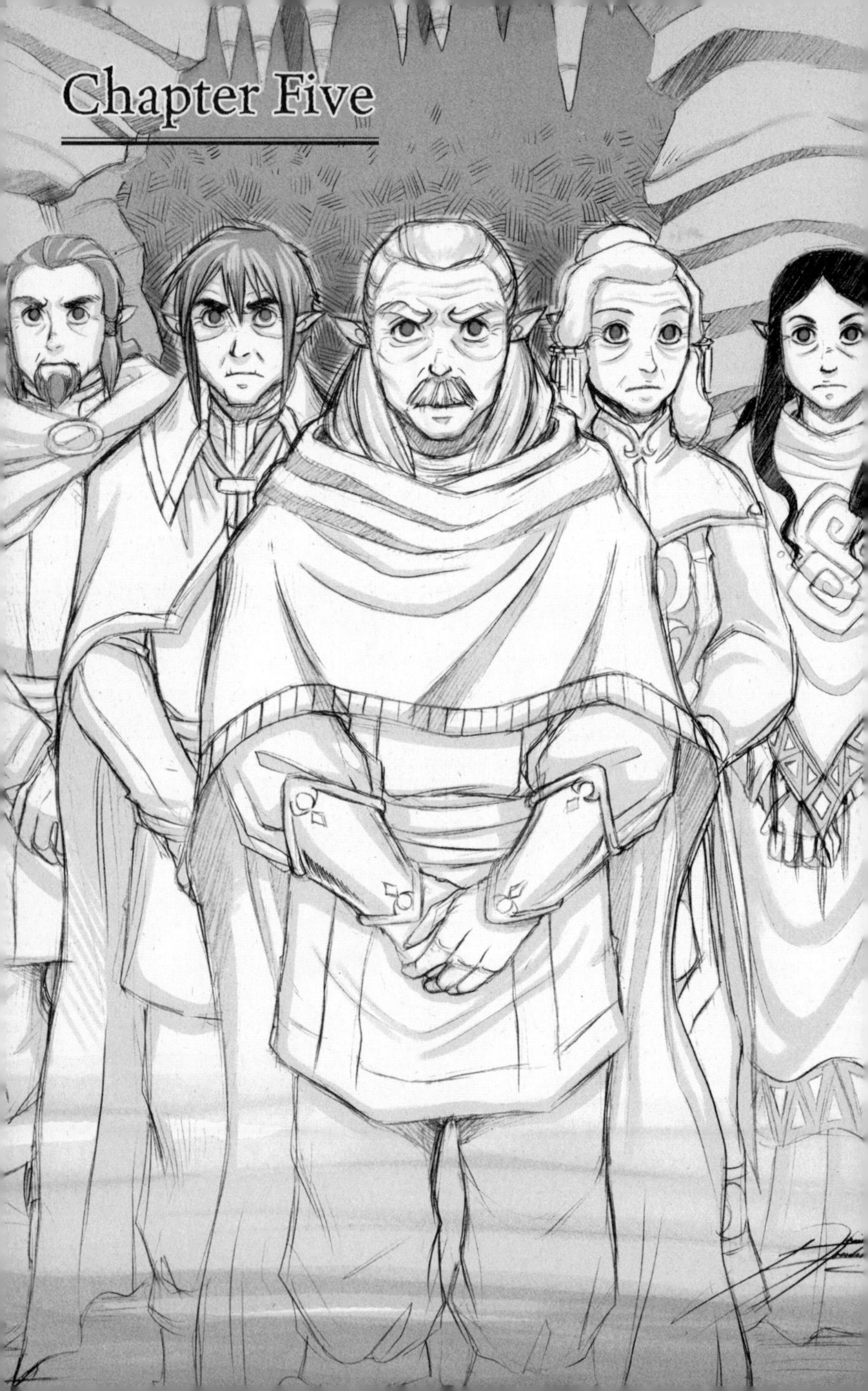

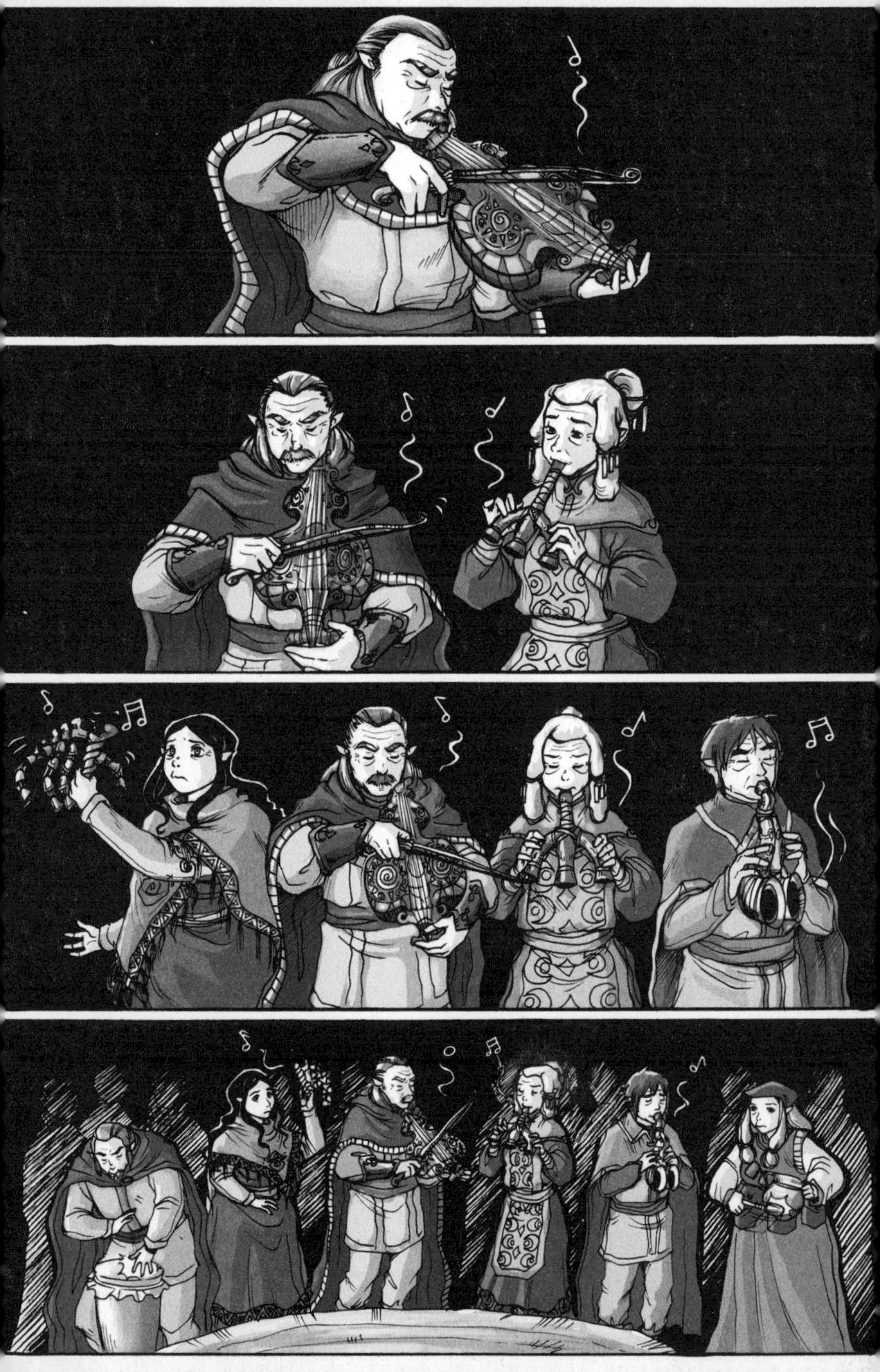

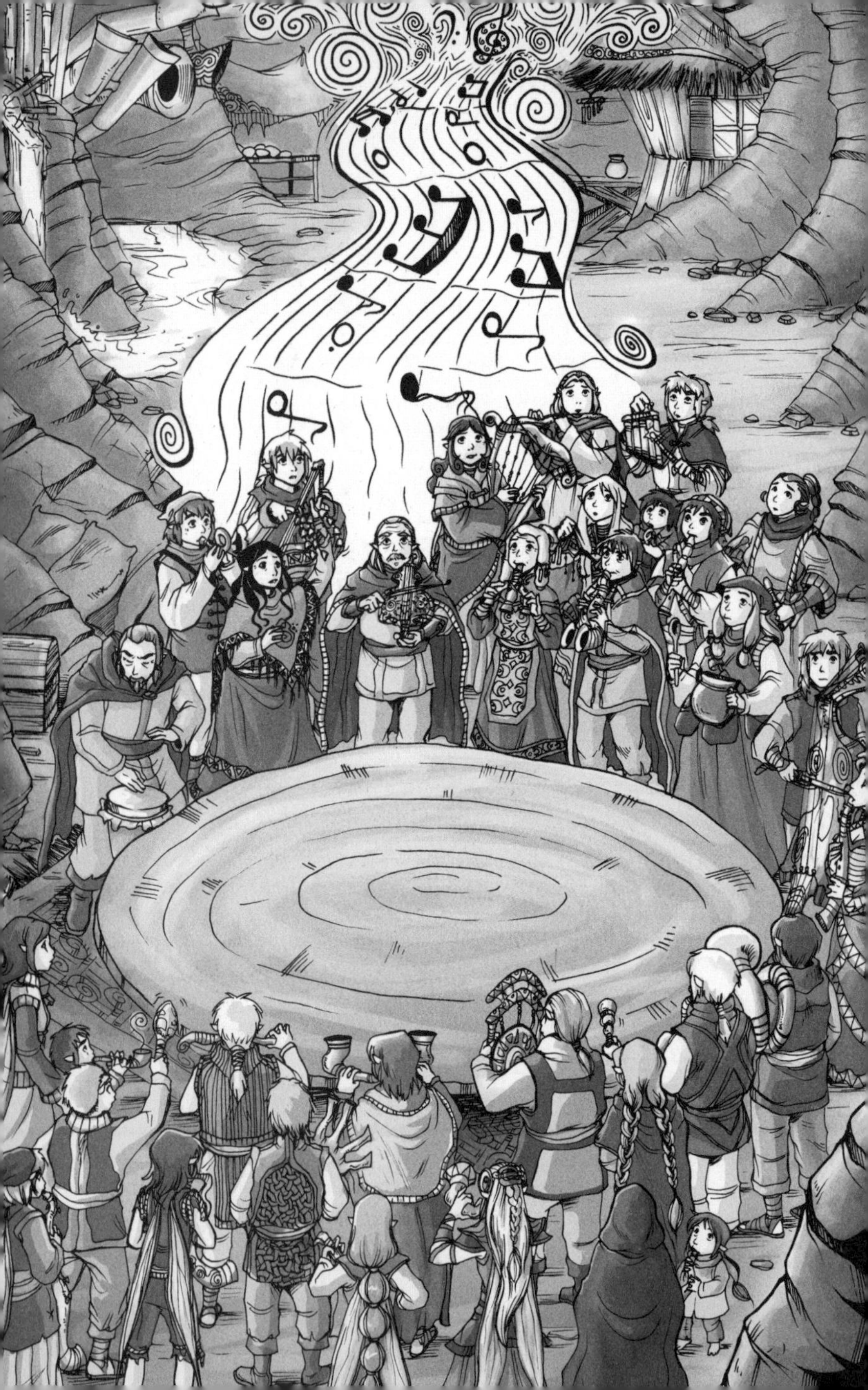

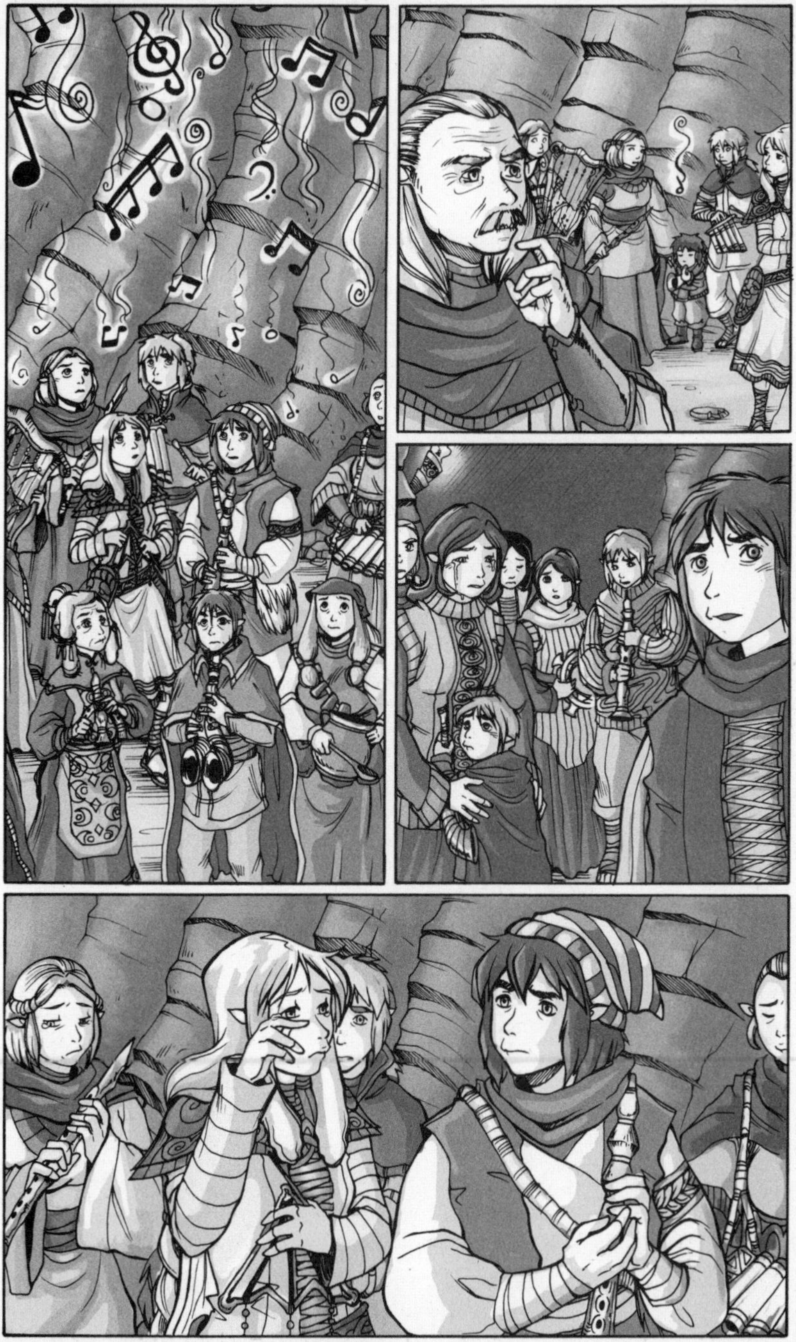

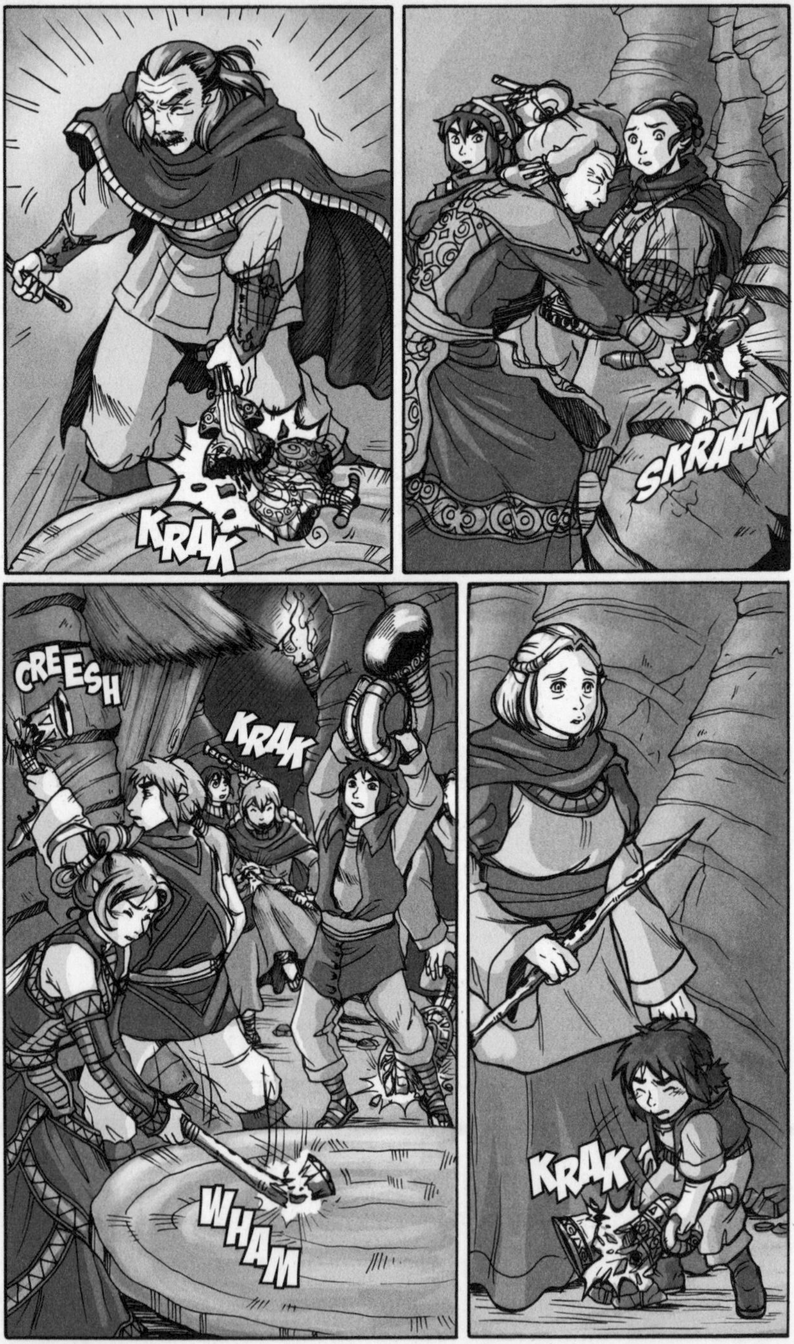
KRAK
SKRAAK
CREESH
KRAK
WHAM
KRAK

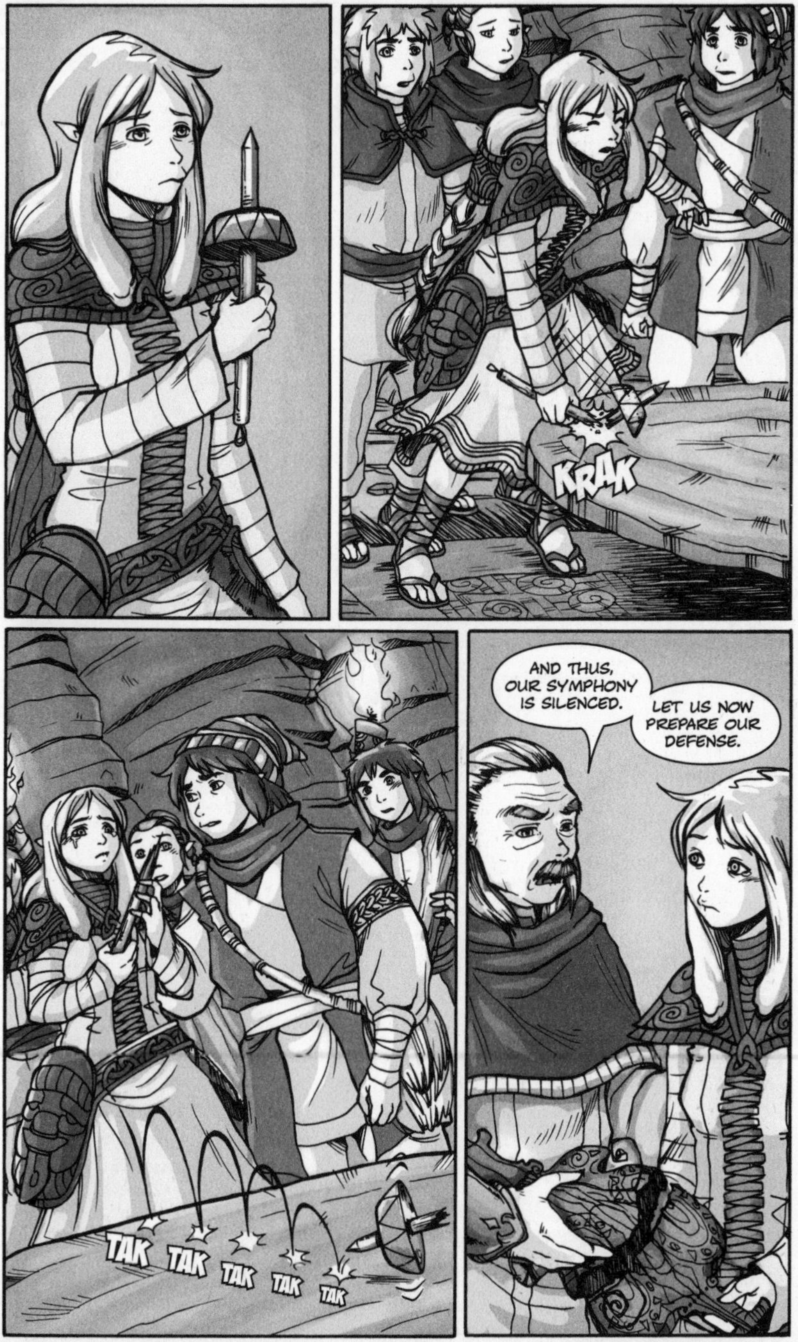
KRAK
TAK TAK TAK TAK TAK
AND THUS, OUR SYMPHONY IS SILENCED.
LET US NOW PREPARE OUR DEFENSE.

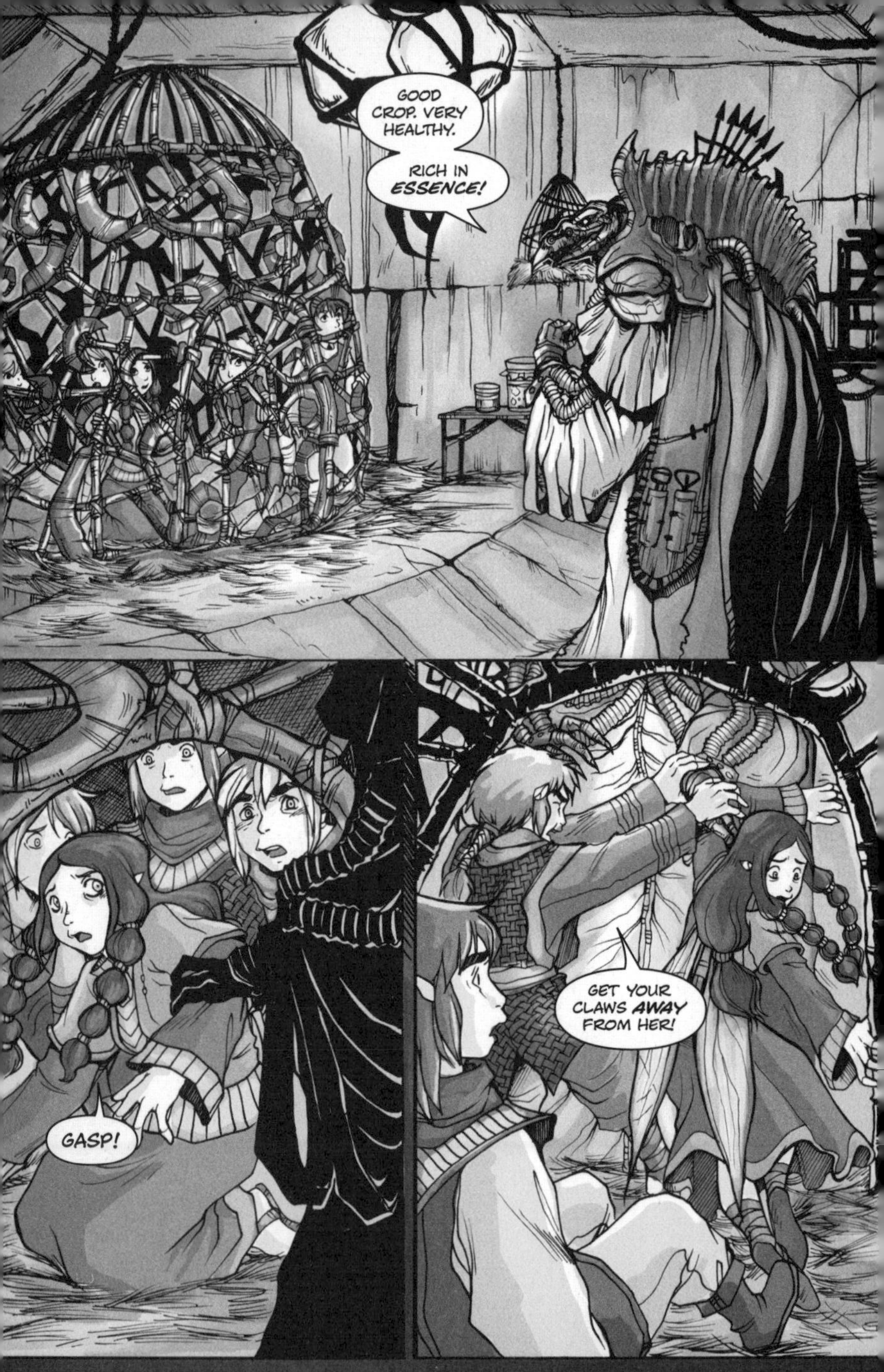
GOOD CROP. VERY HEALTHY.
RICH IN ESSENCE!
GASP!
GET YOUR CLAWS AWAY FROM HER!

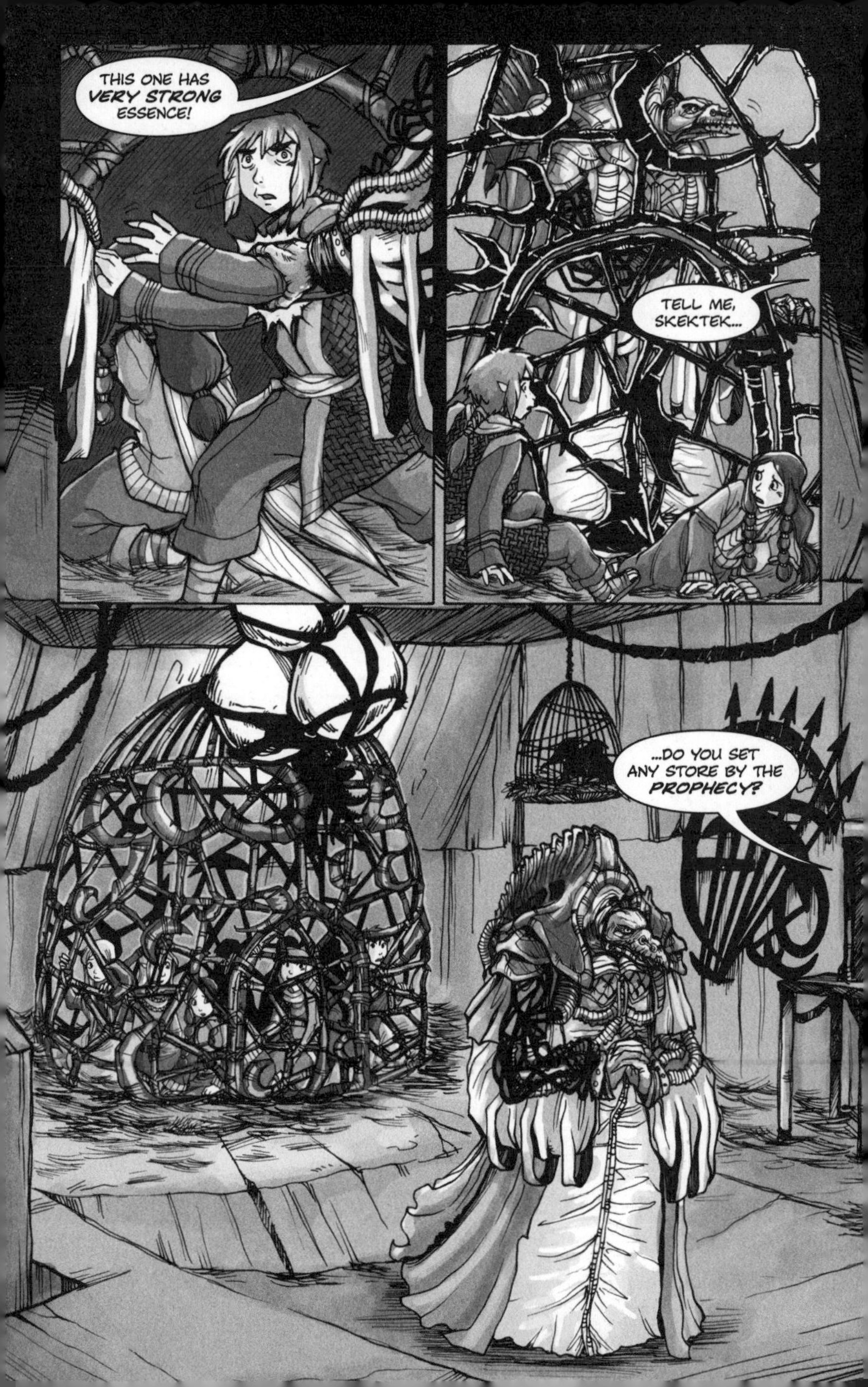
THIS ONE HAS VERY STRONG ESSENCE!
TELL ME, SKEKTEK...
...DO YOU SET ANY STORE BY THE PROPHECY?

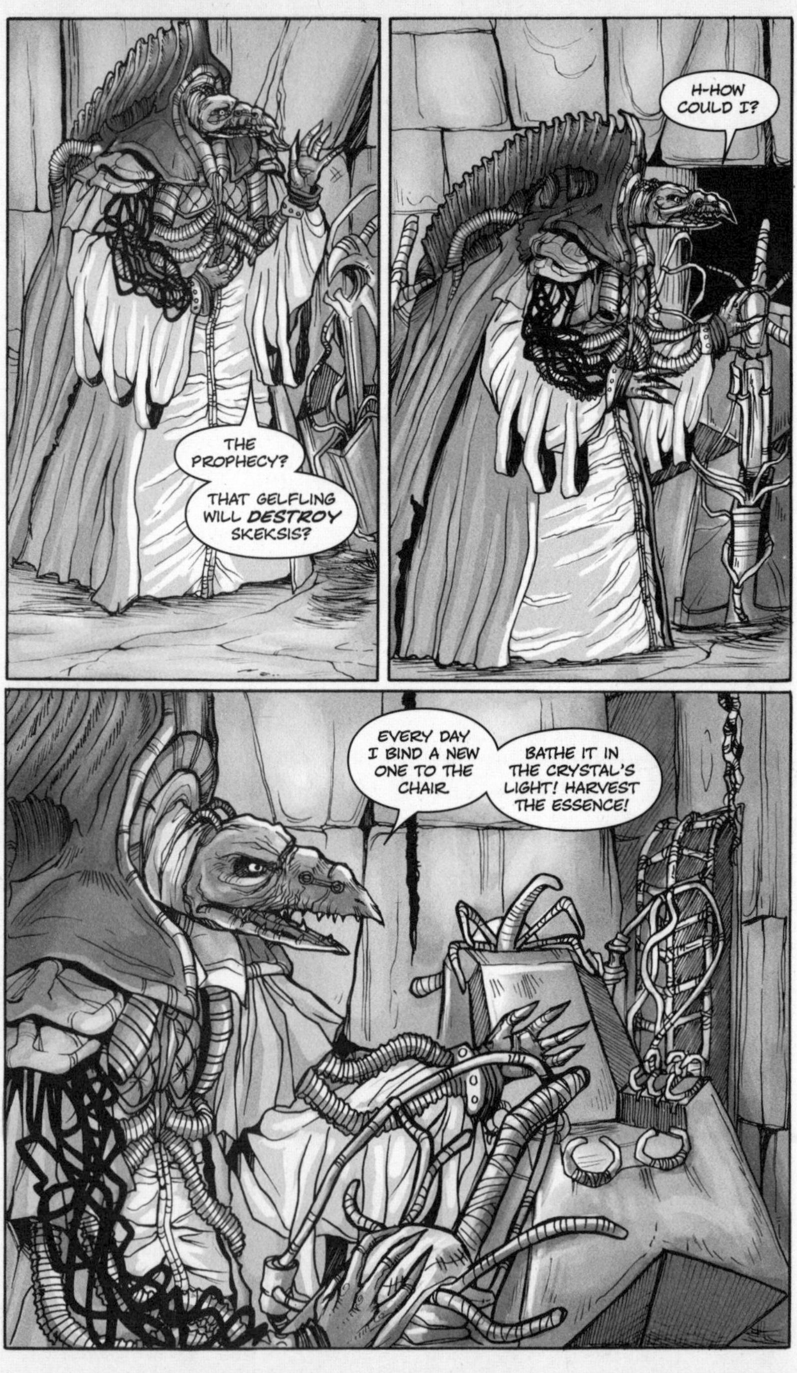
THE PROPHECY?
THAT GELFLING WILL DESTROY SKEKSIS?
H-HOW COULD I?
EVERY DAY I BIND A NEW ONE TO THE CHAIR.
BATHE IT IN THE CRYSTAL'S LIGHT! HARVEST THE ESSENCE!

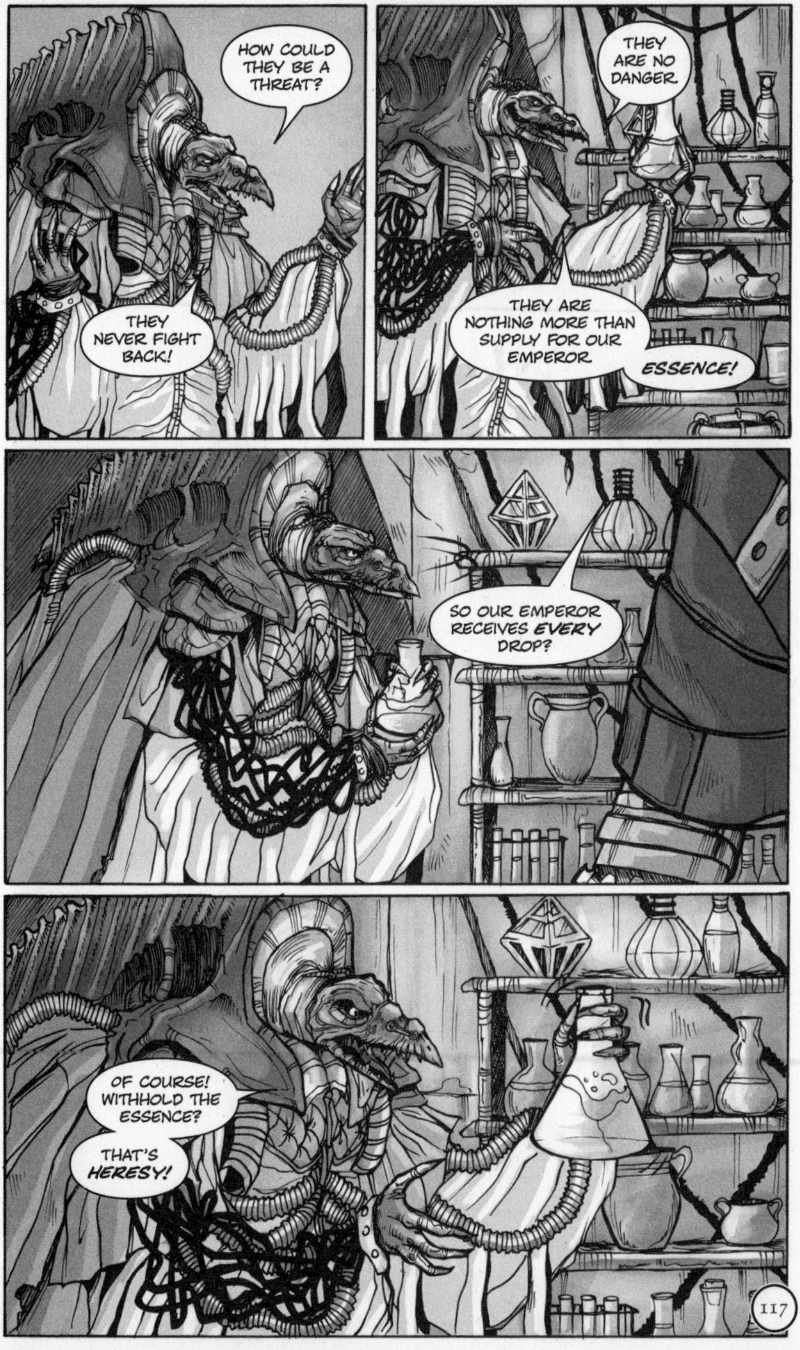
HOW COULD THEY BE A THREAT?
THEY NEVER FIGHT BACK!
THEY ARE NO DANGER
THEY ARE NOTHING MORE THAN SUPPLY FOR OUR EMPEROR
ESSENCE!
SO OUR EMPEROR RECEIVES EVERY DROP?
OF COURSE! WITHHOLD THE ESSENCE?
THAT'S HERESY!

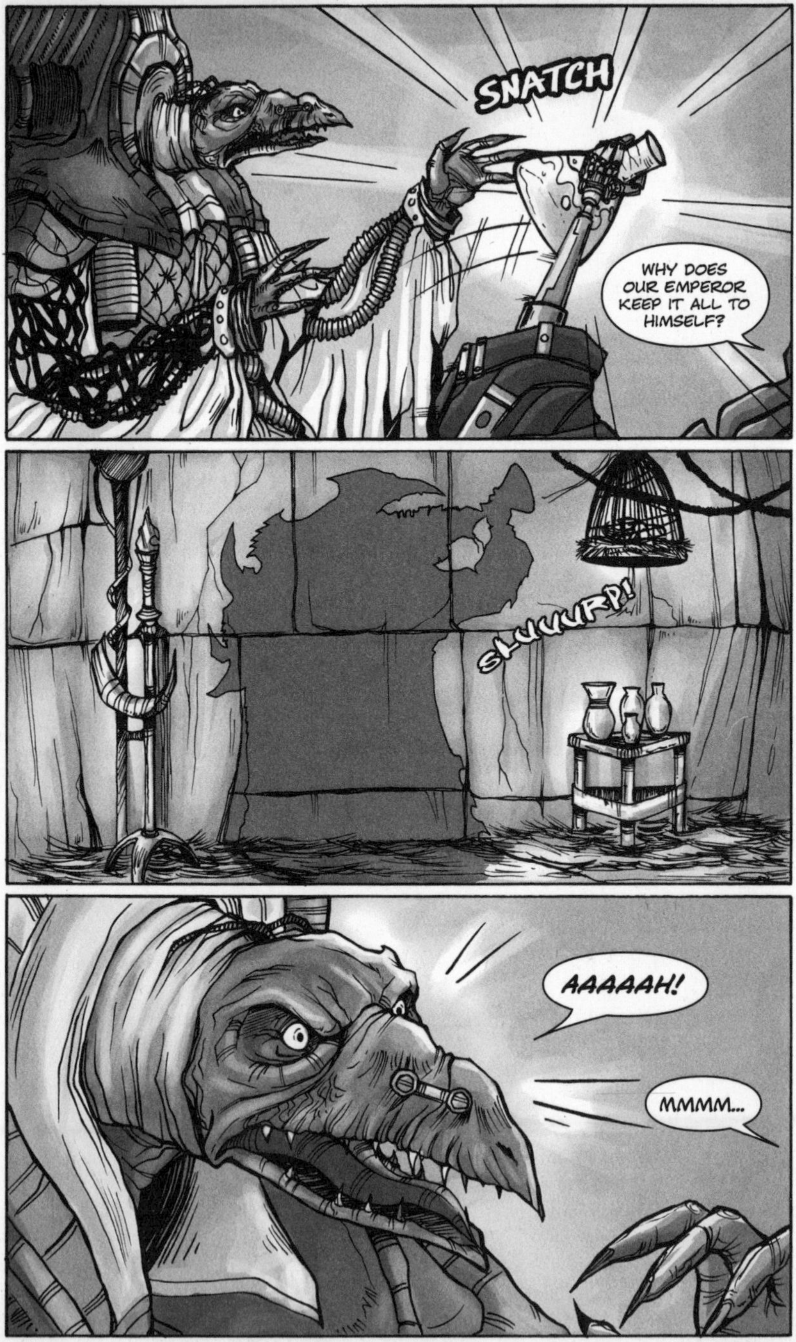
SNATCH
WHY DOES OUR EMPEROR KEEP IT ALL TO HIMSELF?
SLUUURP!
AAAAAH!
MMMM...

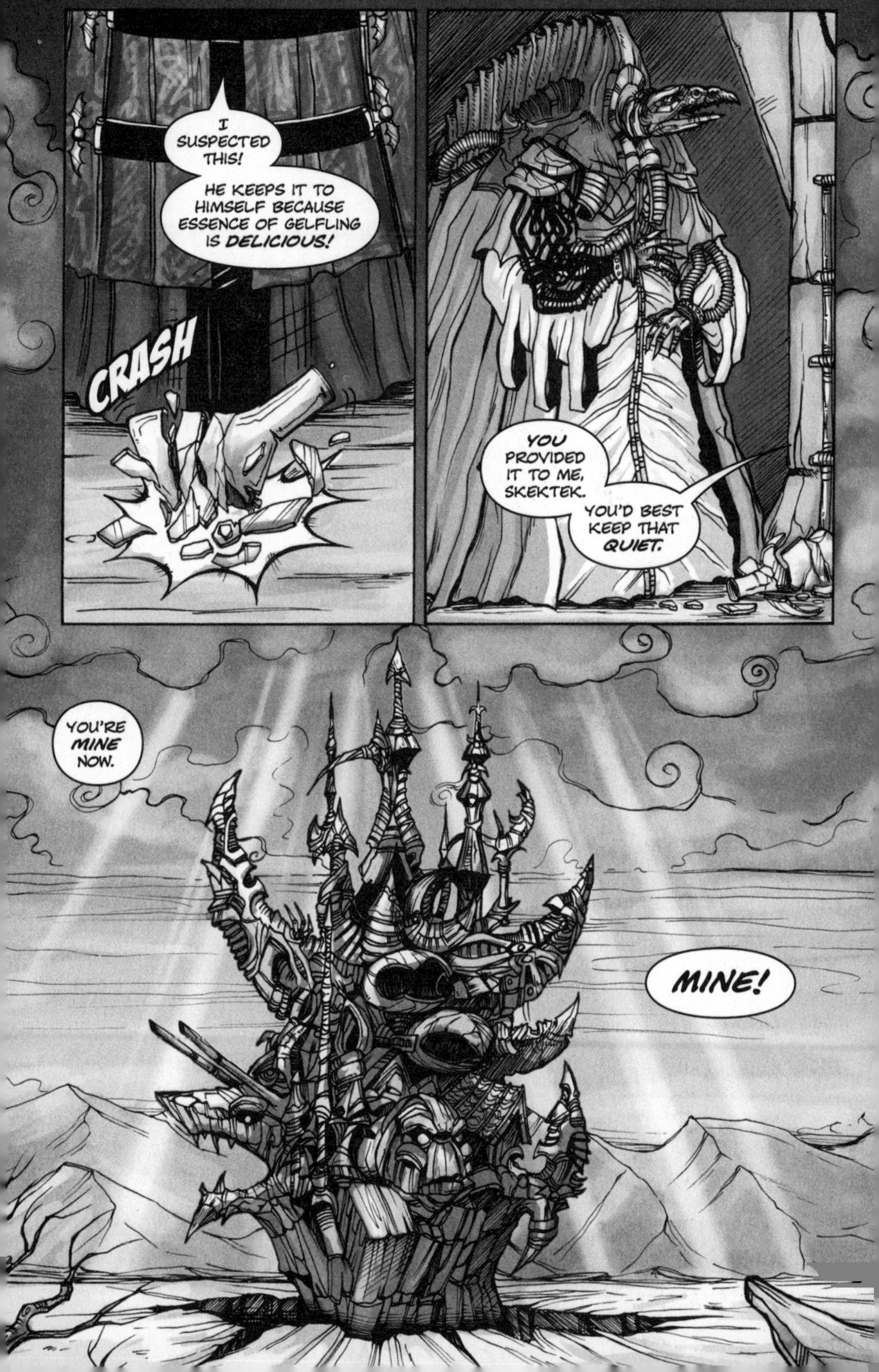
I SUSPECTED THIS!
HE KEEPS IT TO HIMSELF BECAUSE ESSENCE OF GELFLING IS *DELICIOUS!*
CRASH
YOU PROVIDED IT TO ME, SKEKTEK.
YOU'D BEST KEEP THAT *QUIET.*
YOU'RE *MINE* NOW.
MINE!

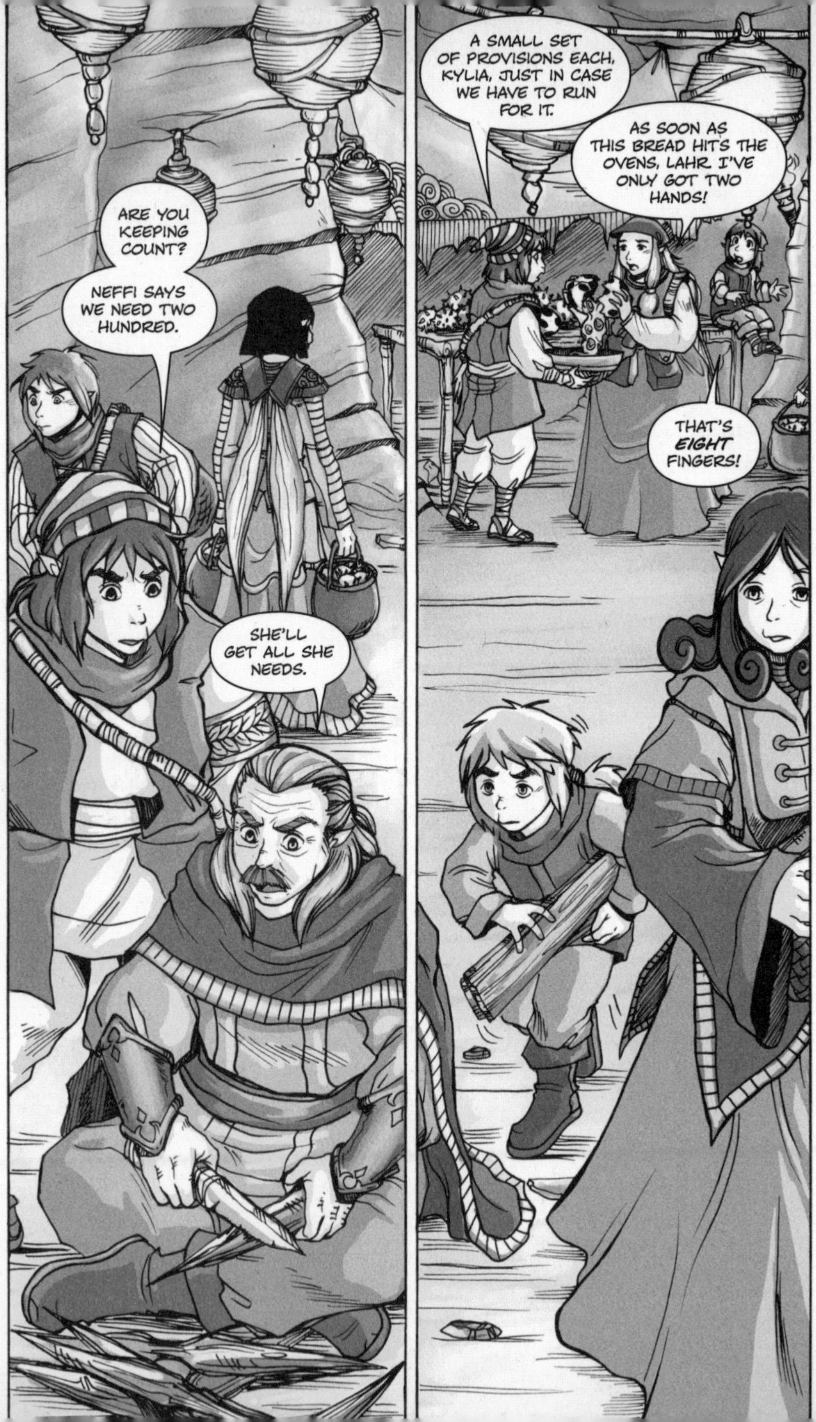
ARE YOU KEEPING COUNT?
NEFFI SAYS WE NEED TWO HUNDRED.
SHE'LL GET ALL SHE NEEDS.
A SMALL SET OF PROVISIONS EACH, KYLIA, JUST IN CASE WE HAVE TO RUN FOR IT.
AS SOON AS THIS BREAD HITS THE OVENS, LAHR. I'VE ONLY GOT TWO HANDS!
THAT'S *EIGHT* FINGERS!

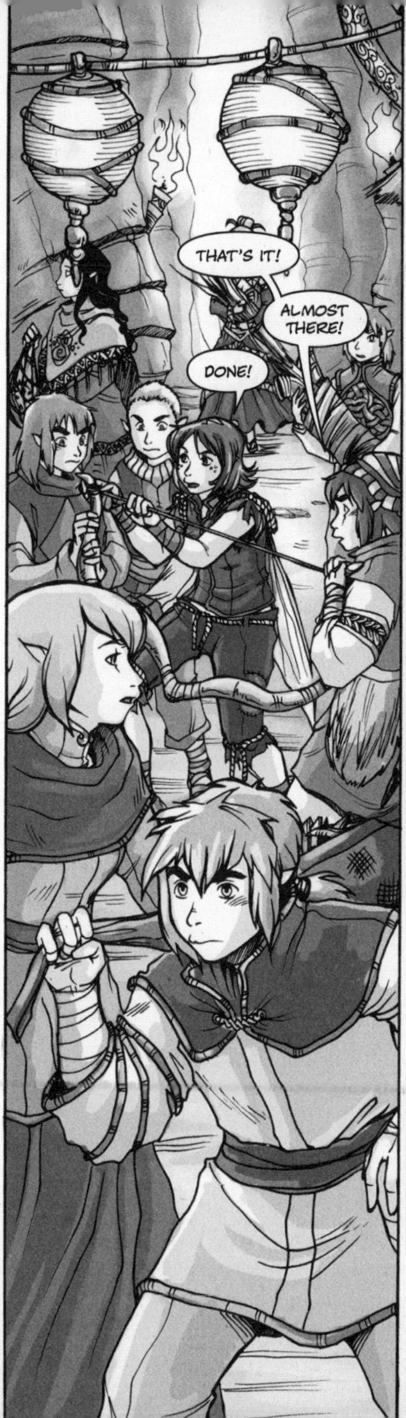
THAT'S IT!
ALMOST THERE!
DONE!
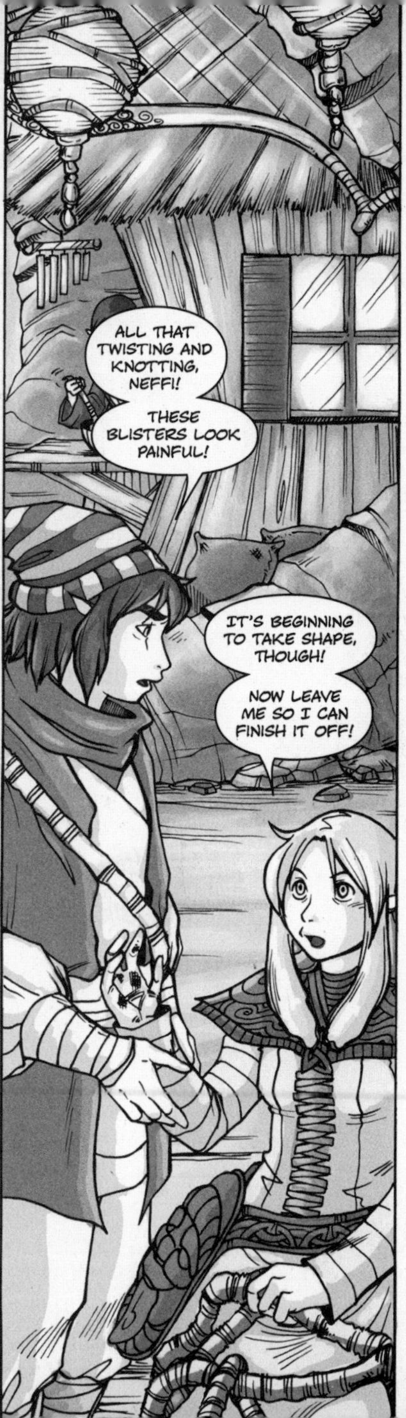
ALL THAT TWISTING AND KNOTTING, NEFFI!
THESE BLISTERS LOOK PAINFUL!
IT'S BEGINNING TO TAKE SHAPE, THOUGH!
NOW LEAVE ME SO I CAN FINISH IT OFF!

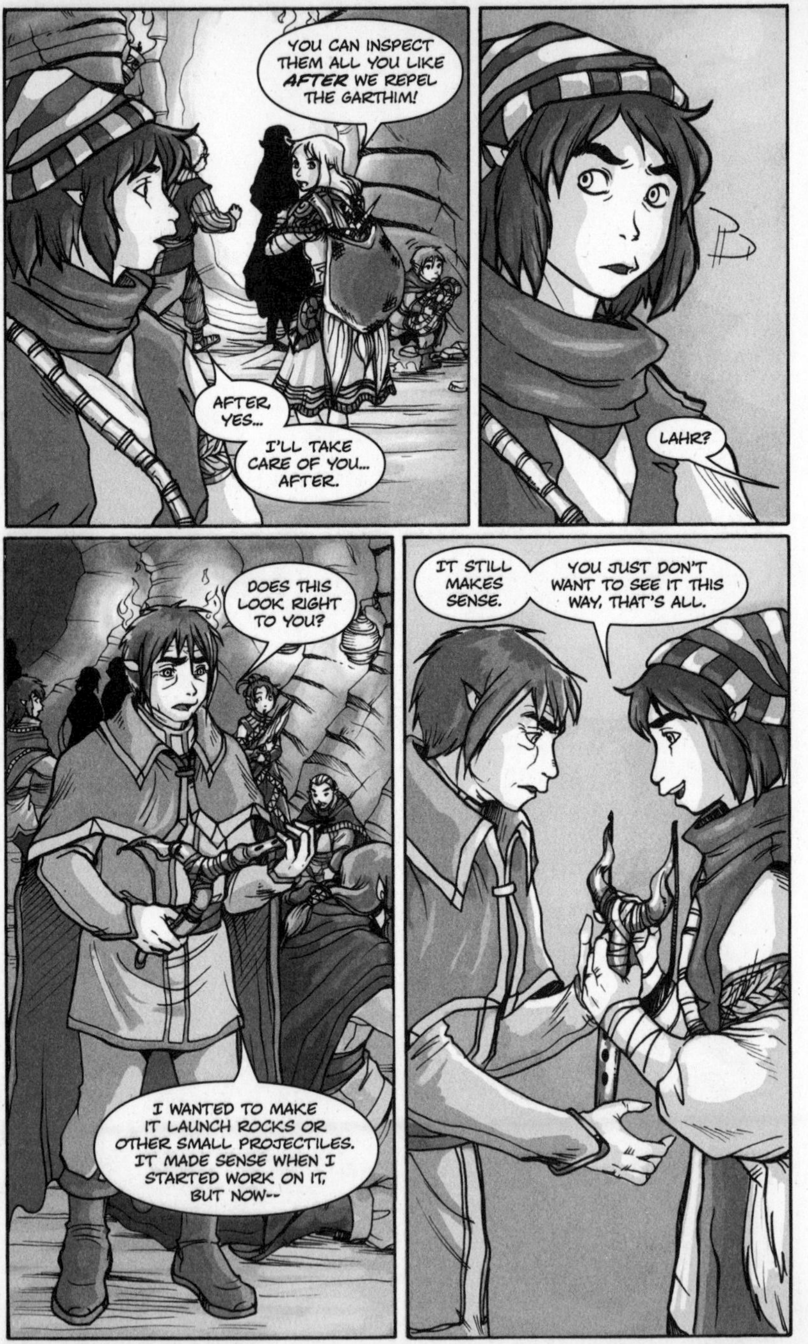
YOU CAN INSPECT THEM ALL YOU LIKE *AFTER* WE REPEL THE GARTHIM!
AFTER, YES...
I'LL TAKE CARE OF YOU... AFTER.
LAHR?
DOES THIS LOOK RIGHT TO YOU?
I WANTED TO MAKE IT LAUNCH ROCKS OR OTHER SMALL PROJECTILES. IT MADE SENSE WHEN I STARTED WORK ON IT, BUT NOW--
IT STILL MAKES SENSE.
YOU JUST DON'T WANT TO SEE IT THIS WAY, THAT'S ALL.

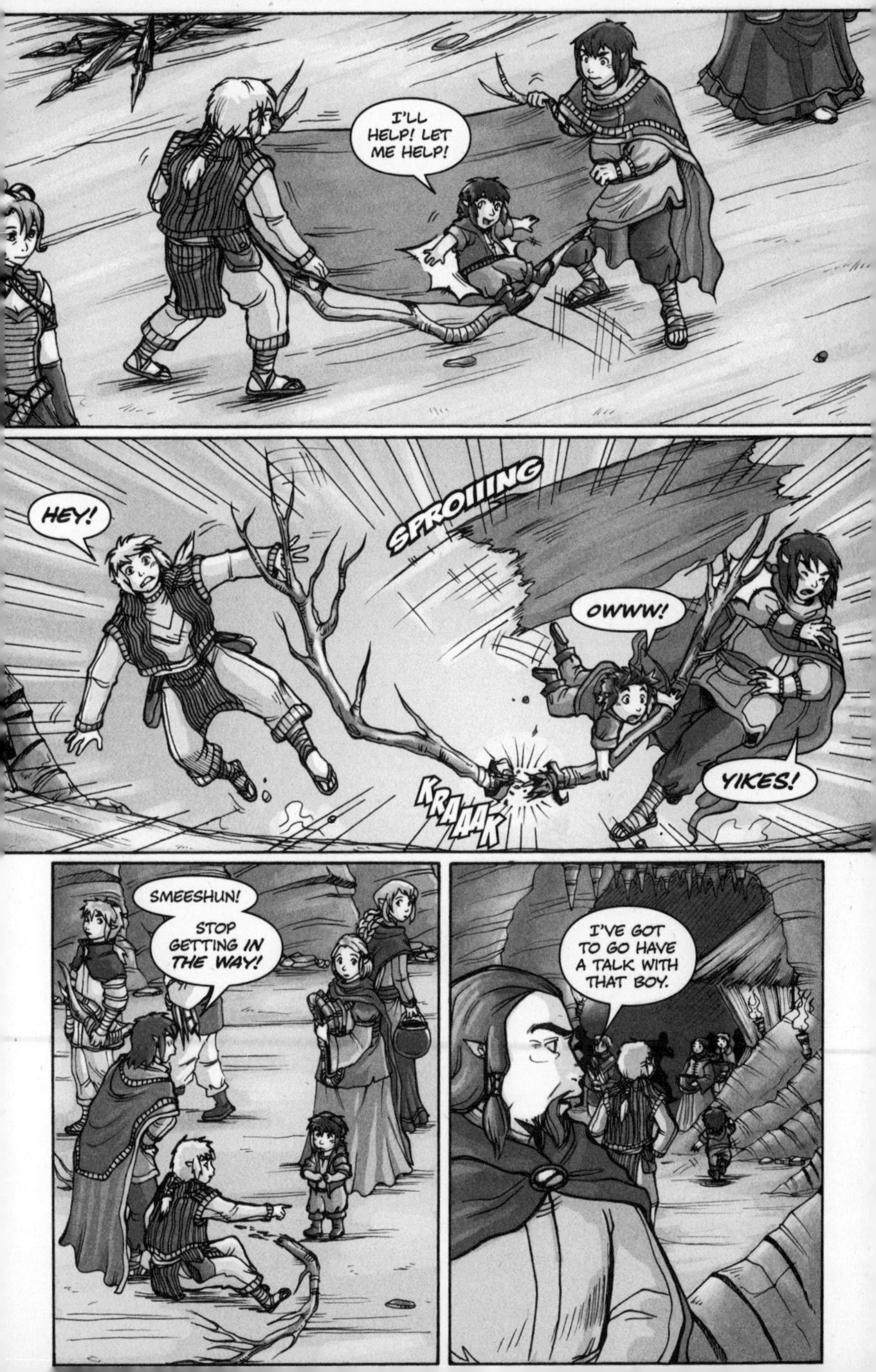
I'LL HELP! LET ME HELP!
HEY!
SPROIIIING
OWWW!
KRAAAK
YIKES!
SMEESHUN!
STOP GETTING IN THE WAY!
I'VE GOT TO GO HAVE A TALK WITH THAT BOY.

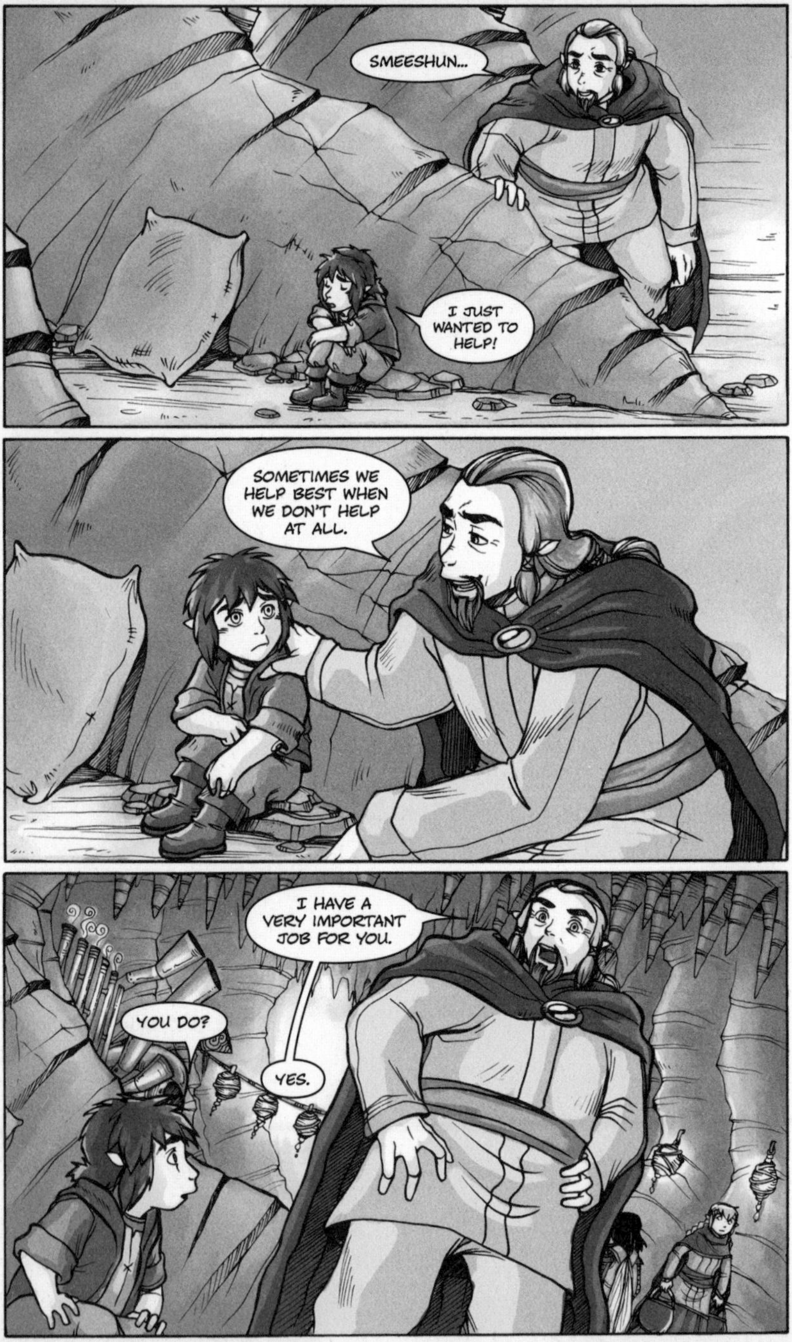
SMEESHUN...
I JUST WANTED TO HELP!
SOMETIMES WE HELP BEST WHEN WE DON'T HELP AT ALL.
I HAVE A VERY IMPORTANT JOB FOR YOU.
YOU DO?
YES.

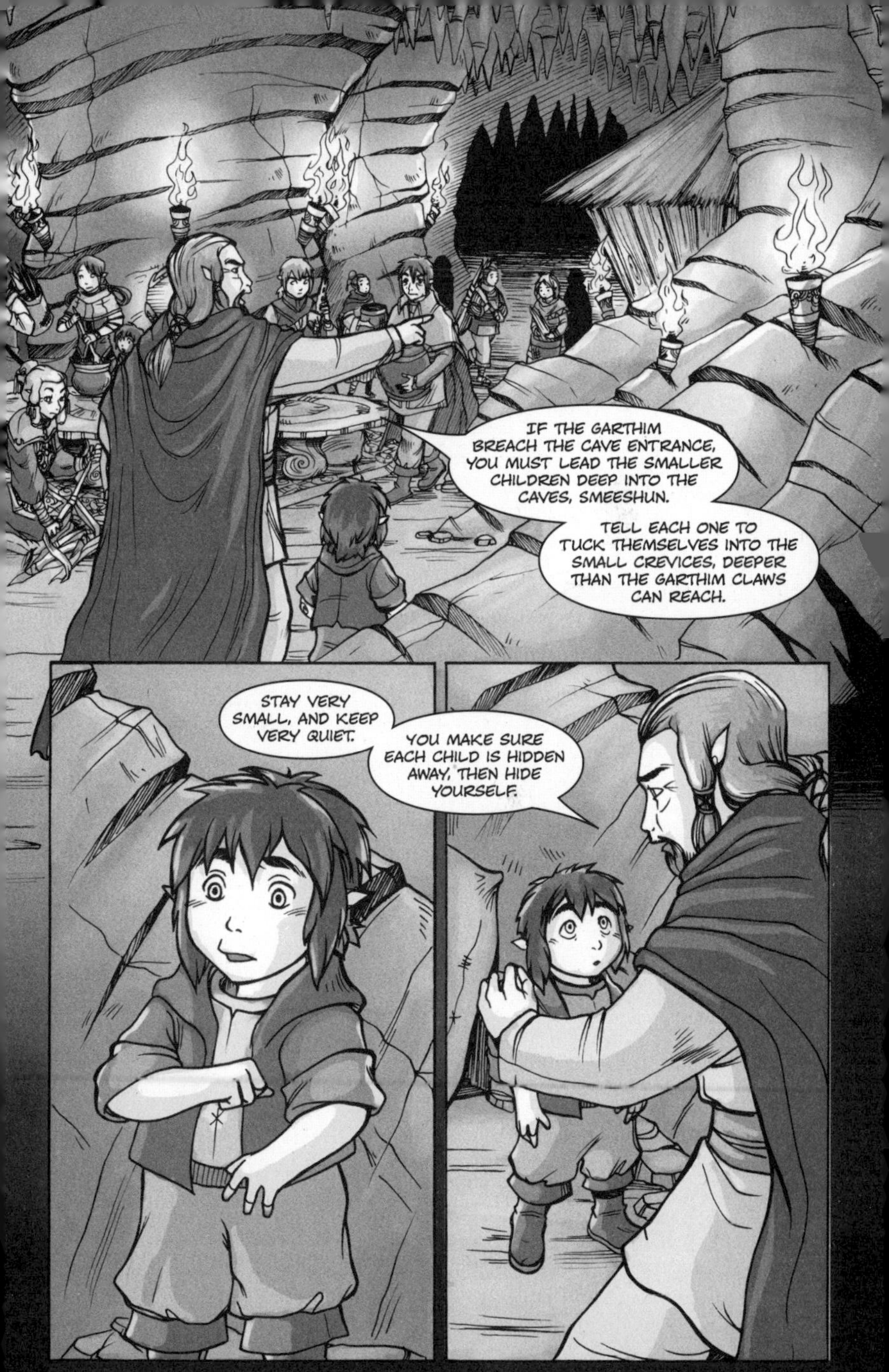
IF THE GARTHIM BREACH THE CAVE ENTRANCE, YOU MUST LEAD THE SMALLER CHILDREN DEEP INTO THE CAVES, SMEESHUN.
TELL EACH ONE TO TUCK THEMSELVES INTO THE SMALL CREVICES, DEEPER THAN THE GARTHIM CLAWS CAN REACH.
STAY VERY SMALL, AND KEEP VERY QUIET.
YOU MAKE SURE EACH CHILD IS HIDDEN AWAY, THEN HIDE YOURSELF.

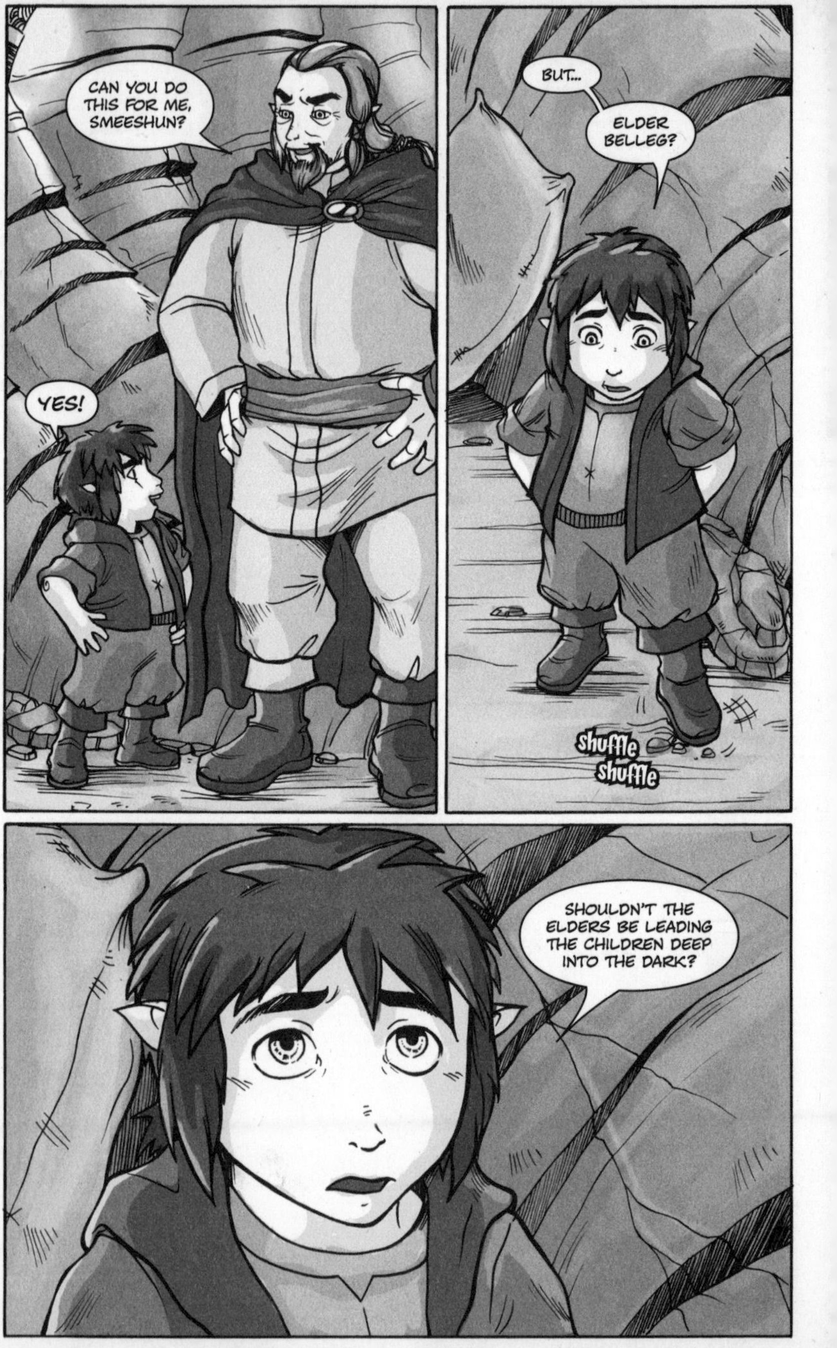
CAN YOU DO THIS FOR ME, SMEESHUN?
YES!
BUT...
ELDER BELLEG?
shuffle shuffle
SHOULDN'T THE ELDERS BE LEADING THE CHILDREN DEEP INTO THE DARK?

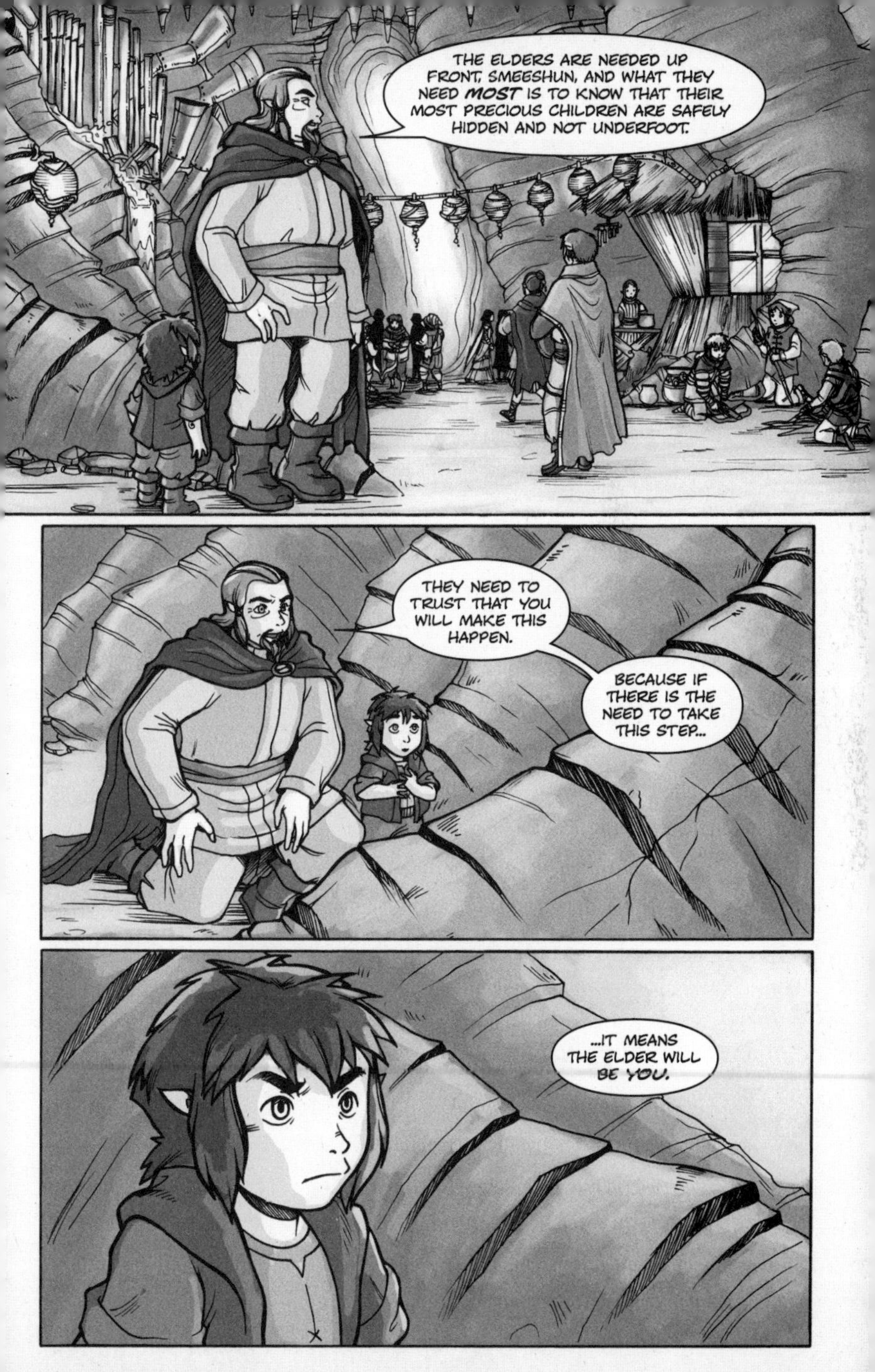
THE ELDERS ARE NEEDED UP FRONT, SMEESHUN, AND WHAT THEY NEED MOST IS TO KNOW THAT THEIR MOST PRECIOUS CHILDREN ARE SAFELY HIDDEN AND NOT UNDERFOOT.
THEY NEED TO TRUST THAT YOU WILL MAKE THIS HAPPEN.
BECAUSE IF THERE IS THE NEED TO TAKE THIS STEP...
...IT MEANS THE ELDER WILL BE YOU.

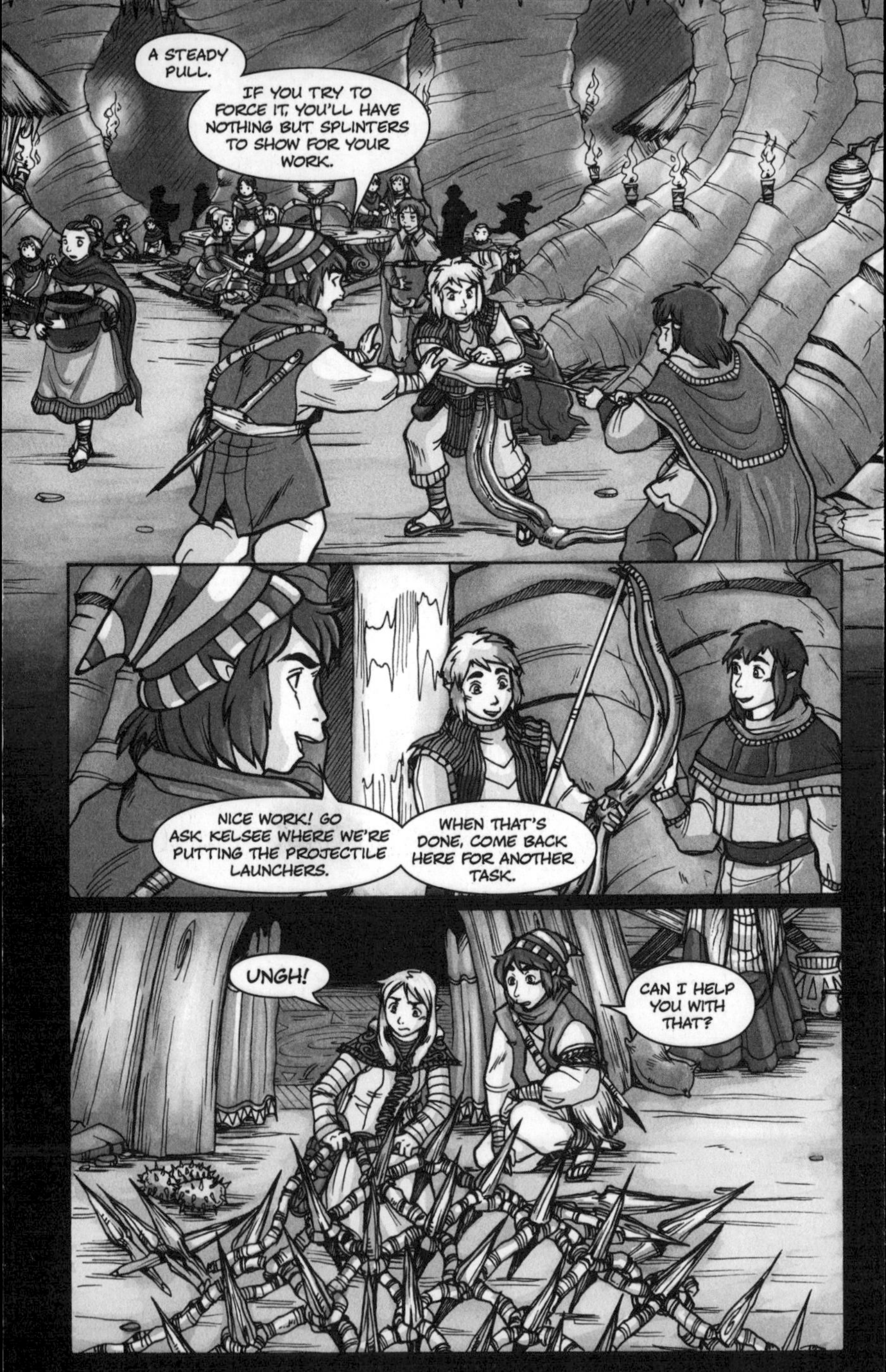
A STEADY PULL.
IF YOU TRY TO FORCE IT, YOU'LL HAVE NOTHING BUT SPLINTERS TO SHOW FOR YOUR WORK.
NICE WORK! GO ASK KELSEE WHERE WE'RE PUTTING THE PROJECTILE LAUNCHERS.
WHEN THAT'S DONE, COME BACK HERE FOR ANOTHER TASK.
UNGH!
CAN I HELP YOU WITH THAT?

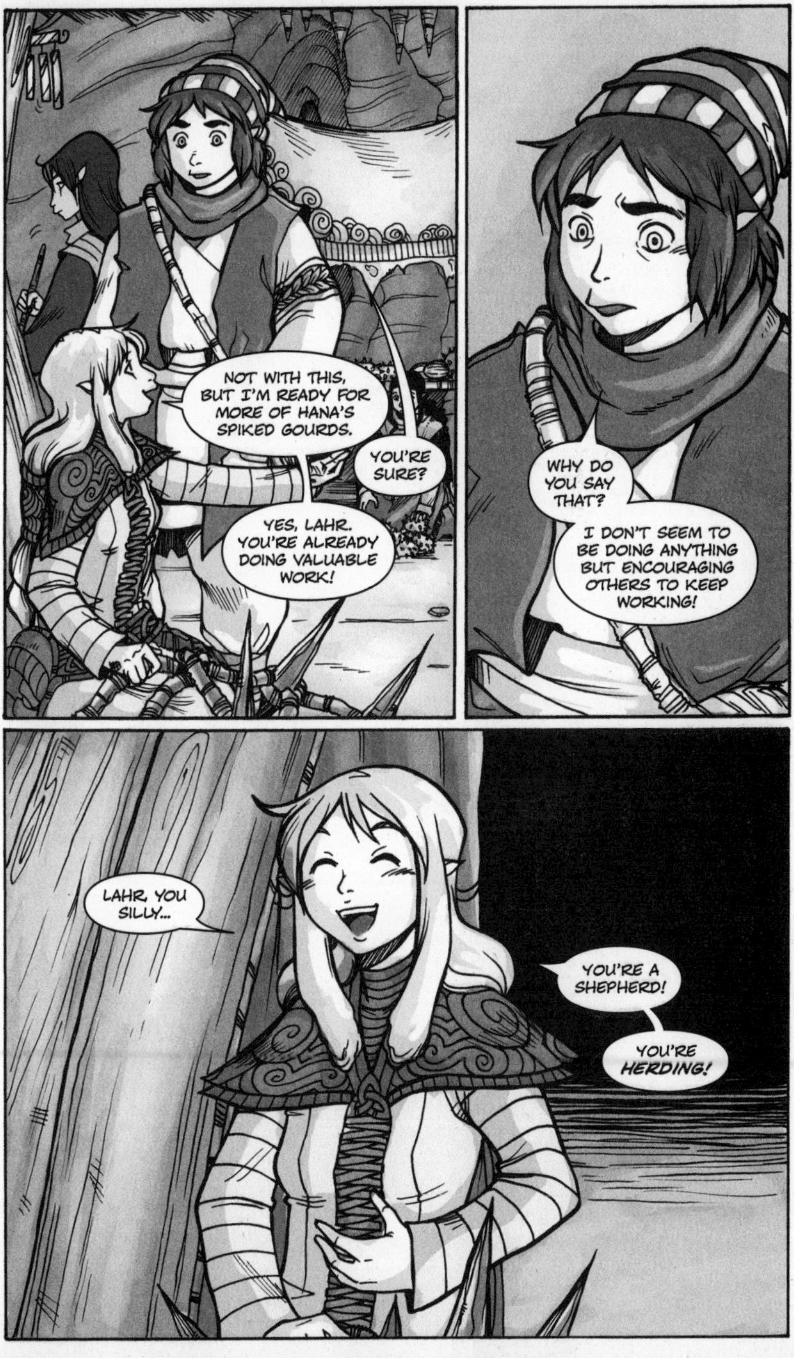
NOT WITH THIS, BUT I'M READY FOR MORE OF HANA'S SPIKED GOURDS.
YOU'RE SURE?
YES, LAHR. YOU'RE ALREADY DOING VALUABLE WORK!
WHY DO YOU SAY THAT?
I DON'T SEEM TO BE DOING ANYTHING BUT ENCOURAGING OTHERS TO KEEP WORKING!
LAHR, YOU SILLY...
YOU'RE A SHEPHERD!
YOU'RE *HERDING!*

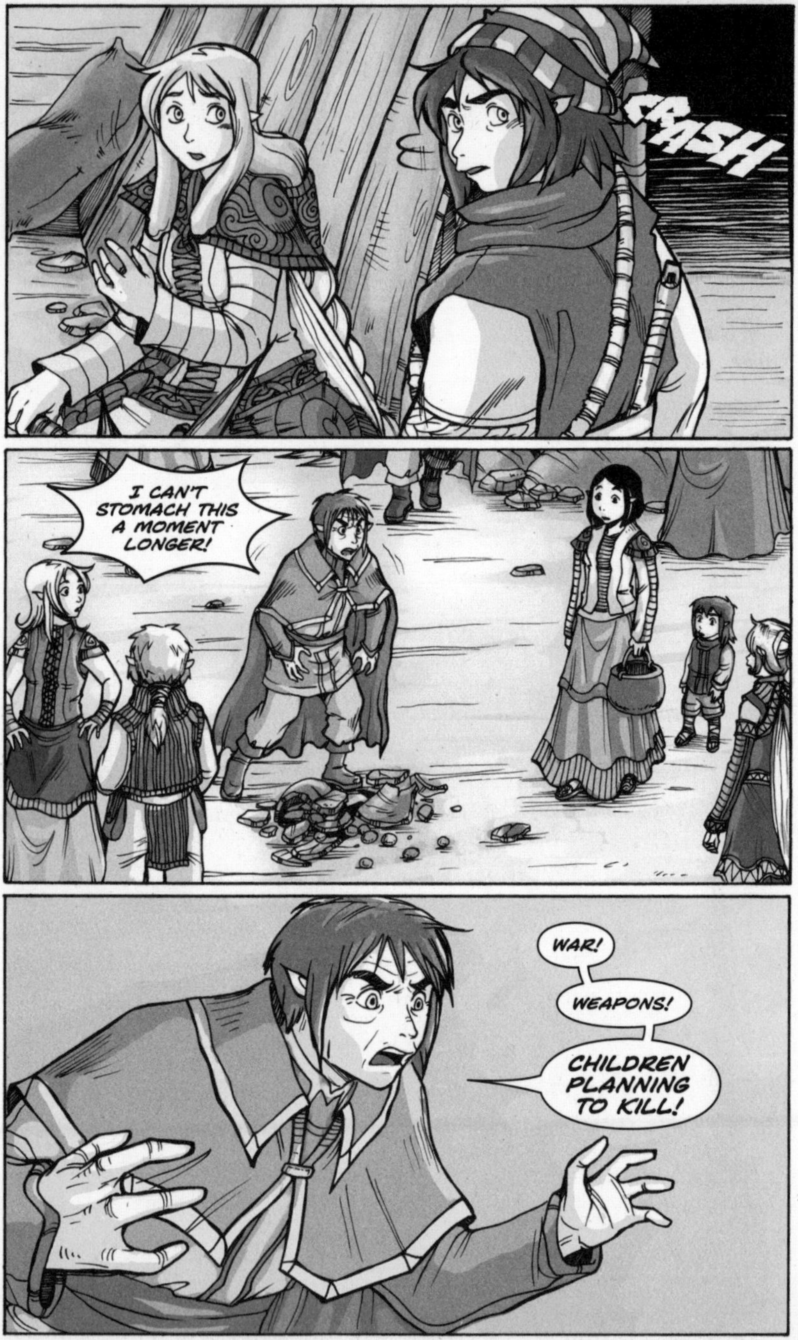
CRASH
I CAN'T STOMACH THIS A MOMENT LONGER!
WAR!
WEAPONS!
CHILDREN PLANNING TO KILL!

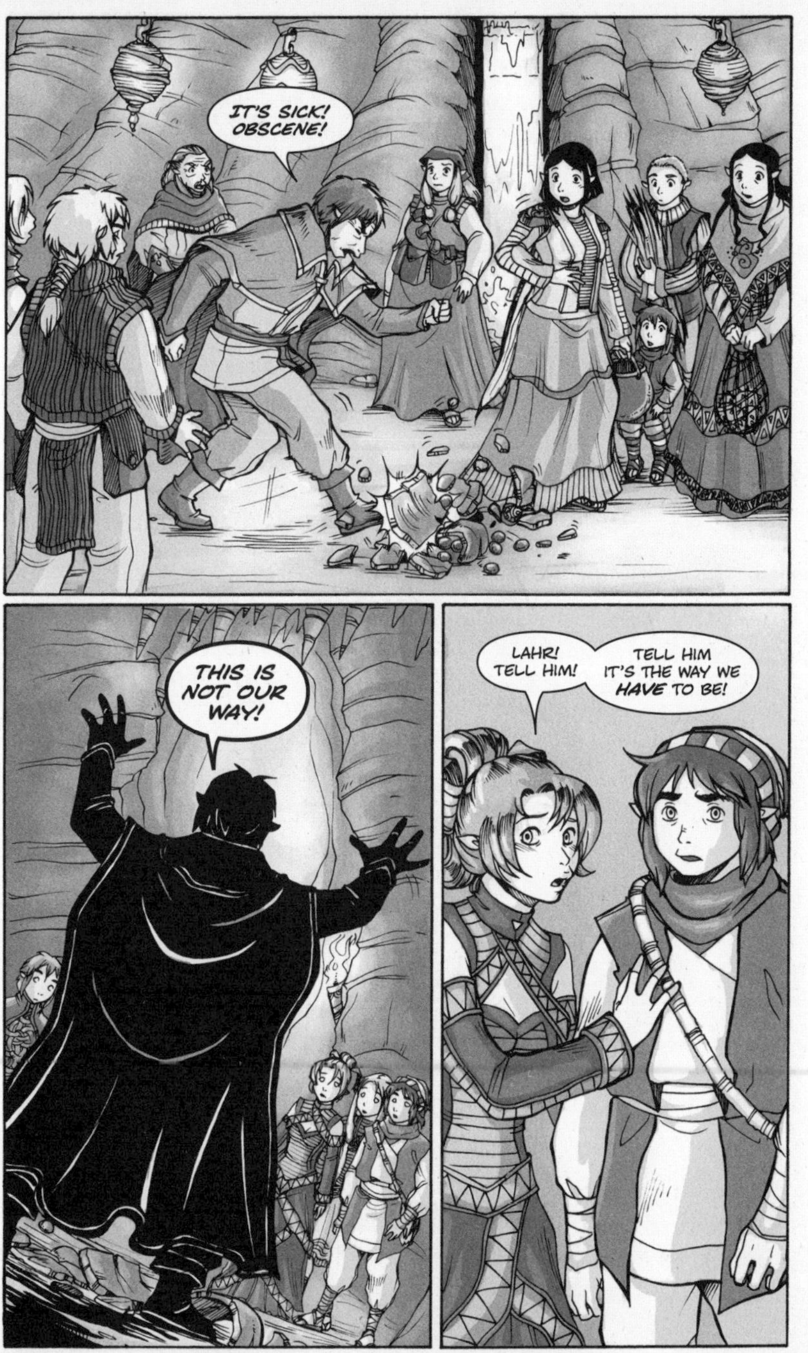
IT'S SICK! OBSCENE!
THIS IS NOT OUR WAY!
LAHR! TELL HIM!
TELL HIM IT'S THE WAY WE *HAVE* TO BE!

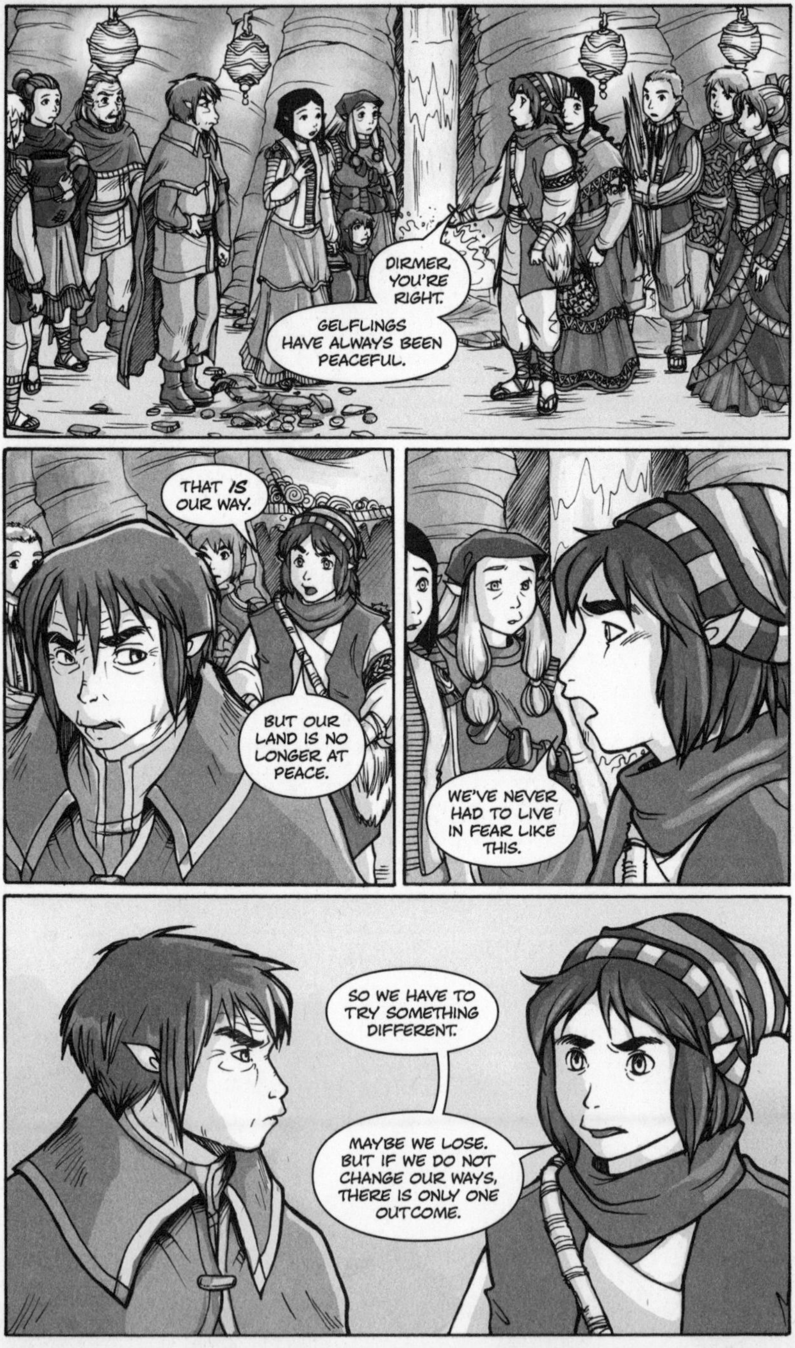
DIRMER, YOU'RE RIGHT.
GELFLINGS HAVE ALWAYS BEEN PEACEFUL.
THAT *IS* OUR WAY.
BUT OUR LAND IS NO LONGER AT PEACE.
WE'VE NEVER HAD TO LIVE IN FEAR LIKE THIS.
SO WE HAVE TO TRY SOMETHING DIFFERENT.
MAYBE WE LOSE. BUT IF WE DO NOT CHANGE OUR WAYS, THERE IS ONLY ONE OUTCOME.

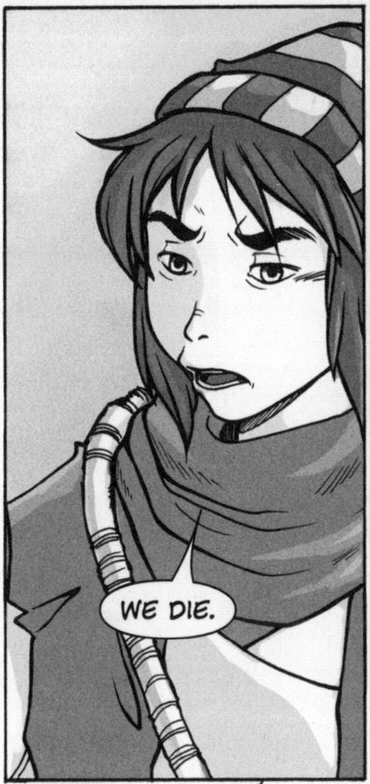
WE DIE.
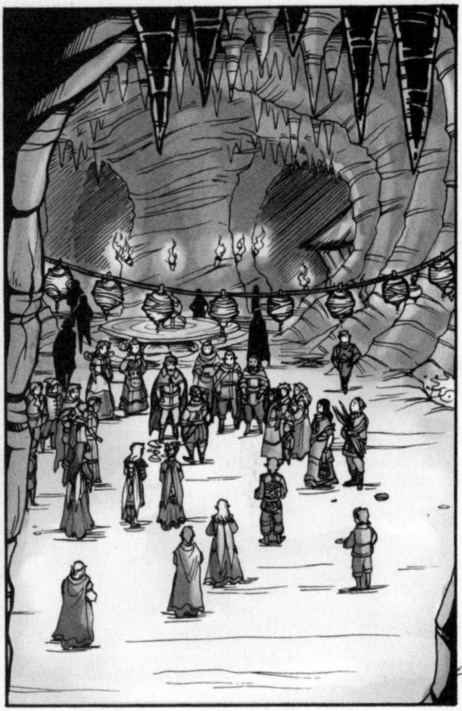
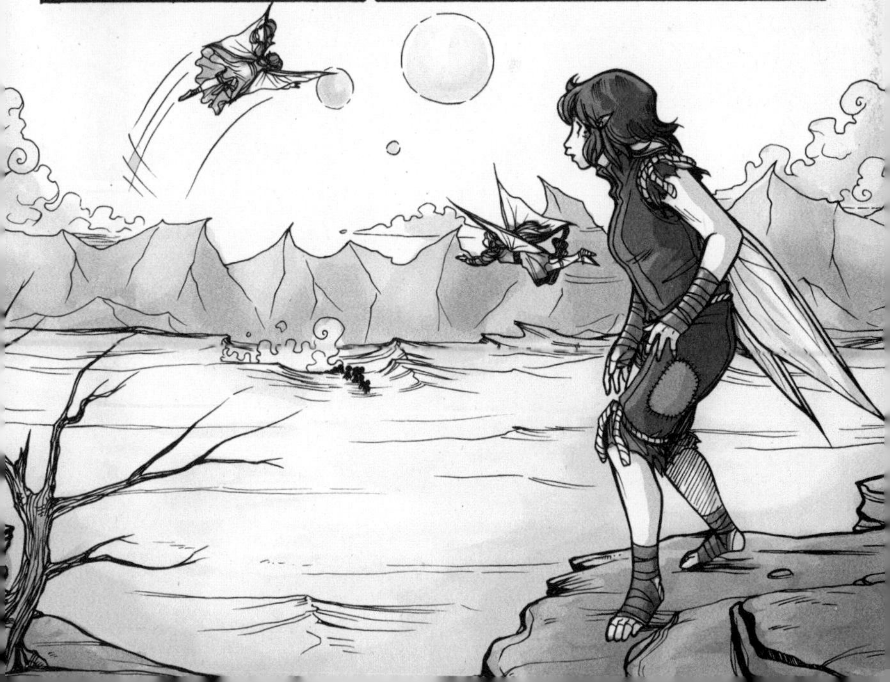

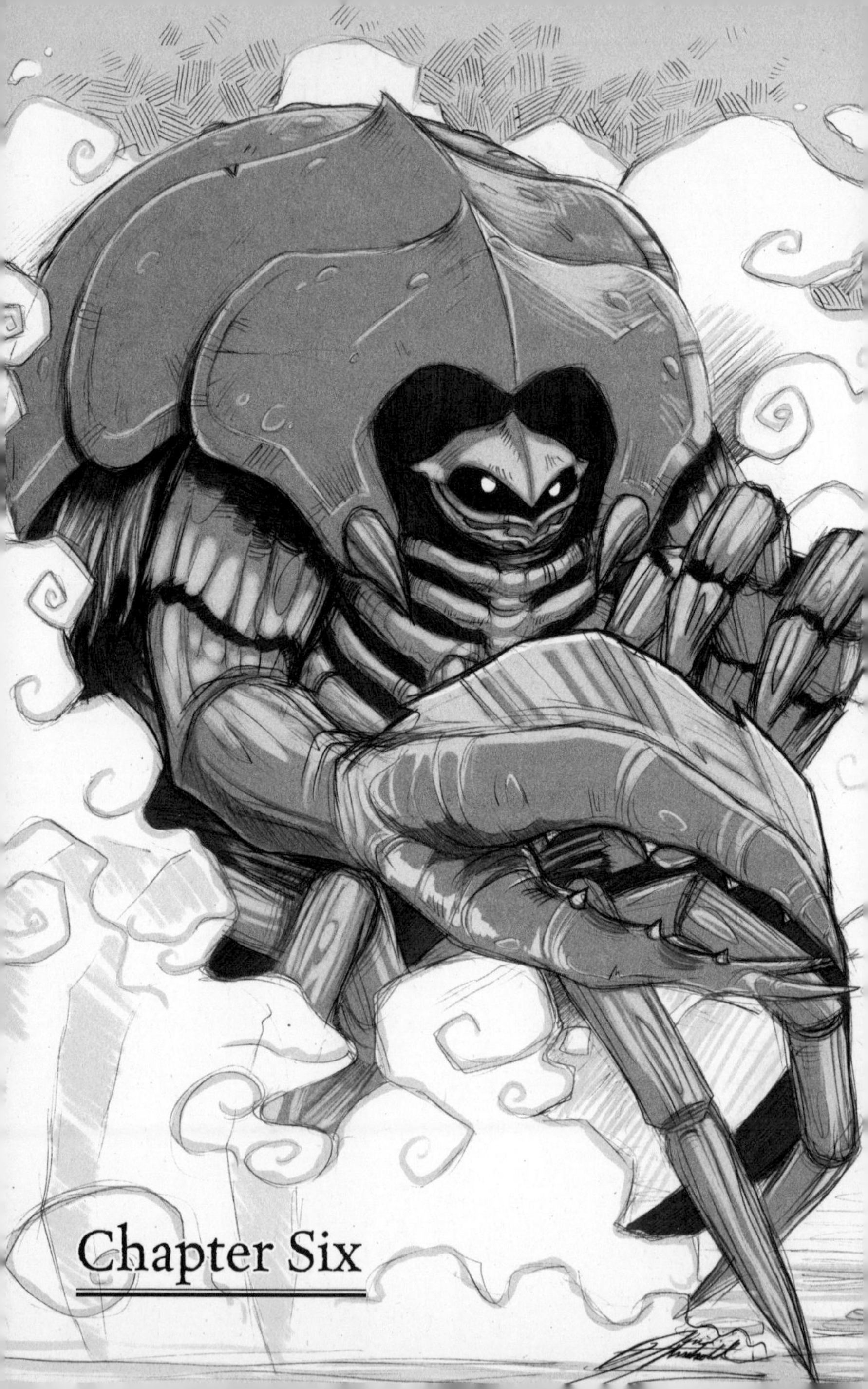

Chapter Six

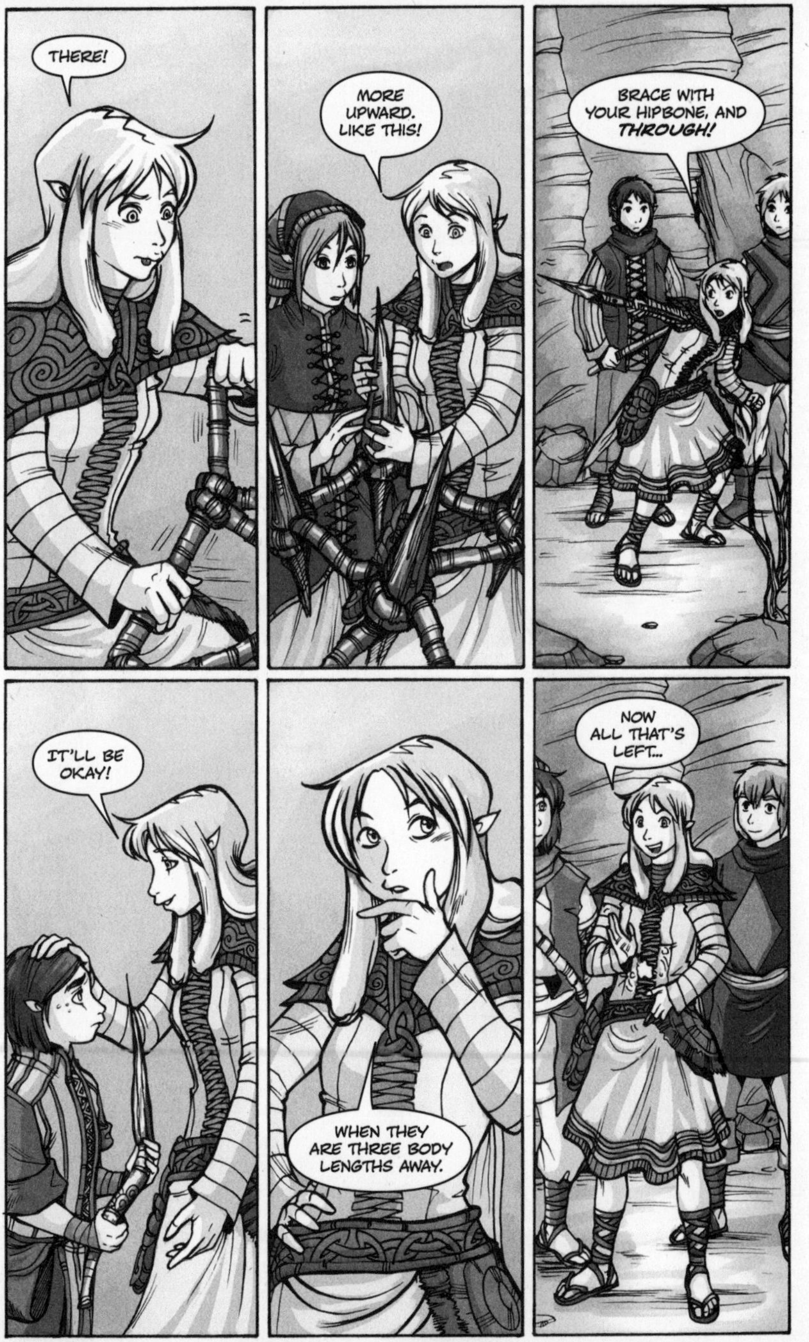
THERE!
MORE UPWARD. LIKE THIS!
BRACE WITH YOUR HIPBONE, AND *THROUGH!*
IT'LL BE OKAY!
WHEN THEY ARE THREE BODY LENGTHS AWAY.
NOW ALL THAT'S LEFT...

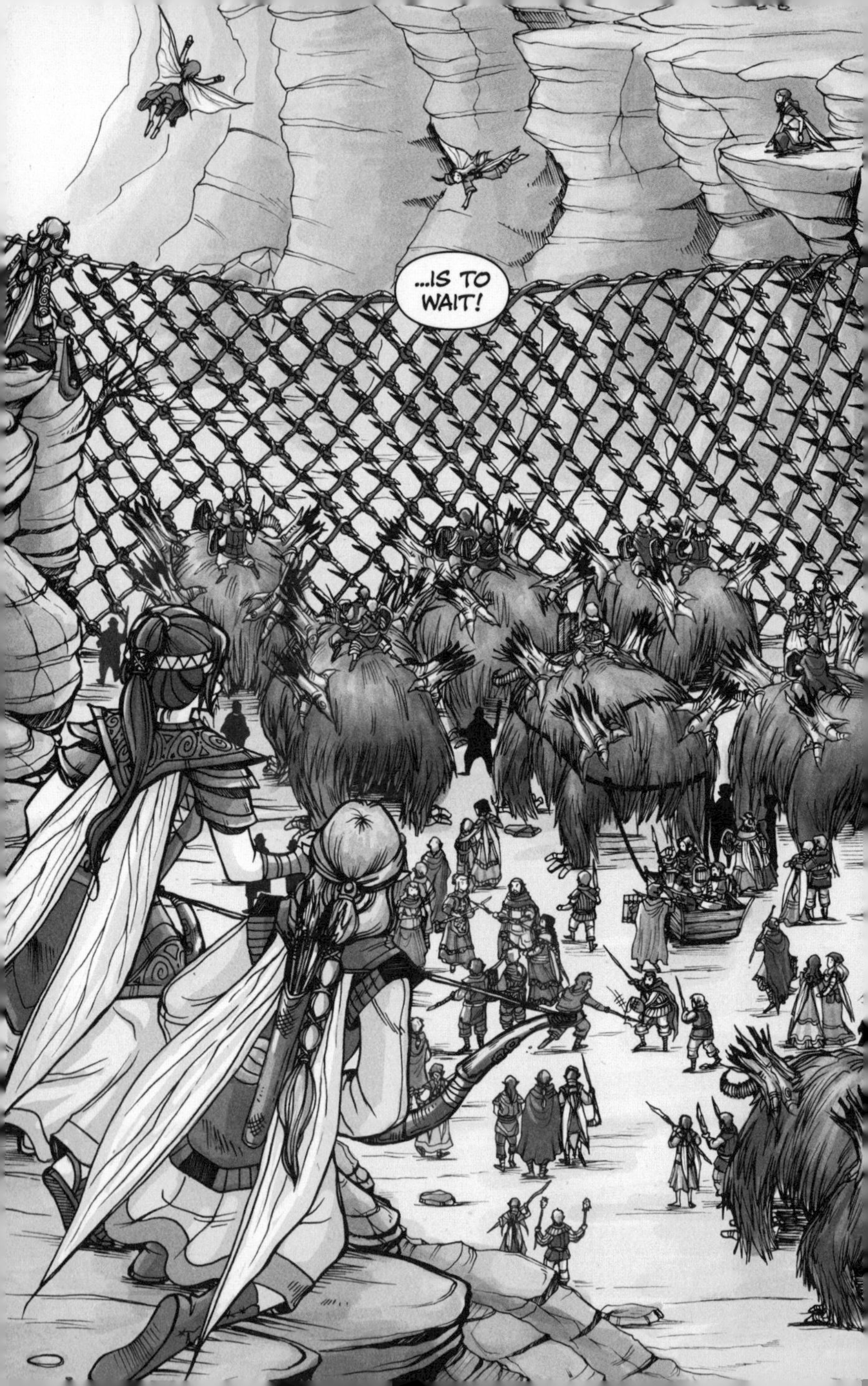
...IS TO WAIT!

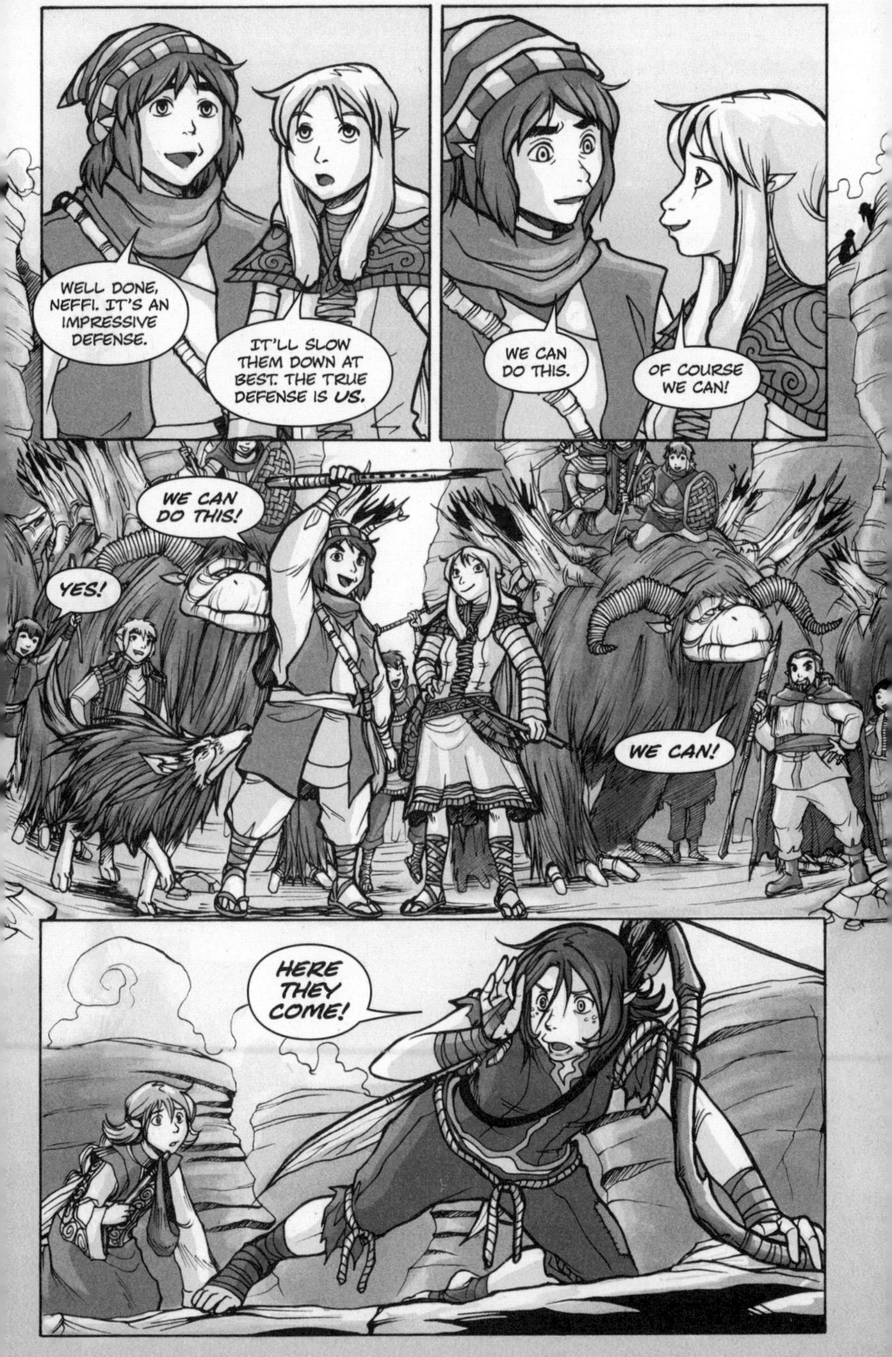
WELL DONE, NEFFI. IT'S AN IMPRESSIVE DEFENSE.
IT'LL SLOW THEM DOWN AT BEST. THE TRUE DEFENSE IS US.
WE CAN DO THIS.
OF COURSE WE CAN!
WE CAN DO THIS!
YES!
WE CAN!
HERE THEY COME!

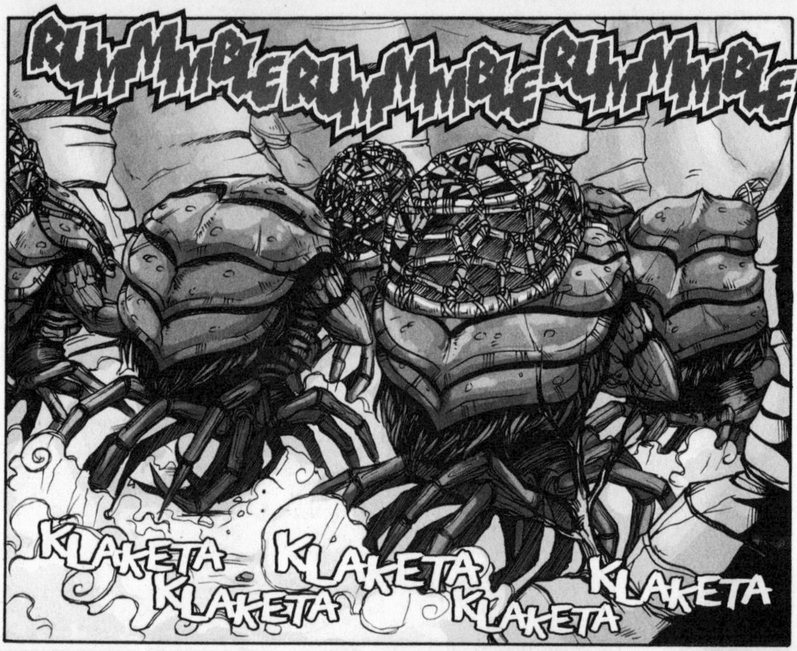
RUMMMBLE RUMMMMBLE RUMMMBLE
KLAKETA KLAKETA
KLAKETA KLAKETA
KLAKETA
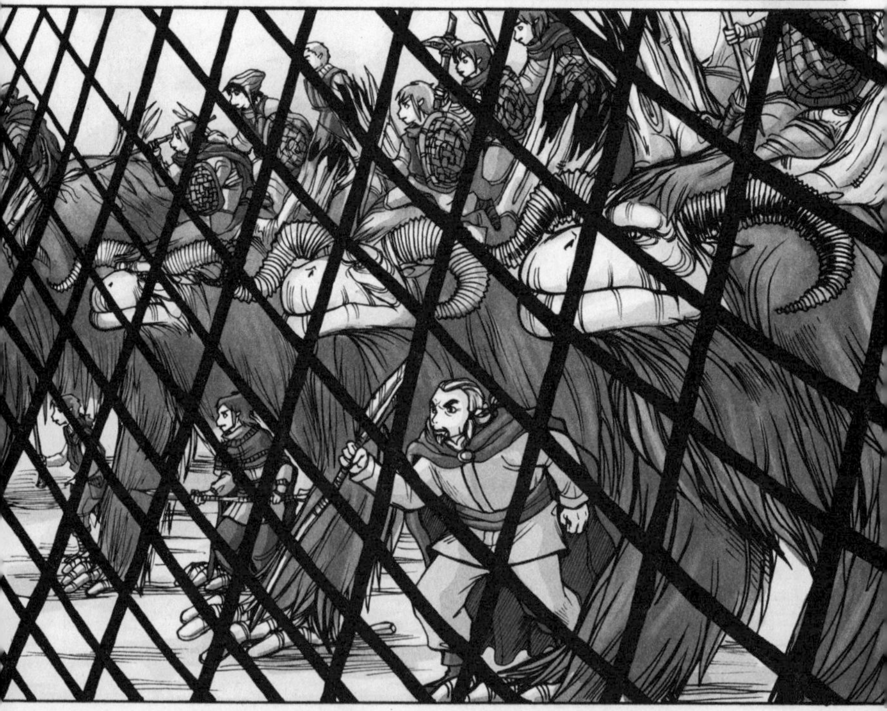

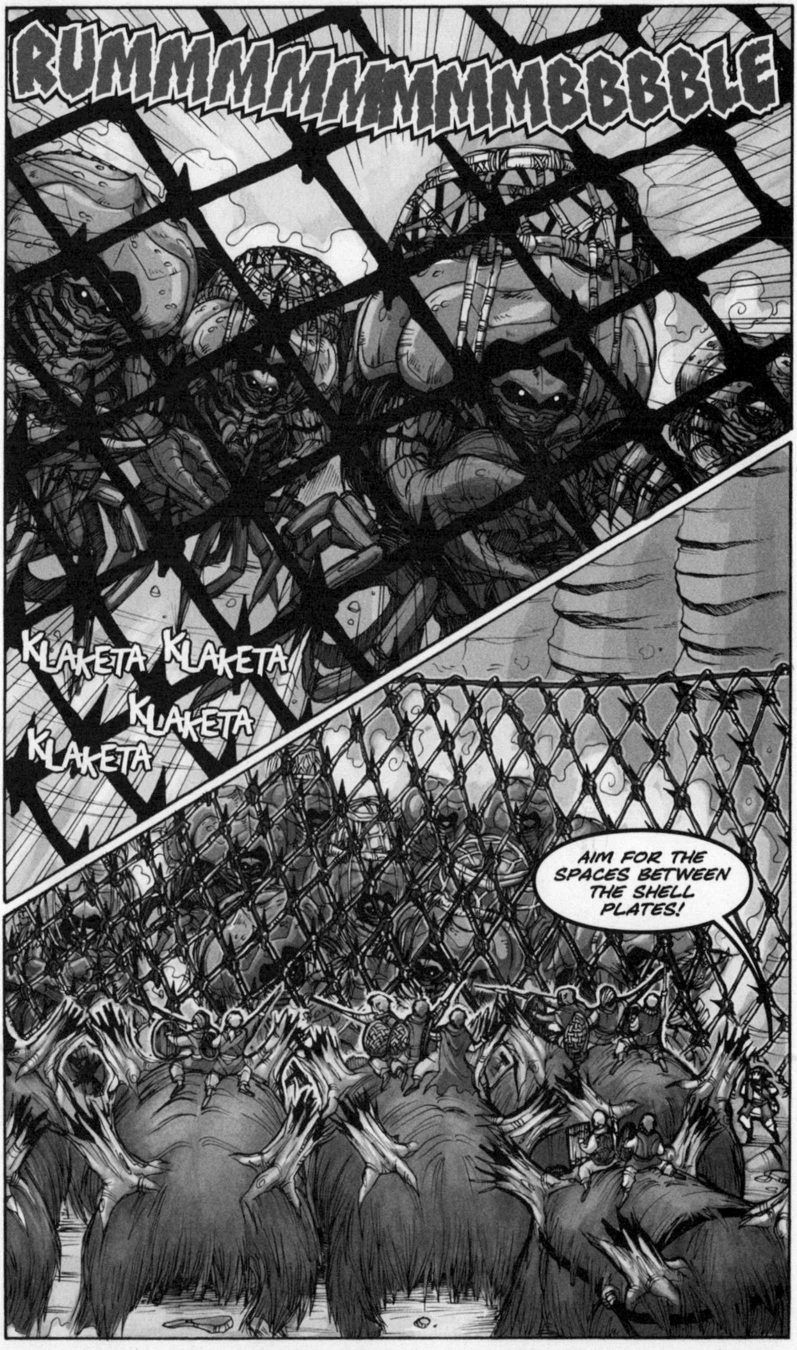
RUMMMMMMMMMBBBBLE
KLAKETA KLAKETA
KLAKETA
KLAKETA
AIM FOR THE SPACES BETWEEN THE SHELL PLATES!

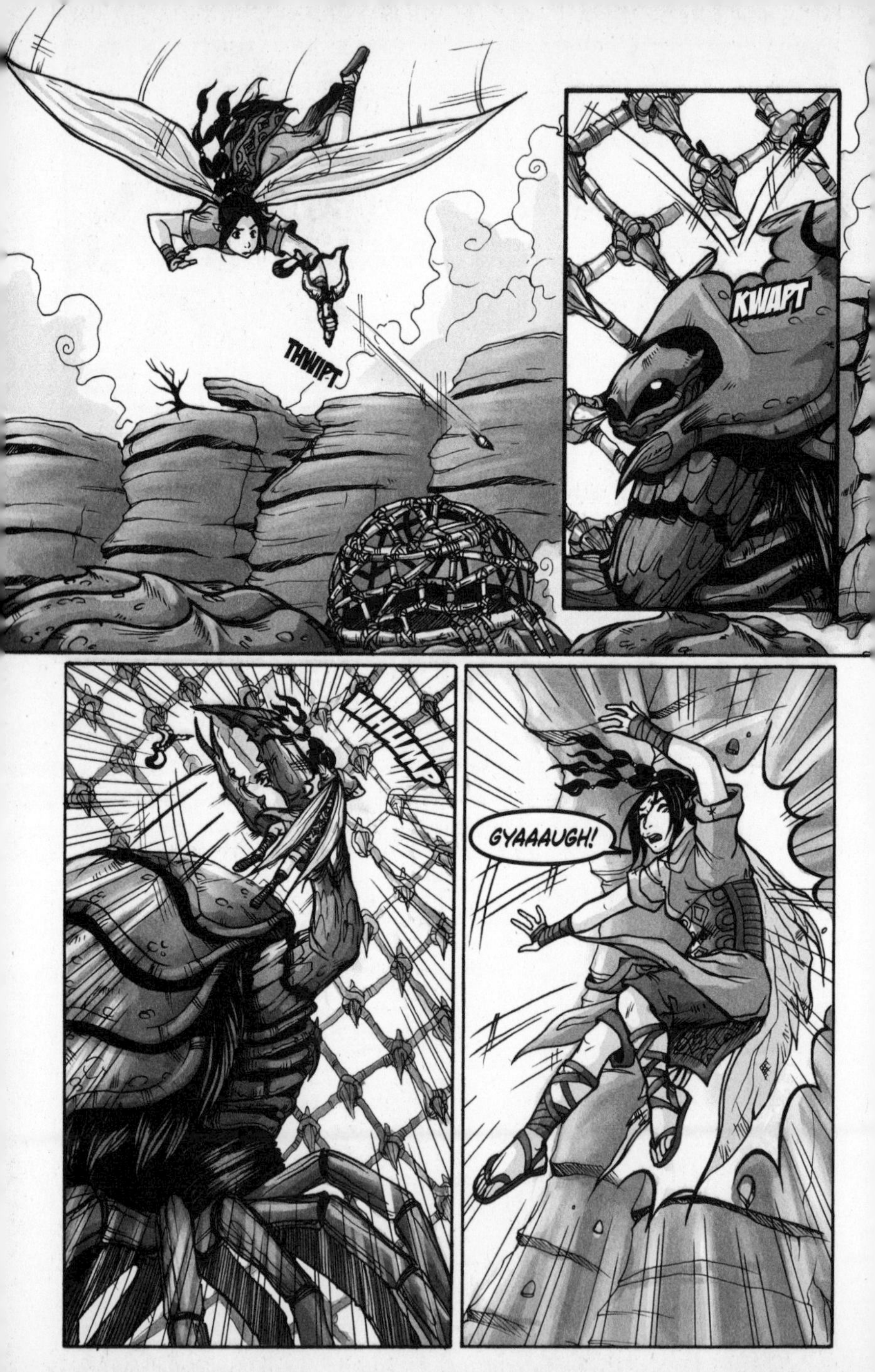
THWIPT
KWAPT
WHUMP
GYAAAUGH!

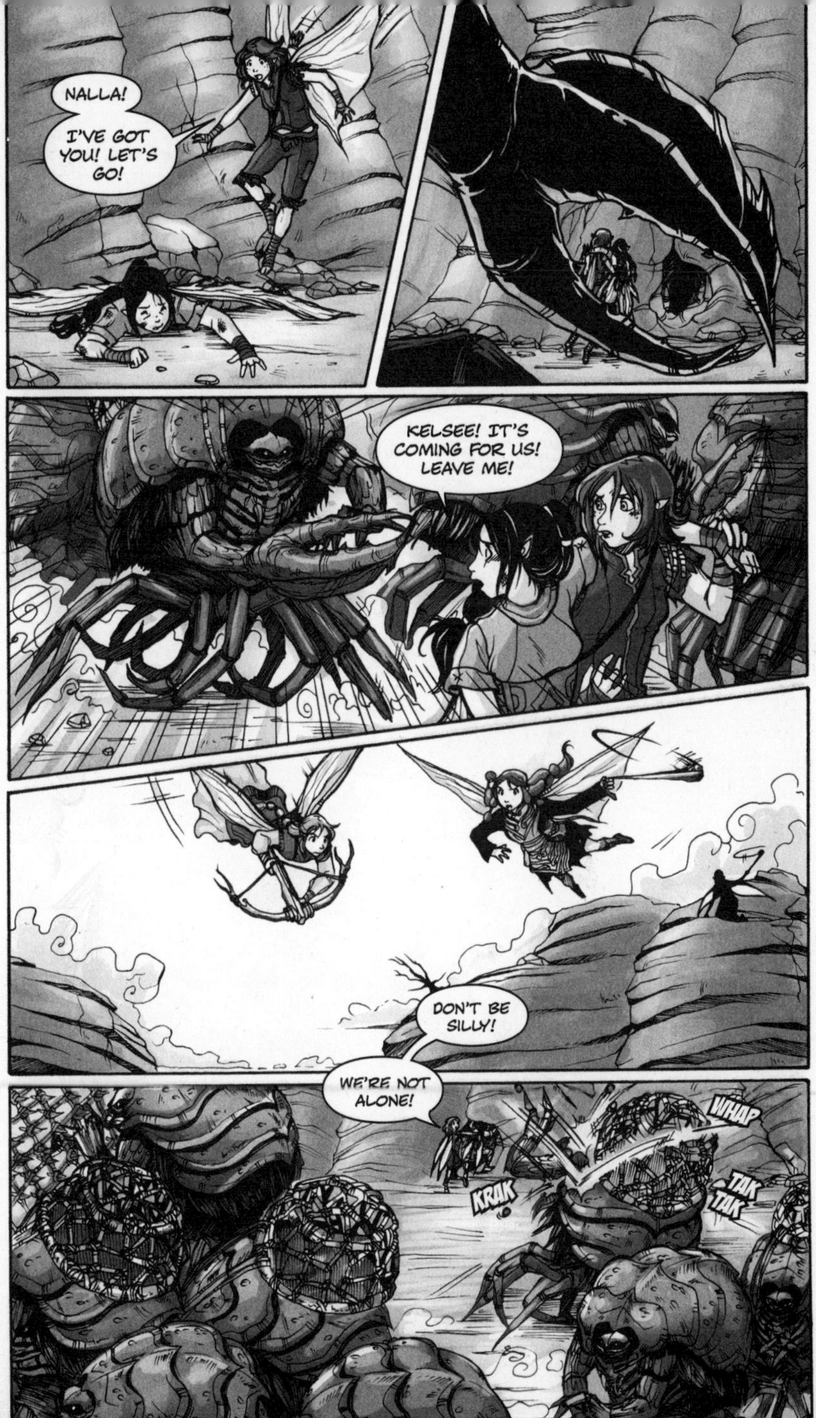
NALLA!
I'VE GOT YOU! LET'S GO!
KELSEE! IT'S COMING FOR US! LEAVE ME!
DON'T BE SILLY!
WE'RE NOT ALONE!
WHAP
KRAK
TAK TAK

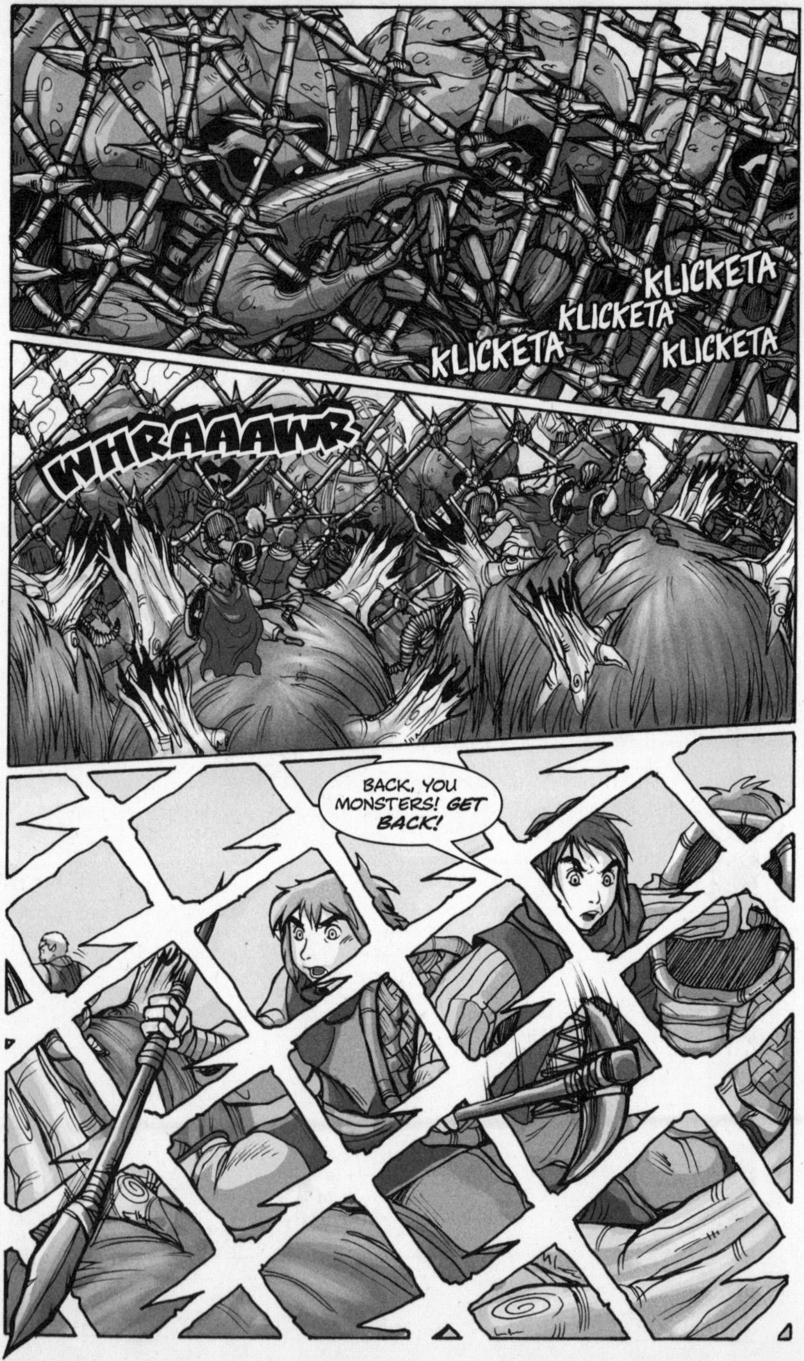
KLICKETA
KLICKETA
KLICKETA
KLICKETA
WHRAAAAWR
BACK, YOU MONSTERS! GET BACK!

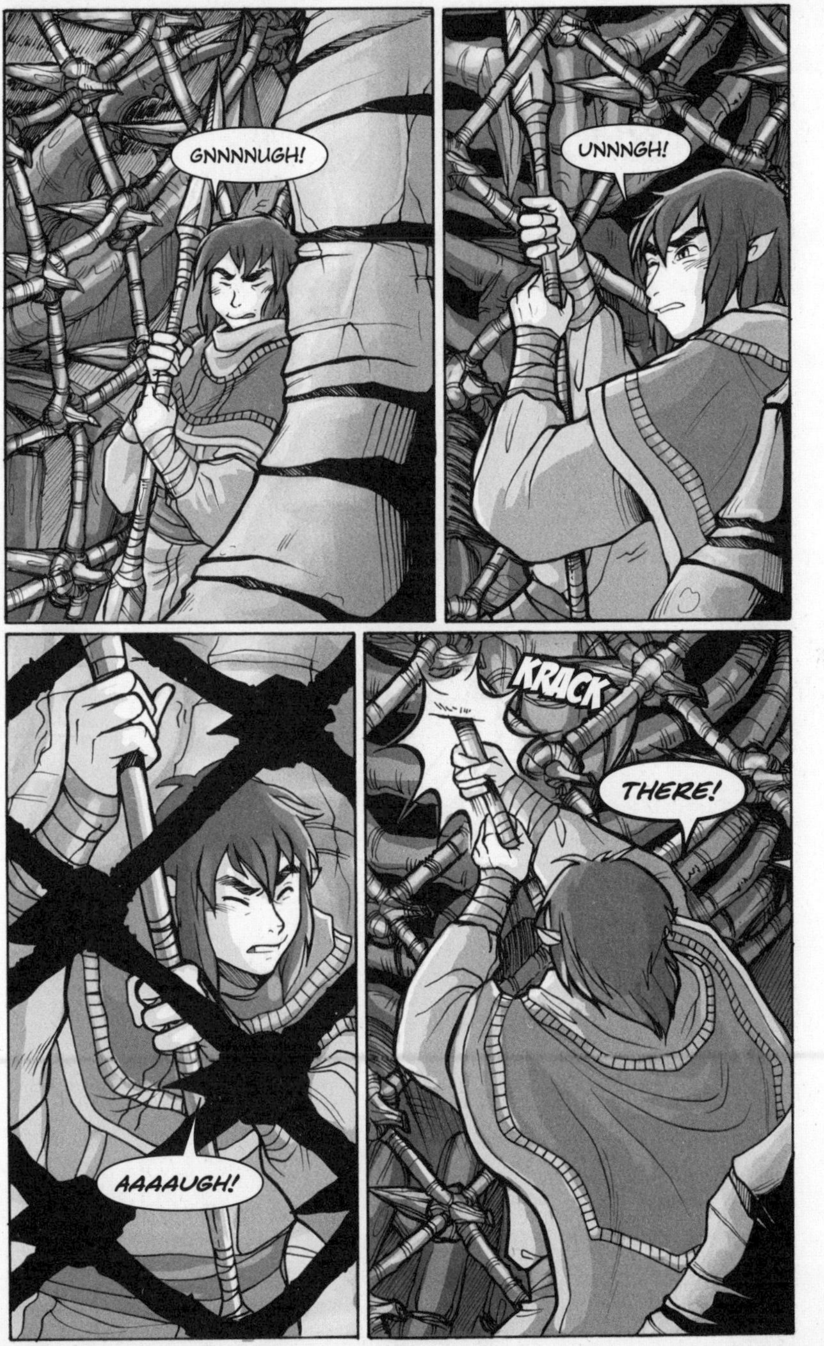
GNNNNUGH!
UNNNGH!
AAAAUGH!
KRACK
THERE!

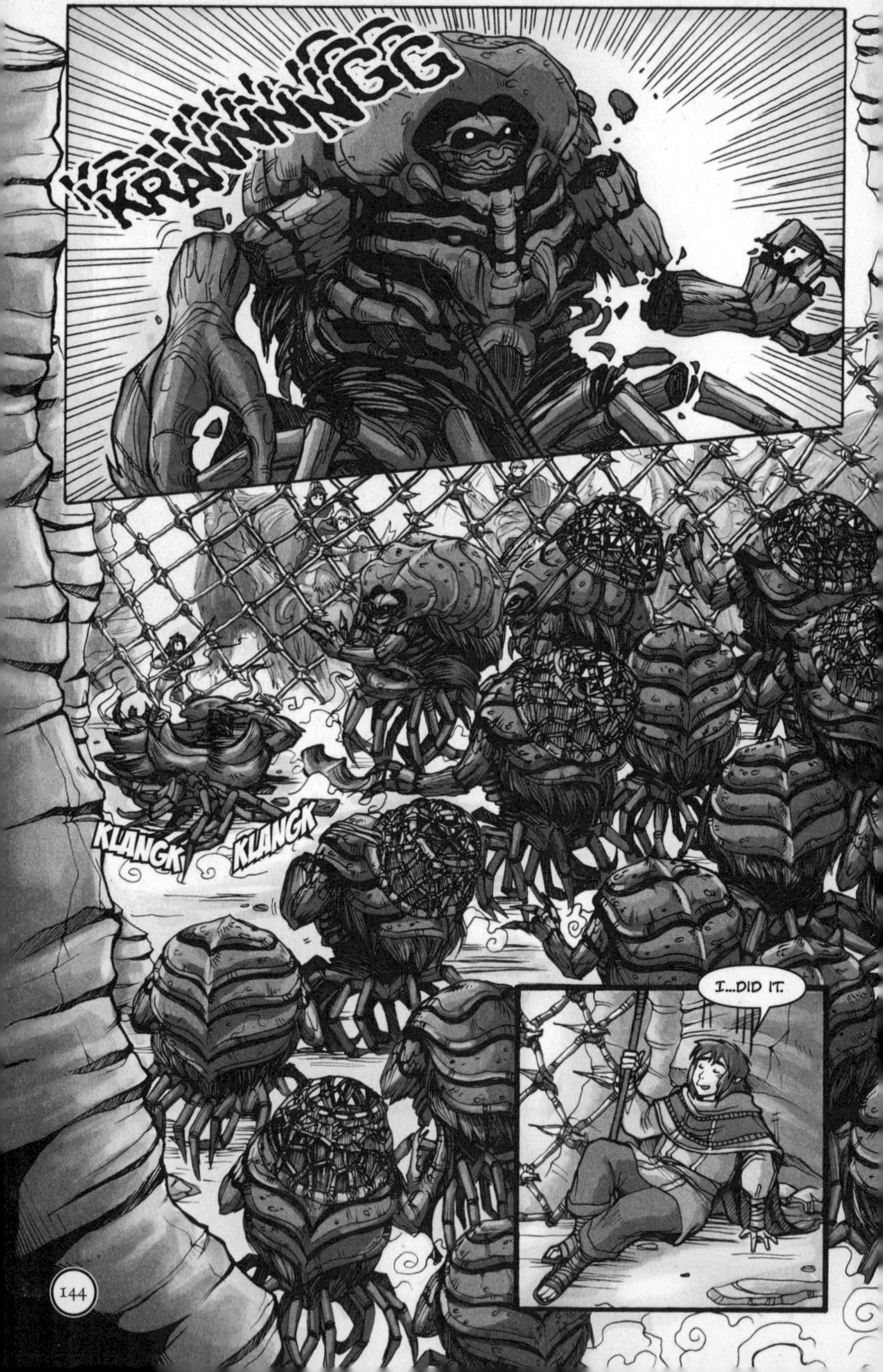
KRANNNNGG
KLANGK
KLANGK
I...DID IT.

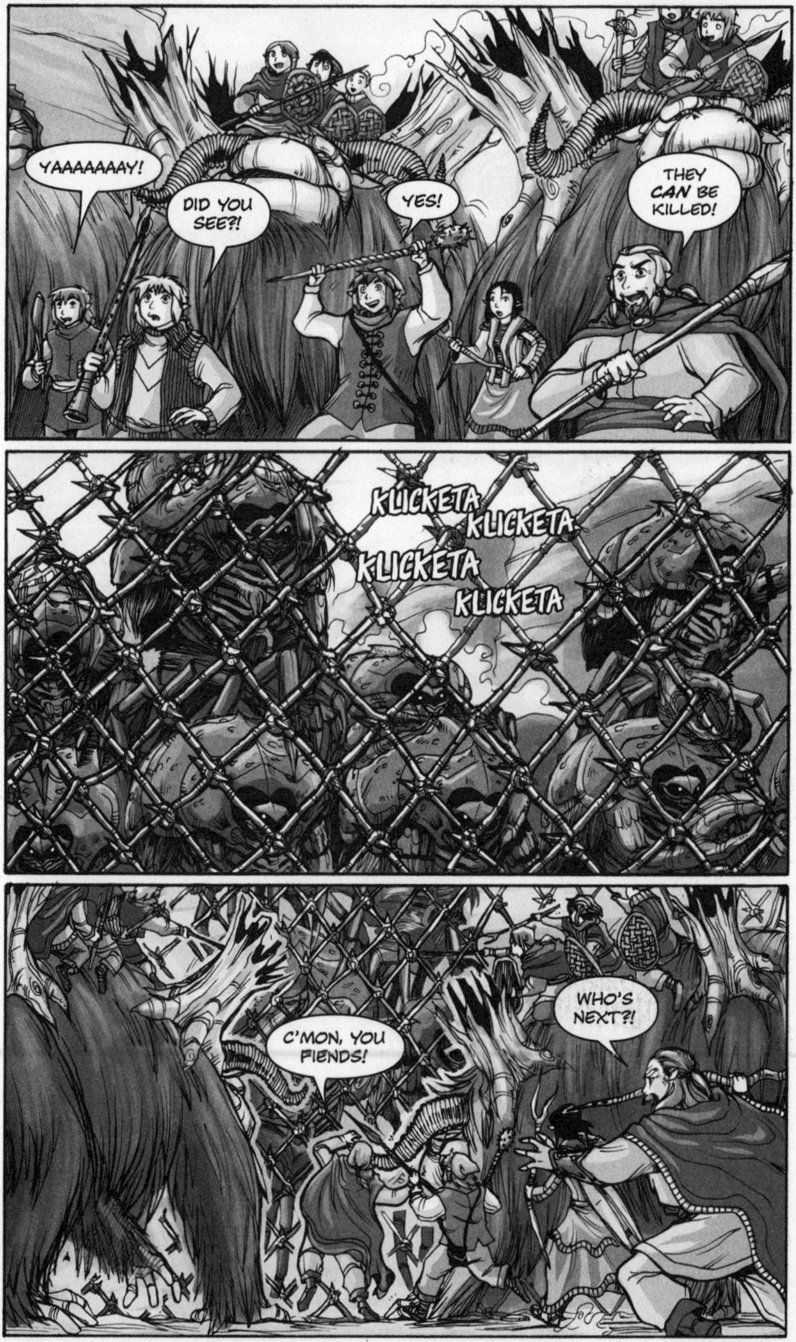
YAAAAAAAY!
DID YOU SEE?!
YES!
THEY *CAN* BE KILLED!
KLICKETA
KLICKETA
KLICKETA
KLICKETA
C'MON, YOU FIENDS!
WHO'S NEXT?!

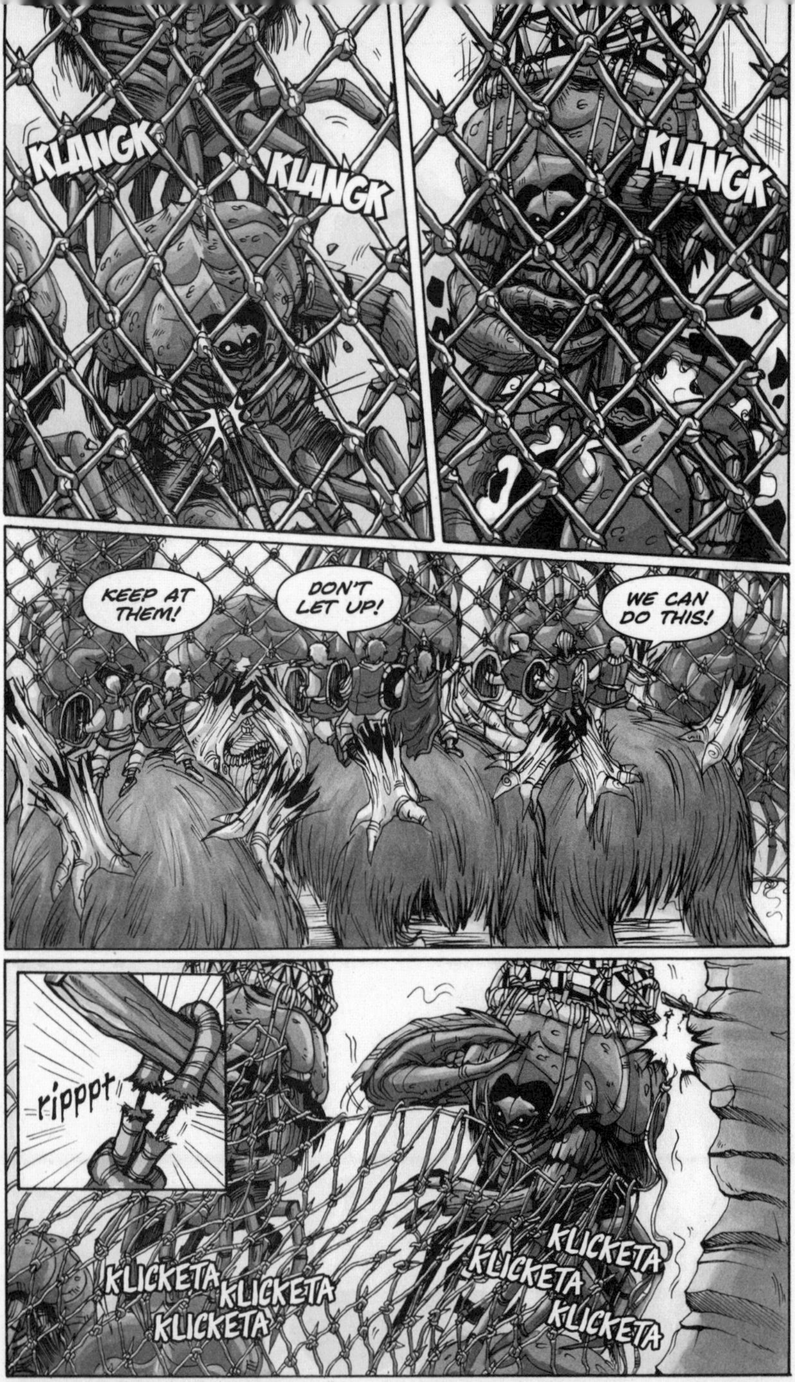
KLANGK
KLANGK
KLANGK
KEEP AT THEM!
DON'T LET UP!
WE CAN DO THIS!
ripppt
KLICKETA
KLICKETA
KLICKETA
KLICKETA
KLICKETA
KLICKETA

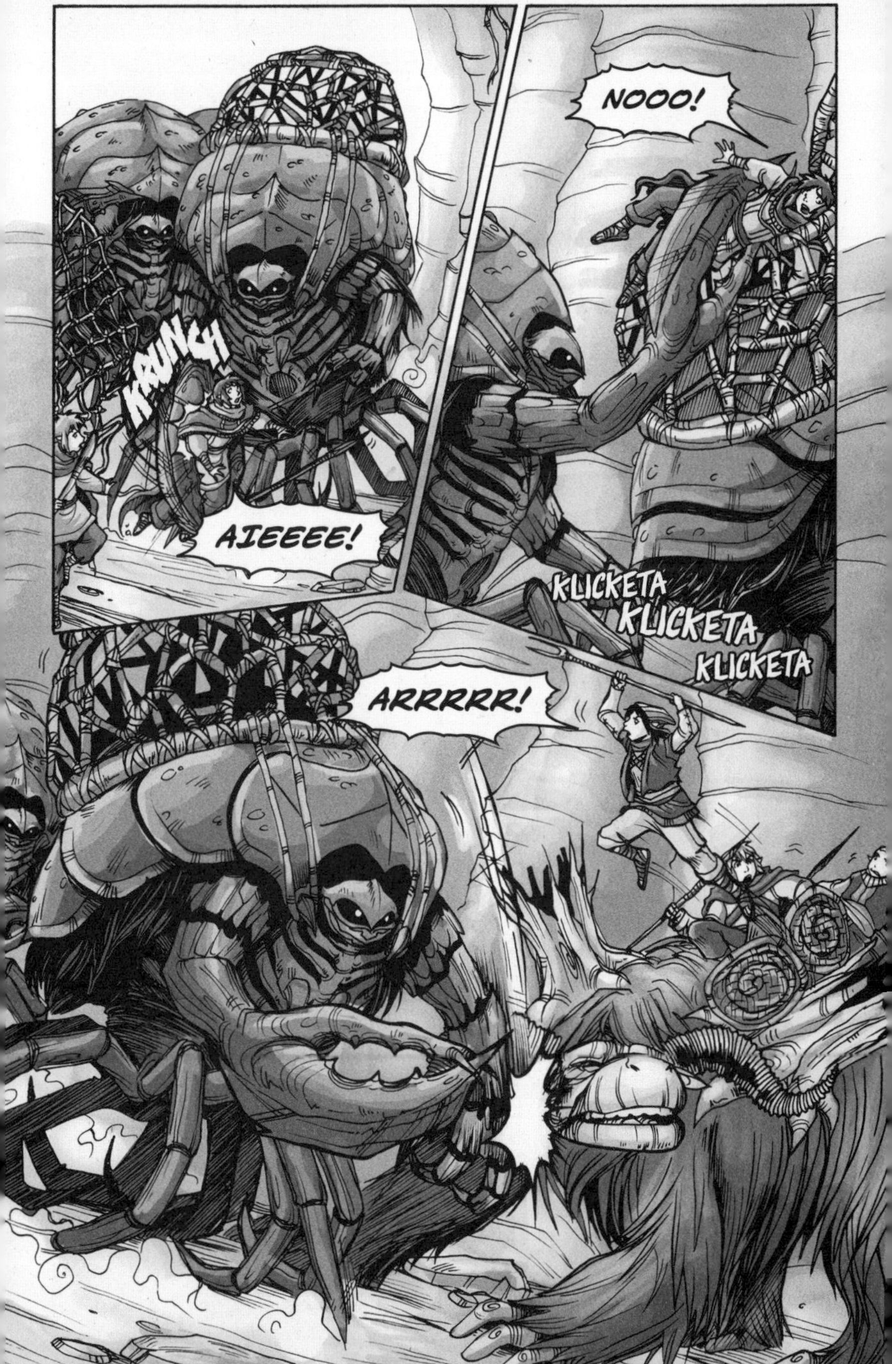
KRUNCH
AIEEEEE!
NOOO!
KLICKETA
KLICKETA
KLICKETA
ARRRRRR!

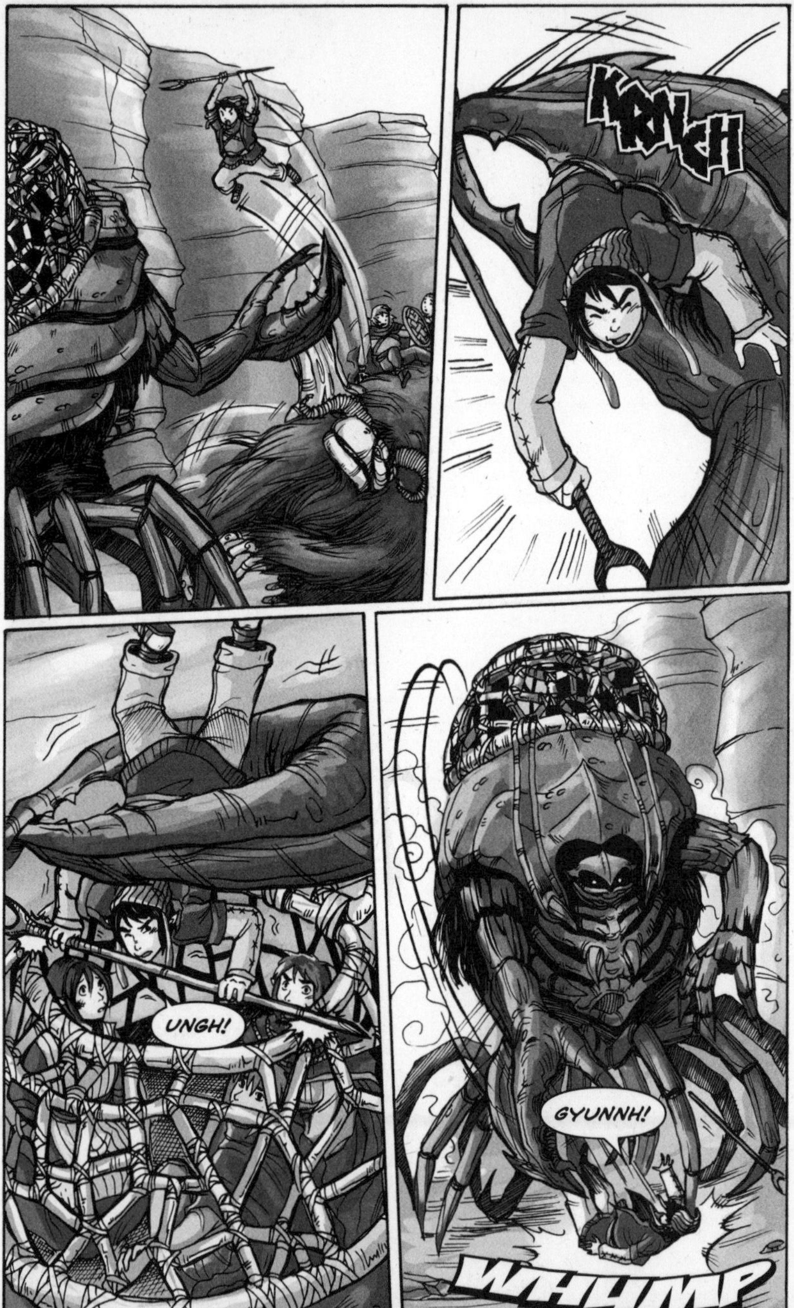
KRUNCH
UNGH!
GYUNNH!
WHUMP

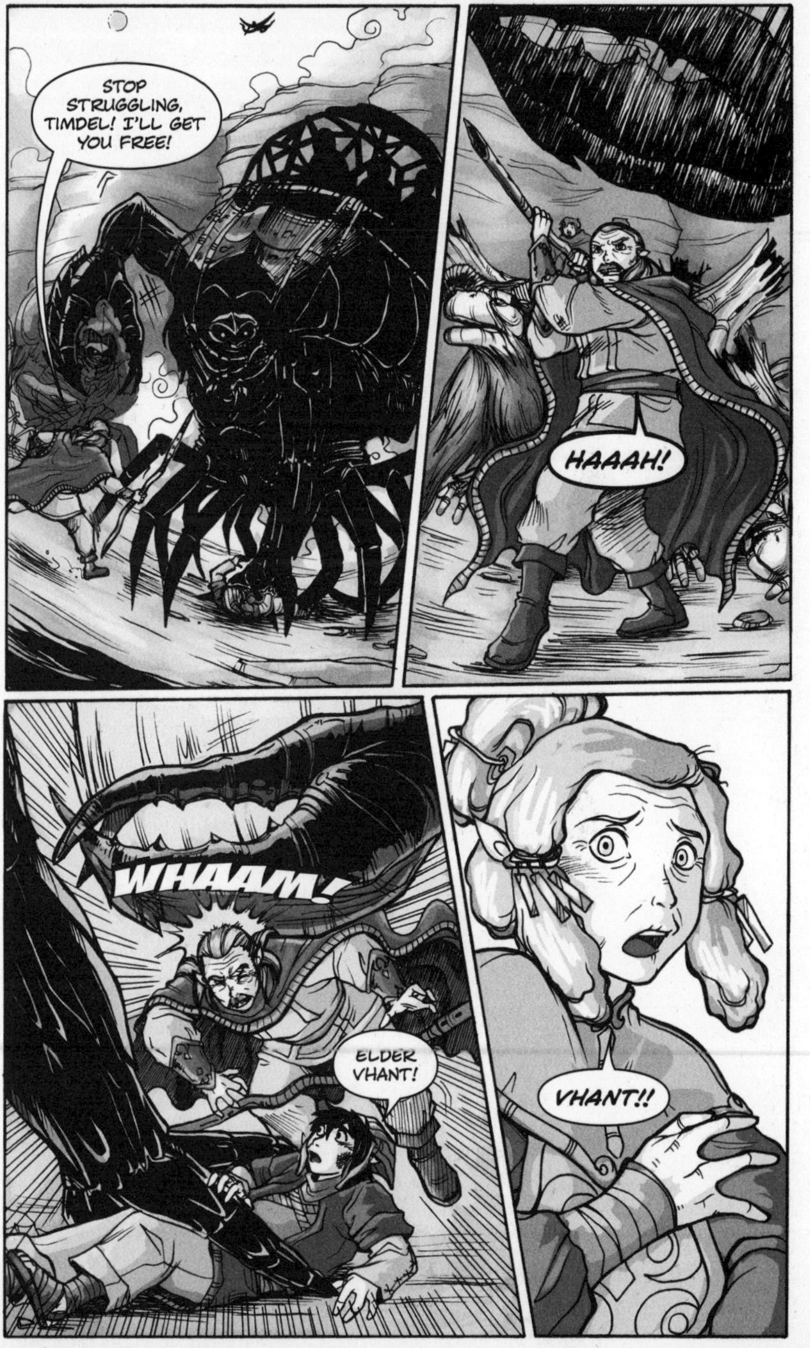
STOP STRUGGLING, TIMDEL! I'LL GET YOU FREE!
HAAAH!
WHAAM!
ELDER VHANT!
VHANT!!

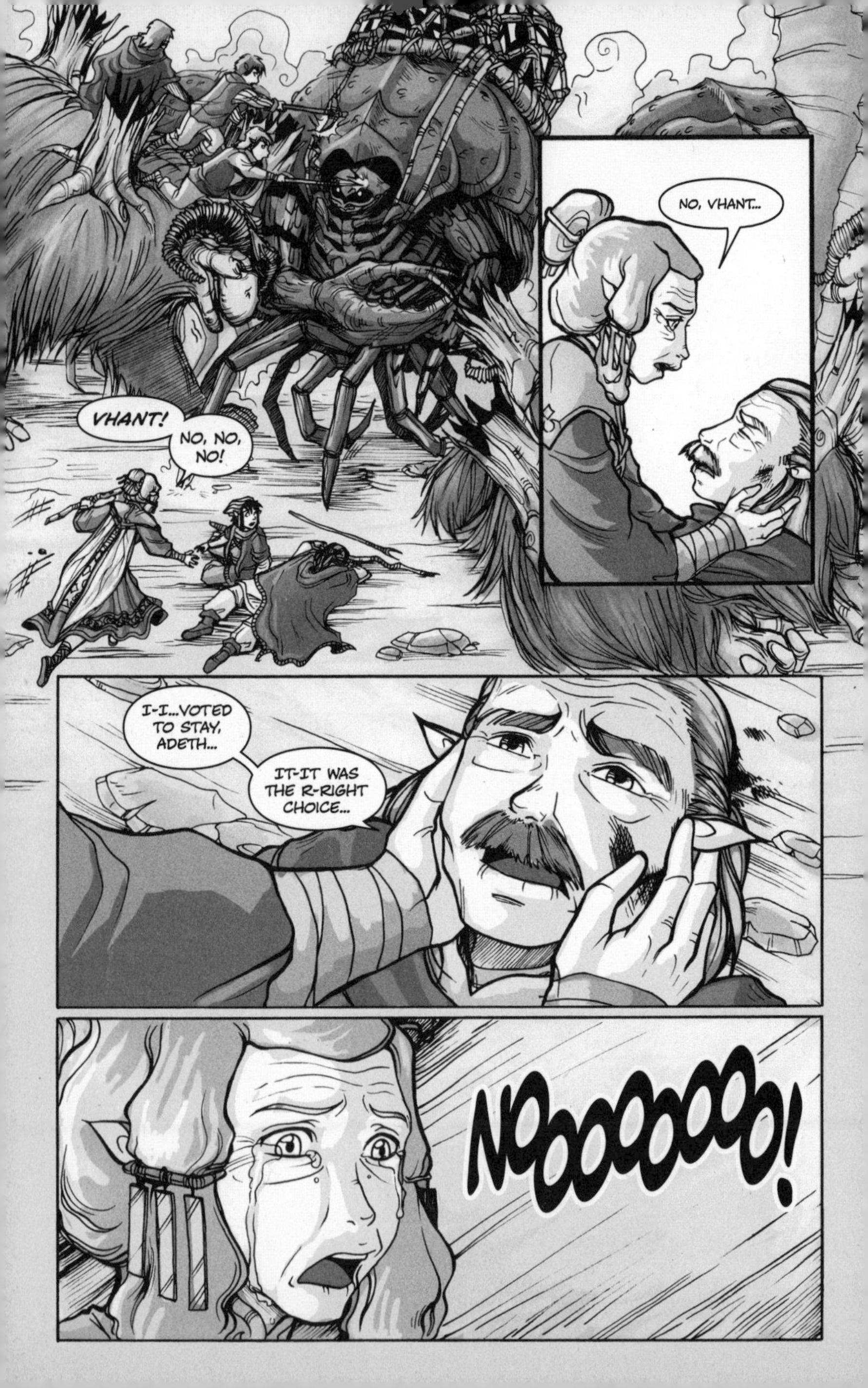
VHANT!
NO, NO, NO!
NO, VHANT...
I-I...VOTED TO STAY, ADETH...
IT-IT WAS THE R-RIGHT CHOICE...
NOOOOOOO!

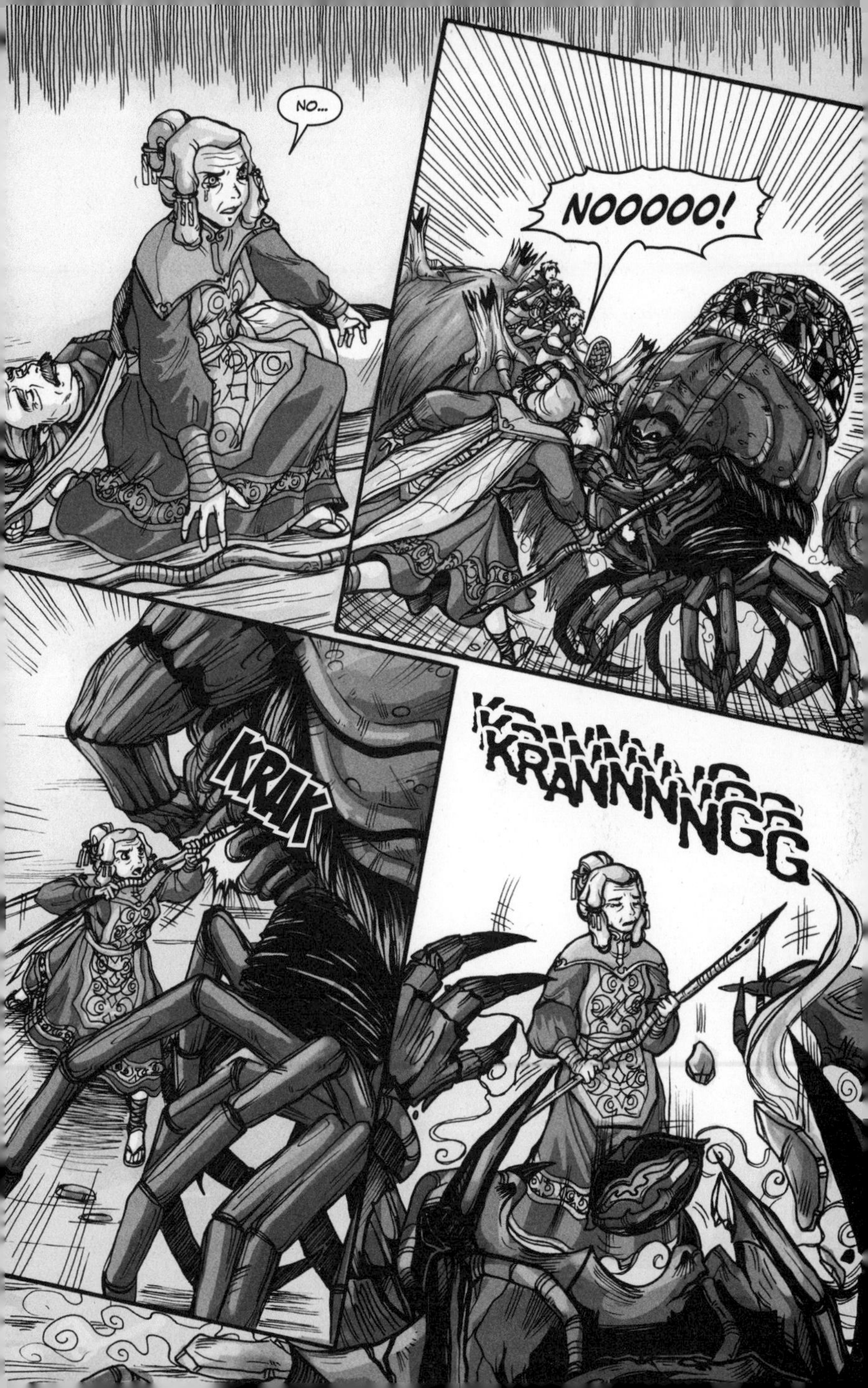
NO...
NOOOOO!
KRAK
KRANNNNNGG

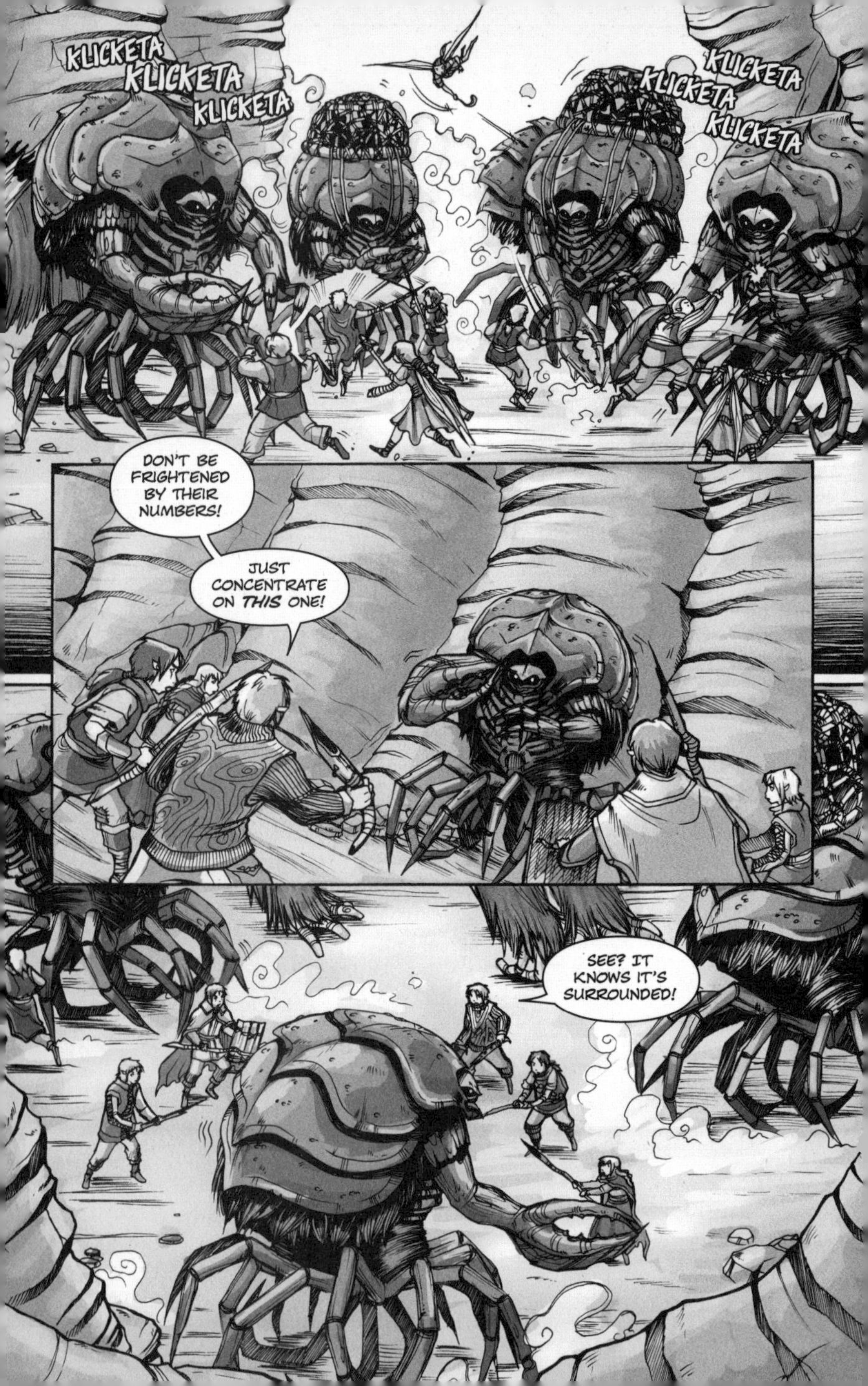
KLICKETA KLICKETA KLICKETA
KLICKETA KLICKETA KLICKETA
DON'T BE FRIGHTENED BY THEIR NUMBERS!
JUST CONCENTRATE ON *THIS* ONE!
SEE? IT KNOWS IT'S SURROUNDED!

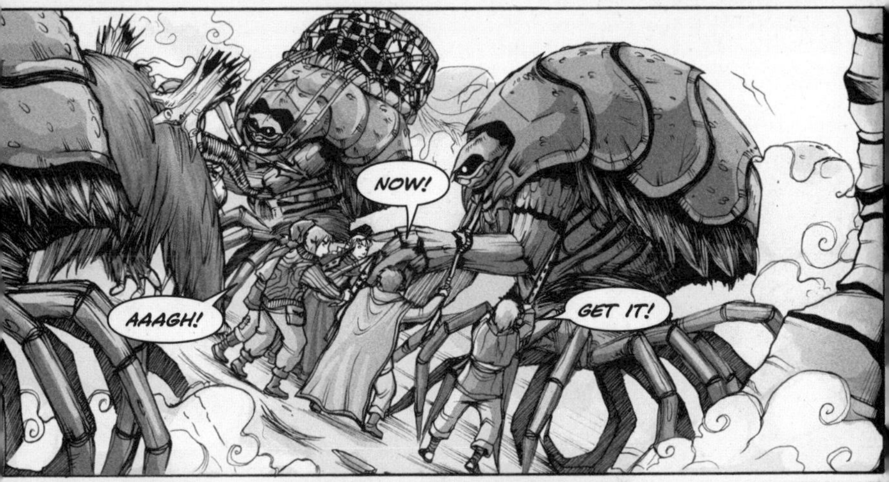
NOW!
AAAGH!
GET IT!

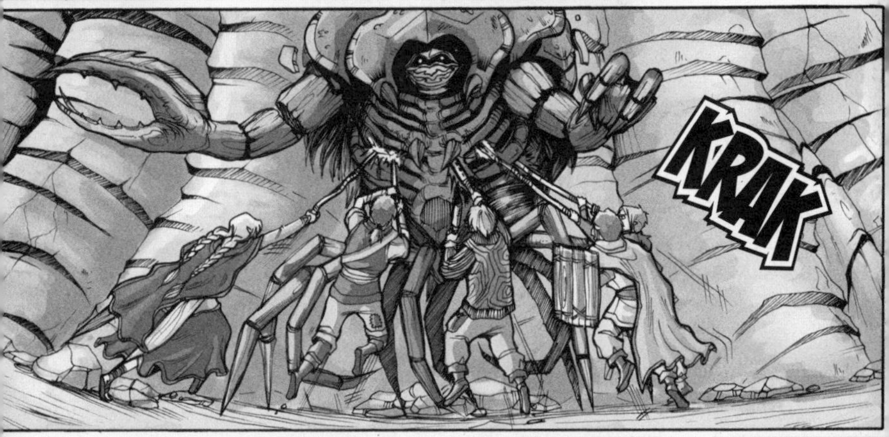
KRAK

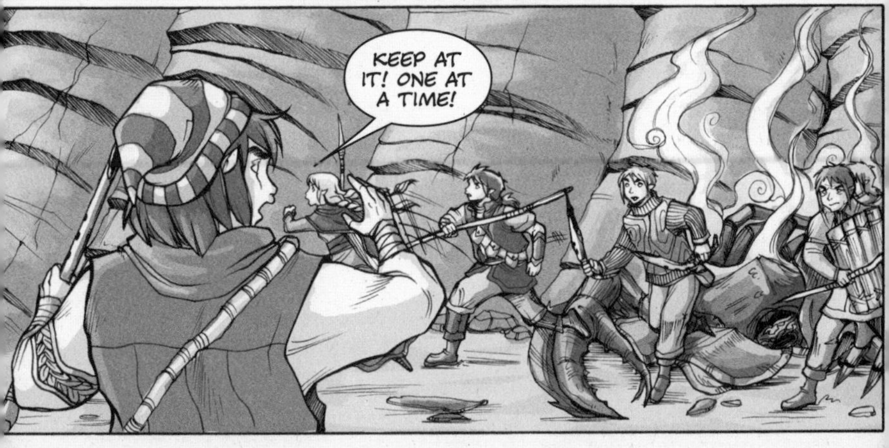
KEEP AT IT! ONE AT A TIME!

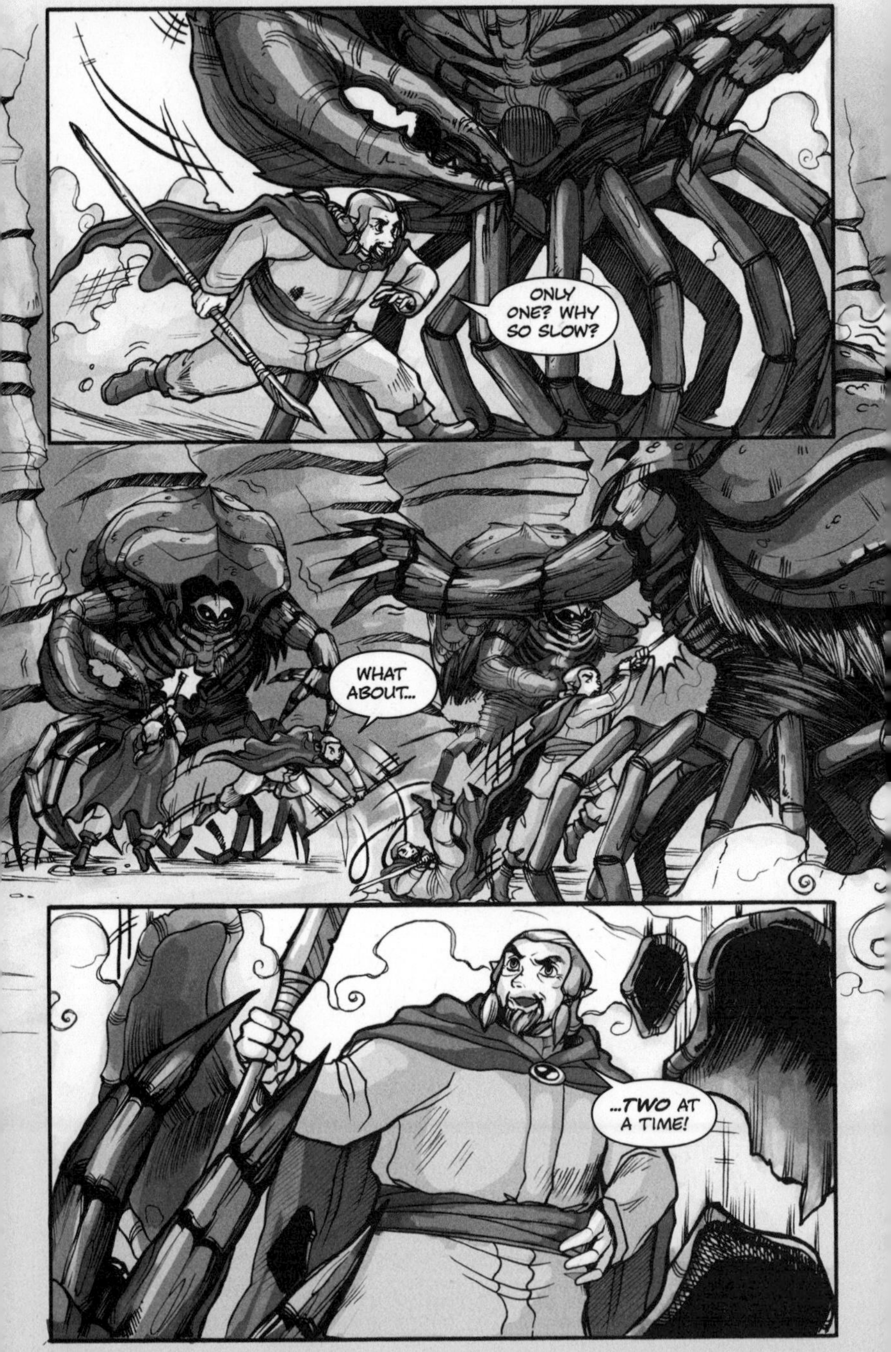
ONLY ONE? WHY SO SLOW?
WHAT ABOUT...
...TWO AT A TIME!

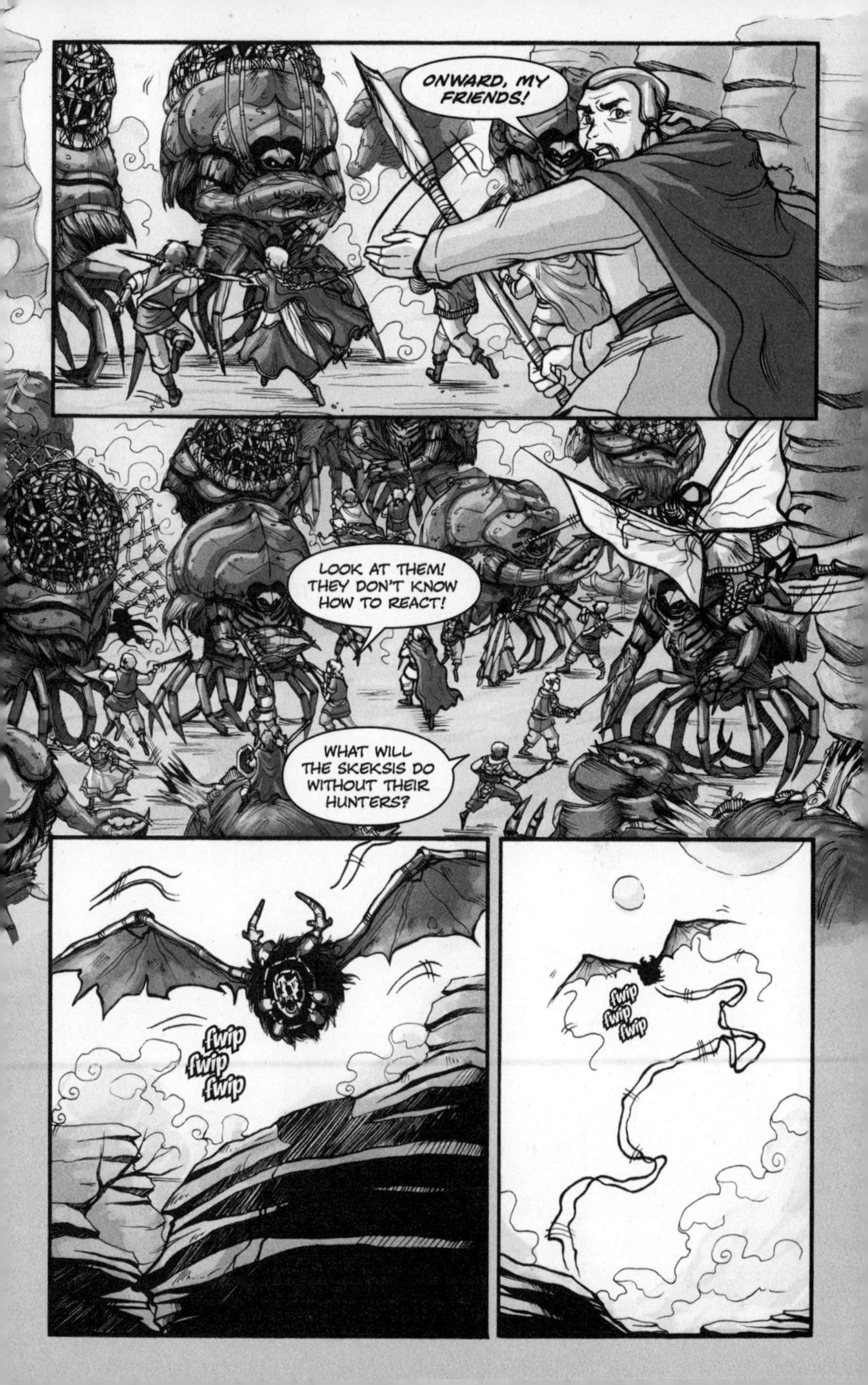
ONWARD, MY FRIENDS!
LOOK AT THEM! THEY DON'T KNOW HOW TO REACT!
WHAT WILL THE SKEKSIS DO WITHOUT THEIR HUNTERS?
fwip fwip fwip
fwip fwip fwip

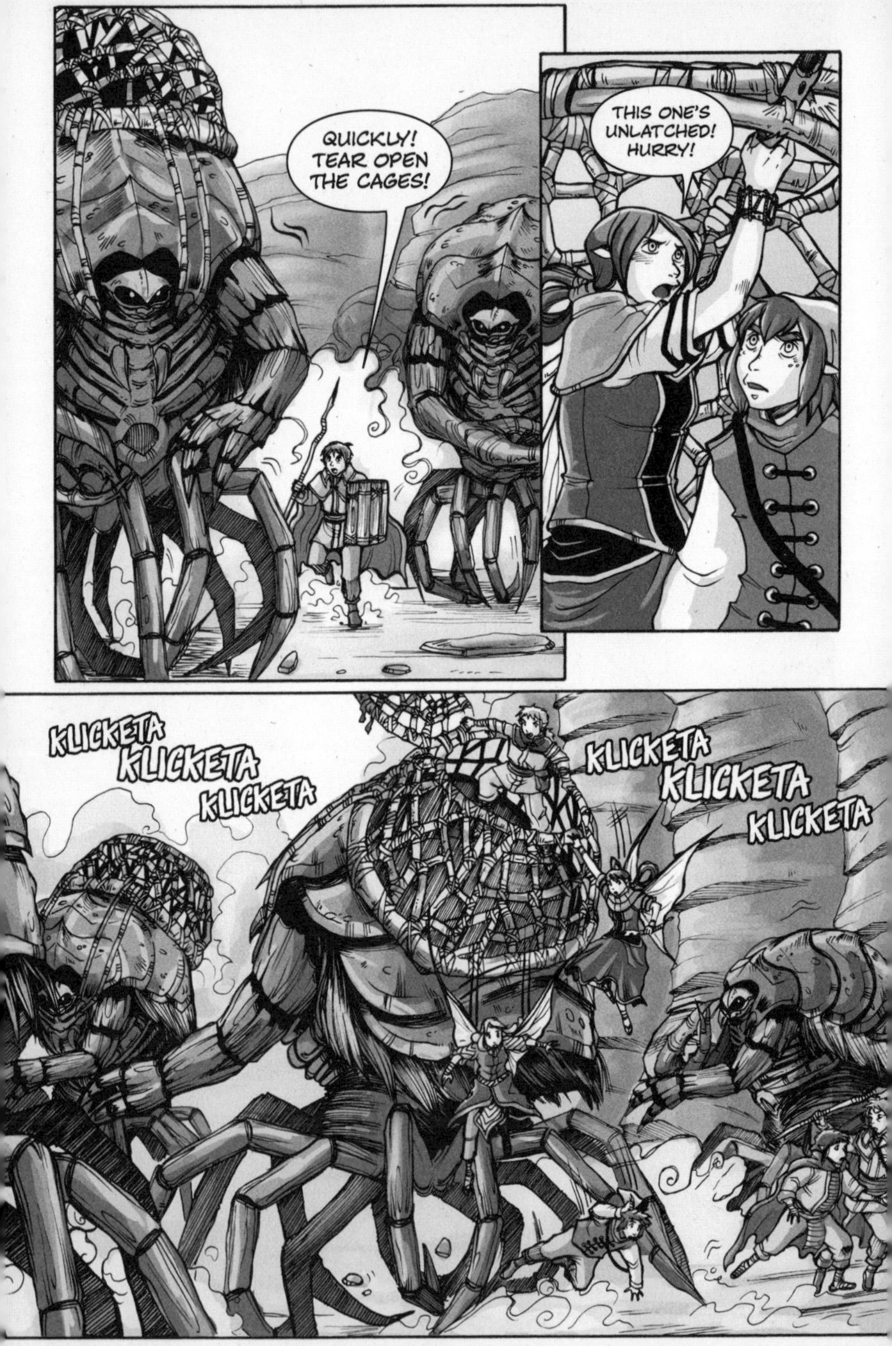
QUICKLY! TEAR OPEN THE CAGES!
THIS ONE'S UNLATCHED! HURRY!
KLICKETA KLICKETA KLICKETA
KLICKETA KLICKETA KLICKETA

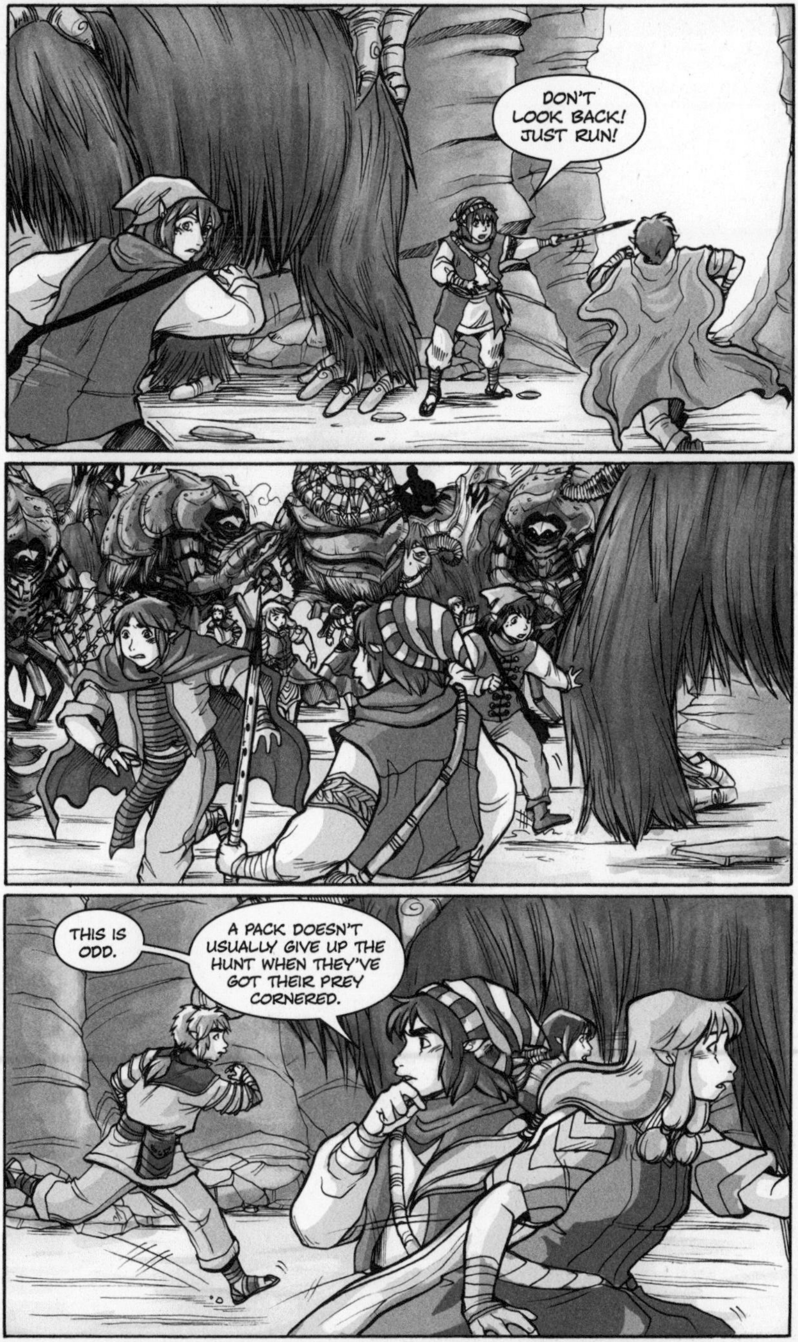
DON'T LOOK BACK! JUST RUN!
THIS IS ODD.
A PACK DOESN'T USUALLY GIVE UP THE HUNT WHEN THEY'VE GOT THEIR PREY CORNERED.

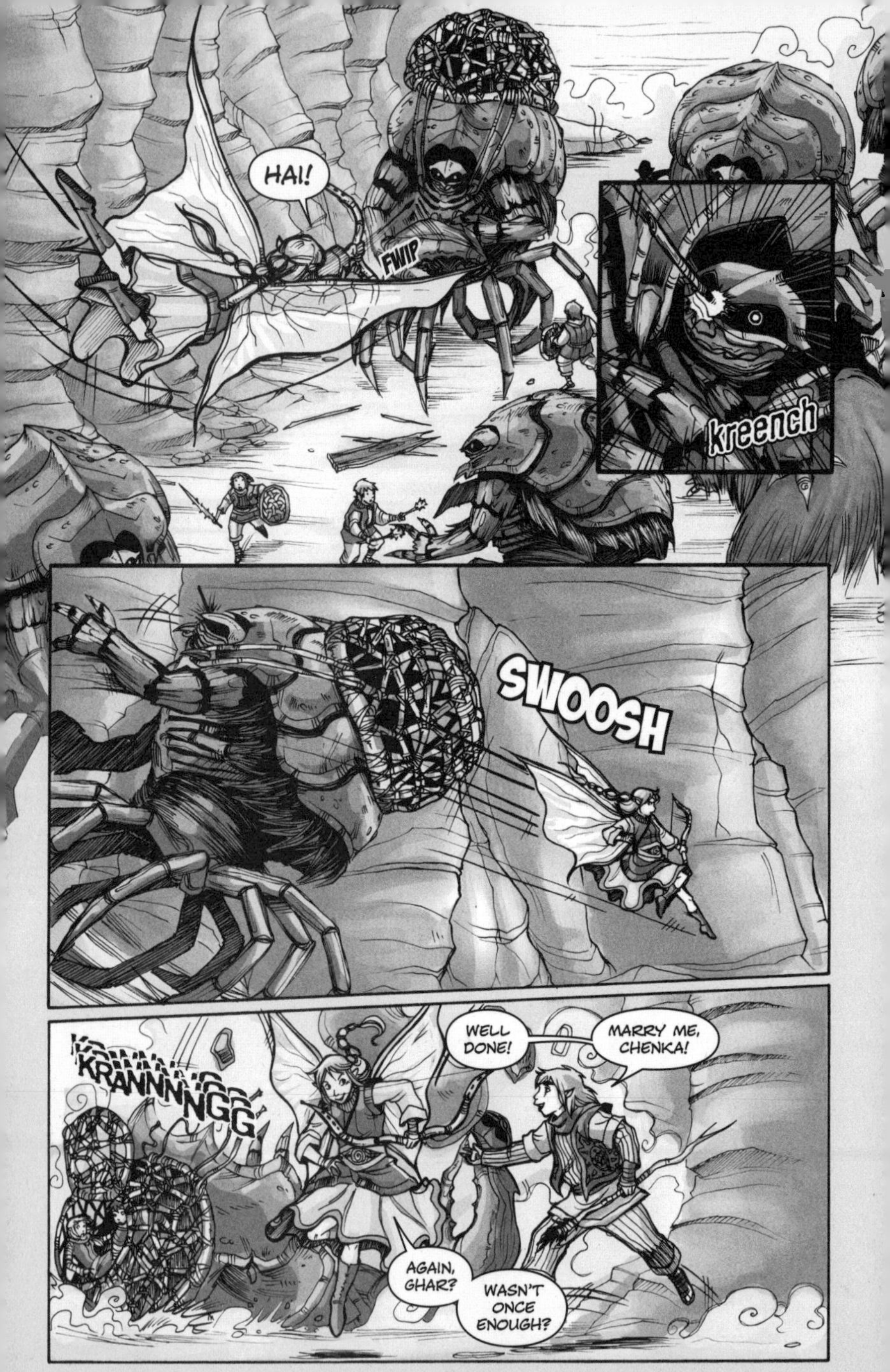
HAI!
FWIP
kreench
SWOOSH
KRANNNNGG
WELL DONE!
MARRY ME, CHENKA!
AGAIN, GHAR?
WASN'T ONCE ENOUGH?

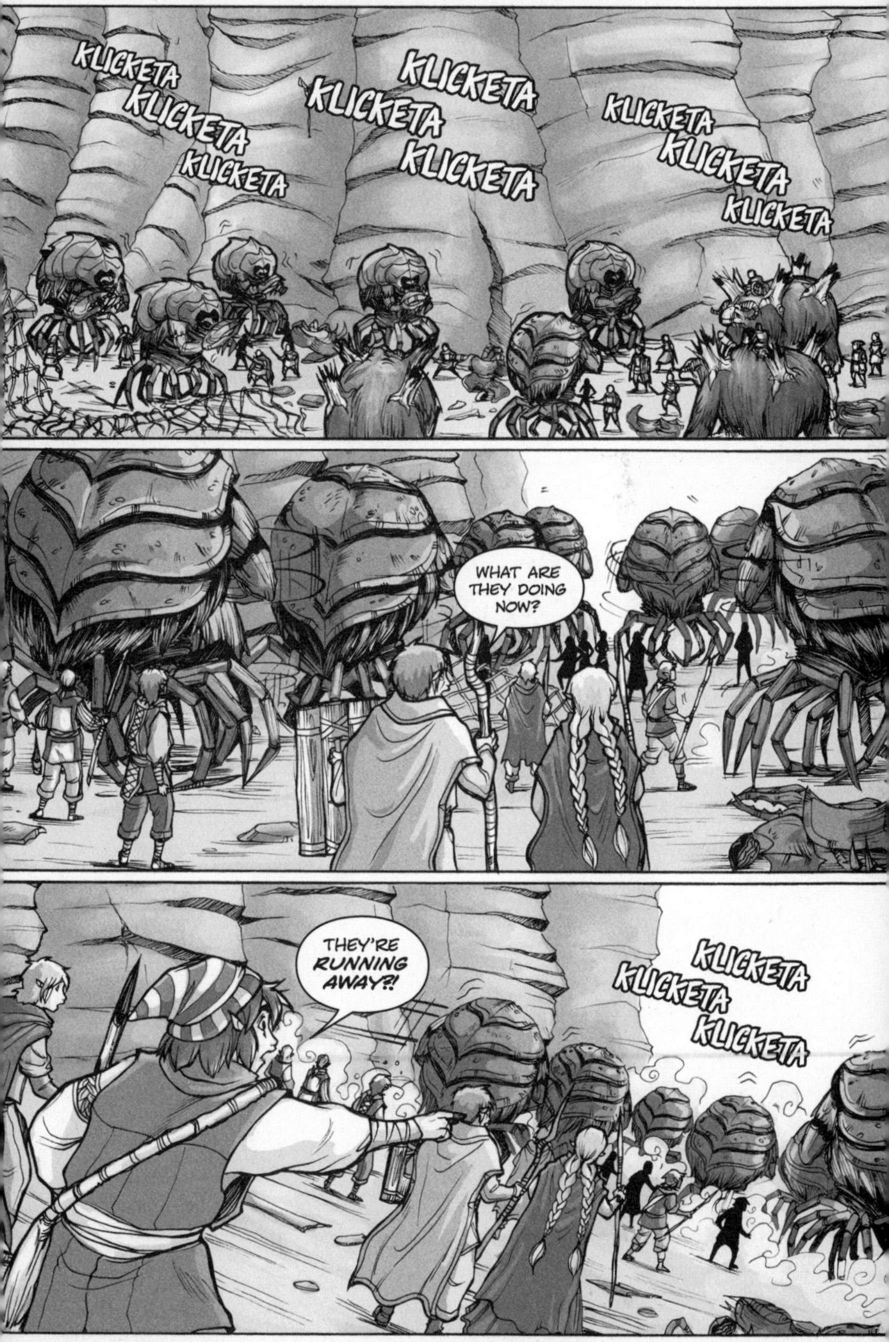
KLICKETA
KLICKETA
KLICKETA
KLICKETA
KLICKETA
KLICKETA
KLICKETA
KLICKETA
KLICKETA
WHAT ARE THEY DOING NOW?
THEY'RE *RUNNING AWAY?!*
KLICKETA
KLICKETA
KLICKETA

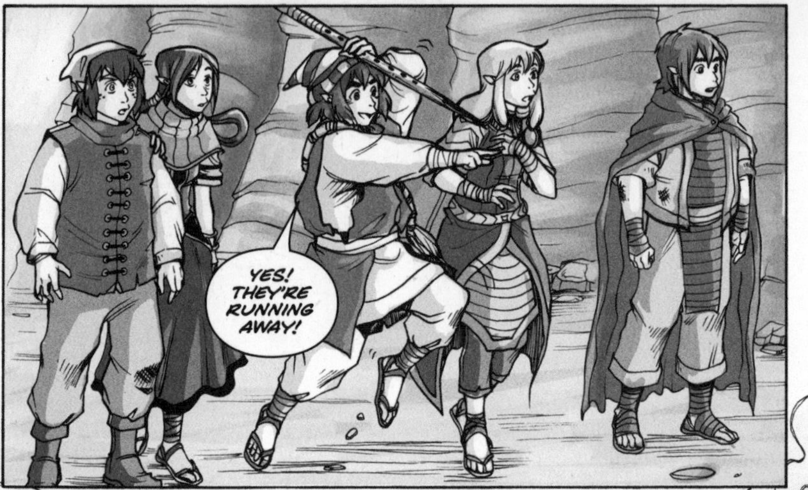
YES! THEY'RE RUNNING AWAY!

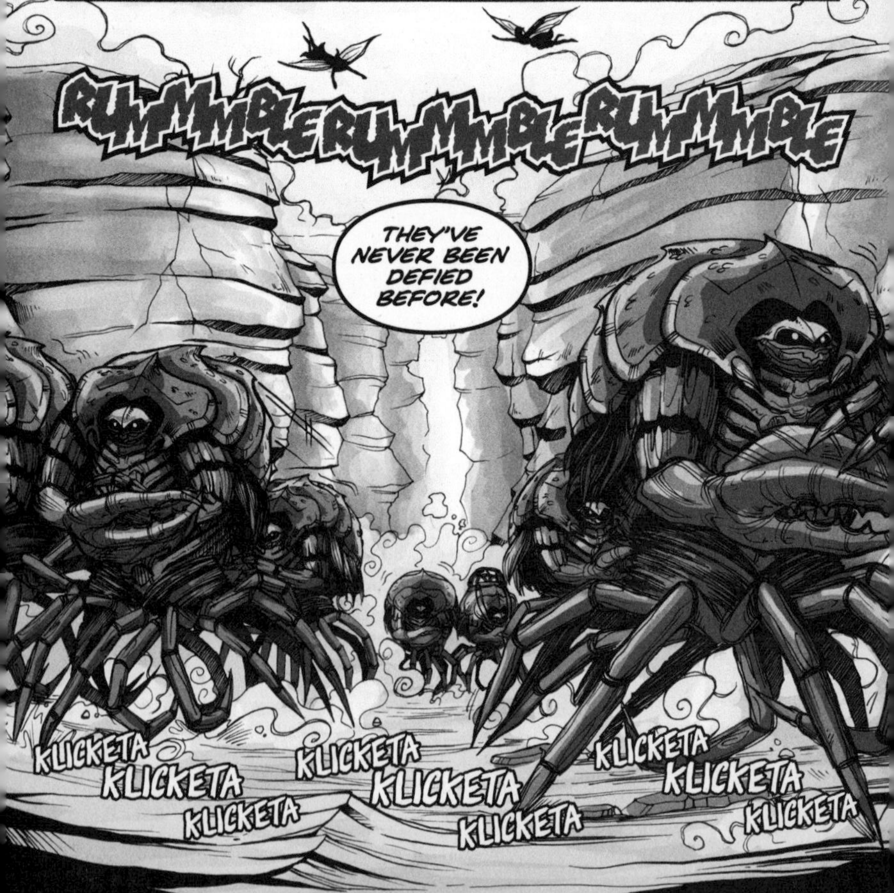
RUMMMMBLE RUMMMMBLE RUMMMMBLE
THEY'VE NEVER BEEN DEFIED BEFORE!
KLICKETA KLICKETA KLICKETA
KLICKETA KLICKETA KLICKETA
KLICKETA KLICKETA KLICKETA

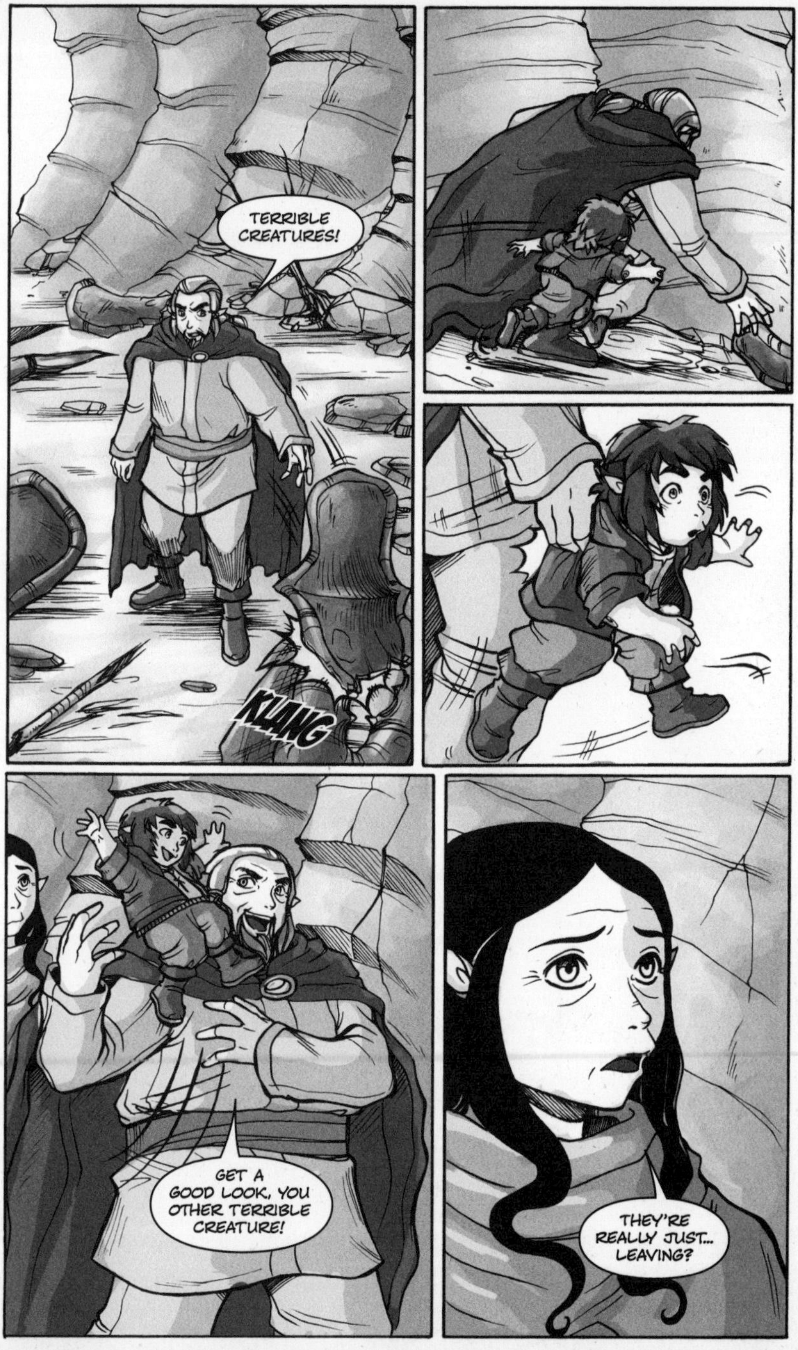

TERRIBLE CREATURES!
KLANG
GET A GOOD LOOK, YOU OTHER TERRIBLE CREATURE!
THEY'RE REALLY JUST... LEAVING?

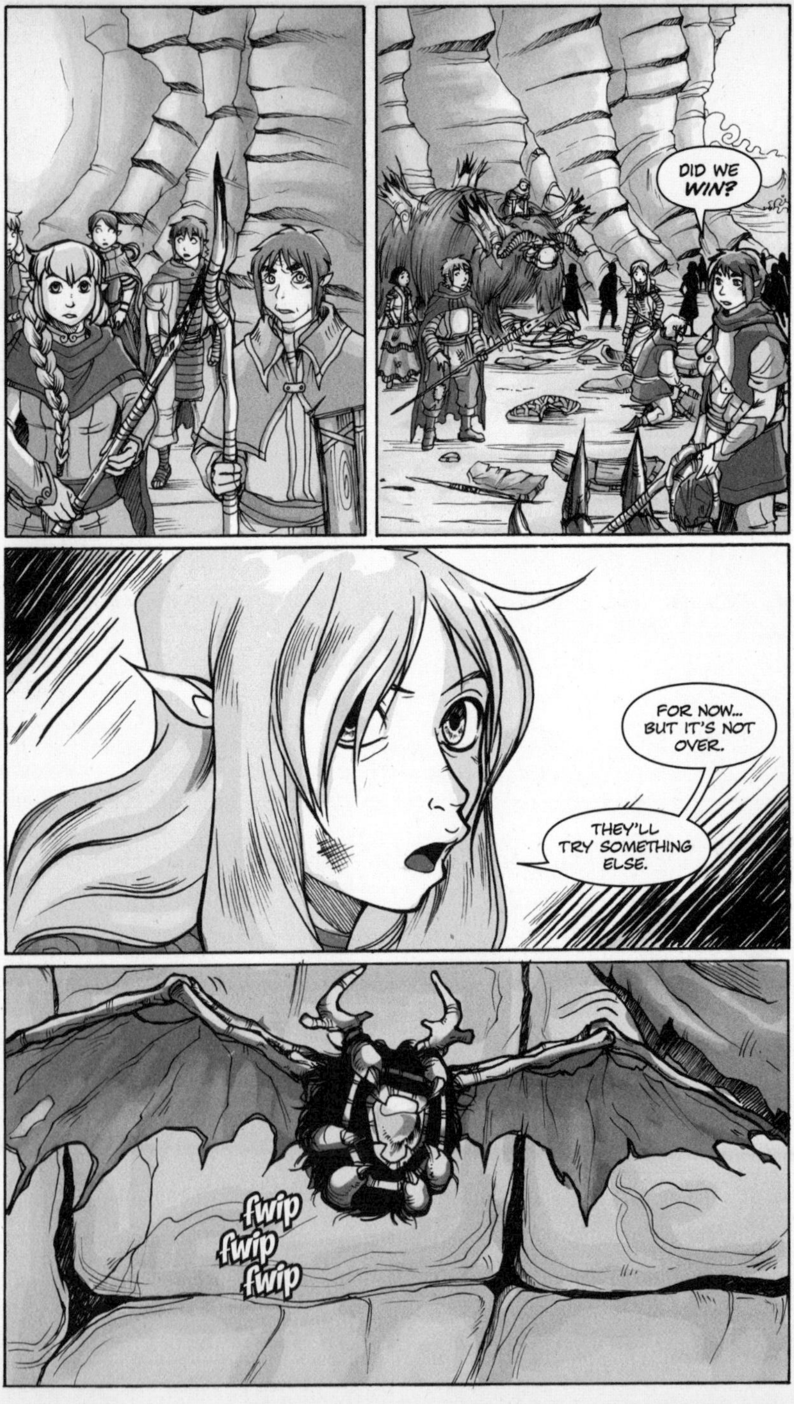
DID WE WIN?
FOR NOW... BUT IT'S NOT OVER.
THEY'LL TRY SOMETHING ELSE.
fwip
fwip
fwip

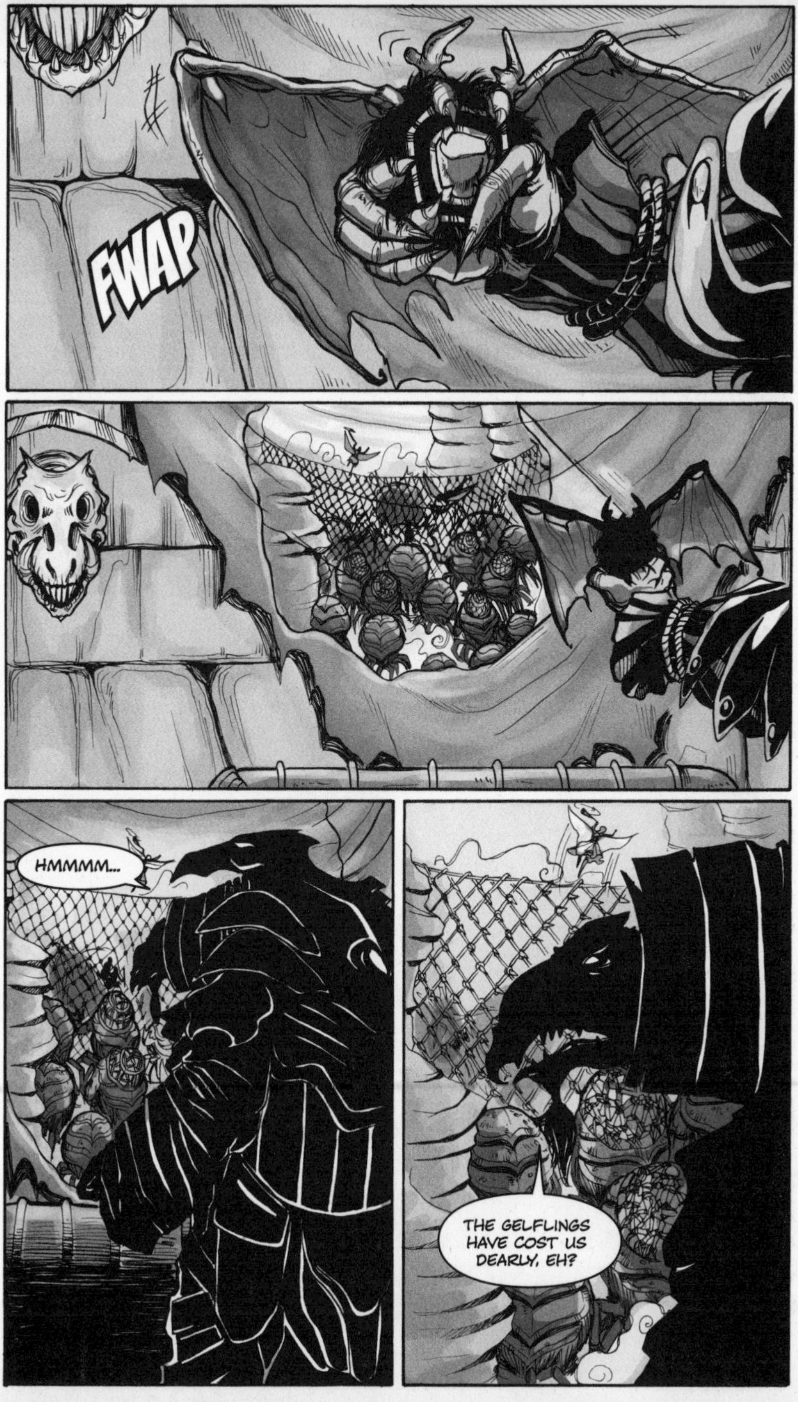
FWAP
HMMMM...
THE GELFLINGS HAVE COST US DEARLY, EH?

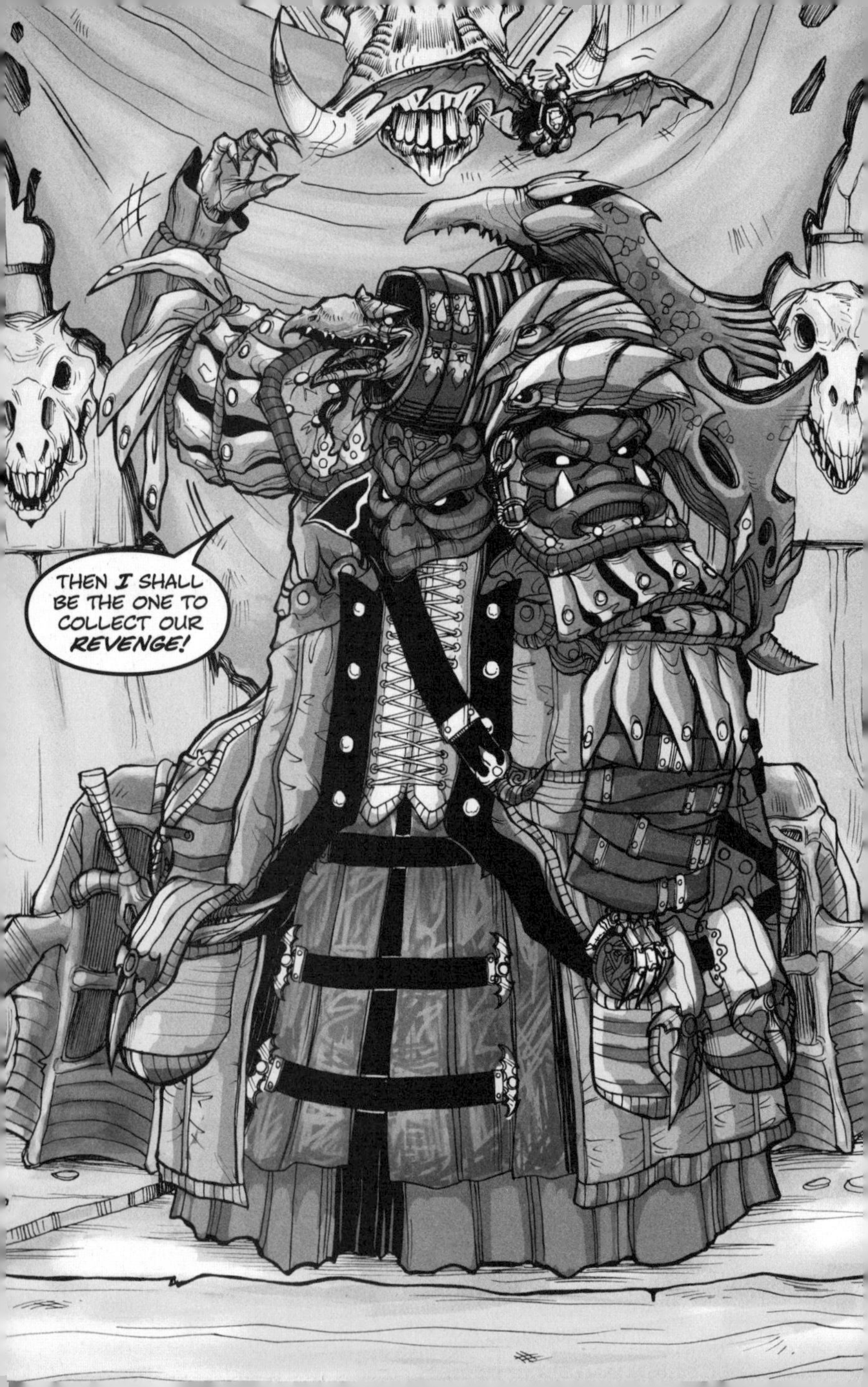
THEN *I* SHALL BE THE ONE TO COLLECT OUR *REVENGE!*

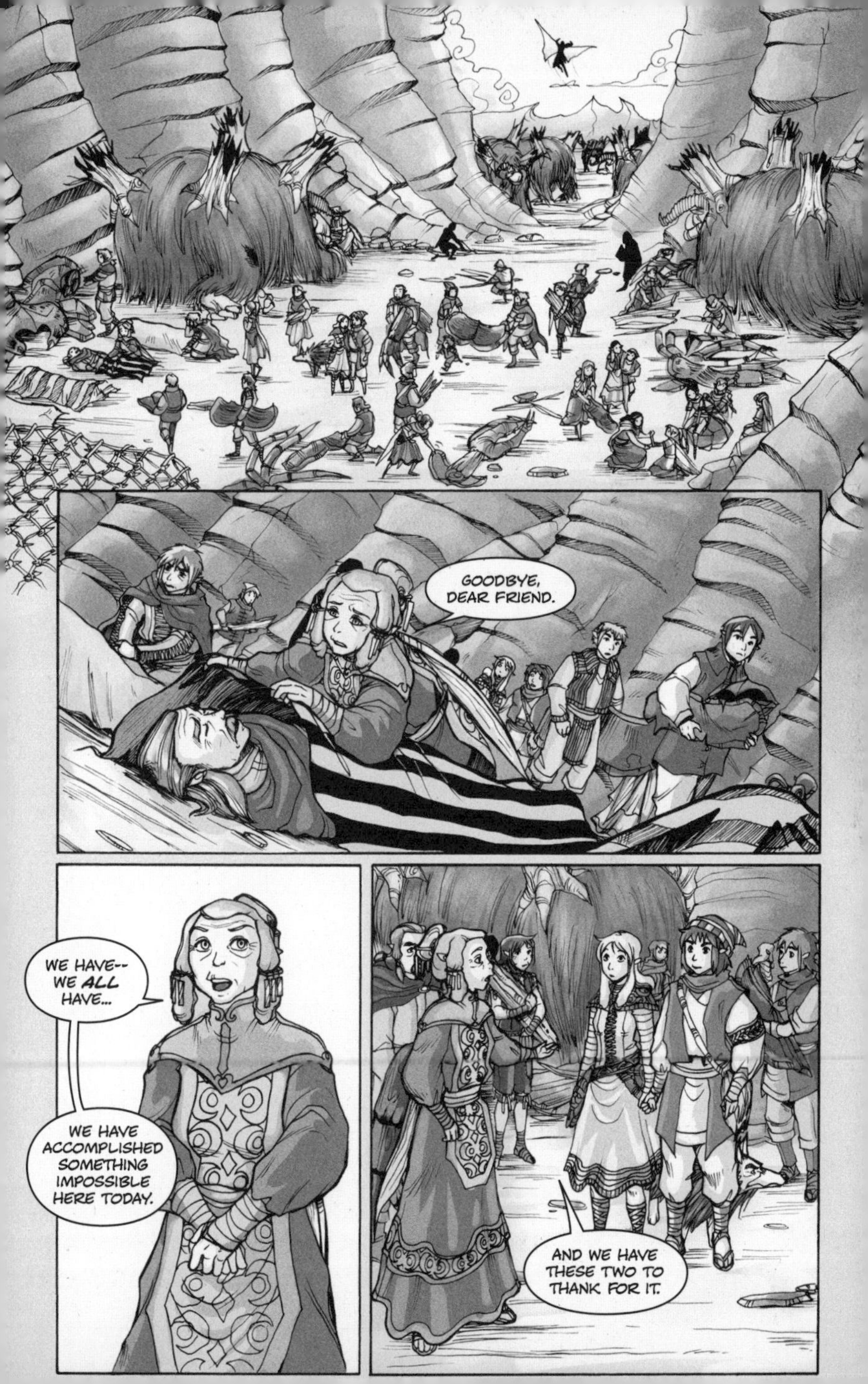
GOODBYE, DEAR FRIEND.
WE HAVE-- WE ALL HAVE...
WE HAVE ACCOMPLISHED SOMETHING IMPOSSIBLE HERE TODAY.
AND WE HAVE THESE TWO TO THANK FOR IT.

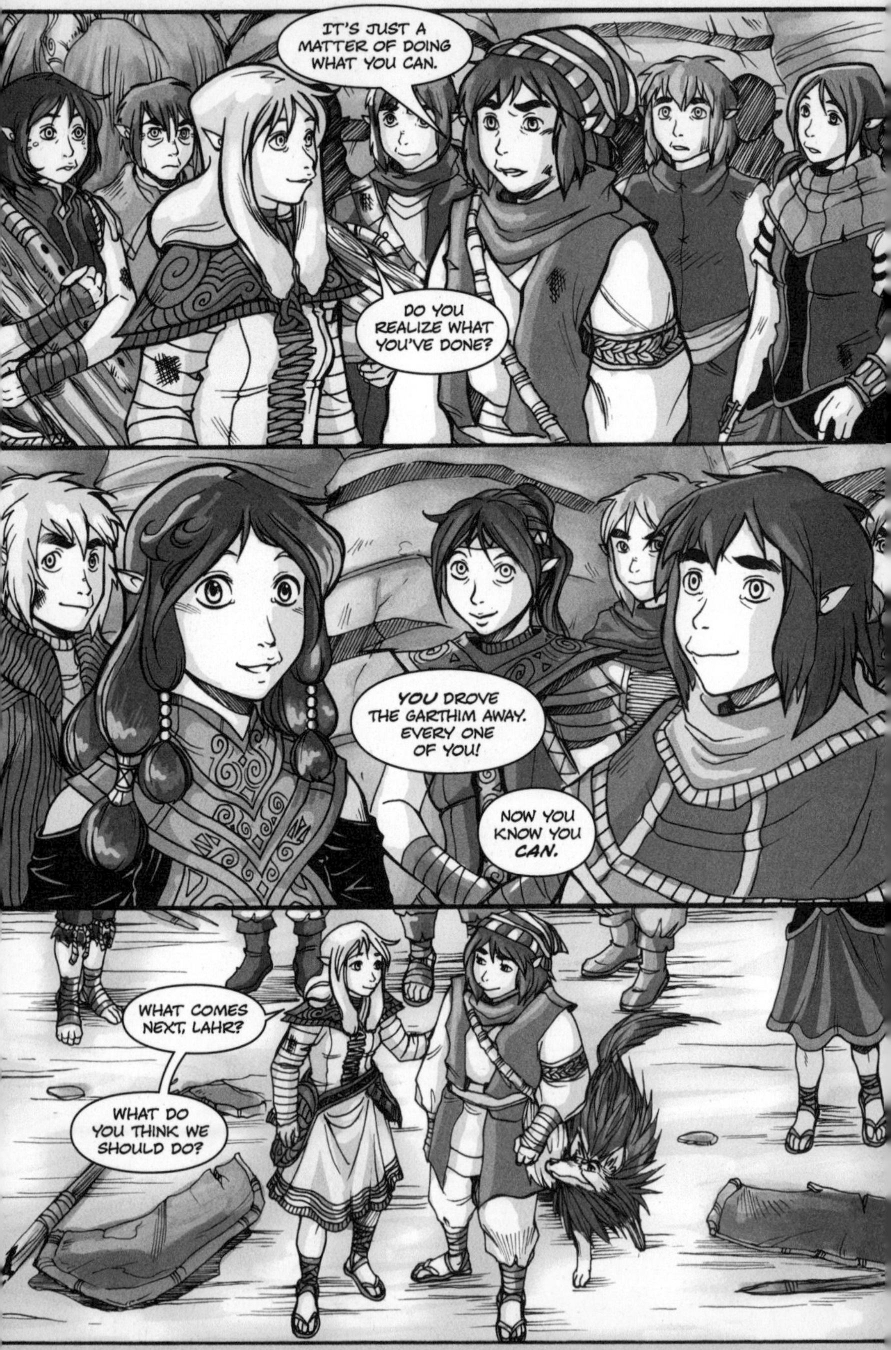
IT'S JUST A MATTER OF DOING WHAT YOU CAN.
DO YOU REALIZE WHAT YOU'VE DONE?
YOU DROVE THE GARTHIM AWAY. EVERY ONE OF YOU!
NOW YOU KNOW YOU CAN.
WHAT COMES NEXT, LAHR?
WHAT DO YOU THINK WE SHOULD DO?

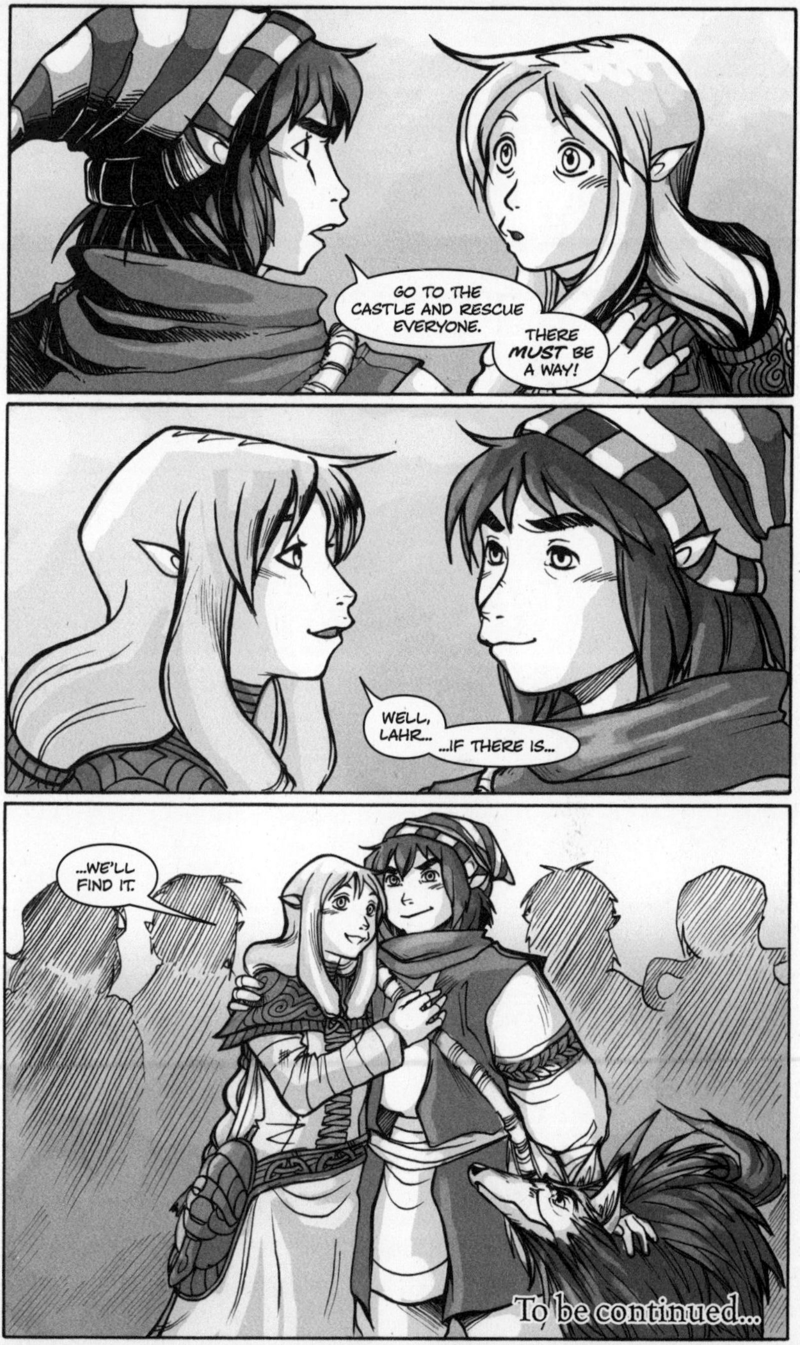
GO TO THE CASTLE AND RESCUE EVERYONE.
THERE *MUST* BE A WAY!
WELL, LAHR...
...IF THERE IS...
...WE'LL FIND IT.
To be continued...

A Mystic Prophecy

When music staves off vile attack
And staff and loom are joined in love,
Two heroes shall on a quest depart,
Observed by beasts from high above.
Two shall enter, two shall return
From castle tall and dungeon deep,
But look to them with fear and dread,
For one hero does a dark secret keep.

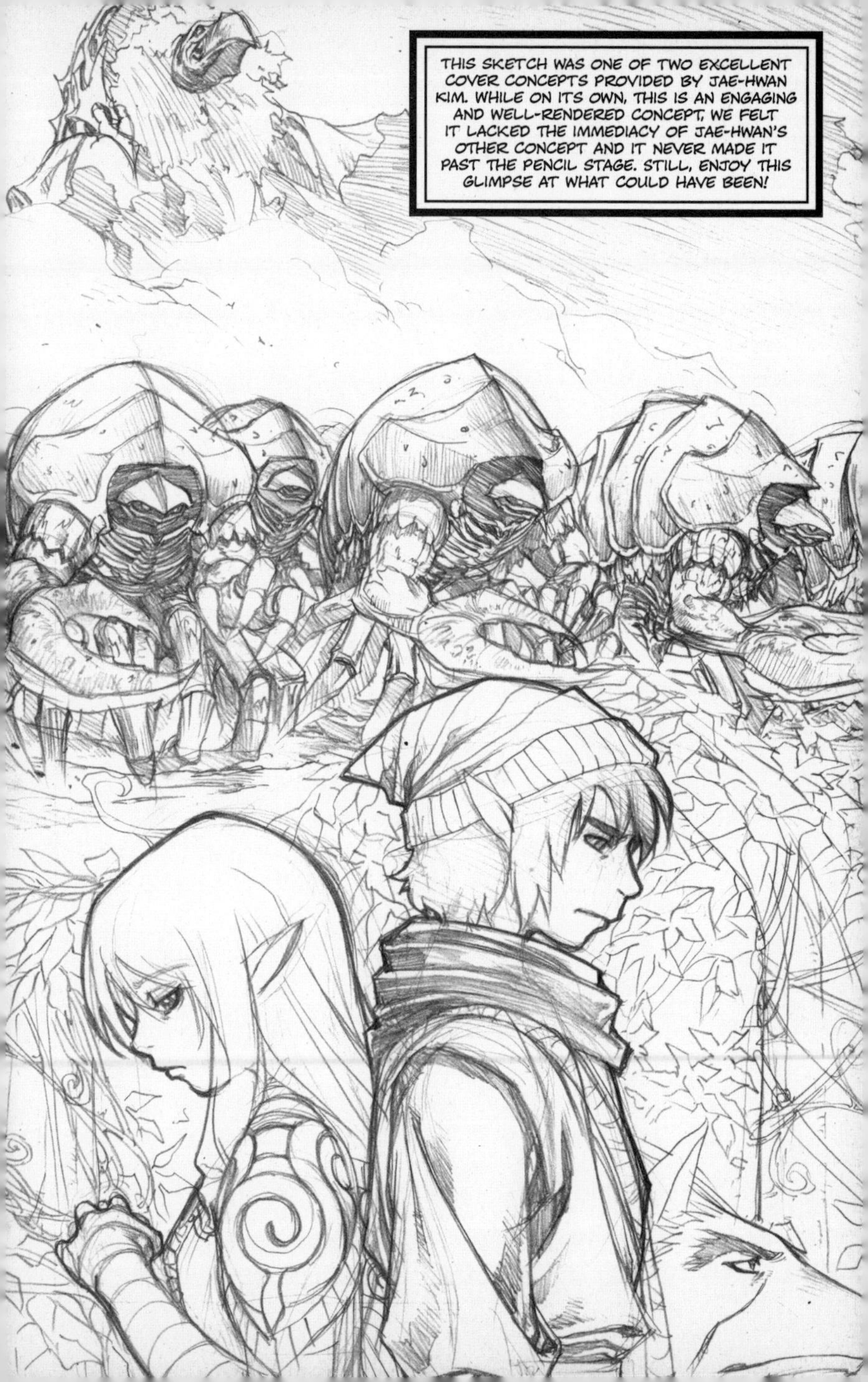

THIS SKETCH WAS ONE OF TWO EXCELLENT COVER CONCEPTS PROVIDED BY JAE-HWAN KIM. WHILE ON ITS OWN, THIS IS AN ENGAGING AND WELL-RENDERED CONCEPT, WE FELT IT LACKED THE IMMEDIACY OF JAE-HWAN'S OTHER CONCEPT AND IT NEVER MADE IT PAST THE PENCIL STAGE. STILL, ENJOY THIS GLIMPSE AT WHAT COULD HAVE BEEN!

Guest Art Gallery

Chris Lie

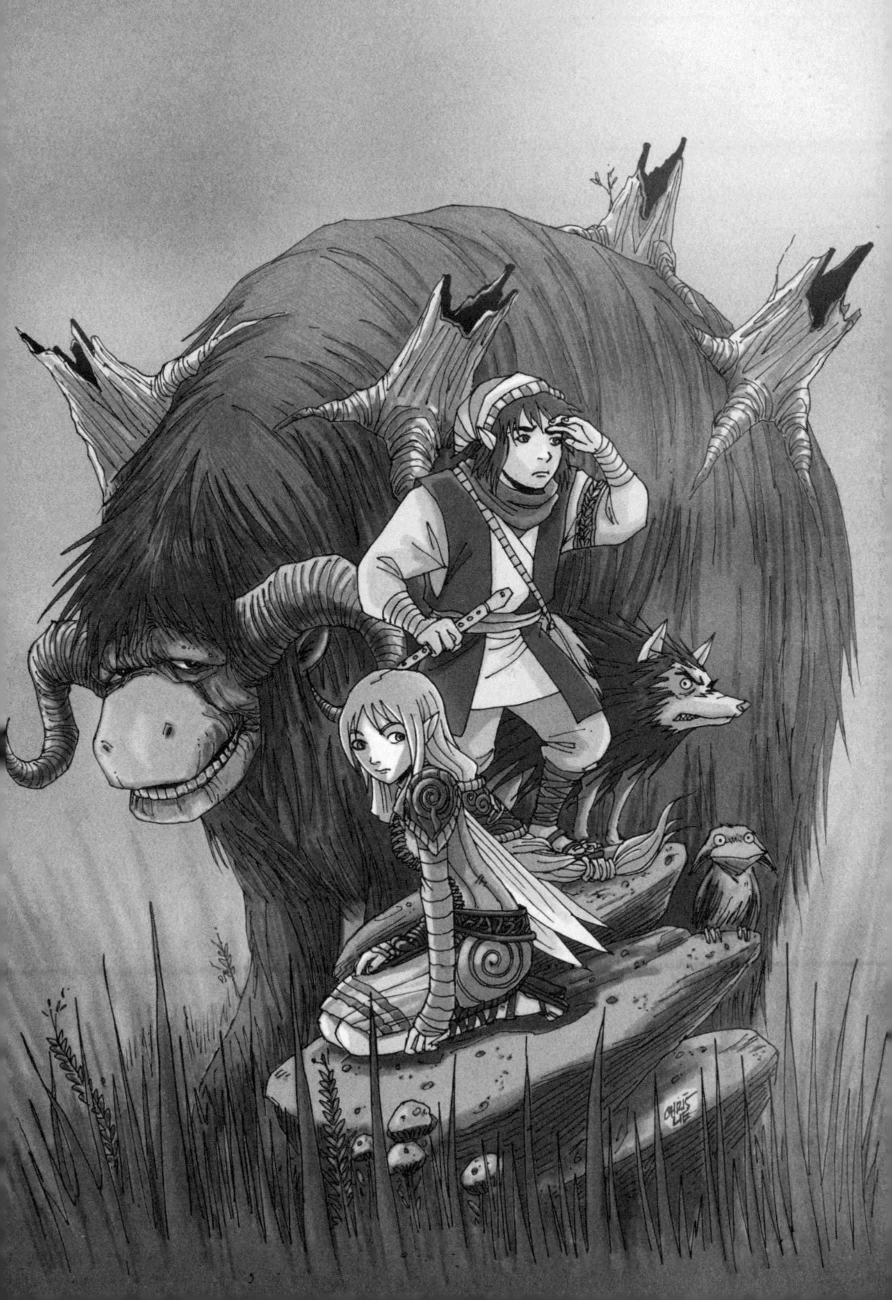
CHRIS LIE

M. Alice LeGrow

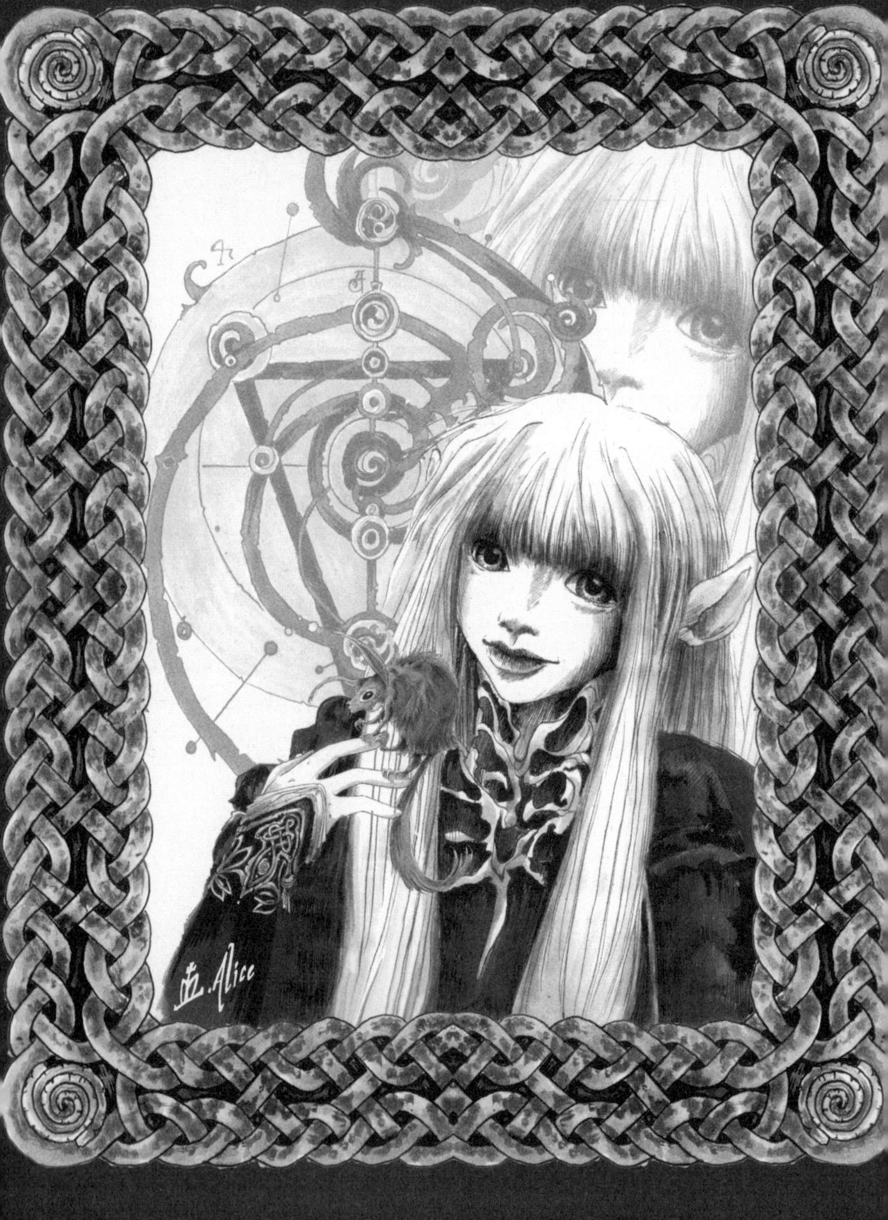

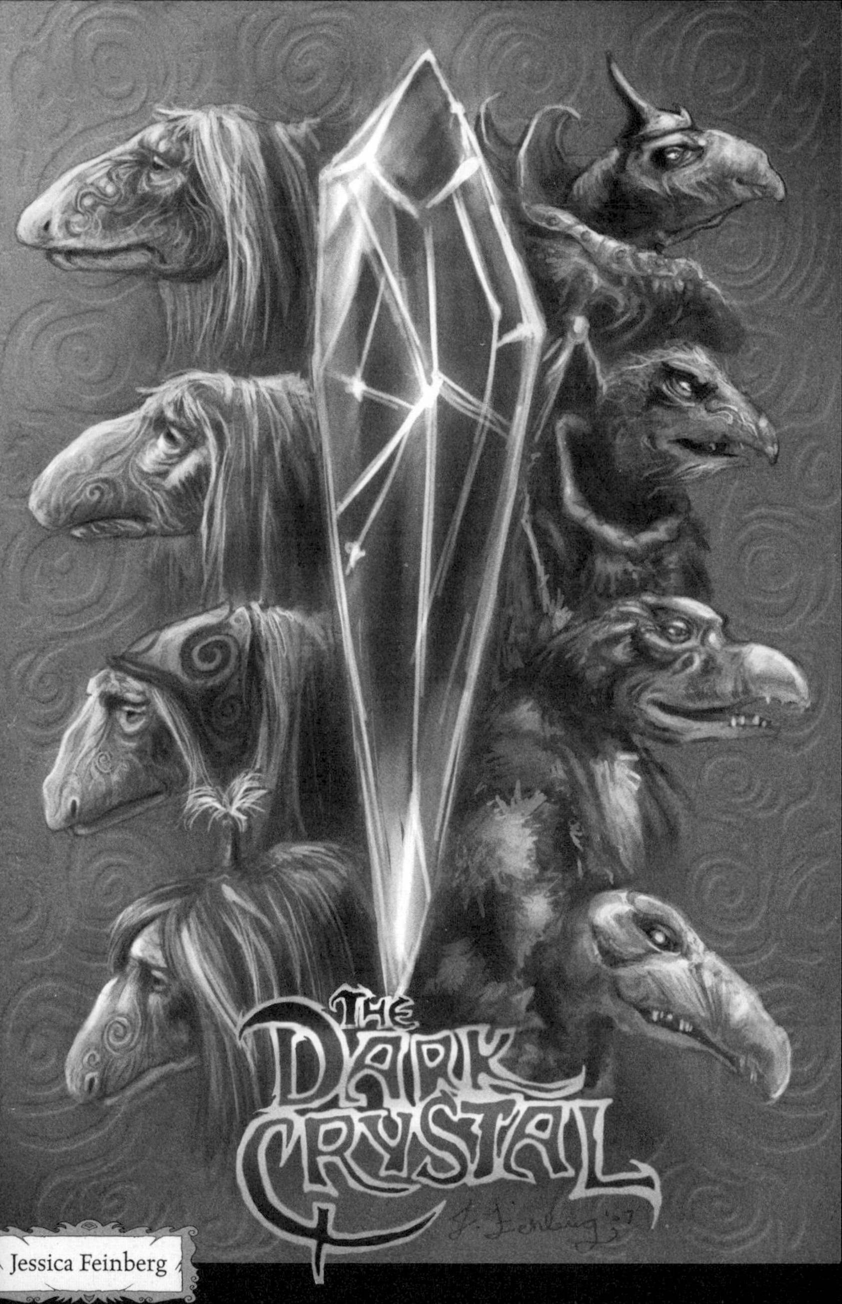
THE
DARK
CRYSTAL

Jessica Feinberg

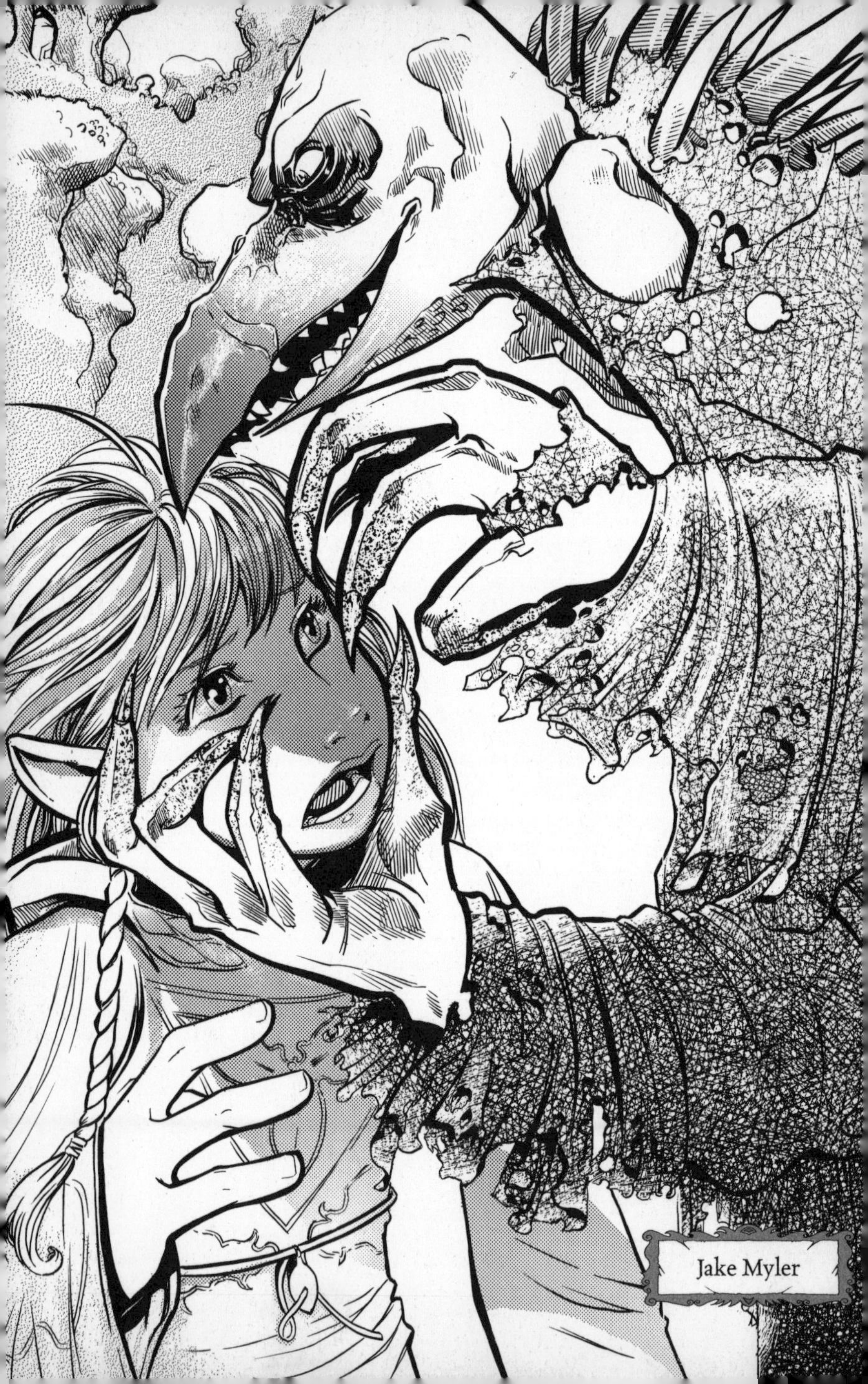
Jake Myler

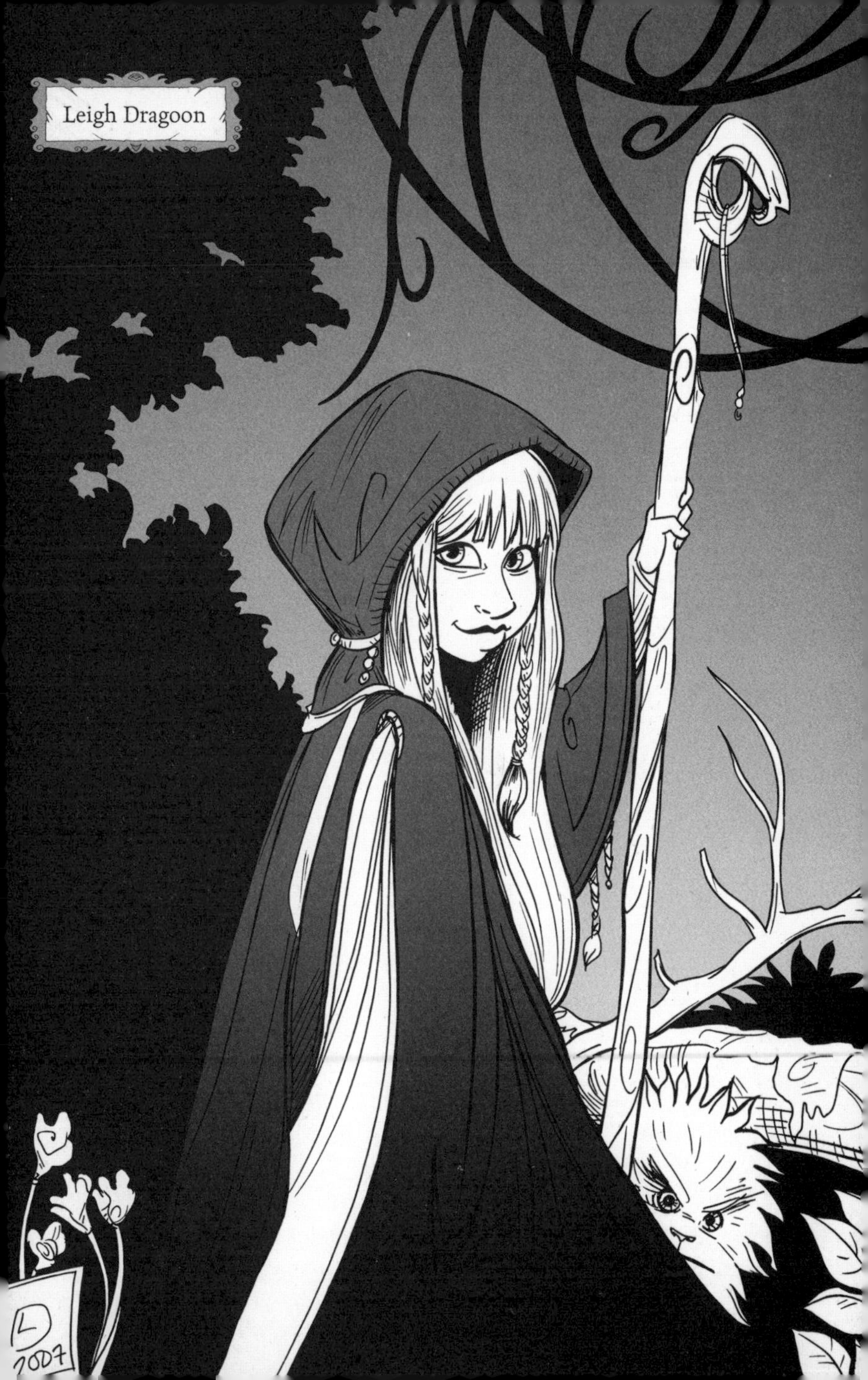
Leigh Dragoon

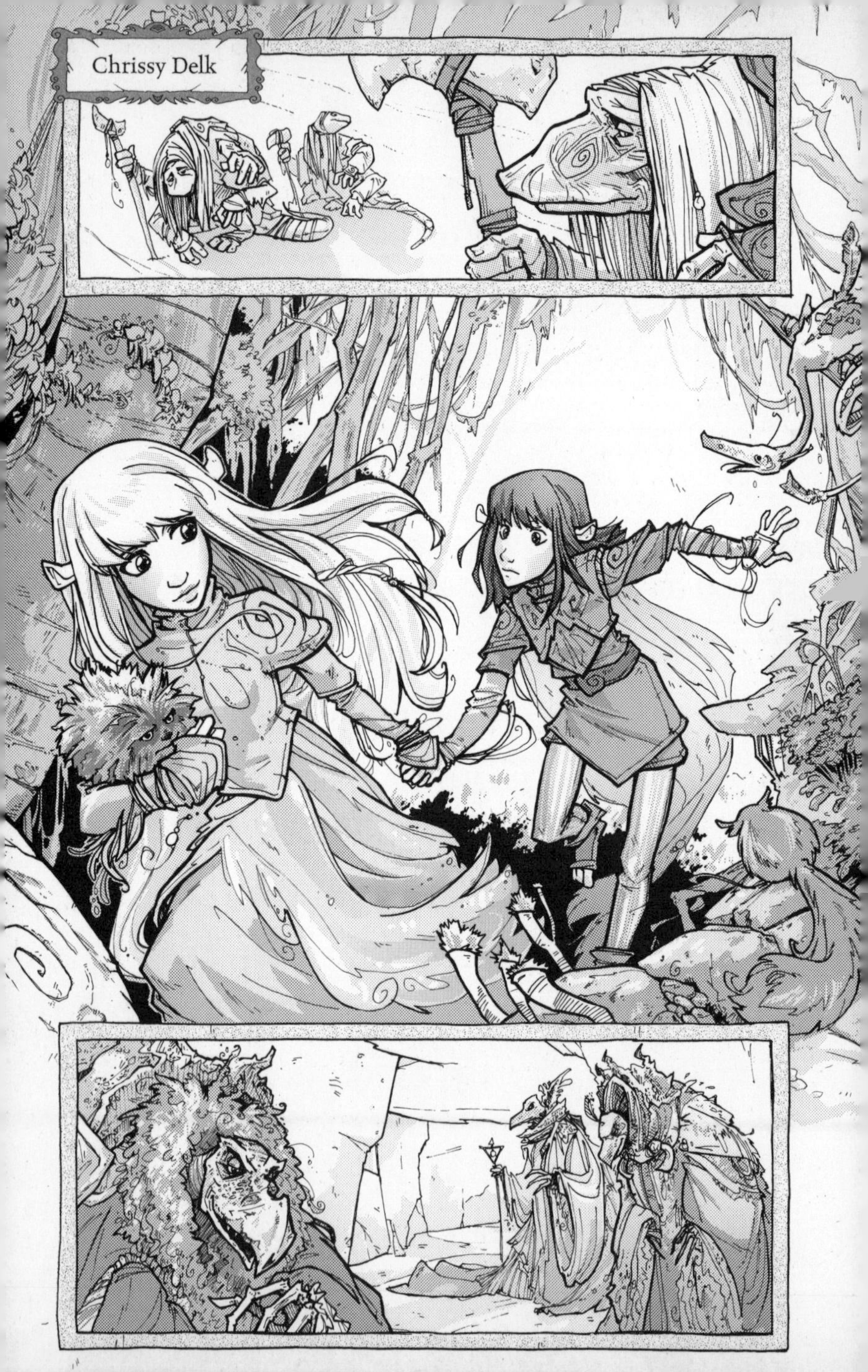
Chrissy Delk

Erica Reis

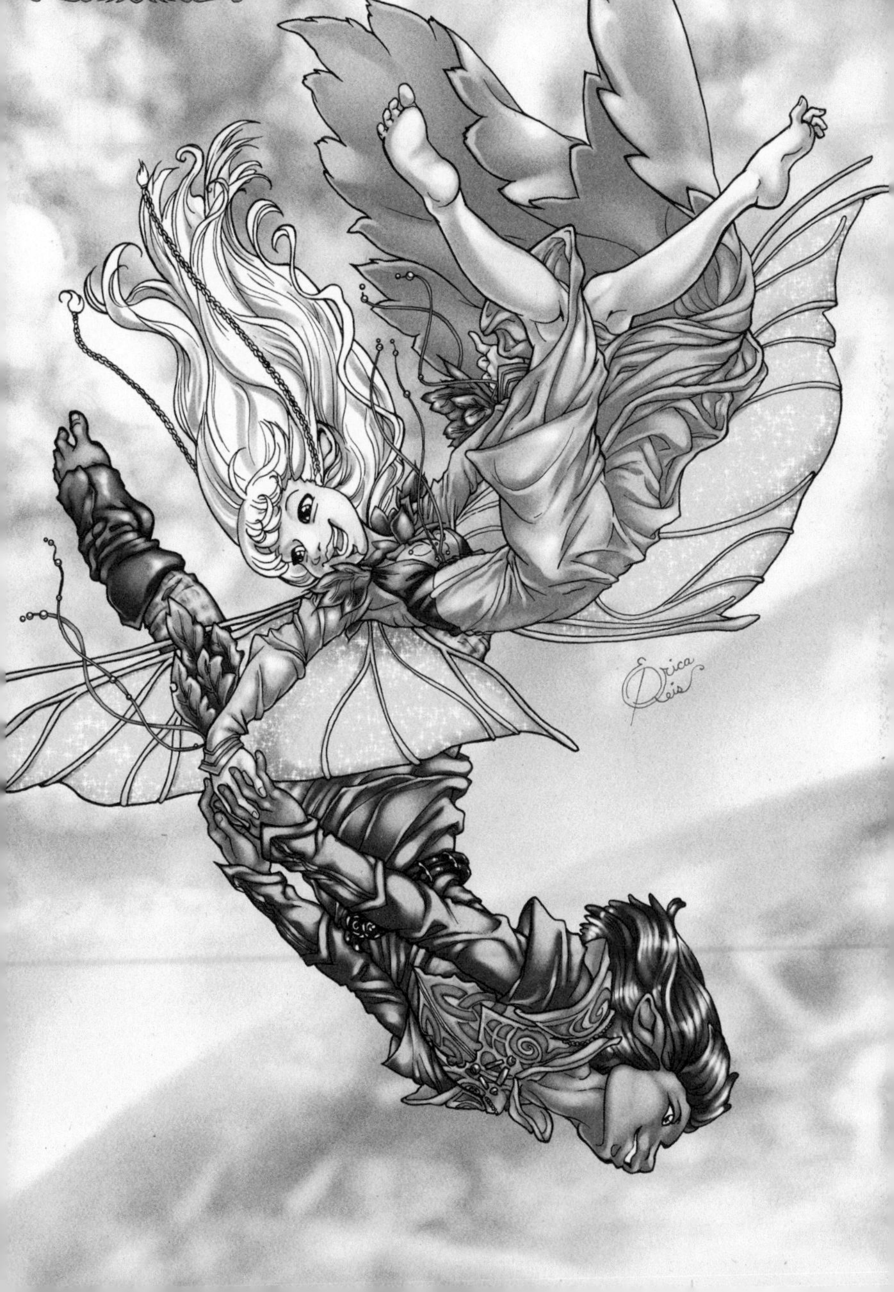
Erica Reis

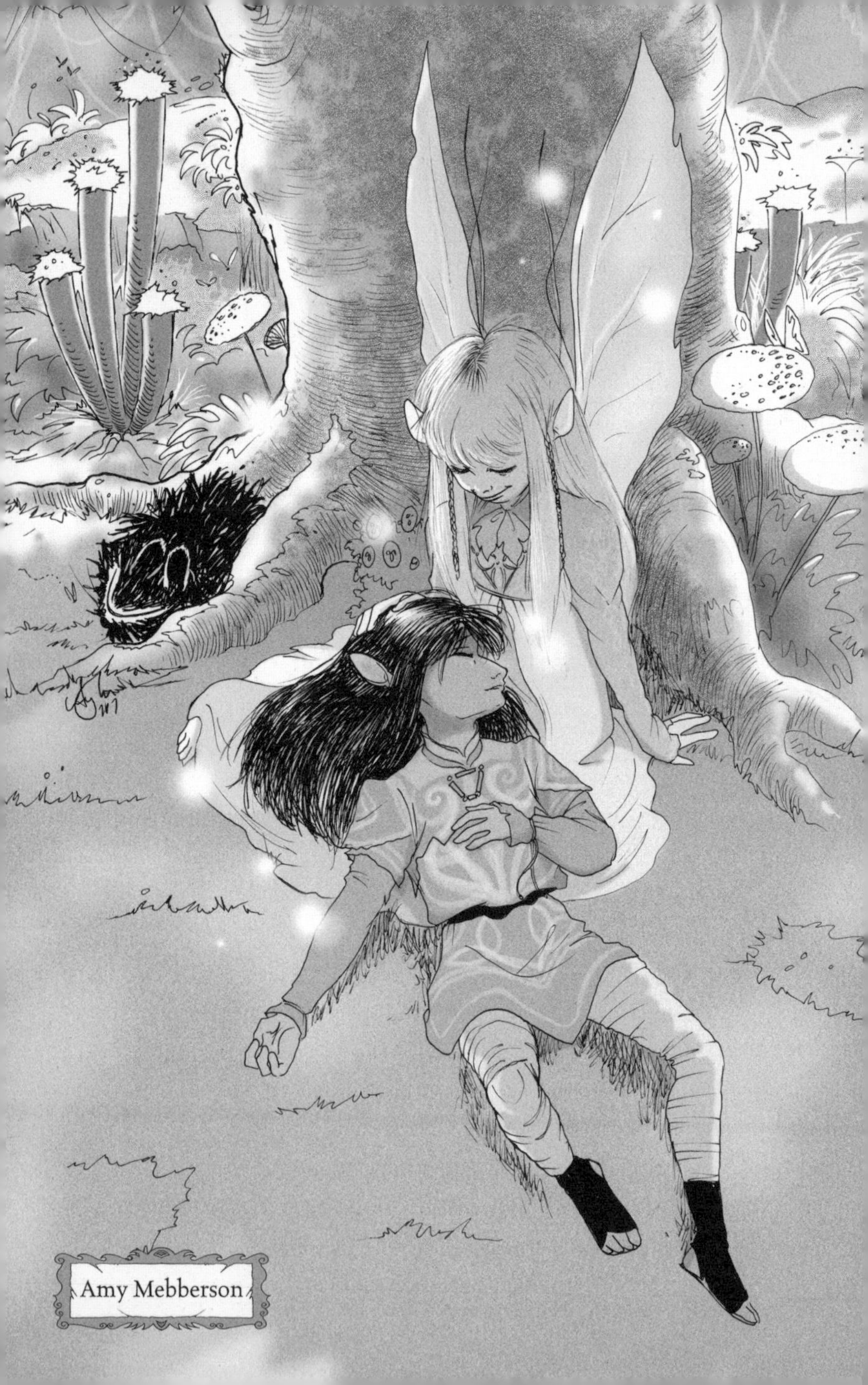
Amy Mebberson

Melissa DeJesus

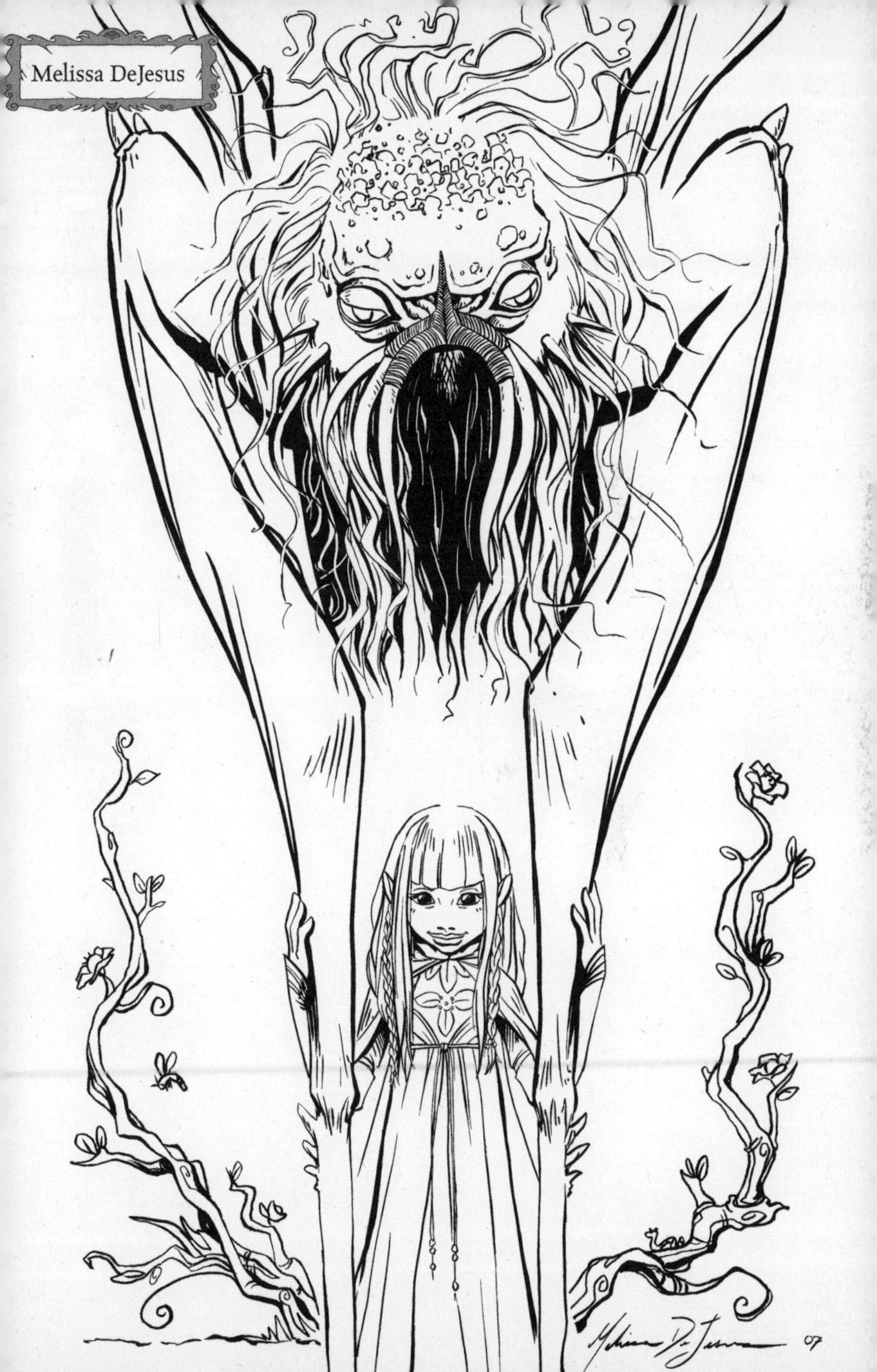

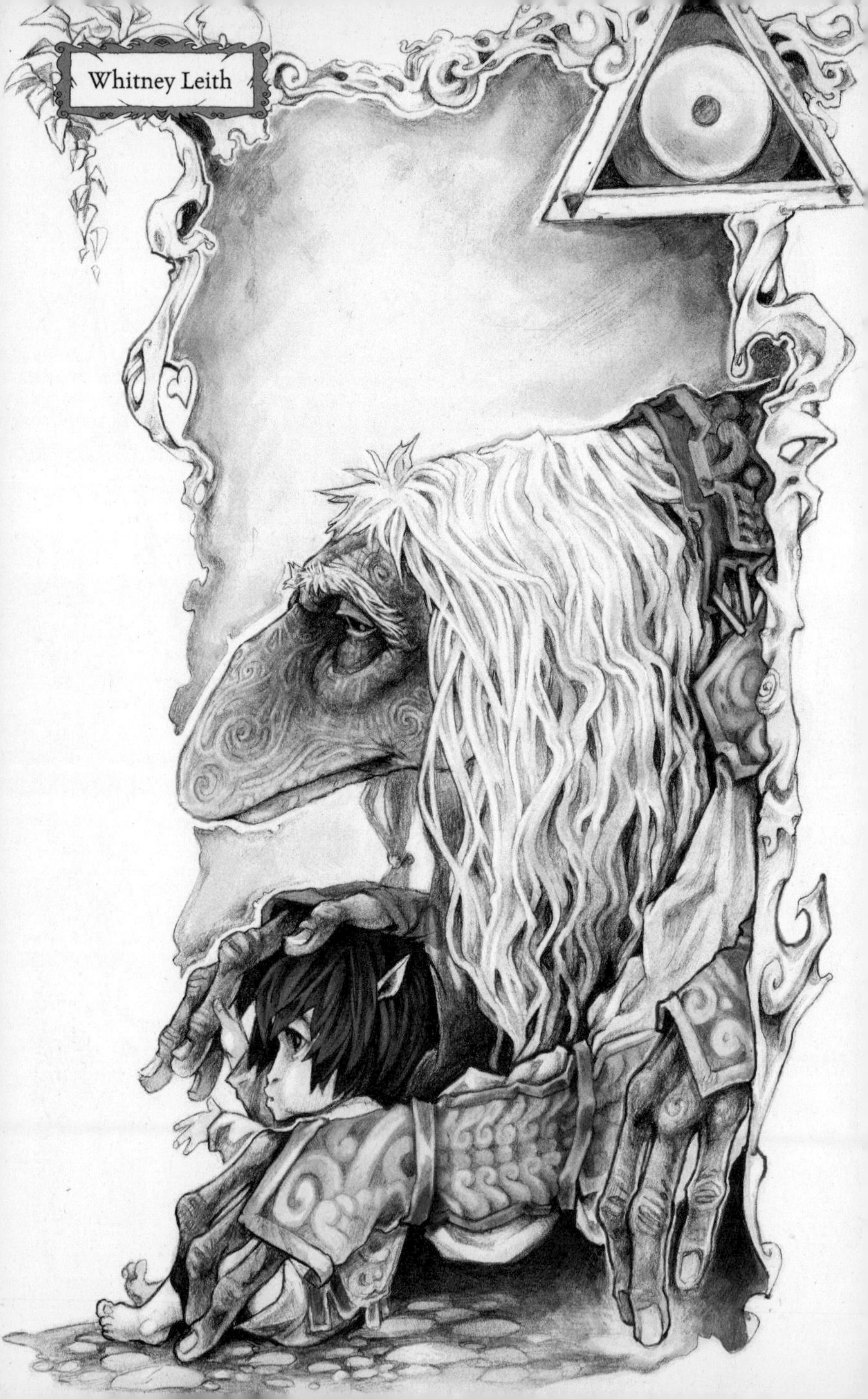
Whitney Leith

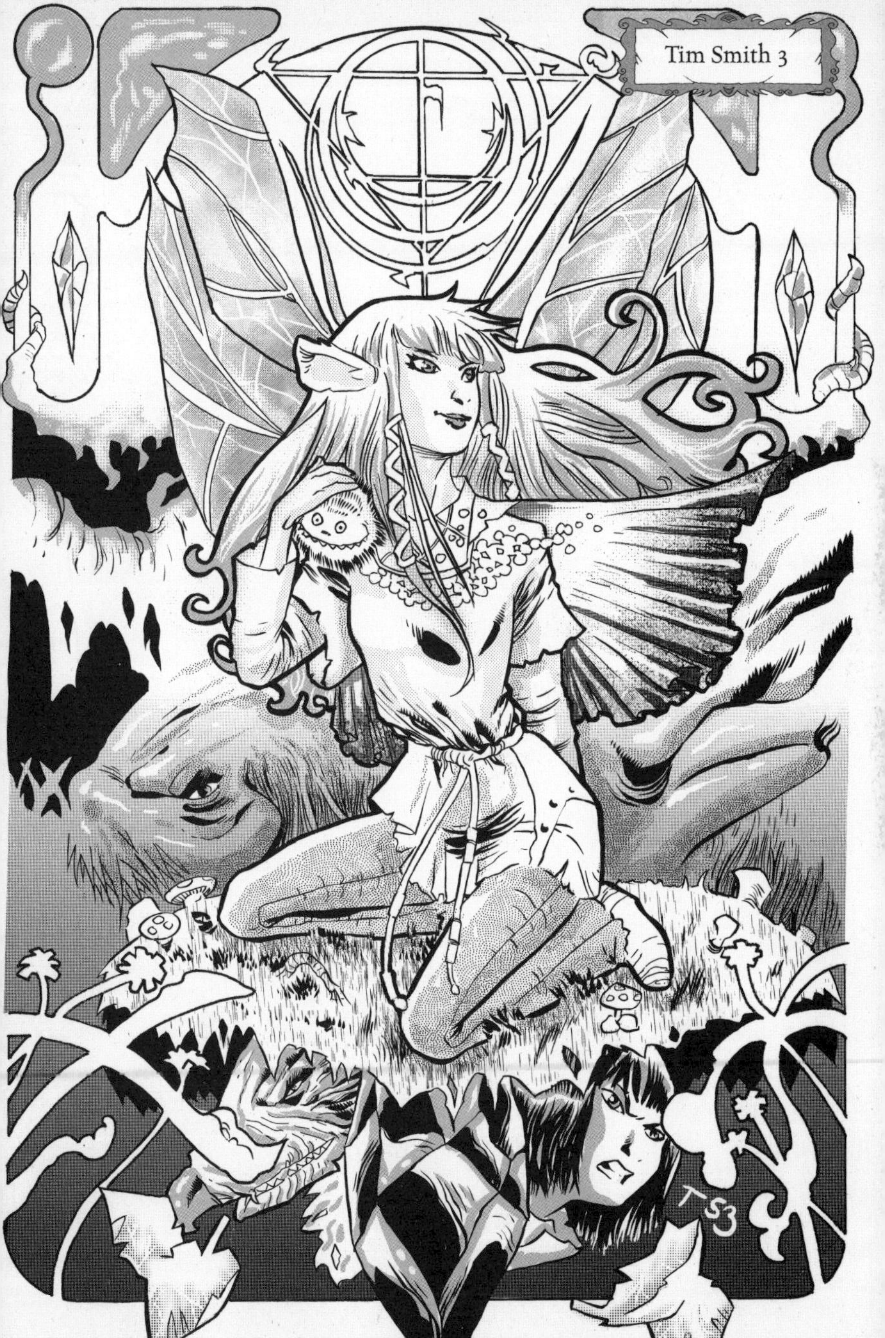
Tim Smith 3

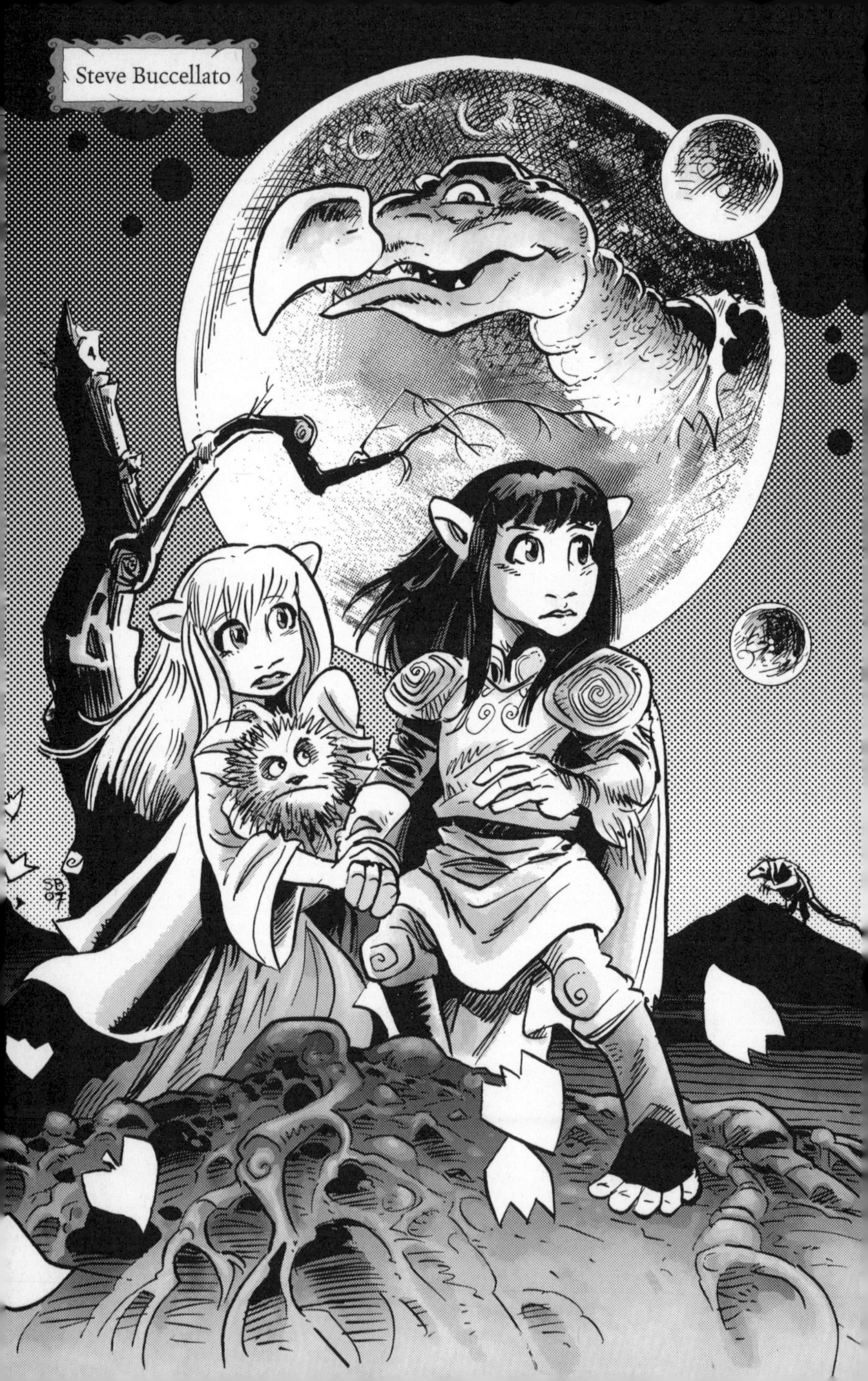

Steve Buccellato

Bret Uher

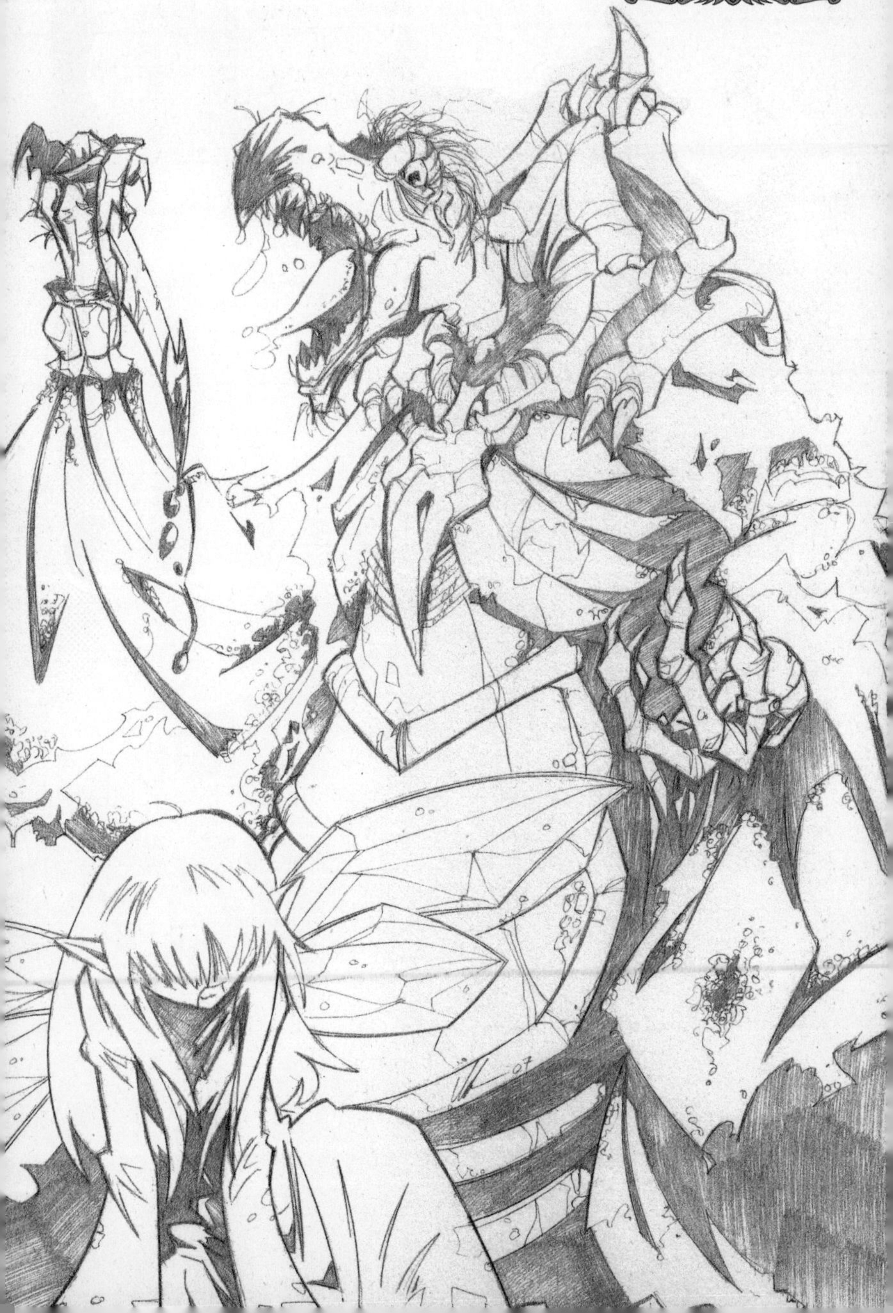

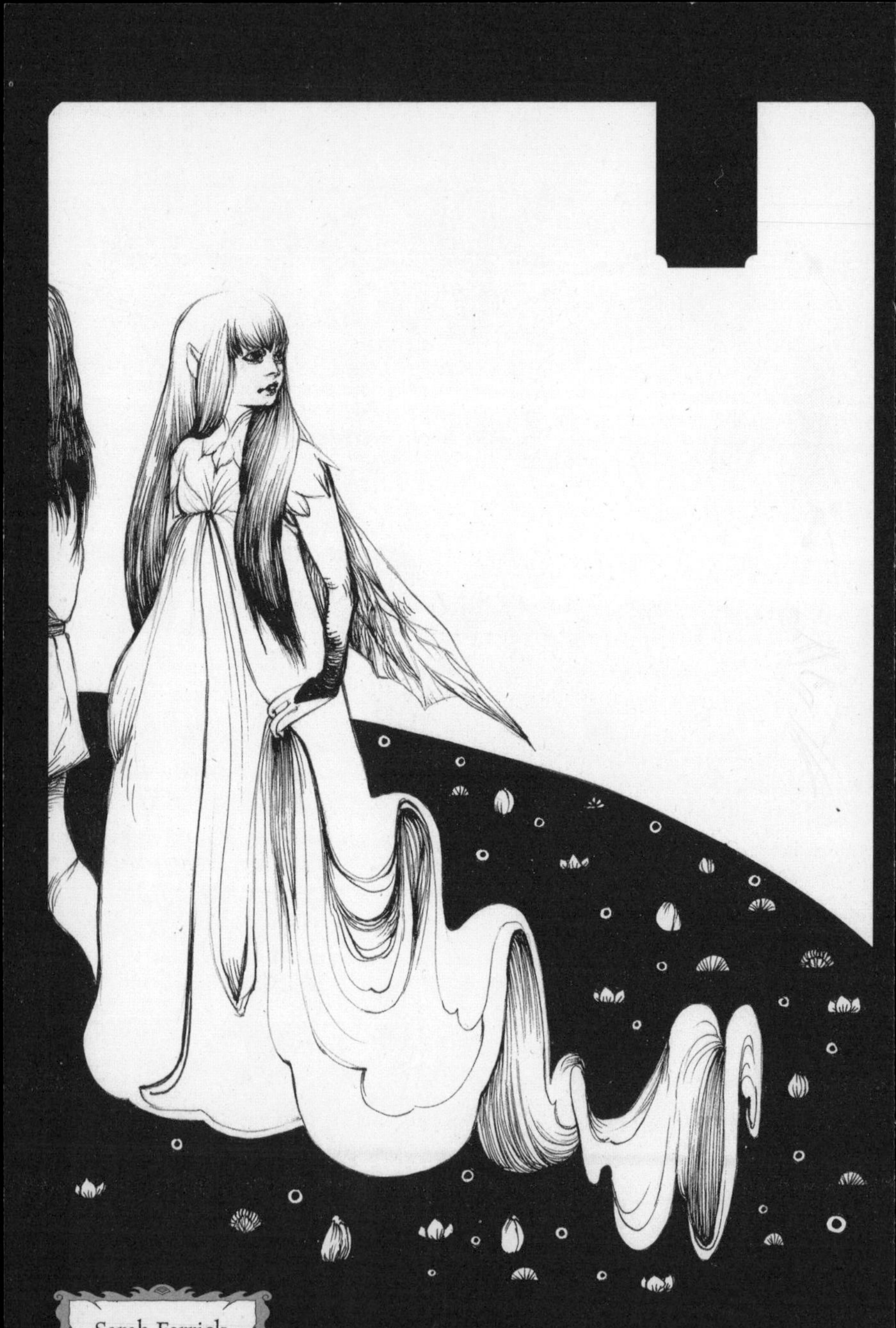

Sarah Ferrick

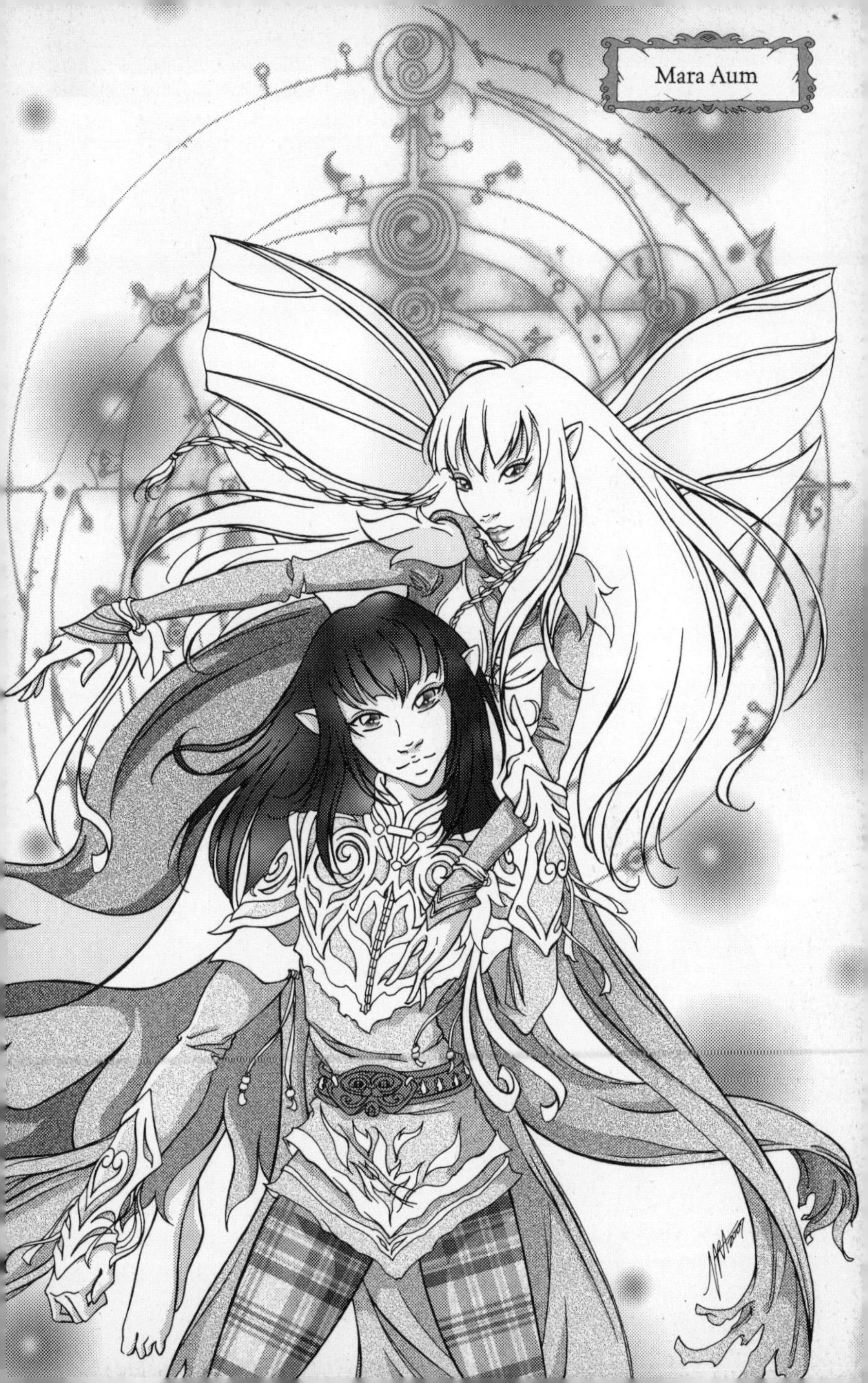
Mara Aum

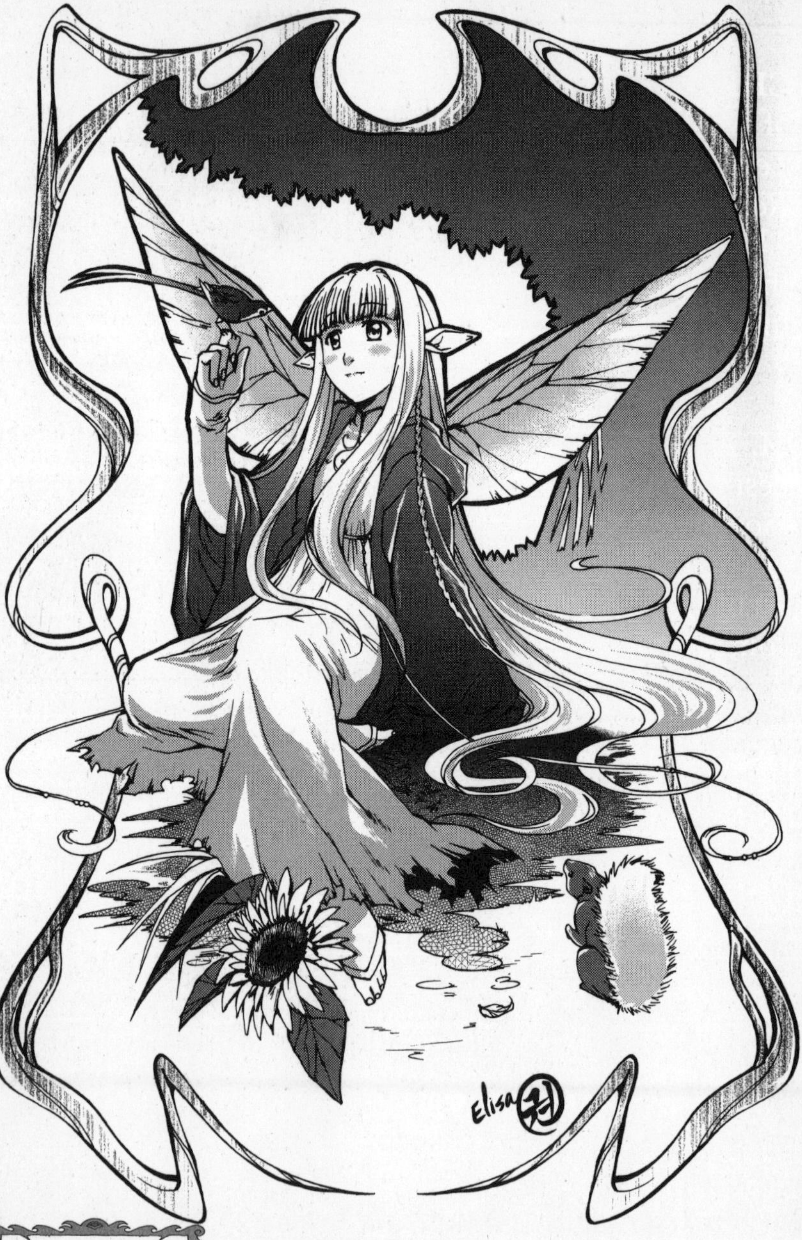
Elisa

Elisa Kwon

CHRIS LIE is a graduate from the Savannah College of Art and Design and the illustrator of *Jim Henson's Legends of The Dark Crystal's* sister title: *Jim Henson's Return to Labyrinth*, available from TOKYOPOP now. Chris is also the artist of several comics published through Devil's Due, including this fall's *Drafted*. Visit his Web site at www.chriscomic.com.

M. ALICE LEGROW is the creator of TOKYOPOP's best-selling manga series *Bizenghast*. Look for her most recent work in *Bizenghast* vol. 4, which ships in December 2007, and in *Bizenghast: Falling Into Fear*, an art book that's available now. Swing by www.bizenghast.com for more information on M. Alice and her art.

JESSICA FEINBERG is a freelance illustrator who just happened to tone the very book you're reading. She's also the English-language localizer for such manga series as *Mitsukazu Mihara: The Embalmer* and *Broken Angels*. Her illustrations are on display at www.artlair.com.

JAKE MYLER is the talented illustrator of TOKYOPOP's dark fantasy *Undertown*. Look for the first volume (which contains an exclusive preview of *Jim Henson's Legends of The Dark Crystal*) in stores now and the second in late 2008. You can find more of Jake's art at www.jakemyler.com.

LEIGH DRAGOON is the creator of the acclaimed Web comic *By the Wayside* and the illustrator of *Freedom Train* for Scholastic Canada's "Timeline" series. The winner of the Friends of Lulu's 2006 Kim Yale Award for Best New Talent, Leigh is currently busy scripting the manga continuation of Frewin Jones' *The Faerie Path* for TOKYOPOP and HarperCollins. Visit her at www.leighdragoon.com.

CHRISSY DELK is a recent graduate from the Savannah College of Art and Design. She's the co-creator of *Paintings of You*, available now from Iris Print, and *Wonderland*, a fantasy Web comic. Art from both is on display at www.chrissydelk.com.

ERICA REIS is also a recent graduate of the Savannah College of Art and Design and is the creator of *Sea Princess Azuri*, the second volume of which is available now from TOKYOPOP. Discover the underwater world of the Orcans (and say hi to Erica) at www.seaprincessazuri.com.

AMY MEBBERSON is a winner of the *Rising Stars of Manga* contest and the co-creator of TOKYOPOP's original manga series *Divalicious!*, as well as the popular Web comic *As If!* Her most recent Web comic, *Thorn*, can be found on her Web site: www.mimisgrotto.com.

MELISSA DEJESUS is the artist of TOKYOPOP's fanservice-filled fantasy series *Sokora Refugees*, which is available now from TOKYOPOP. She's also the illustrator of the daily comic strip *My Cage*, which is currently taking American newspapers by storm. Learn more about it at www.myspace.com/mycagecomic.

WHITNEY LEITH was a finalist in TOKYOPOP's third *Rising Stars of Manga* contest with her short manga "Cupid's Folly." She's currently collaborating on the upcoming fantasy comic *Junk Punk*. You can find more of her art at http://ayamefataru.deviantart.com.

TIM SMITH 3 is the creator of the original manga series *Grimm & Co.*, coming soon from TOKYOPOP. He's also worked on *The Hardy Boys* and *Tales from the Crypt* for Papercutz. His Web domain is www.timsmith3.com.

STEVE BUCCELLATO is the creator of *Battle of the Bands*, a new original harem manga from TOKYOPOP. He's also the creator of *Comiculture*, a comic anthology magazine, and *Weasel Guy*, published by Image Comics. You can visit Steve online at www.stevebuccellato.com.

BRETT UHER lives in Alaska and is a graduate of the Joe Kubert School of Cartoon and Graphic Art. His first comic was "Christmas Shopping," a short published through Antarctic Press in 2004, but he's currently busy illustrating *Dark Moon Diary*, a spooky new manga series available now from TOKYOPOP.

SARAH FERRICK was a finalist in TOKYOPOP's *Rising Stars of Manga* contest at the tender age of 15. She's since gone on to publish two short comics: "Locker No. 246" (which can be found in the back of TOKYOPOP's *The Dreaming*) and "The Girl with Wings." Both can be read at http://tea-for-one.xepher.net.

MARA AUM is the artist of TOKYOPOP's *Reign Over Destiny*, a short manga produced for the Make-a-Wish Foundation. She also inked and toned Brett Uher's lively pencils in TOKYOPOP's *Dark Moon Diary*. Mara's Web gallery can be found at http://irrydanni.deviantart.com.

ELISA KWON was born in South Korea, and is currently living in Brazil. She provided concept art for *Mercenaries*, a comic that was published by TALISMÃ. A recent college graduate, you can find more of her art at http://tiggerfactory.deviantart.com.